The Girl I Saved on the Train Turned Out to Be My Childhood Friend 1

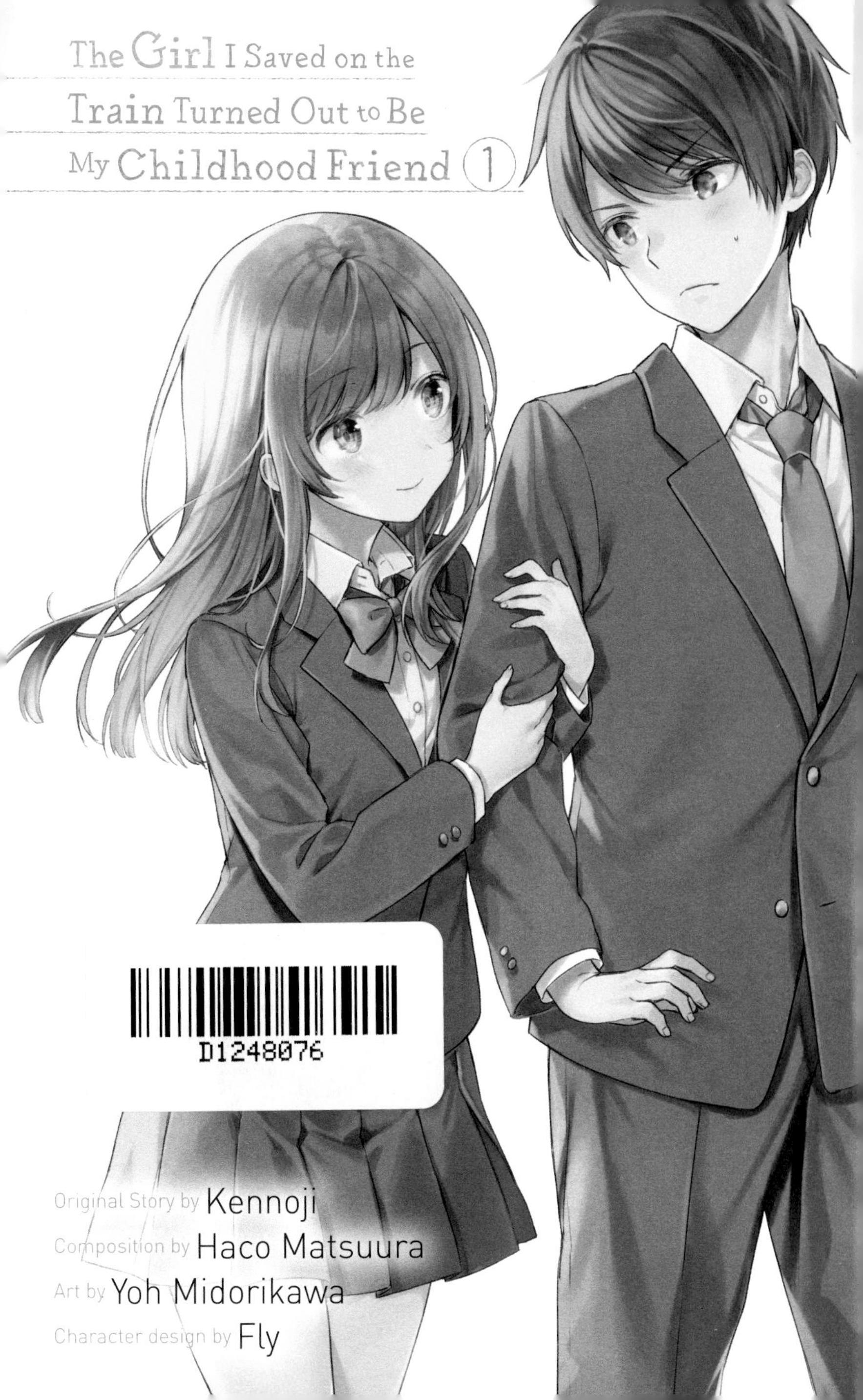

Original Story by Kennoji
Composition by Haco Matsuura
Art by Yoh Midorikawa
Character design by Fly

CONTENTS

#1 Same Old Train, Brand-New Girl — 003

#2 Lunch Friends — 029

#3 Death (from Embarrassment) — 057

#4 "That Type" vs. the Gyaru — 081

#5 First Visit in Four Years — 095

#6 A Piece of Our Promises — 109

#7 Accident — 125

#8 Mr. Reoffender and Ms. Diligent — 143

#9 Looking Back — 163

Extra Bad Girl, Good Girl — 175

When we get
into high school,
I will kiss ~~Hina-chan~~

#1 Same Old Train, Brand-New Girl

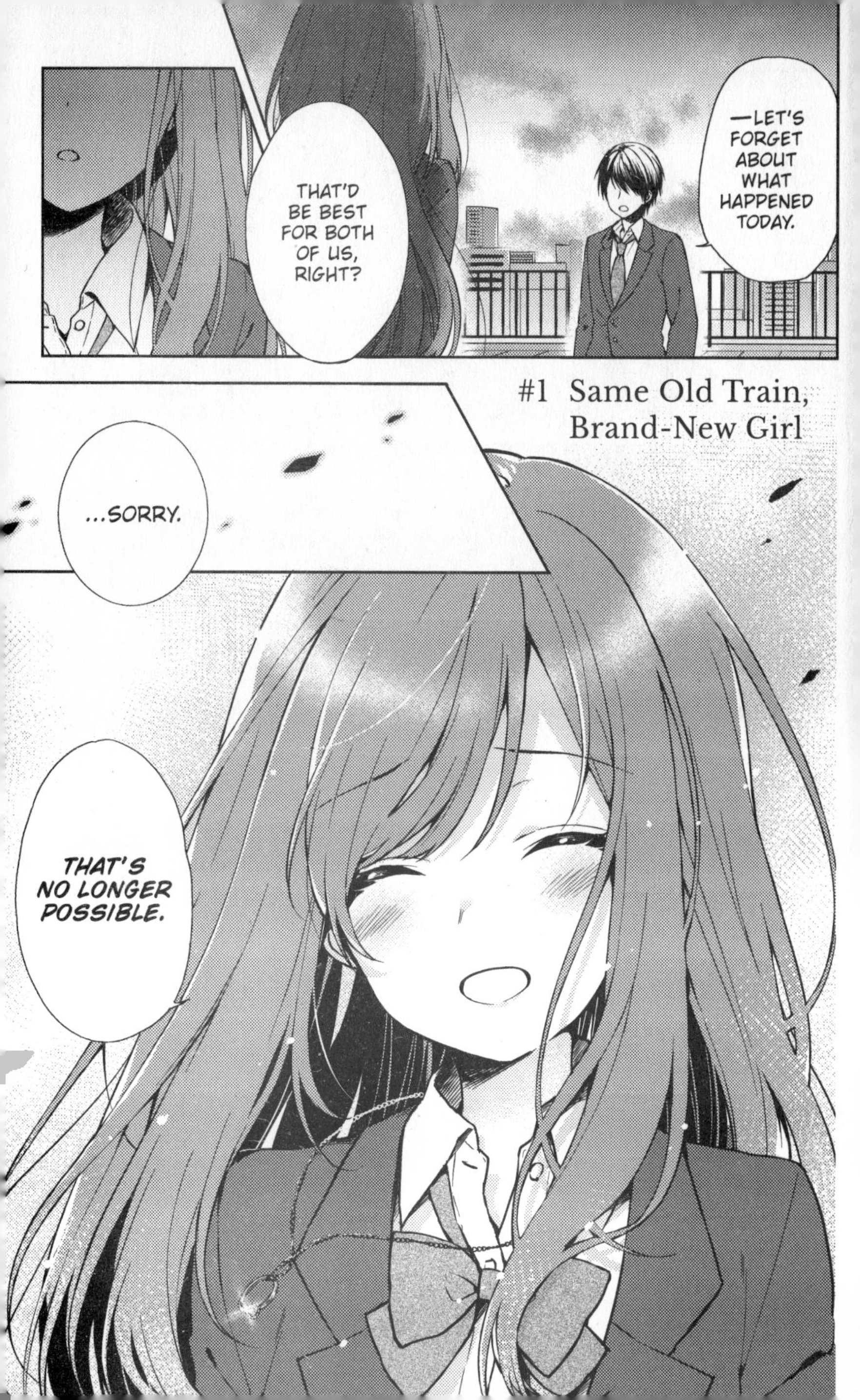
—LET'S FORGET ABOUT WHAT HAPPENED TODAY.
THAT'D BE BEST FOR BOTH OF US, RIGHT?
...SORRY.
THAT'S NO LONGER POSSIBLE.

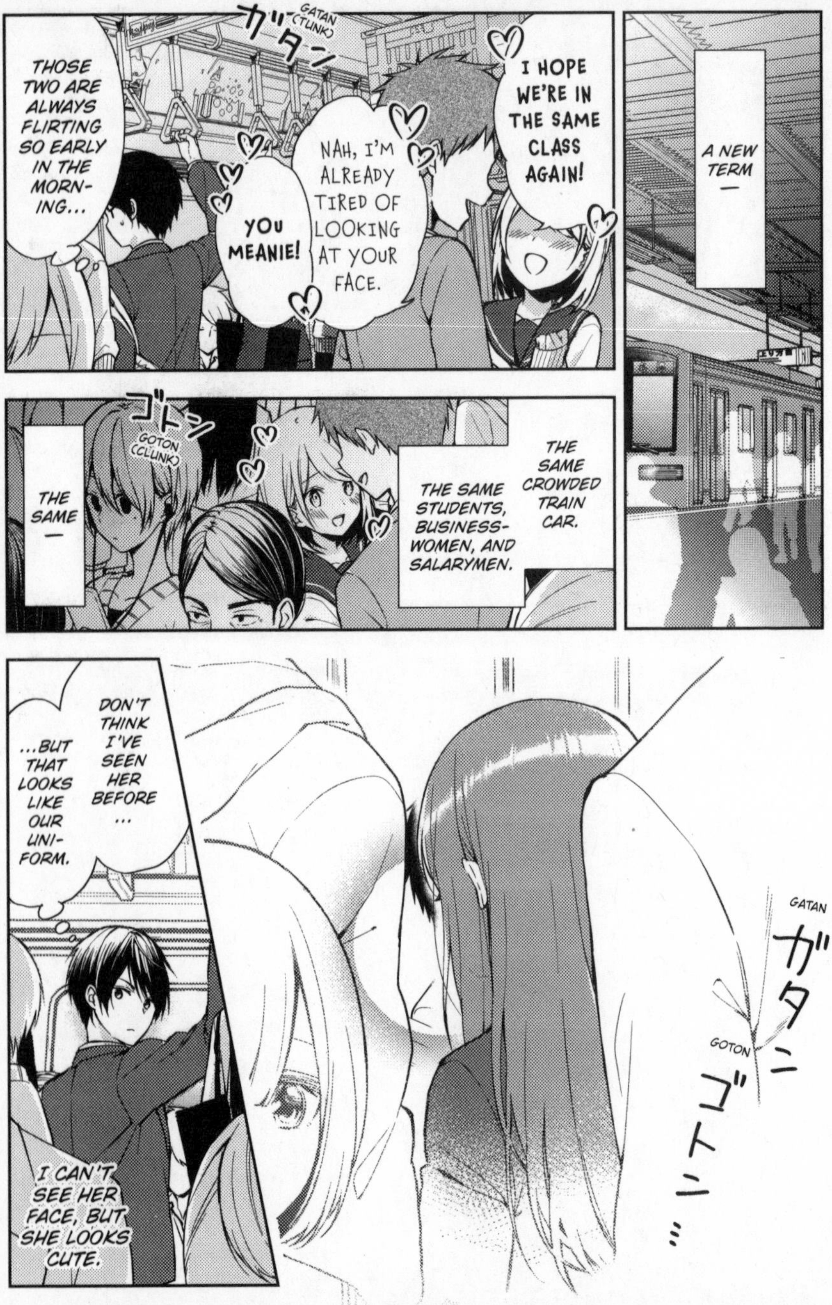
A NEW TERM —
I HOPE WE'RE IN THE SAME CLASS AGAIN!
ガタン
GATAN (TUNK)
NAH, I'M ALREADY TIRED OF LOOKING AT YOUR FACE.
YOU MEANIE!
THOSE TWO ARE ALWAYS FLIRTING SO EARLY IN THE MORNING...
THE SAME CROWDED TRAIN CAR.
THE SAME STUDENTS, BUSINESS-WOMEN, AND SALARYMEN.
ゴトン
GOTON (CLUNK)
THE SAME —
ガタン
GATAN
ゴトン…
GOTON
DON'T THINK I'VE SEEN HER BEFORE ...
...BUT THAT LOOKS LIKE OUR UNIFORM.
I CAN'T SEE HER FACE, BUT SHE LOOKS CUTE.

SOME-THING...

...SEEMS OFF—

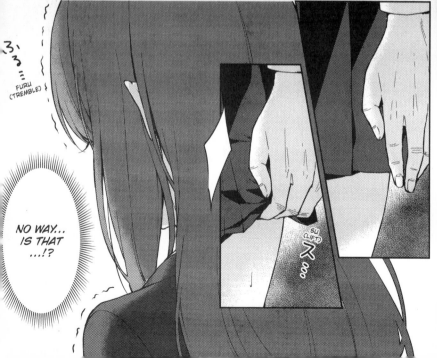

FURU
(TREMBLE)

NO WAY...
IS THAT
...!?

SU
(LIFT)

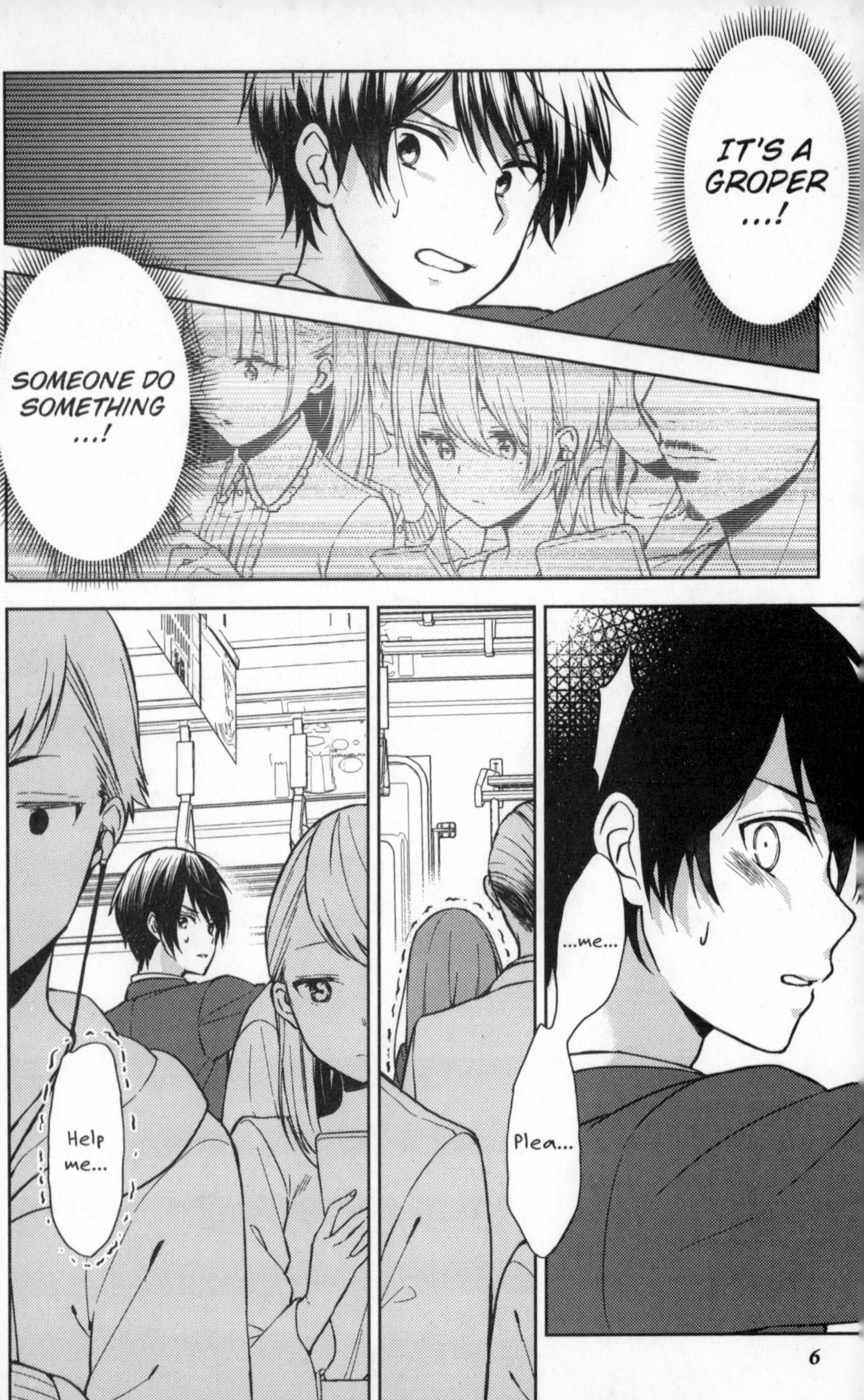
IT'S A GROPER ...!
SOMEONE DO SOMETHING ...!
...me...
Plea...
Help me...

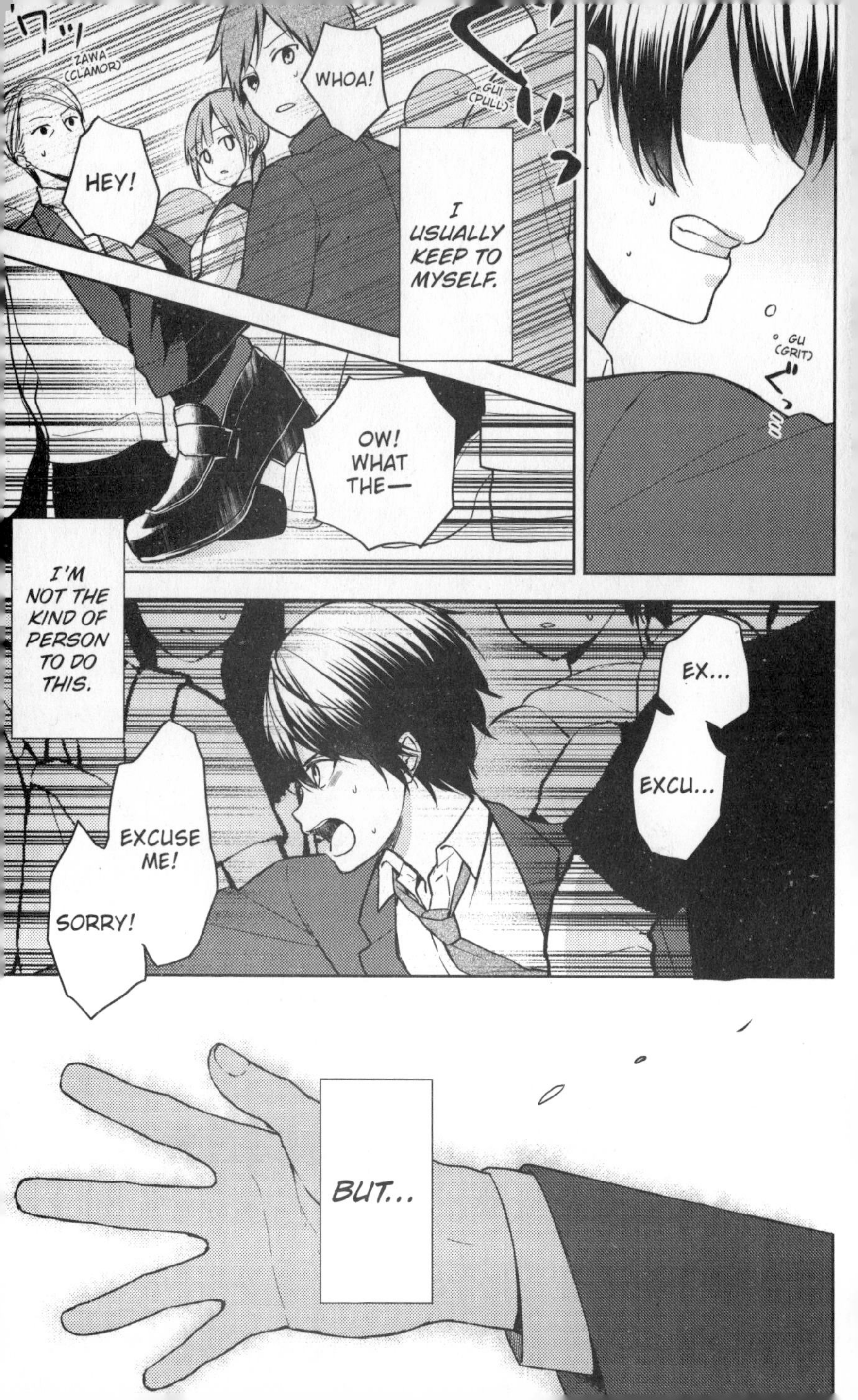
GU (GRIT)
GUI (PULL)
I USUALLY KEEP TO MYSELF.
WHOA!
ZAWA (CLAMOR)
HEY!
OW! WHAT THE—
EX...
EXCU...
EXCUSE ME!
SORRY!
I'M NOT THE KIND OF PERSON TO DO THIS.
BUT...

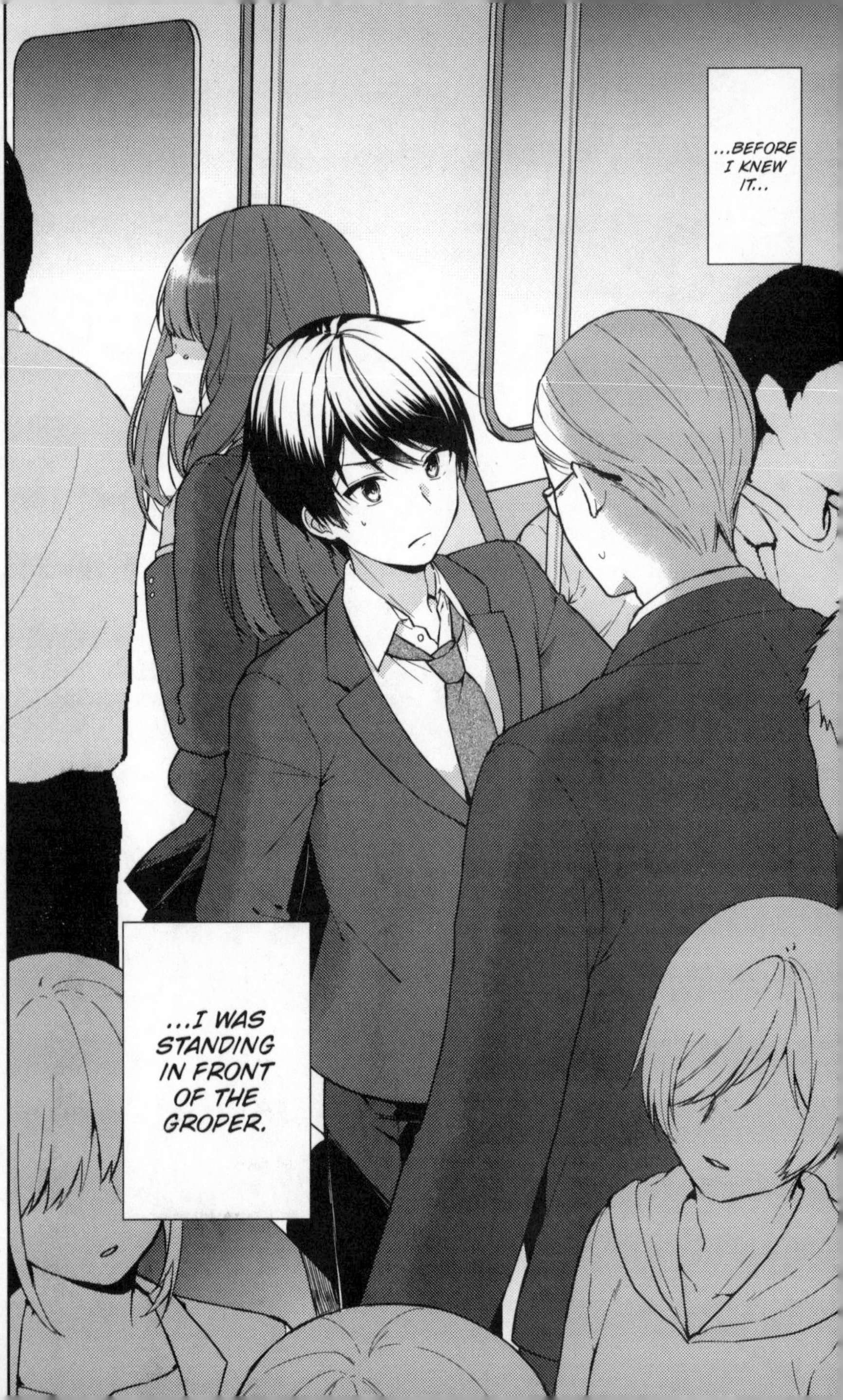
...BEFORE I KNEW IT...
...I WAS STANDING IN FRONT OF THE GROPER.

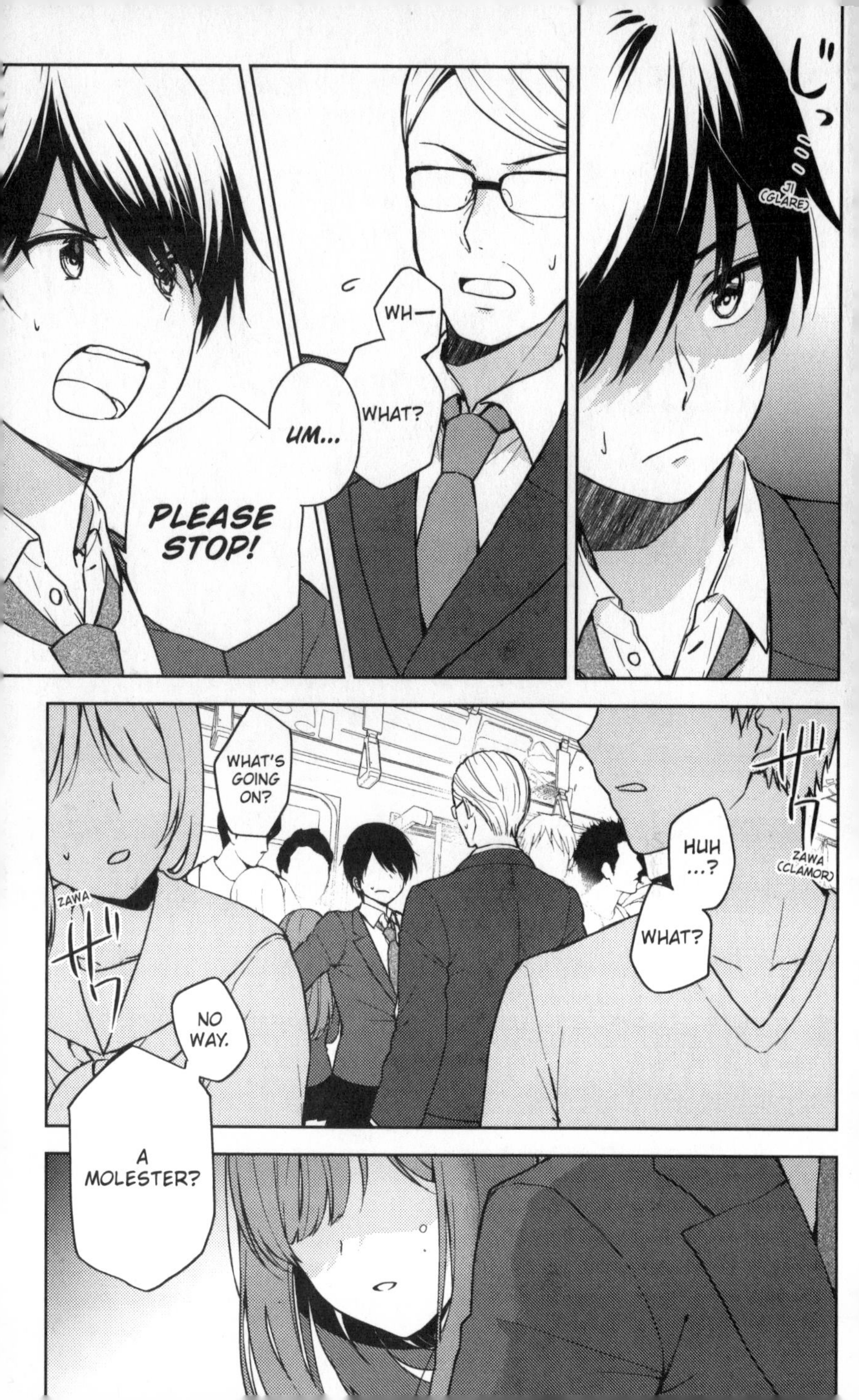
じっ
JI (GLARE)
WH—
WHAT?
UM...
PLEASE STOP!
ザワ
ZAWA (CLAMOR)
HUH ...?
WHAT?
WHAT'S GOING ON?
ザワ
ZAWA
NO WAY.
A MOLESTER?

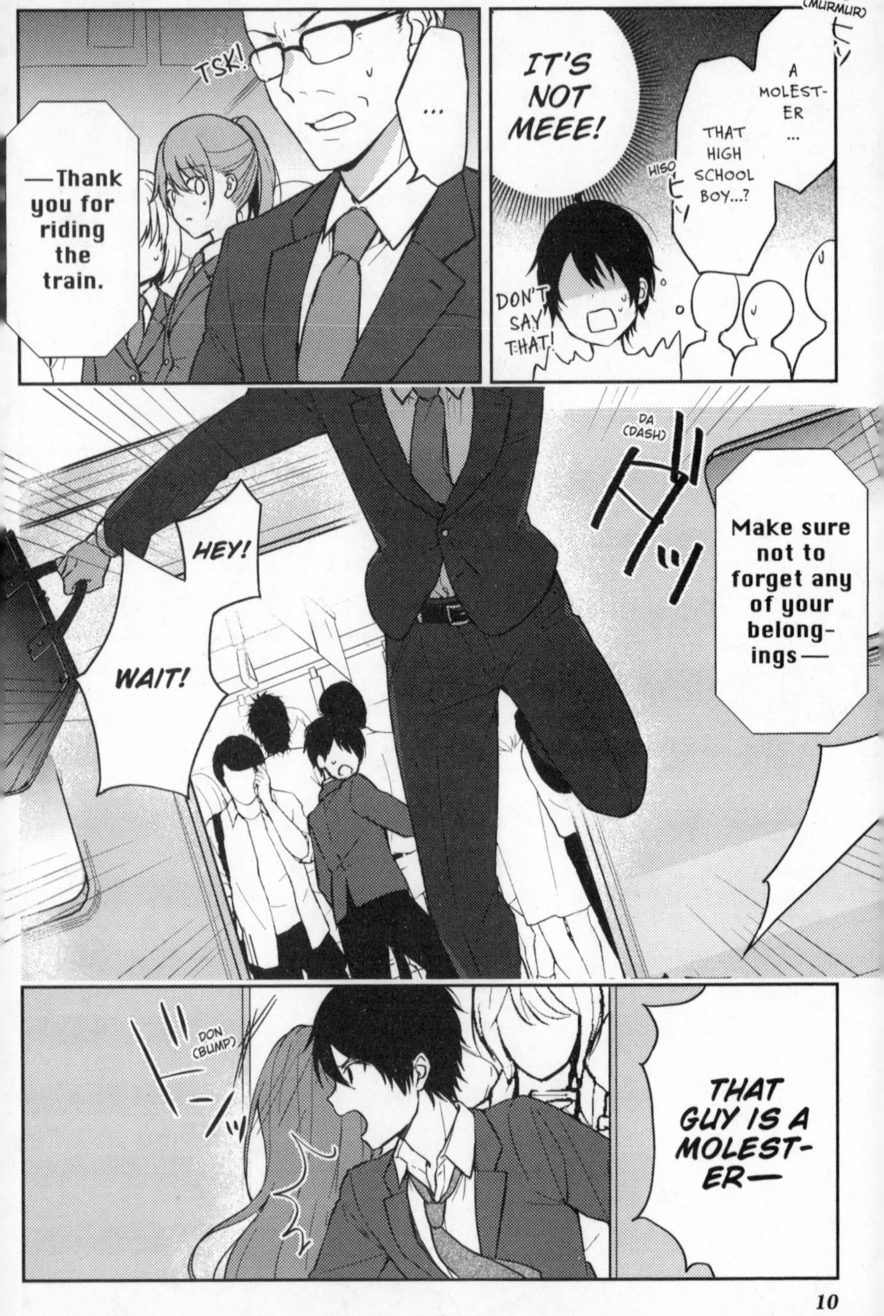
HISO (MURMUR)
A MOLEST-ER...
THAT HIGH SCHOOL BOY...?
HISO
IT'S NOT MEEE!
DON'T SAY THAT!
...
TSK!
—Thank you for riding the train.
DA (DASH)
Make sure not to forget any of your belong-ings—
HEY!
WAIT!
THAT GUY IS A MOLEST-ER—
DON (BUMP)

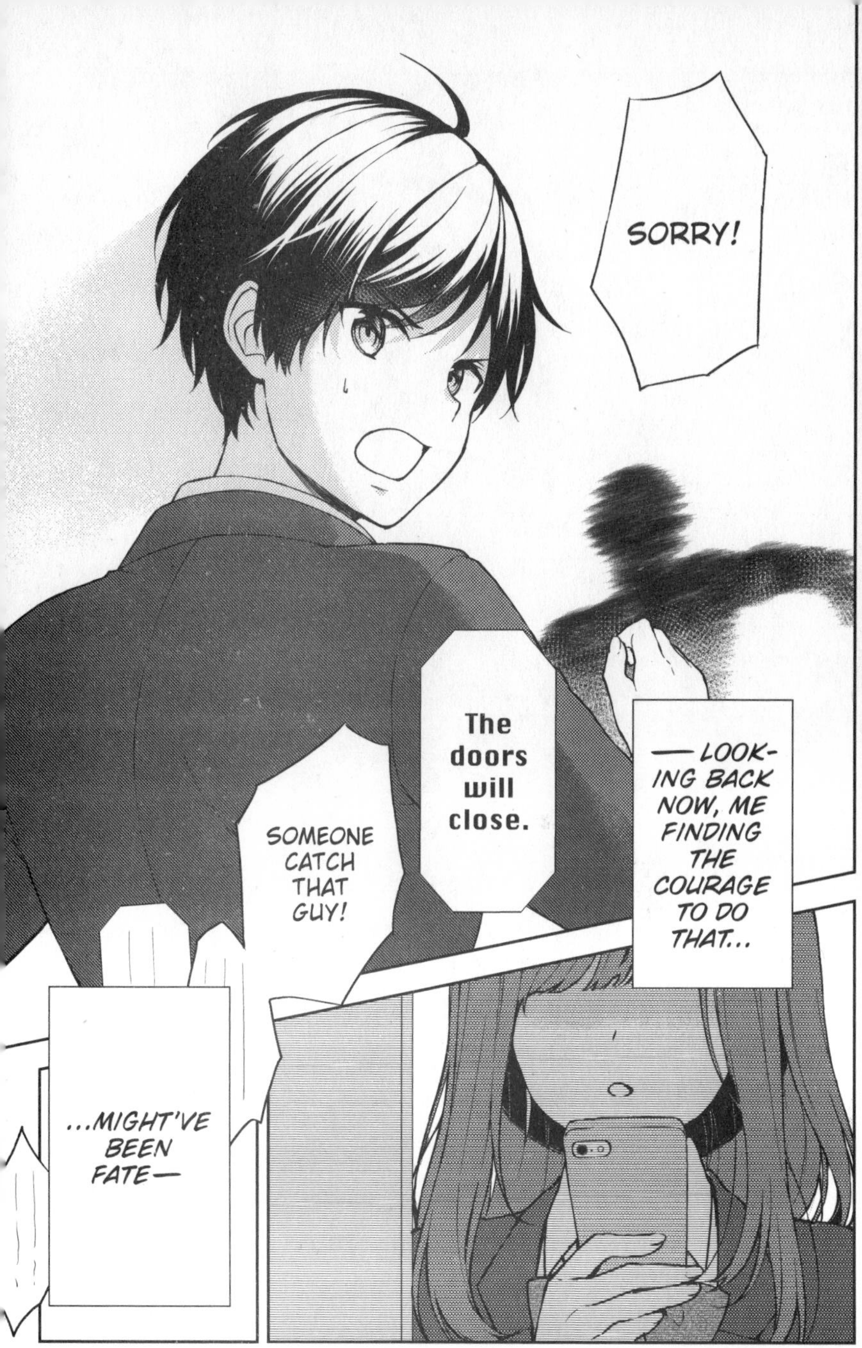
SORRY!
The doors will close.
SOMEONE CATCH THAT GUY!
—LOOKING BACK NOW, ME FINDING THE COURAGE TO DO THAT...
...MIGHT'VE BEEN FATE—

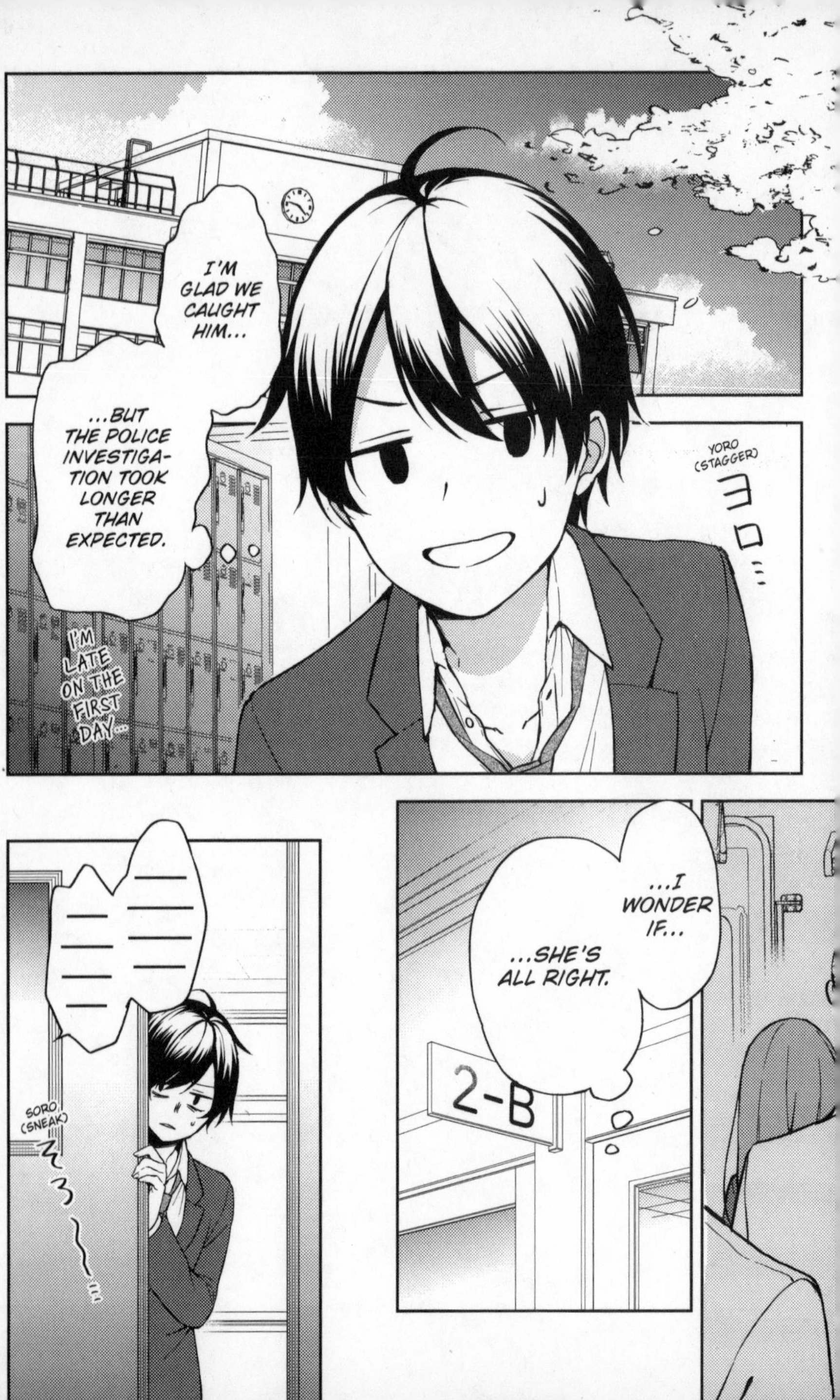
I'M GLAD WE CAUGHT HIM...
...BUT THE POLICE INVESTIGATION TOOK LONGER THAN EXPECTED.
YORO (STAGGER)
ヨロ…
I'M LATE ON THE FIRST DAY...
...I WONDER IF...
...SHE'S ALL RIGHT.
2-B
————
SORO (SNEAK)
そろ～～…

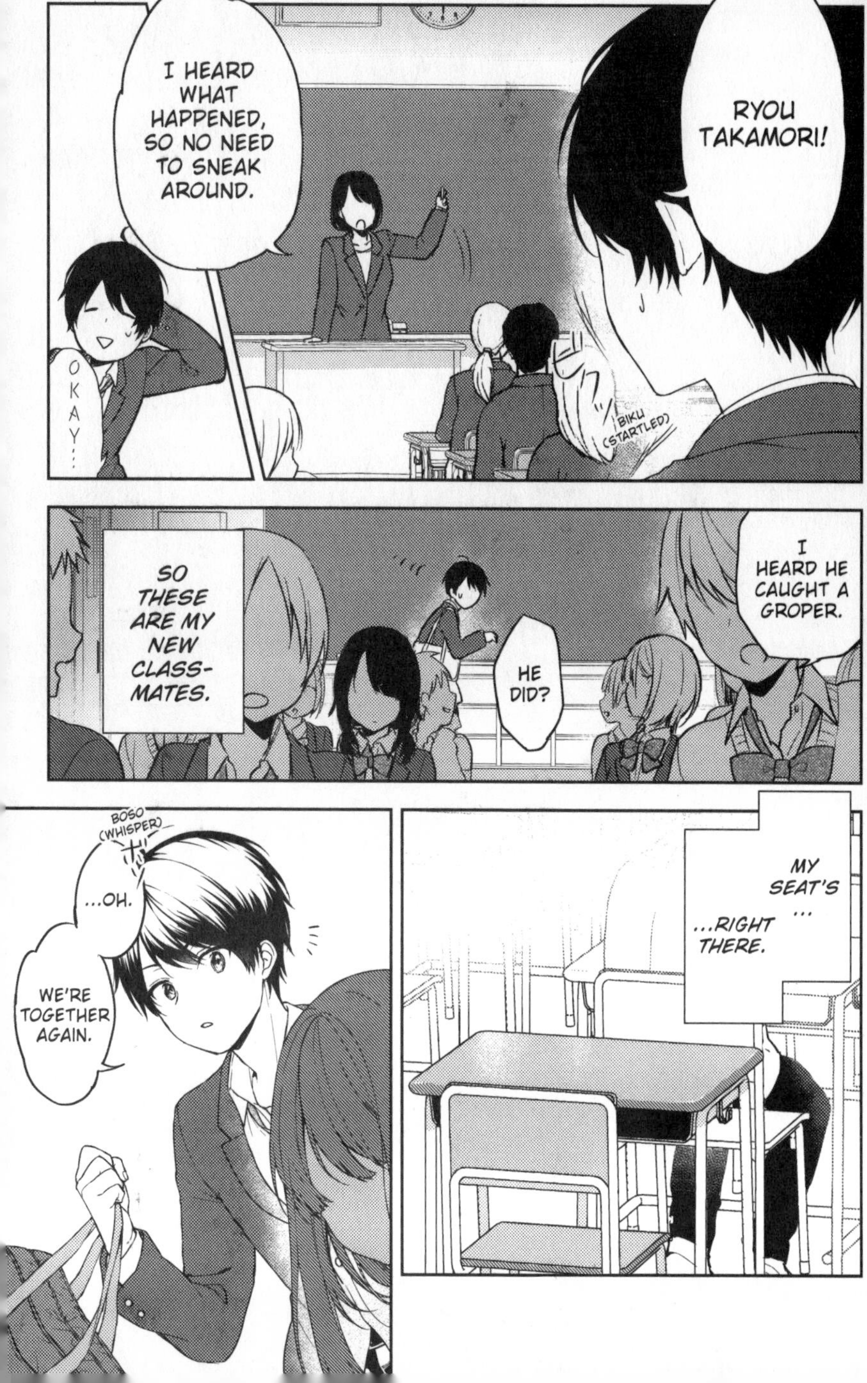
RYOU TAKAMORI!
BIKU (STARTLED)
I HEARD WHAT HAPPENED, SO NO NEED TO SNEAK AROUND.
OKAY...
I HEARD HE CAUGHT A GROPER.
HE DID?
SO THESE ARE MY NEW CLASS-MATES.
MY SEAT'S...
...RIGHT THERE.
BOSO (WHISPER)
...OH.
WE'RE TOGETHER AGAIN.

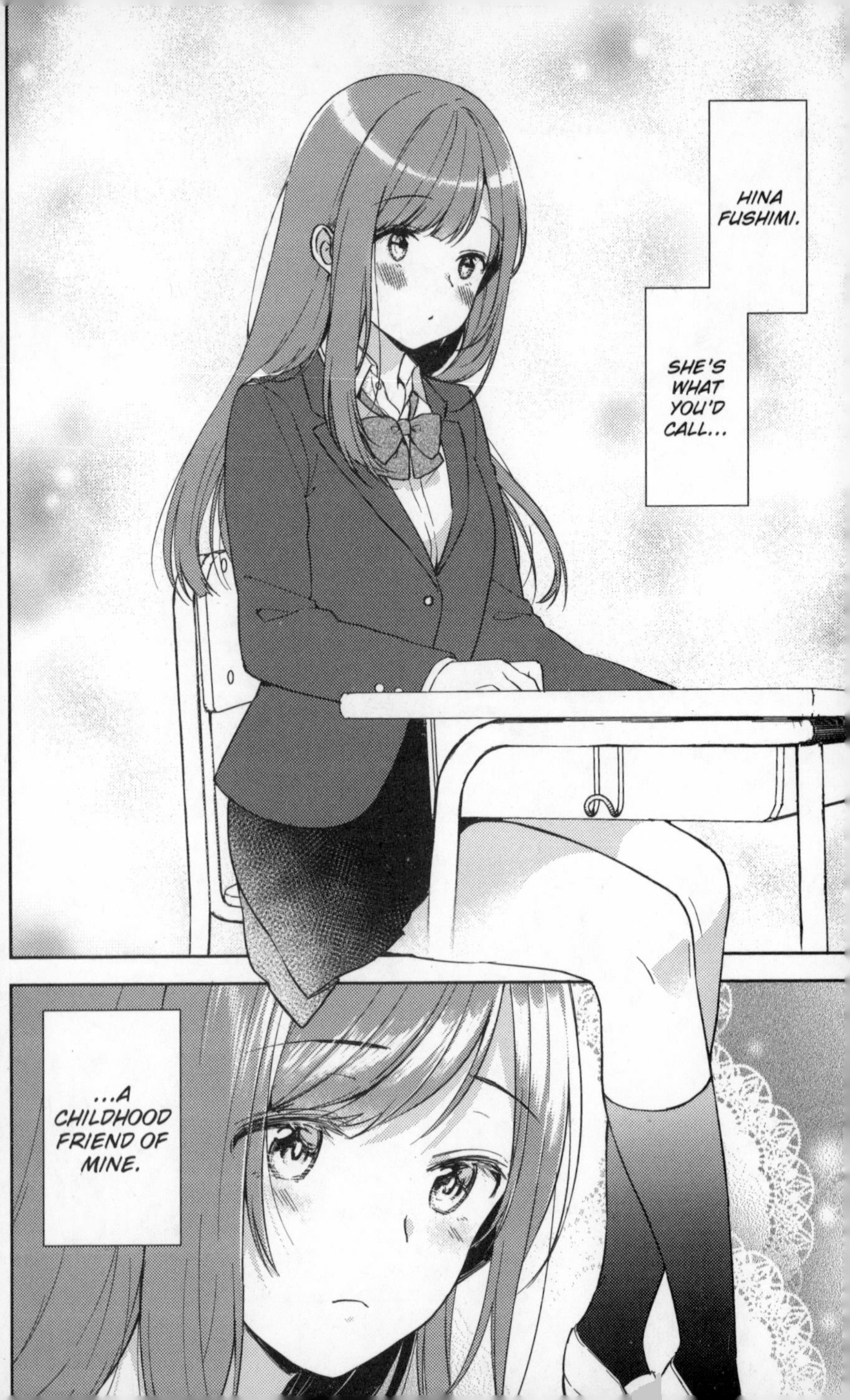
HINA FUSHIMI.
SHE'S WHAT YOU'D CALL...
...A CHILDHOOD FRIEND OF MINE.

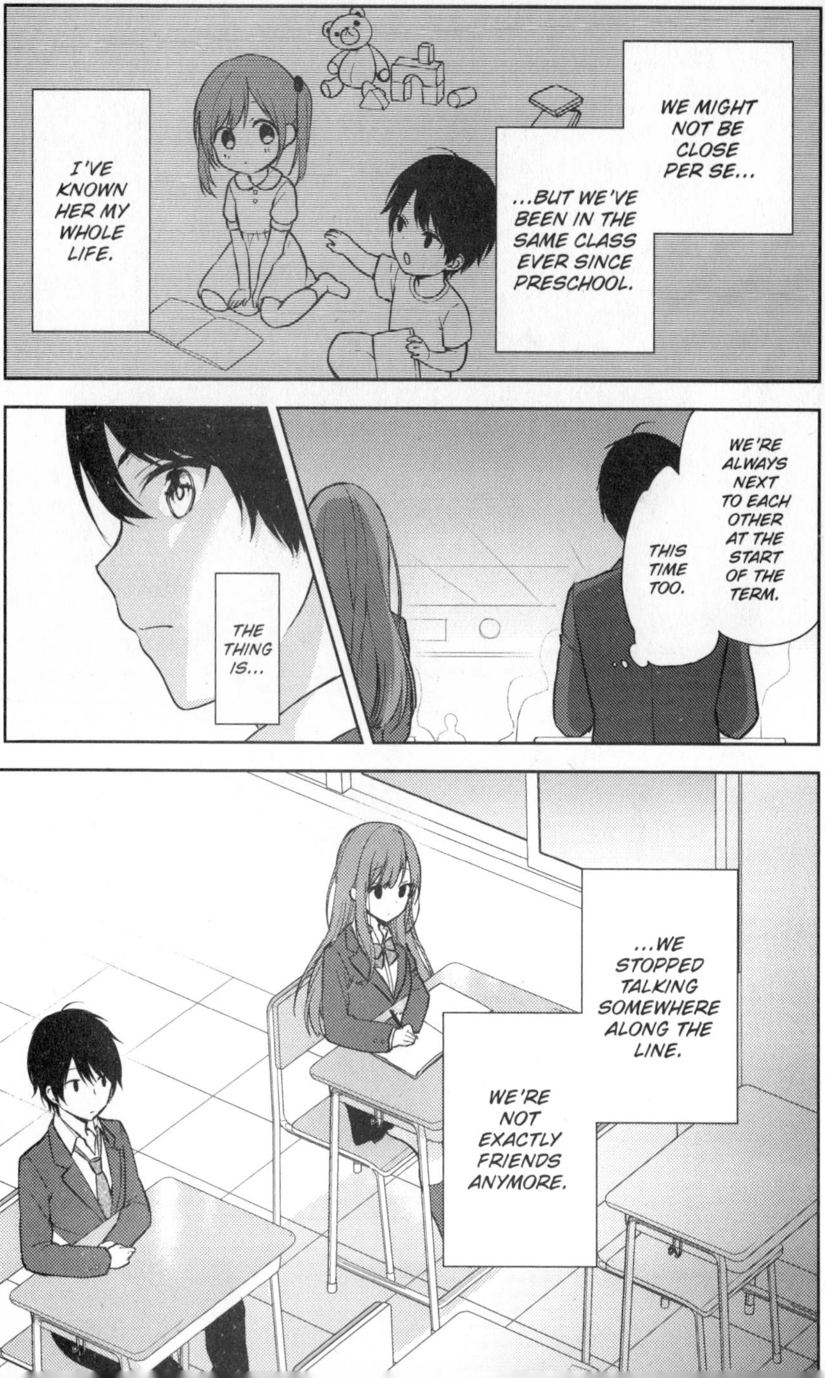
WE MIGHT NOT BE CLOSE PER SE...
...BUT WE'VE BEEN IN THE SAME CLASS EVER SINCE PRESCHOOL.
I'VE KNOWN HER MY WHOLE LIFE.
WE'RE ALWAYS NEXT TO EACH OTHER AT THE START OF THE TERM.
THIS TIME TOO.
THE THING IS...
...WE STOPPED TALKING SOMEWHERE ALONG THE LINE.
WE'RE NOT EXACTLY FRIENDS ANYMORE.

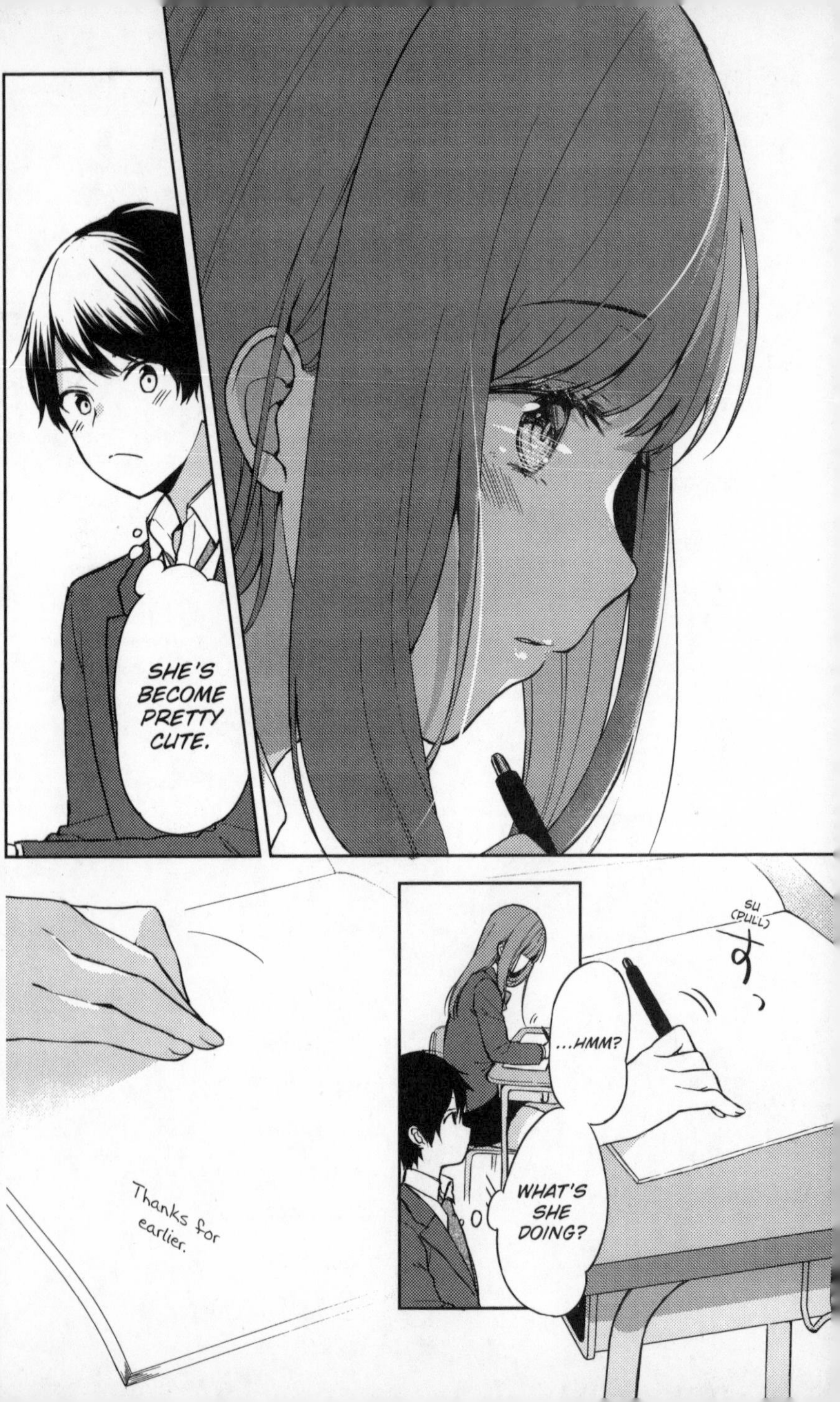
SHE'S BECOME PRETTY CUTE.
SU (PULL)
...HMM?
WHAT'S SHE DOING?
Thanks for earlier.

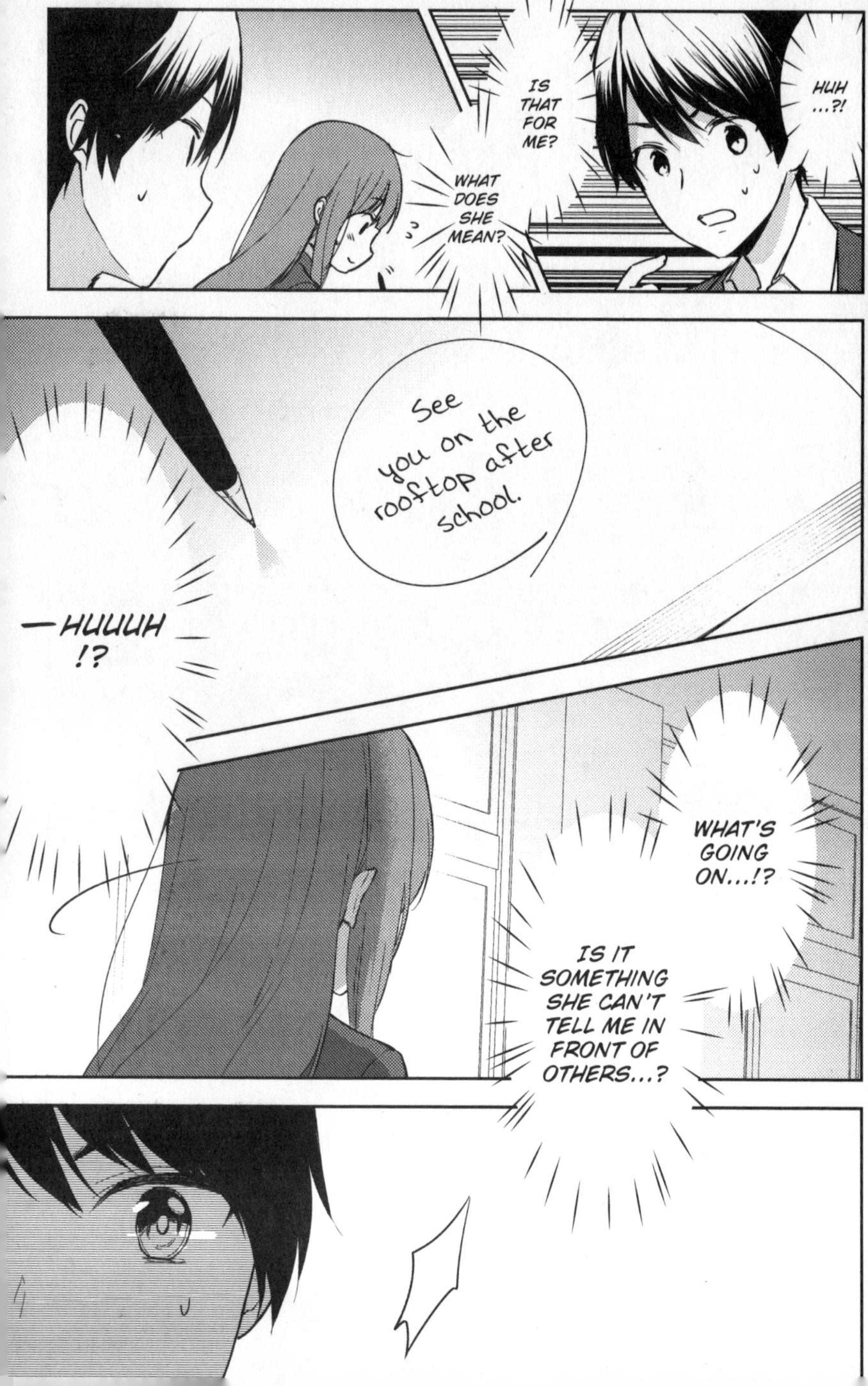
HUH...?!
IS THAT FOR ME?
WHAT DOES SHE MEAN?
See you on the rooftop after school.
—HUUUH!?
WHAT'S GOING ON...!?
IS IT SOMETHING SHE CAN'T TELL ME IN FRONT OF OTHERS...?

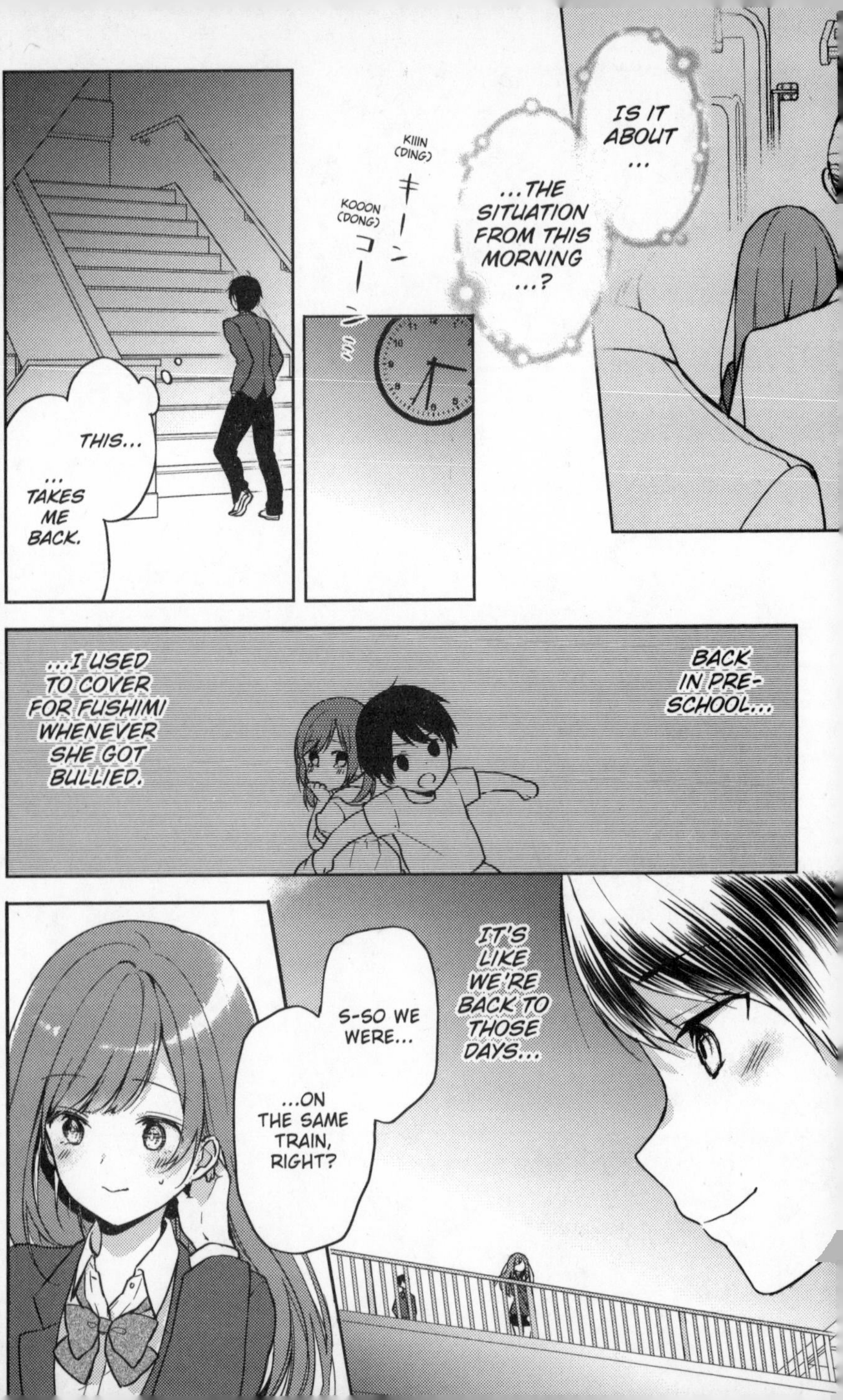
IS IT ABOUT ...
...THE SITUATION FROM THIS MORNING ...?
KIIIN (DING)
キーン
KOOON (DONG)
コーン
THIS...
... TAKES ME BACK.
BACK IN PRE-SCHOOL...
...I USED TO COVER FOR FUSHIMI WHENEVER SHE GOT BULLIED.
IT'S LIKE WE'RE BACK TO THOSE DAYS...
S-SO WE WERE...
...ON THE SAME TRAIN, RIGHT?

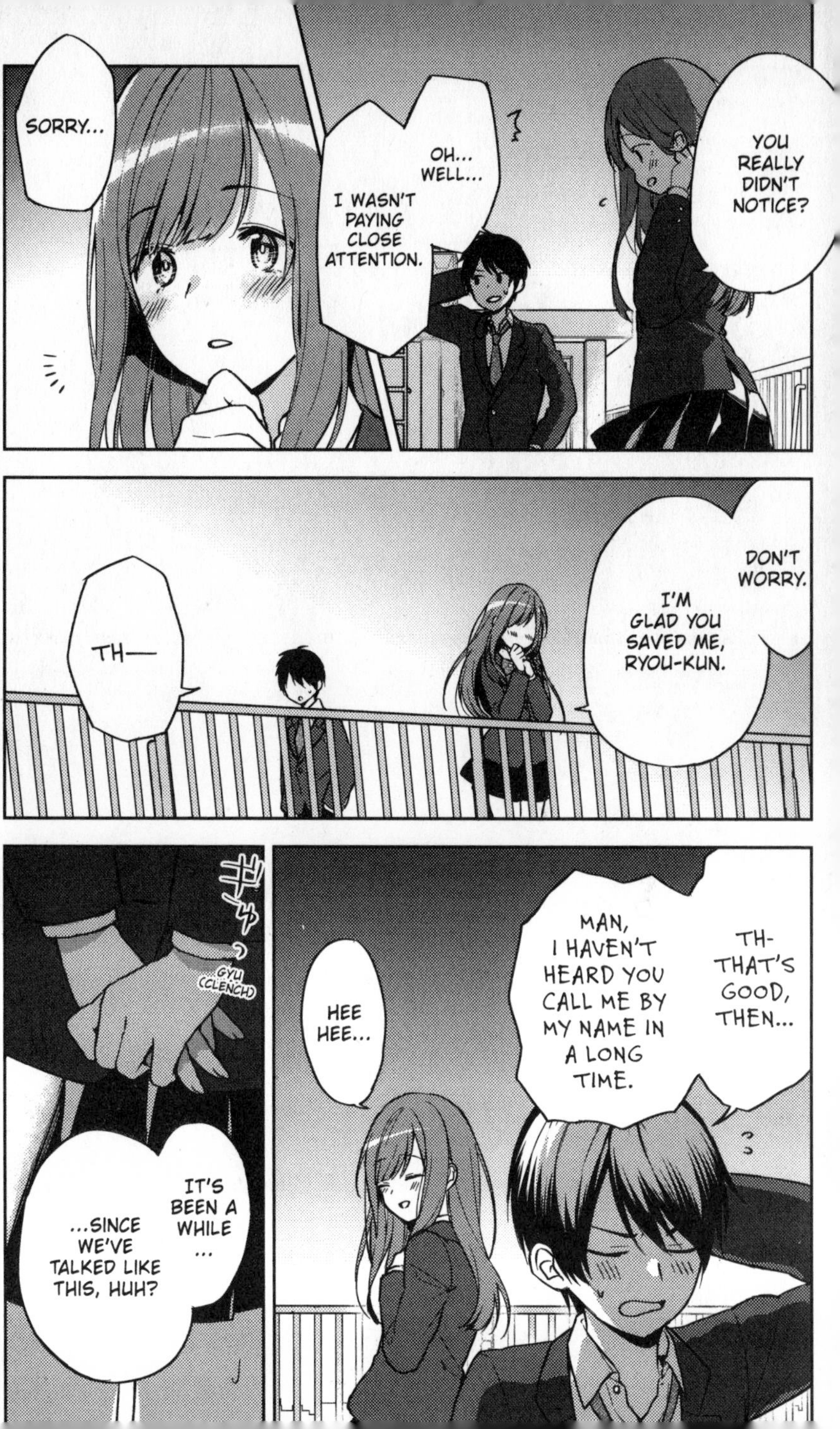
YOU REALLY DIDN'T NOTICE?
OH... WELL...
I WASN'T PAYING CLOSE ATTENTION.
SORRY...
DON'T WORRY.
I'M GLAD YOU SAVED ME, RYOU-KUN.
TH—
TH- THAT'S GOOD, THEN...
MAN, I HAVEN'T HEARD YOU CALL ME BY MY NAME IN A LONG TIME.
HEE HEE...
ギュッ
GYU (CLENCH)
IT'S BEEN A WHILE...
...SINCE WE'VE TALKED LIKE THIS, HUH?

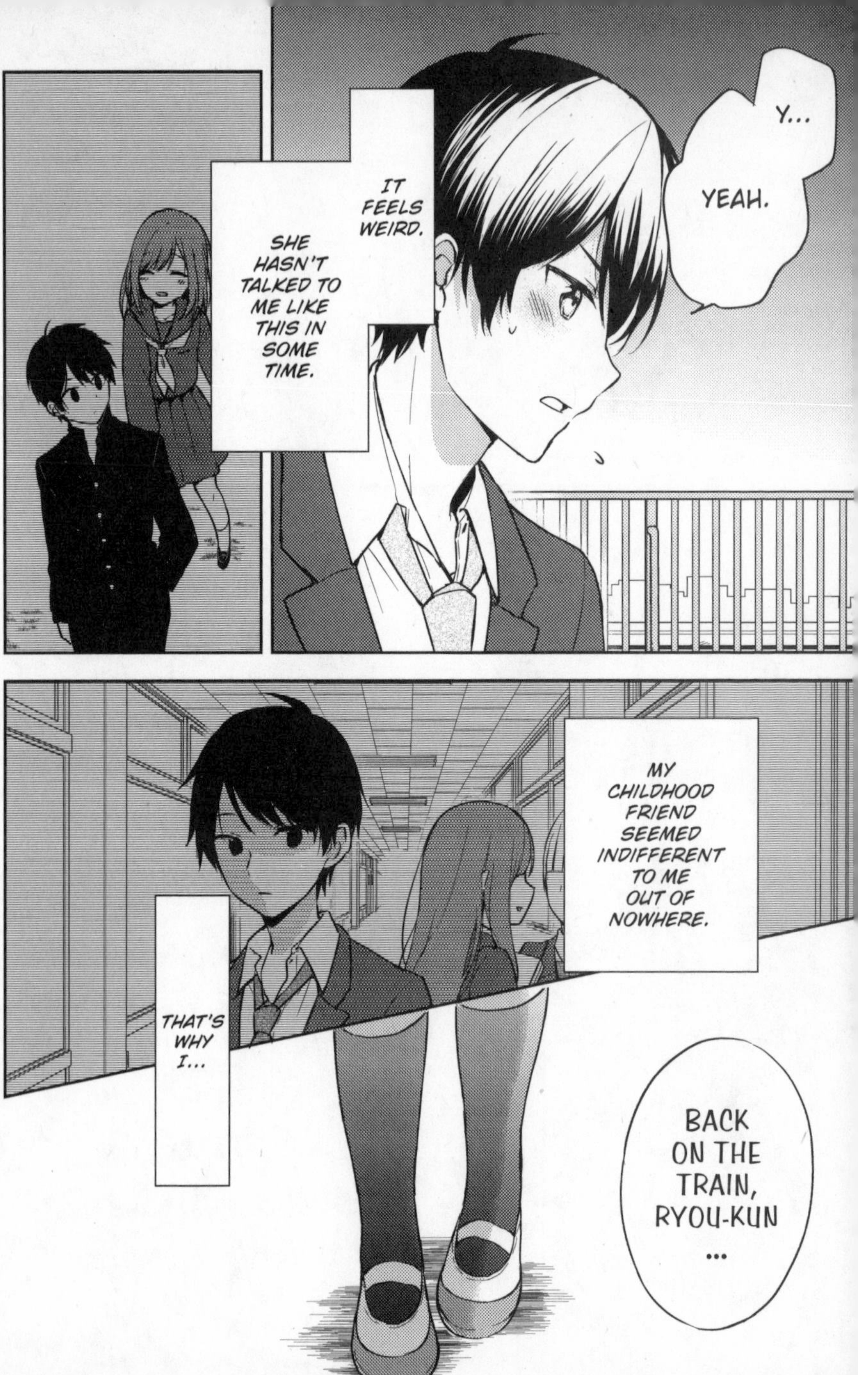
Y...
YEAH.
IT FEELS WEIRD.
SHE HASN'T TALKED TO ME LIKE THIS IN SOME TIME.
MY CHILDHOOD FRIEND SEEMED INDIFFERENT TO ME OUT OF NOWHERE.
THAT'S WHY I...
BACK ON THE TRAIN, RYOU-KUN ...

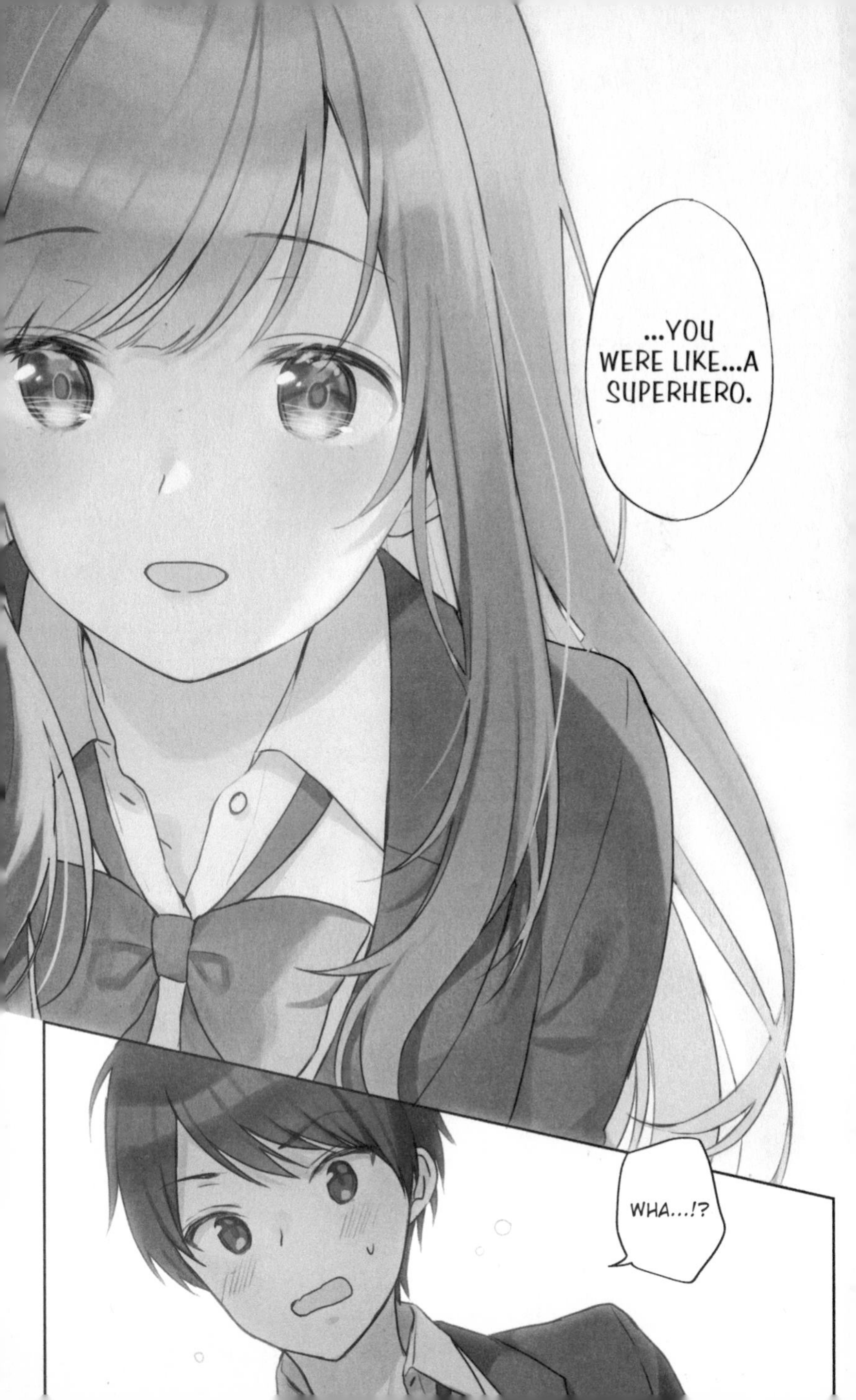
...YOU WERE LIKE...A SUPERHERO.
WHA...!?

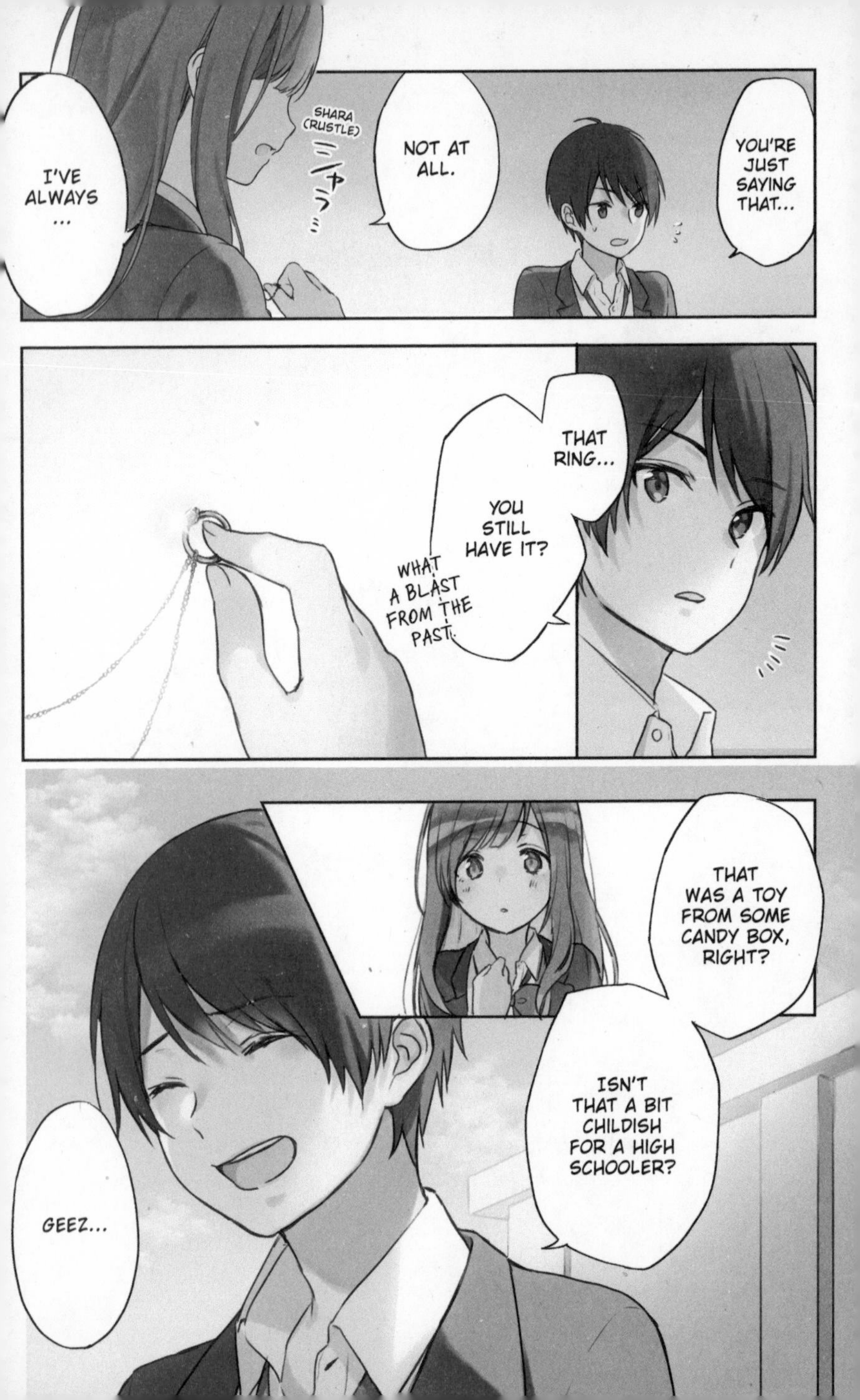
YOU'RE JUST SAYING THAT...
NOT AT ALL.
SHARA (RUSTLE)
シャラ
I'VE ALWAYS ...
THAT RING...
YOU STILL HAVE IT?
WHAT A BLAST FROM THE PAST.
THAT WAS A TOY FROM SOME CANDY BOX, RIGHT?
ISN'T THAT A BIT CHILDISH FOR A HIGH SCHOOLER?
GEEZ...

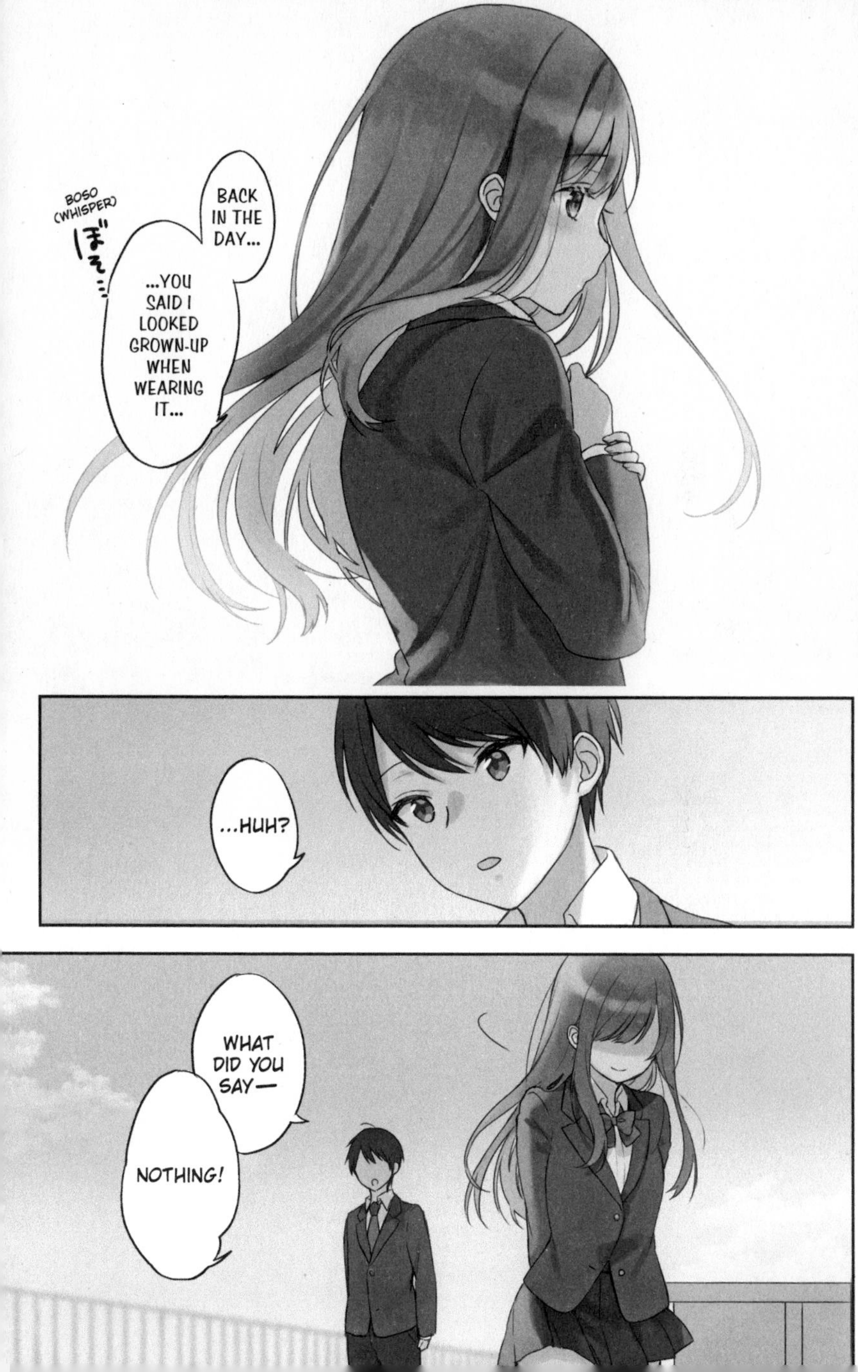
BACK IN THE DAY...
...YOU SAID I LOOKED GROWN-UP WHEN WEARING IT...
BOSO (WHISPER)
ぼそ…
...HUH?
WHAT DID YOU SAY—
NOTHING!

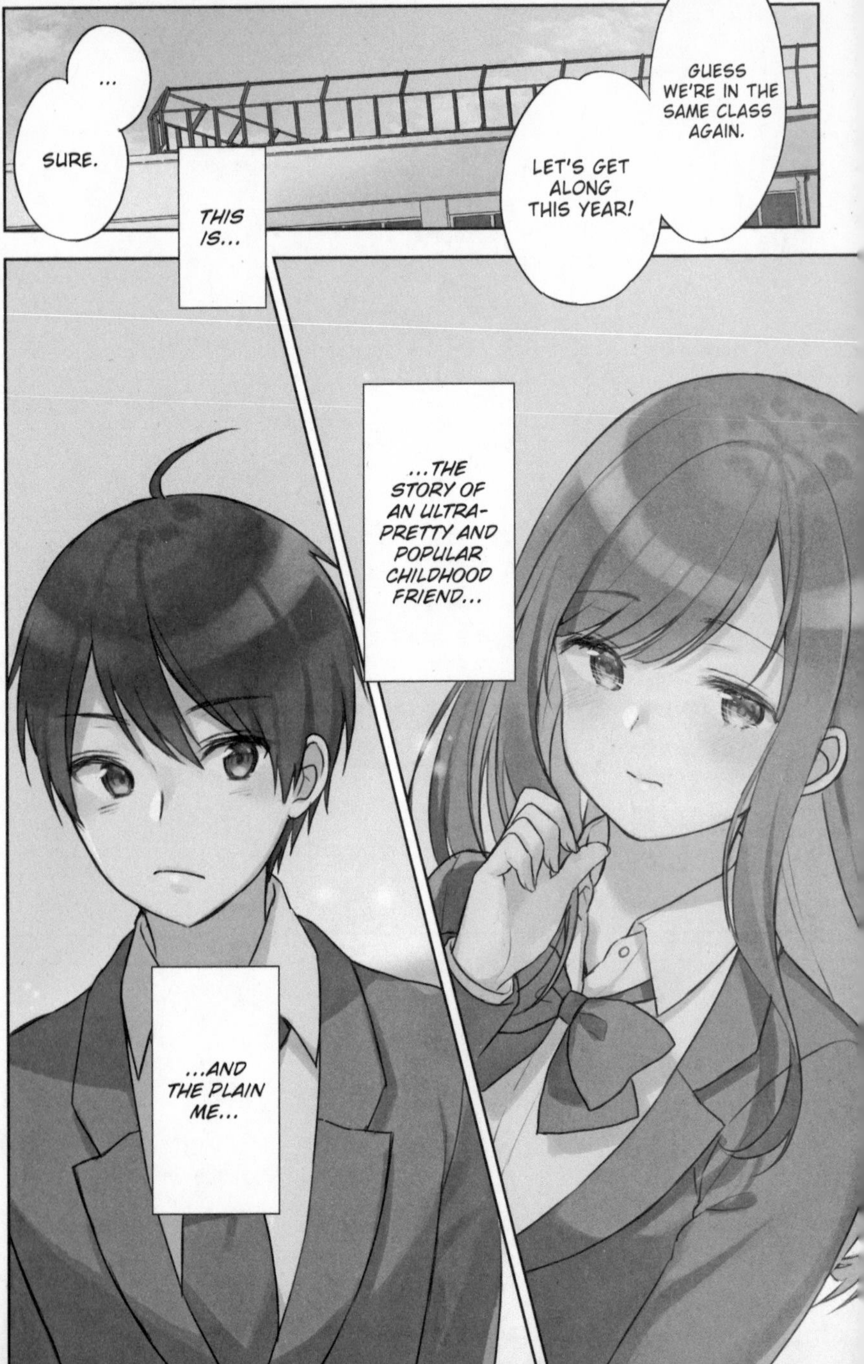
GUESS WE'RE IN THE SAME CLASS AGAIN.
LET'S GET ALONG THIS YEAR!
...
SURE.
THIS IS...
...THE STORY OF AN ULTRA-PRETTY AND POPULAR CHILDHOOD FRIEND...
...AND THE PLAIN ME...

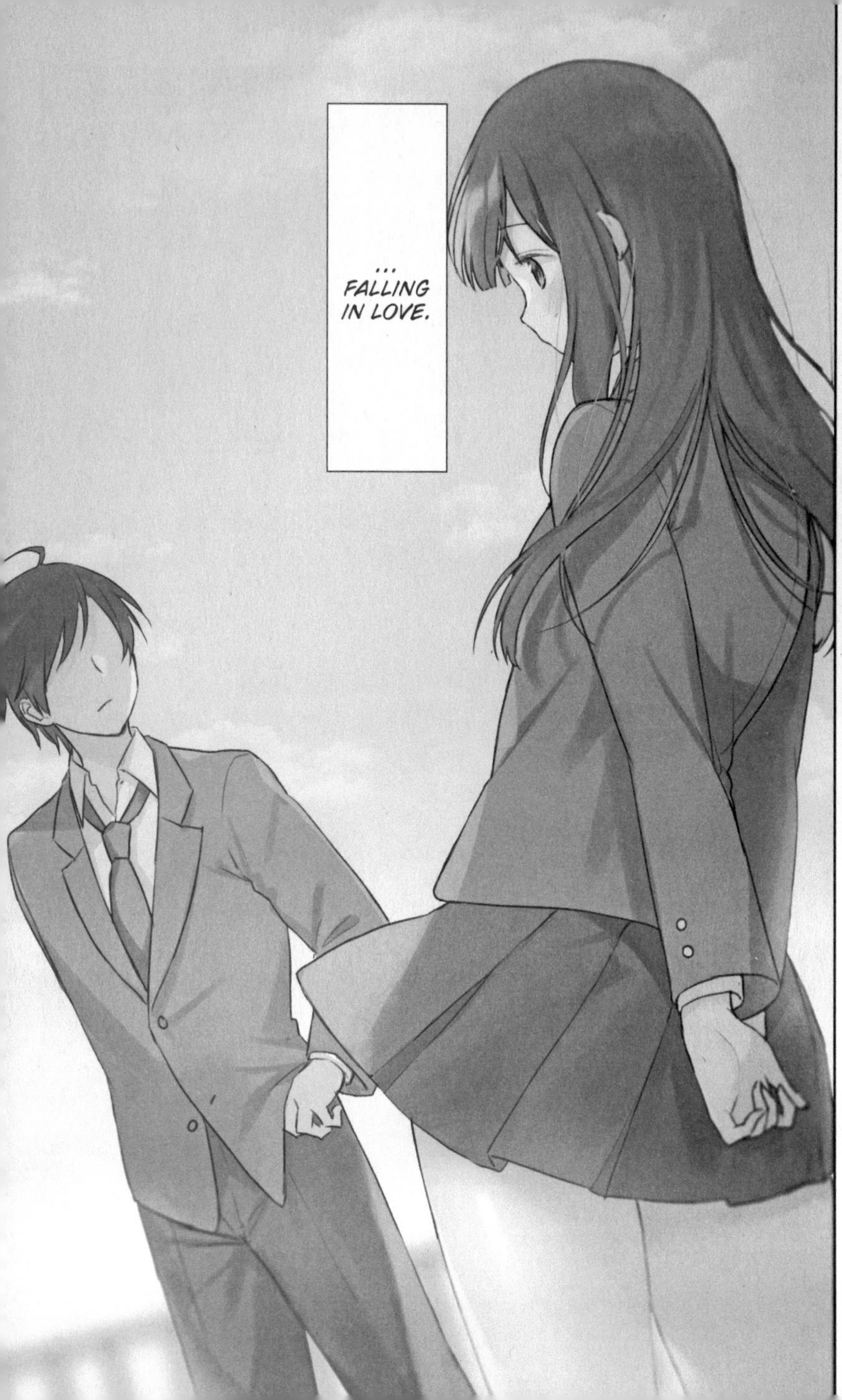
...FALLING IN LOVE.

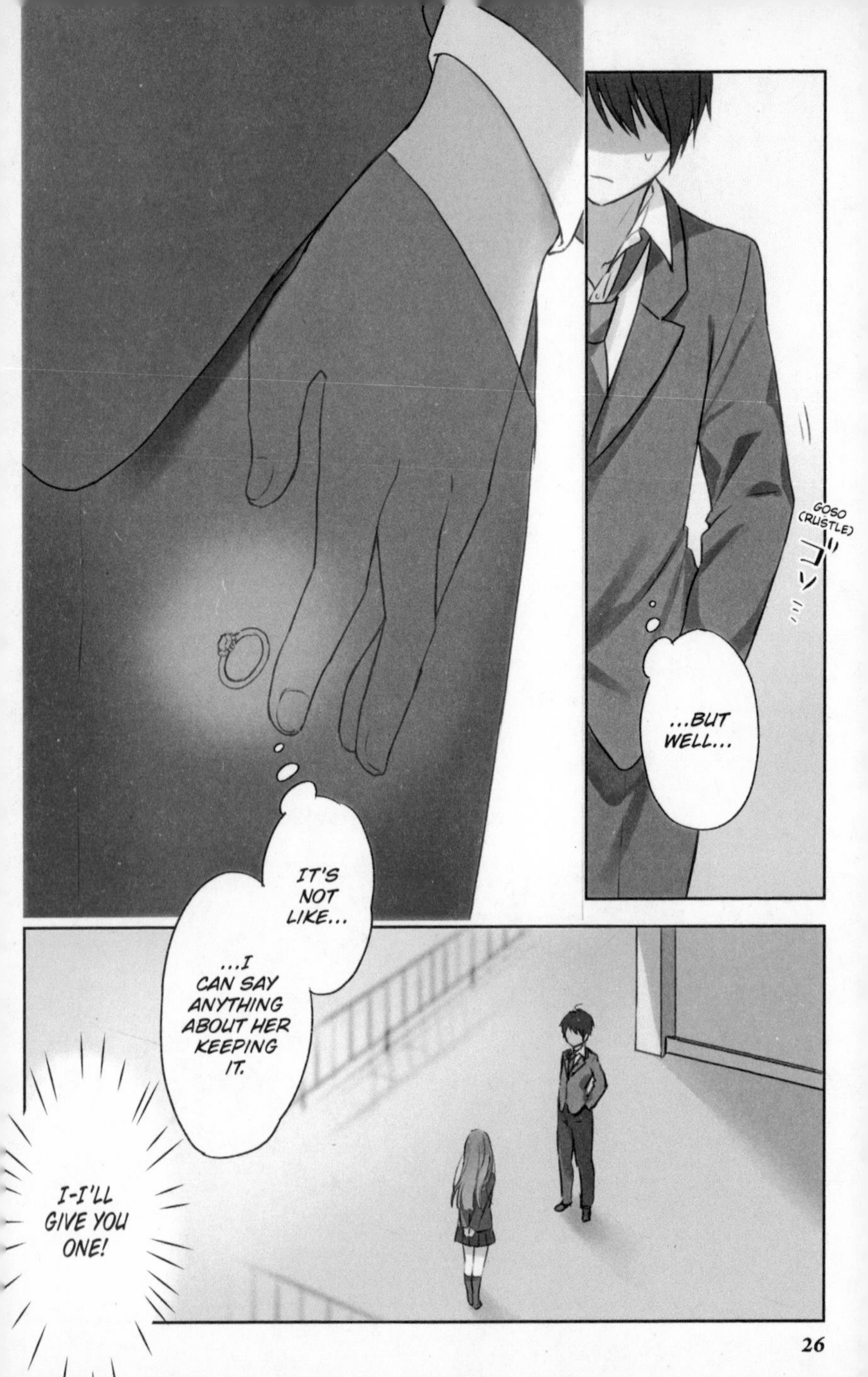
GOSO (RUSTLE)
ゴソ
...BUT WELL...
IT'S NOT LIKE...
...I CAN SAY ANYTHING ABOUT HER KEEPING IT.
I-I'LL GIVE YOU ONE!

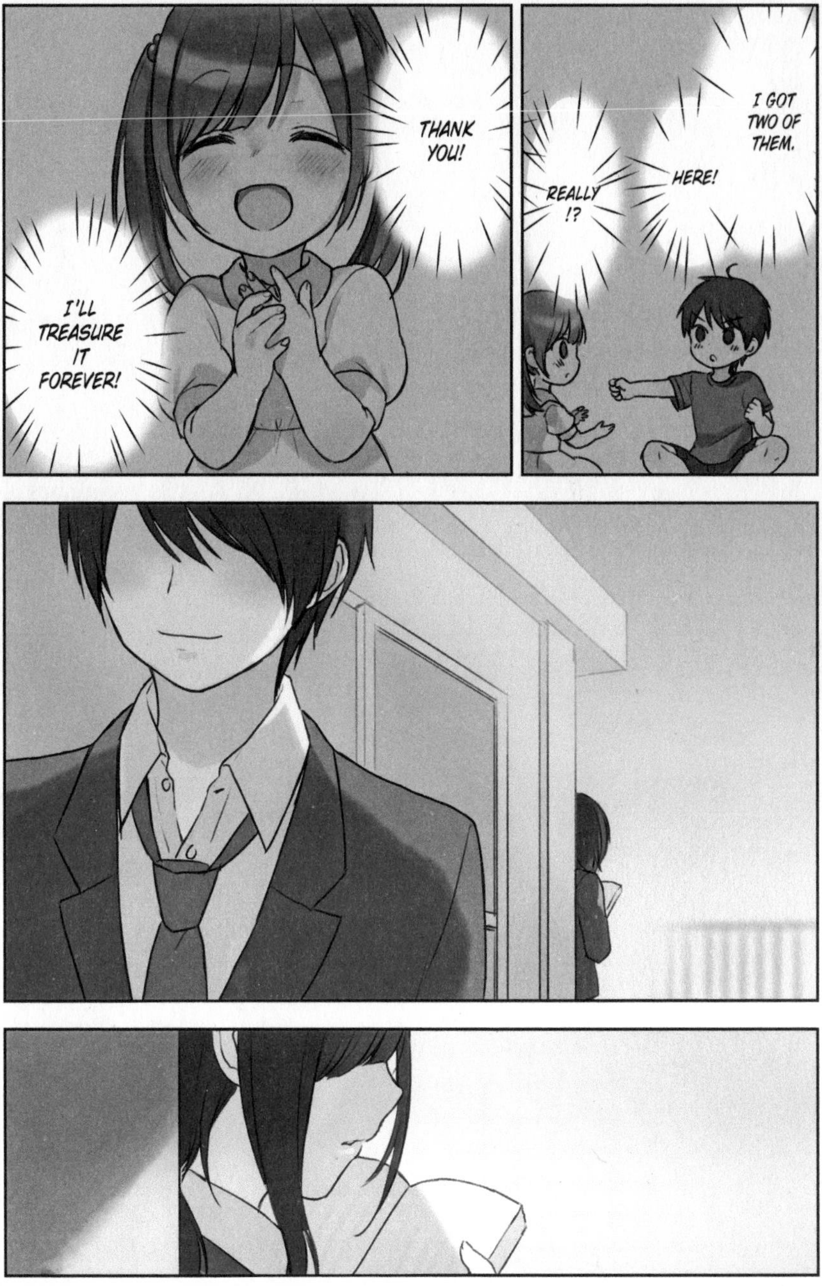
I GOT TWO OF THEM.
HERE!
REALLY !?
THANK YOU!
I'LL TREASURE IT FOREVER!

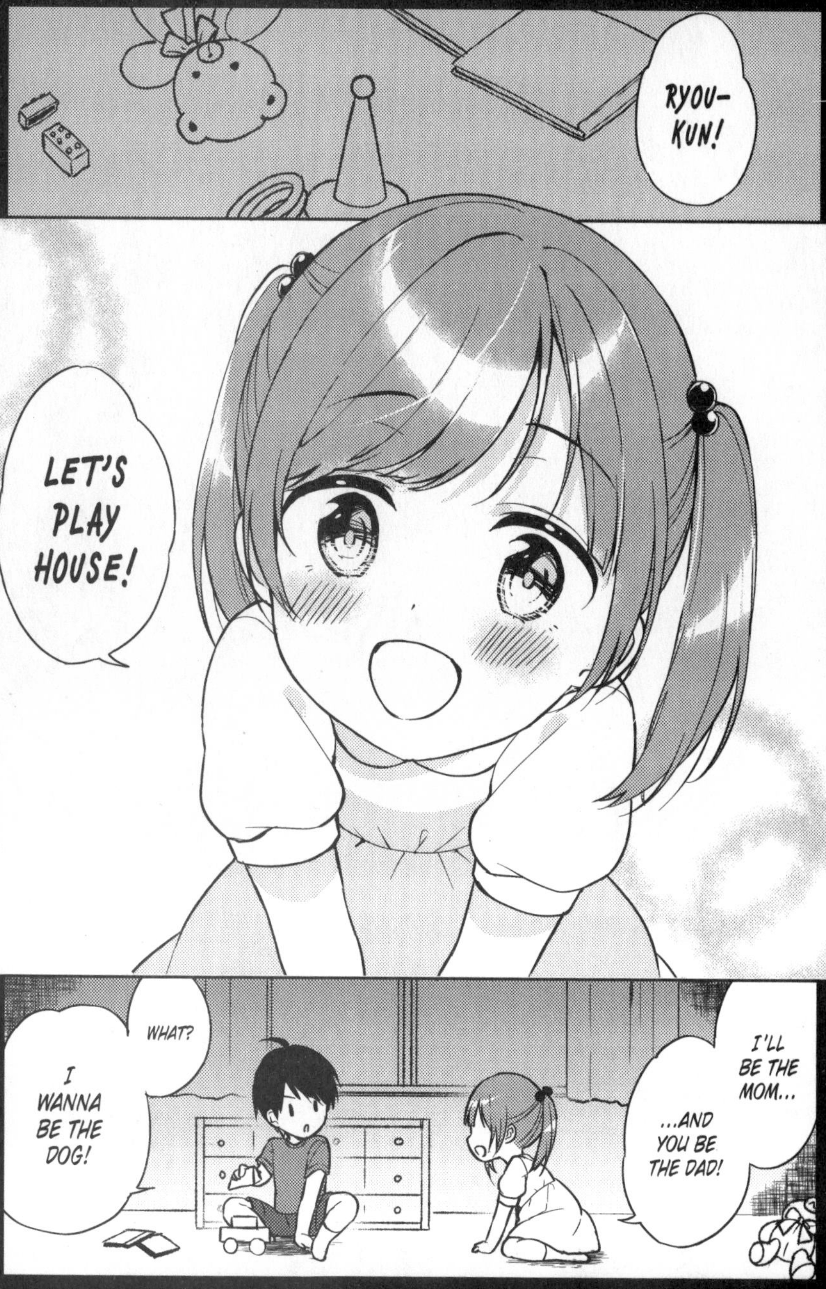
RYOU-KUN!
LET'S PLAY HOUSE!
I'LL BE THE MOM...
...AND YOU BE THE DAD!
WHAT?
I WANNA BE THE DOG!

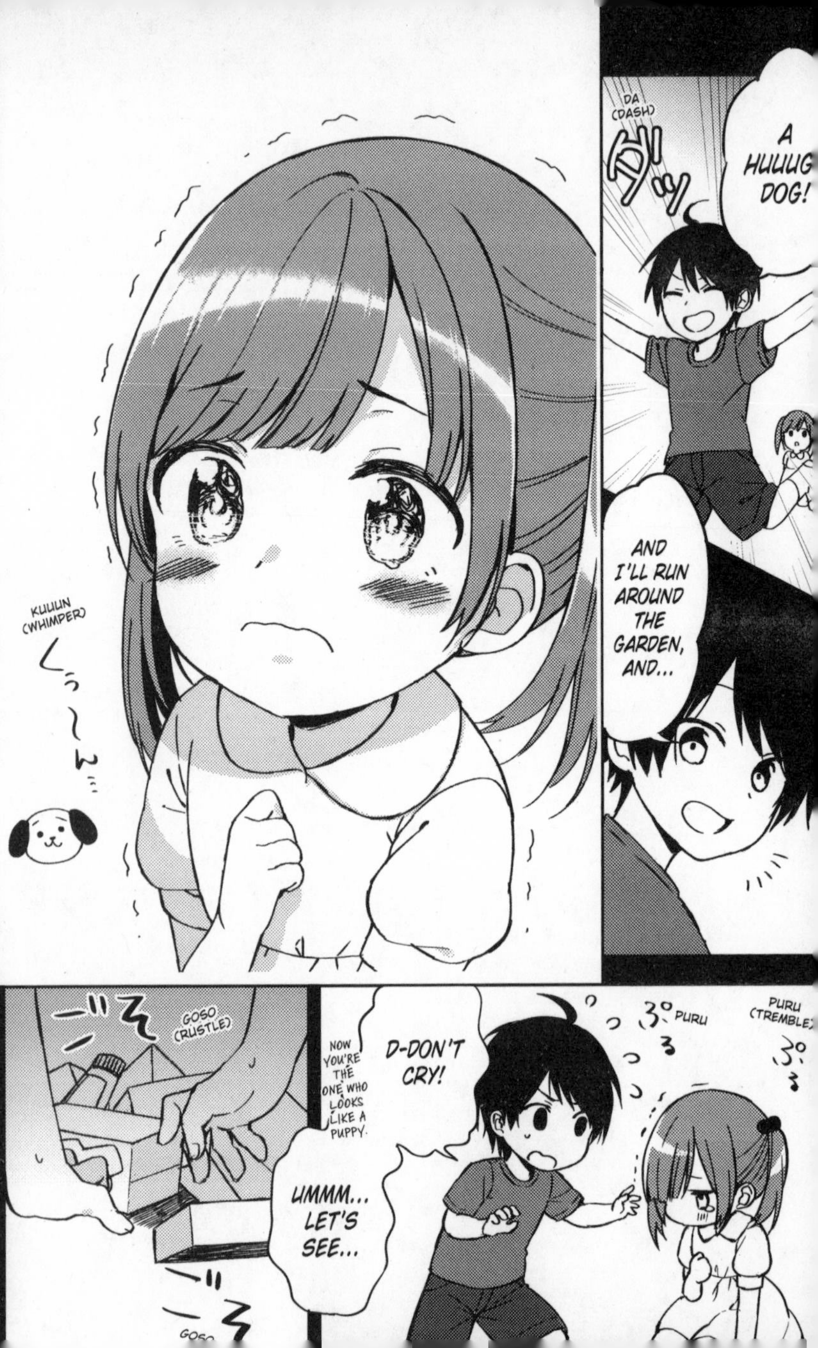
A HUUUG DOG!
DA (DASH)
AND I'LL RUN AROUND THE GARDEN, AND...
KUUUN (WHIMPER)
PURU (TREMBLE)
PURU
D-DON'T CRY!
NOW YOU'RE THE ONE WHO LOOKS LIKE A PUPPY.
UMMM... LET'S SEE...
GOSO (RUSTLE)
GOSO

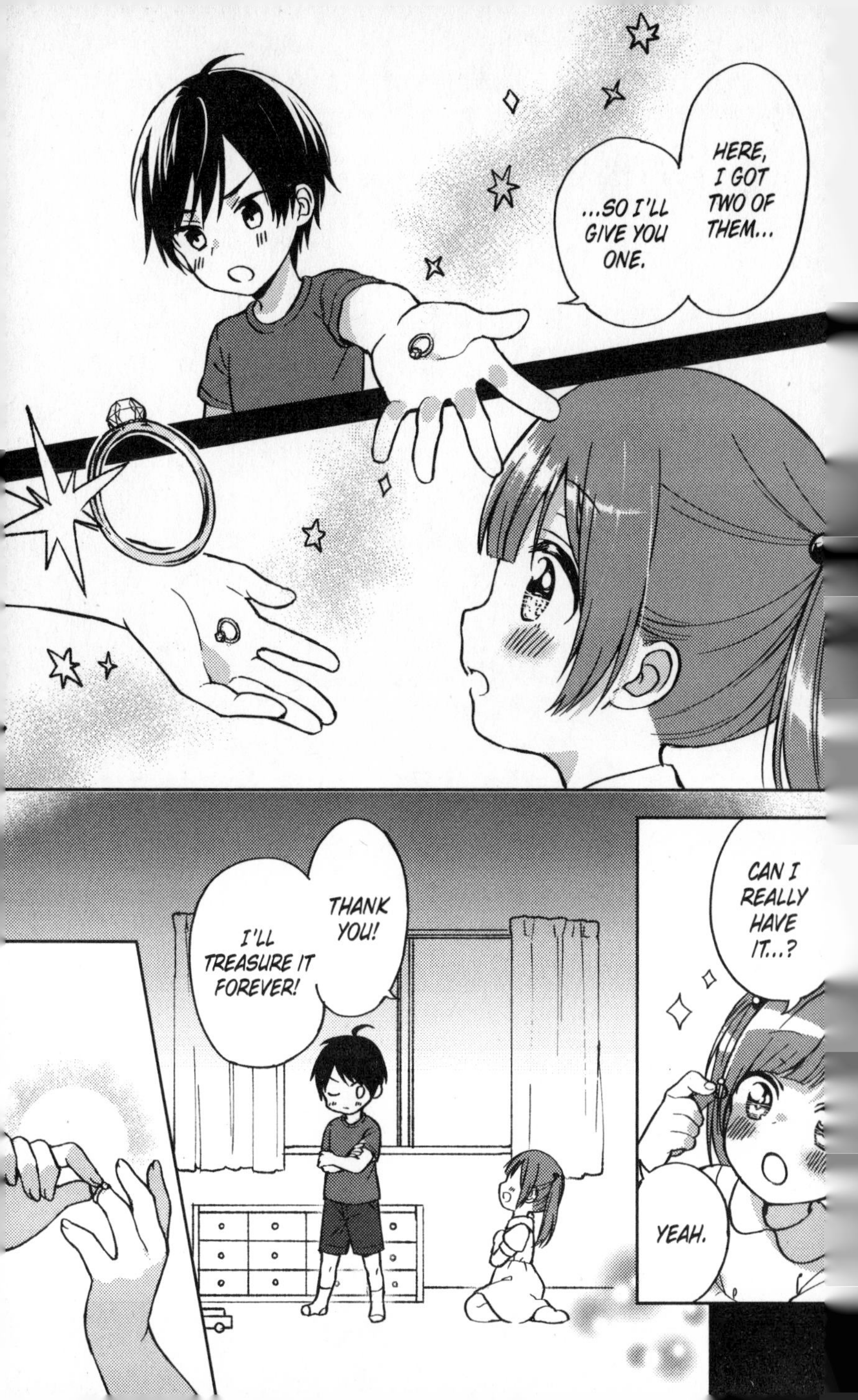
HERE, I GOT TWO OF THEM...
...SO I'LL GIVE YOU ONE.
CAN I REALLY HAVE IT...?
YEAH.
THANK YOU!
I'LL TREASURE IT FOREVER!

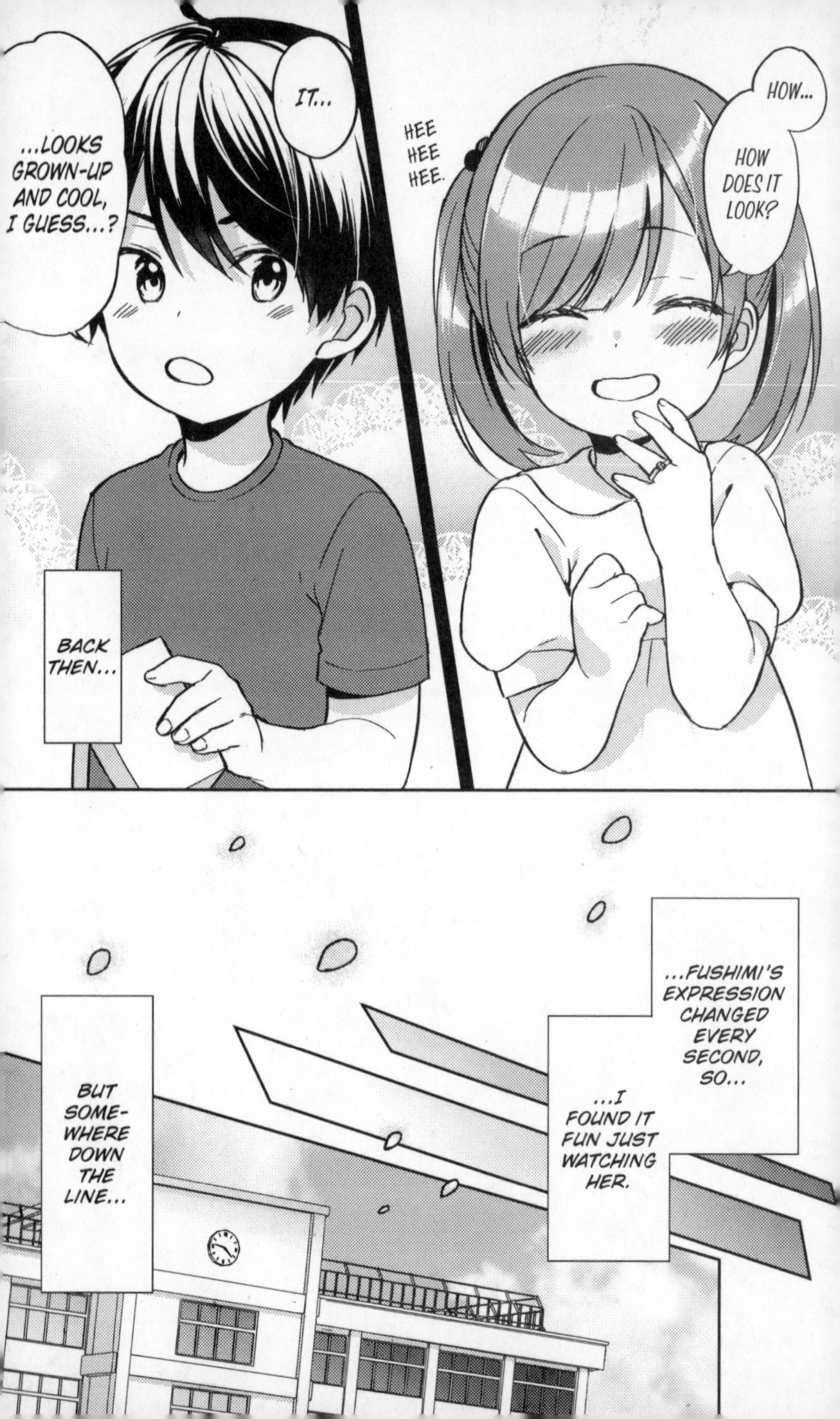
HOW...
HOW DOES IT LOOK?
HEE HEE HEE.
IT...
...LOOKS GROWN-UP AND COOL, I GUESS...?
BACK THEN...
...FUSHIMI'S EXPRESSION CHANGED EVERY SECOND, SO...
...I FOUND IT FUN JUST WATCHING HER.
BUT SOMEWHERE DOWN THE LINE...

#2 Lunch Friends

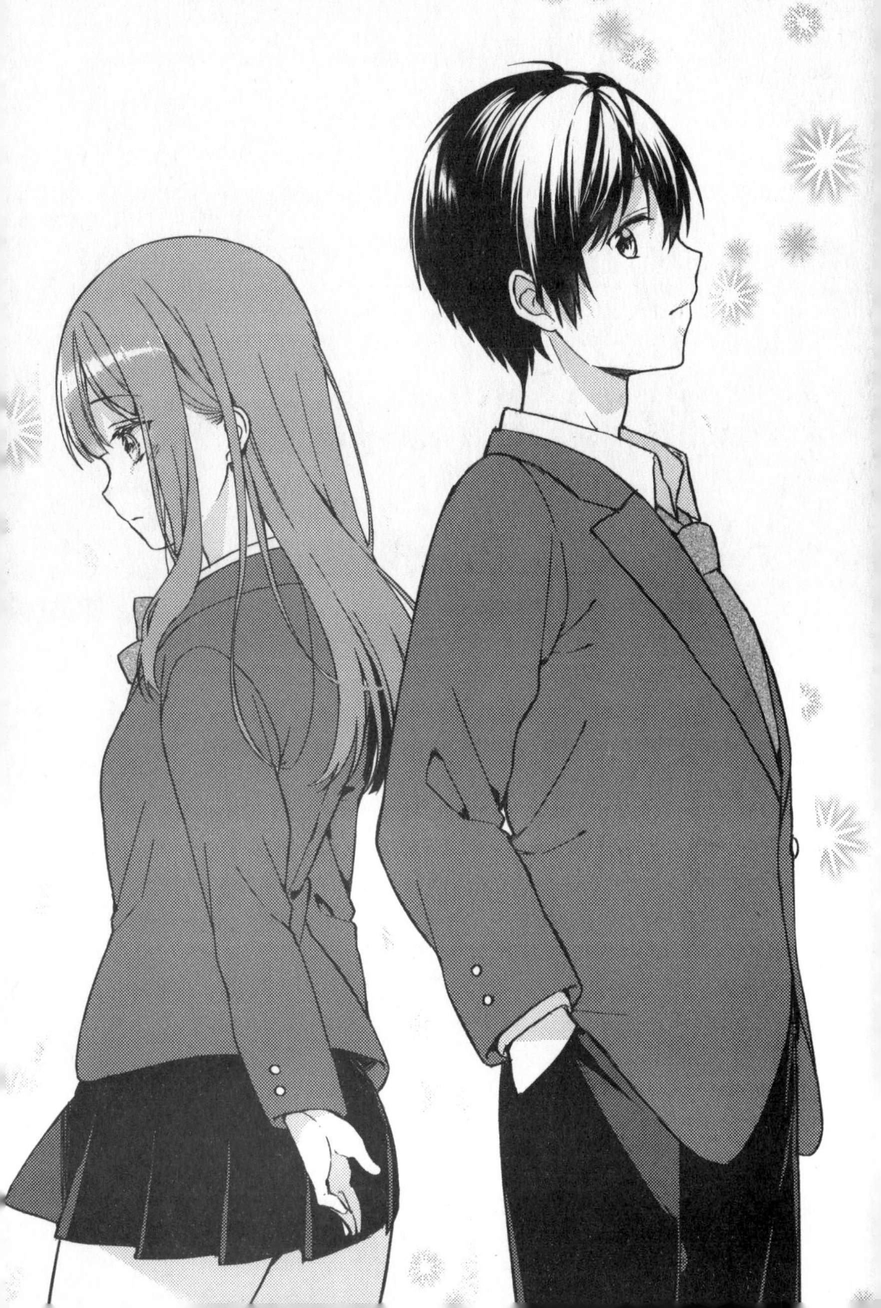

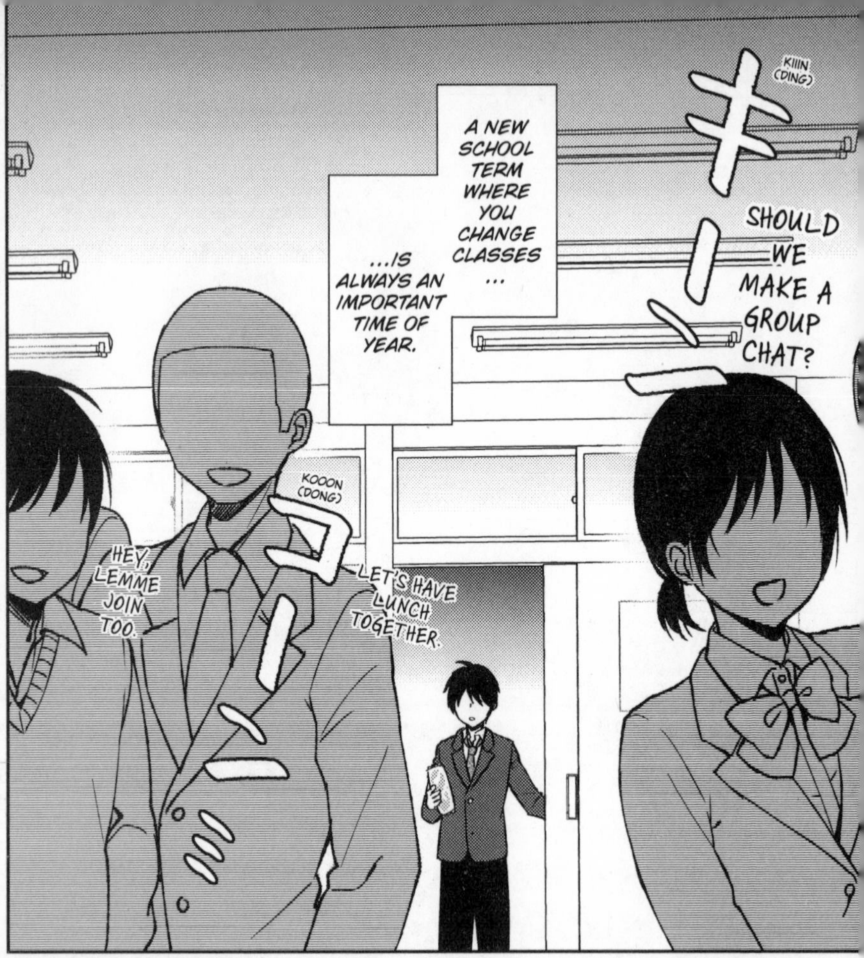
KIIIN (DING)
SHOULD WE MAKE A GROUP CHAT?
A NEW SCHOOL TERM WHERE YOU CHANGE CLASSES...
...IS ALWAYS AN IMPORTANT TIME OF YEAR.
KOOON (DONG)
LET'S HAVE LUNCH TOGETHER.
HEY, LEMME JOIN TOO.

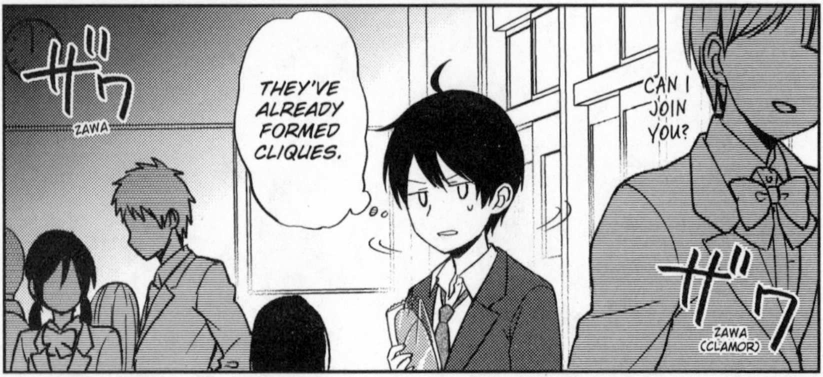
CAN I JOIN YOU?
ザワ
ZAWA (CLAMOR)
THEY'VE ALREADY FORMED CLIQUES.
ザワ
ZAWA

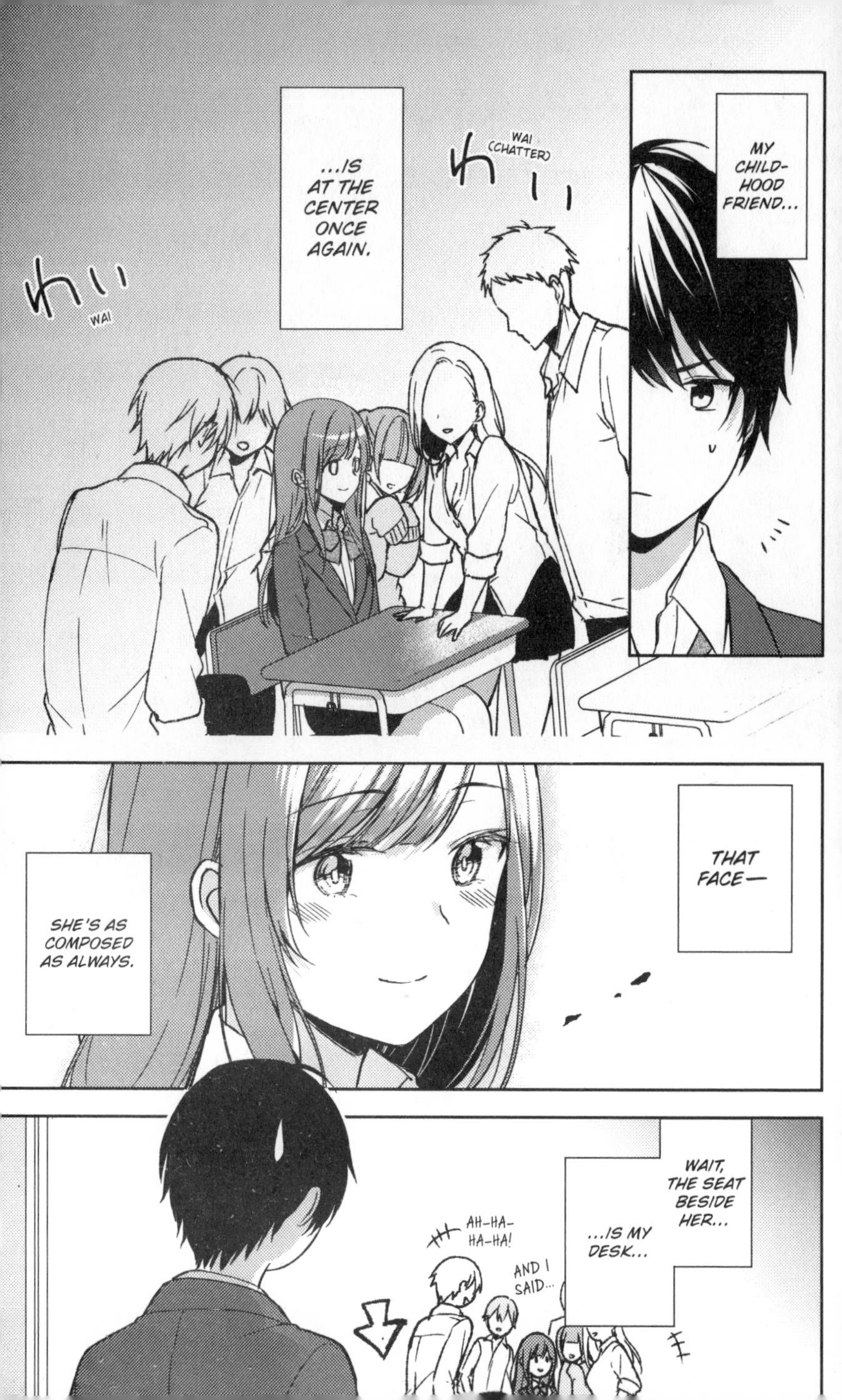
MY CHILDHOOD FRIEND...
WAI (CHATTER)
...IS AT THE CENTER ONCE AGAIN.
WAI
THAT FACE—
SHE'S AS COMPOSED AS ALWAYS.
WAIT, THE SEAT BESIDE HER...
...IS MY DESK...
AH-HA-HA-HA!
AND I SAID...

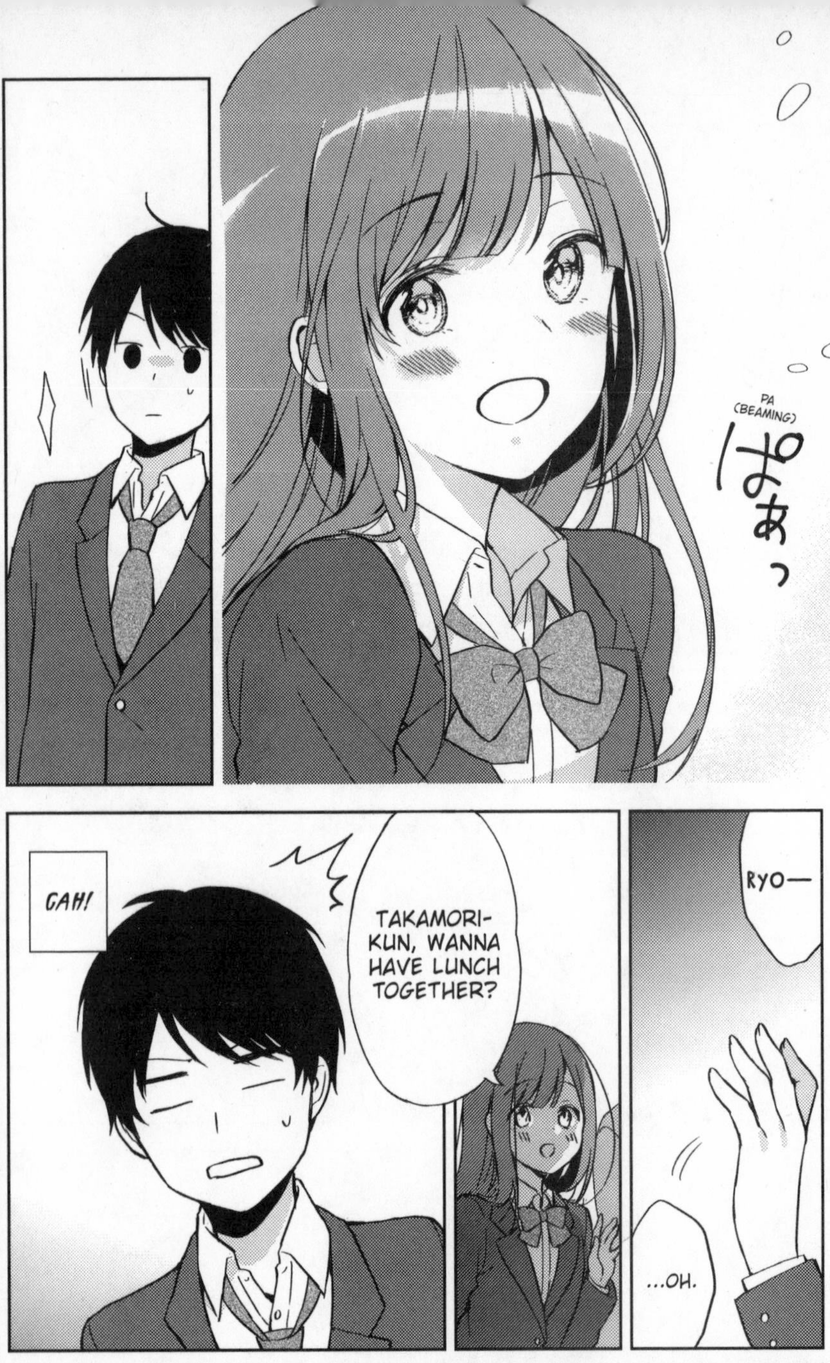
PA (BEAMING)
ぱあっ
RYO—
...OH.
TAKAMORI-KUN, WANNA HAVE LUNCH TOGETHER?
GAH!

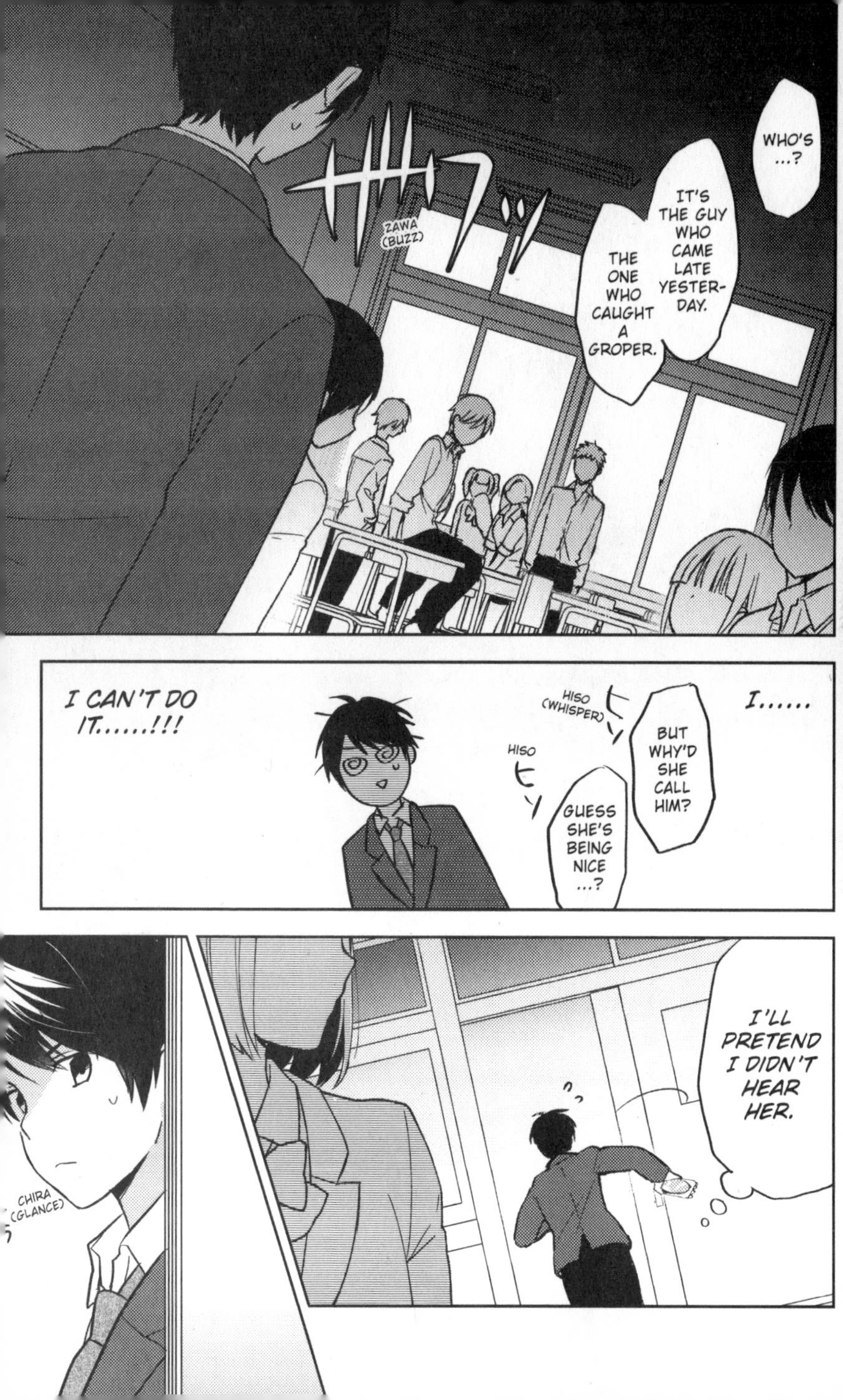
WHO'S ...?
IT'S THE GUY WHO CAME LATE YESTER-DAY.
THE ONE WHO CAUGHT A GROPER.
ZAWA (BUZZ)
I......
HISO (WHISPER)
BUT WHY'D SHE CALL HIM?
HISO
GUESS SHE'S BEING NICE ...?
I CAN'T DO IT......!!!
I'LL PRETEND I DIDN'T HEAR HER.
CHIRA (GLANCE)

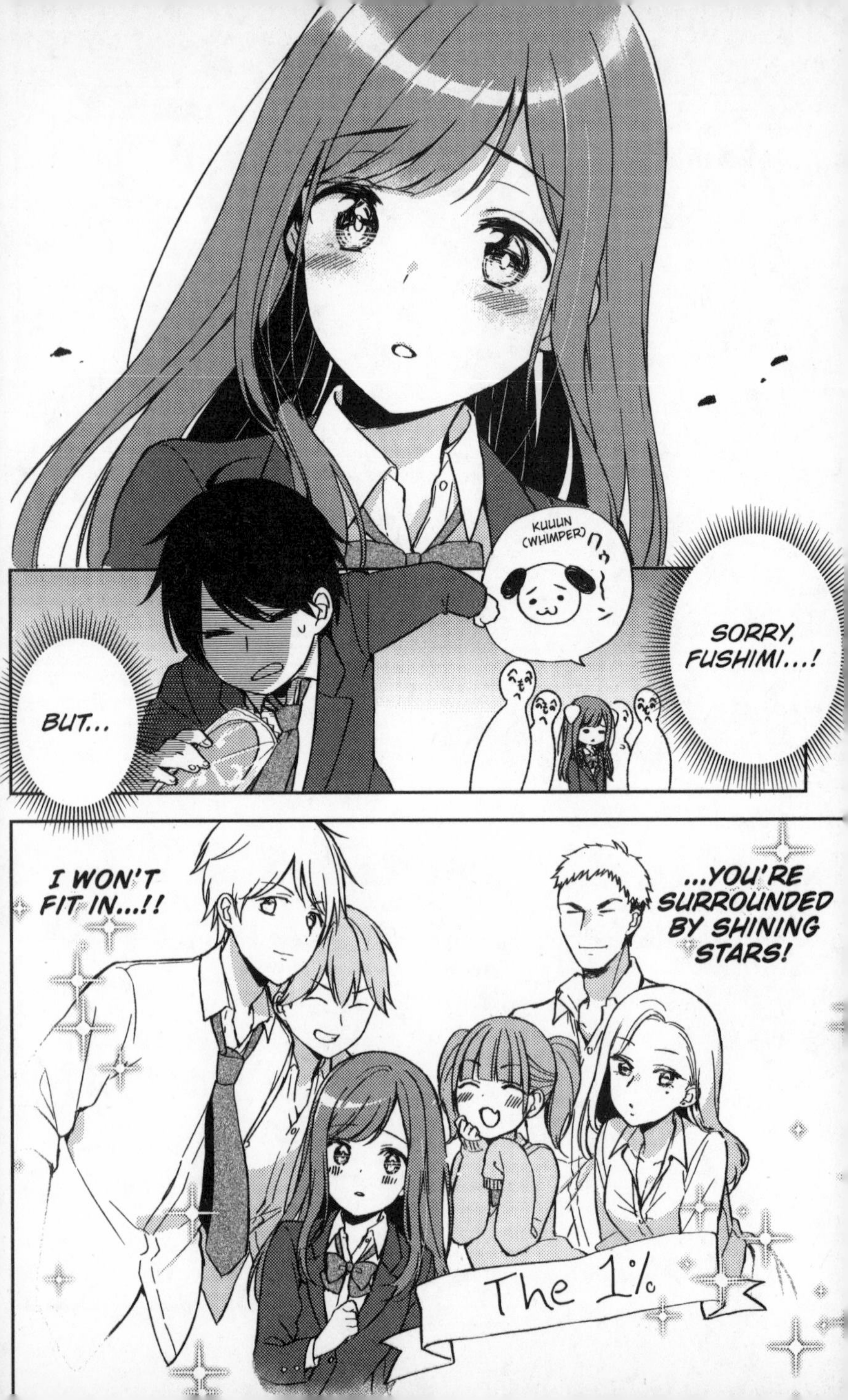
SORRY, FUSHIMI...!
KUUUN (WHIMPER)
BUT...
...YOU'RE SURROUNDED BY SHINING STARS!
I WON'T FIT IN...!!
The 1%

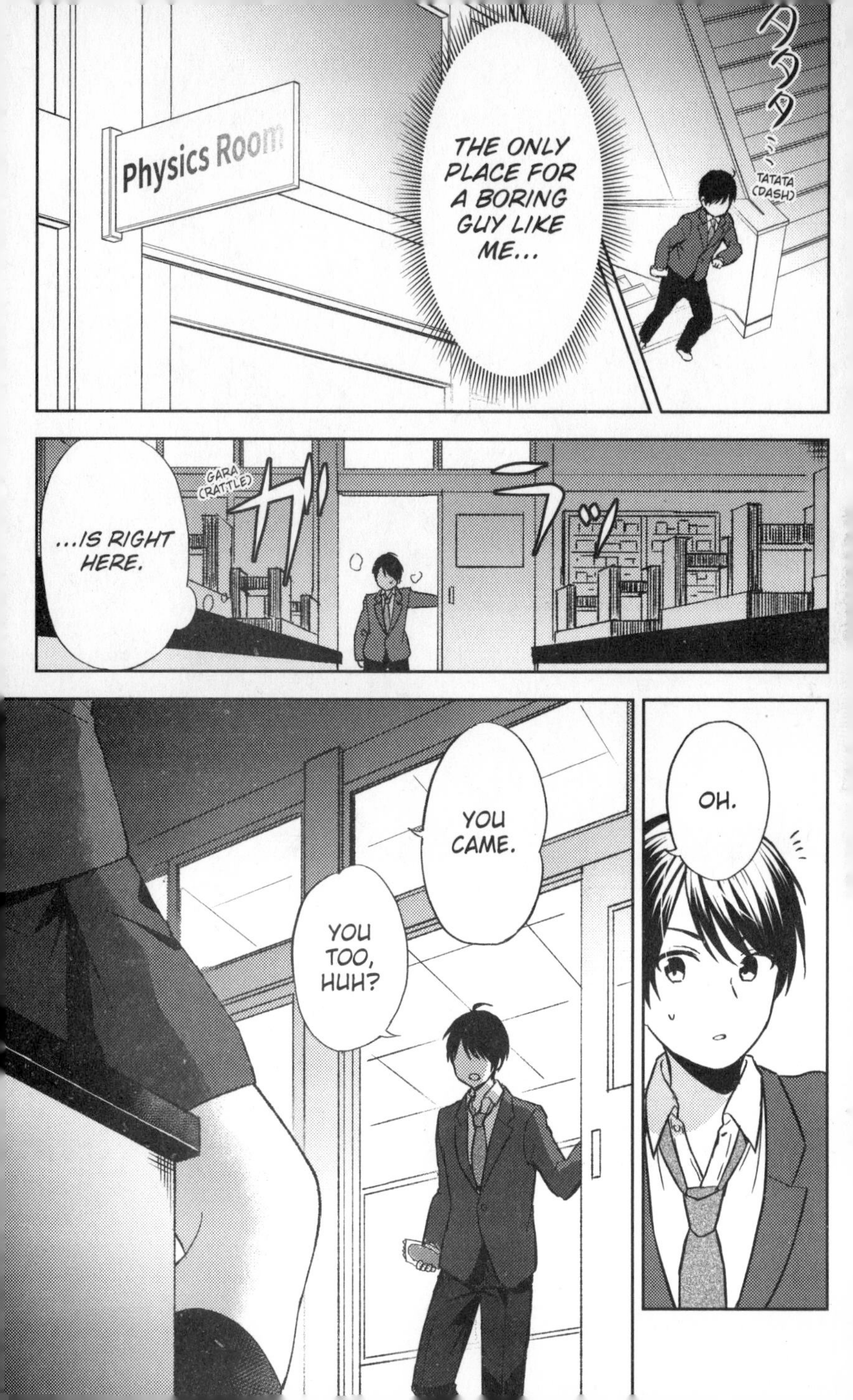
TATATA (DASH)
THE ONLY PLACE FOR A BORING GUY LIKE ME...
Physics Room
GARA (RATTLE)
...IS RIGHT HERE.
OH.
YOU CAME.
YOU TOO, HUH?

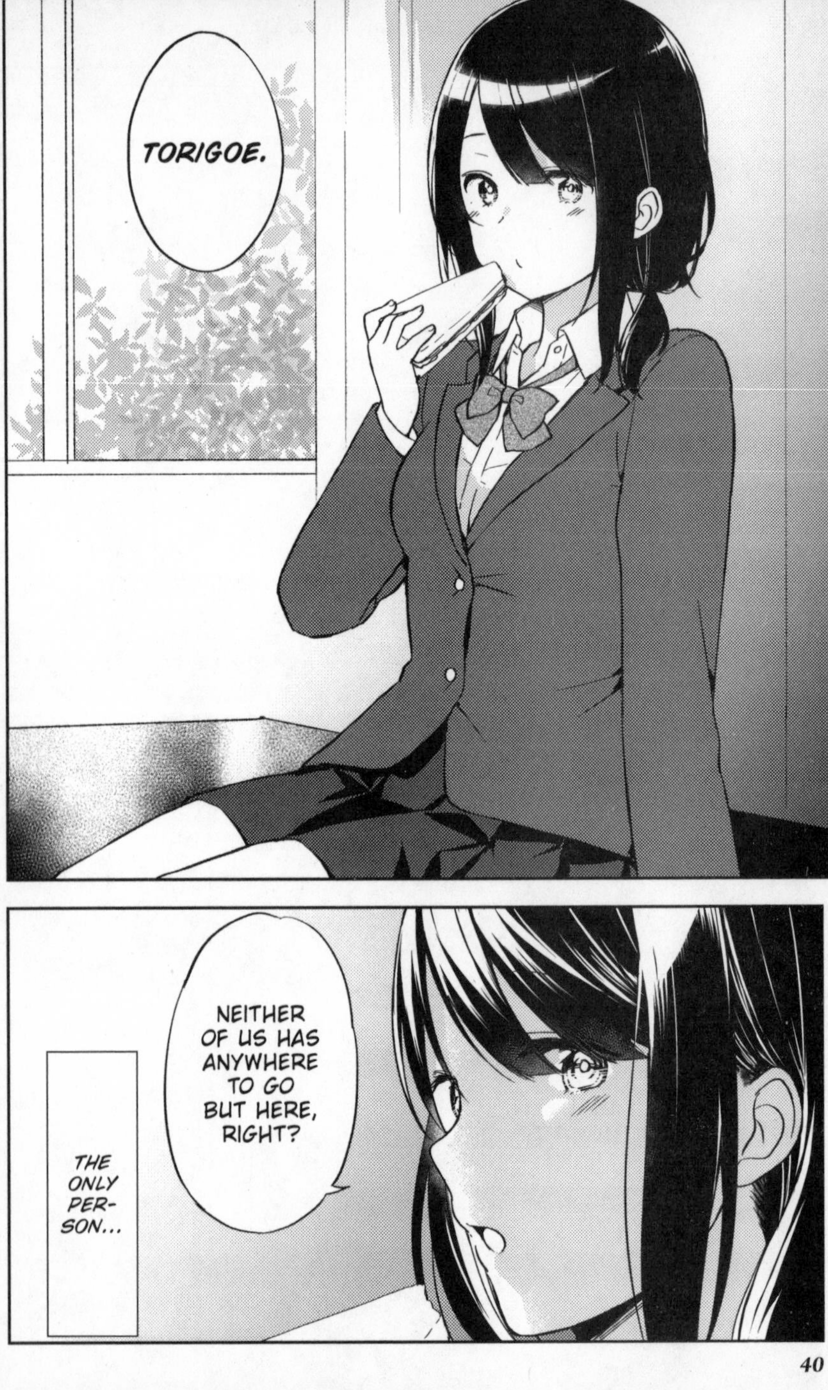
TORIGOE.
NEITHER OF US HAS ANYWHERE TO GO BUT HERE, RIGHT?
THE ONLY PER-SON...

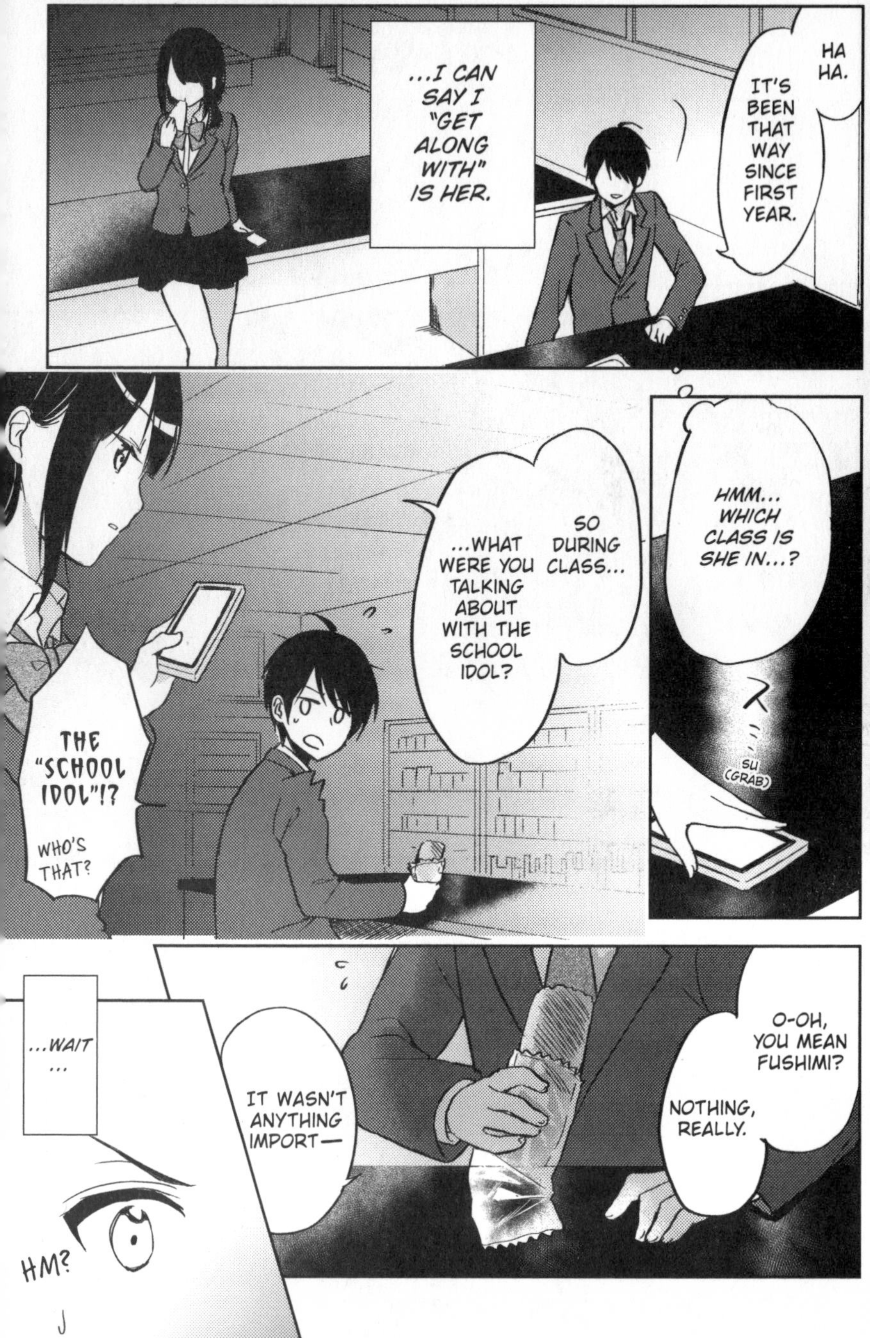
HA HA.
IT'S BEEN THAT WAY SINCE FIRST YEAR.
...I CAN SAY I "GET ALONG WITH" IS HER.
HMM... WHICH CLASS IS SHE IN...?
SU (GRAB)
SO DURING CLASS...
...WHAT WERE YOU TALKING ABOUT WITH THE SCHOOL IDOL?
THE "SCHOOL IDOL"!?
WHO'S THAT?
O-OH, YOU MEAN FUSHIMI?
NOTHING, REALLY.
IT WASN'T ANYTHING IMPORT—
...WAIT ...
HM?

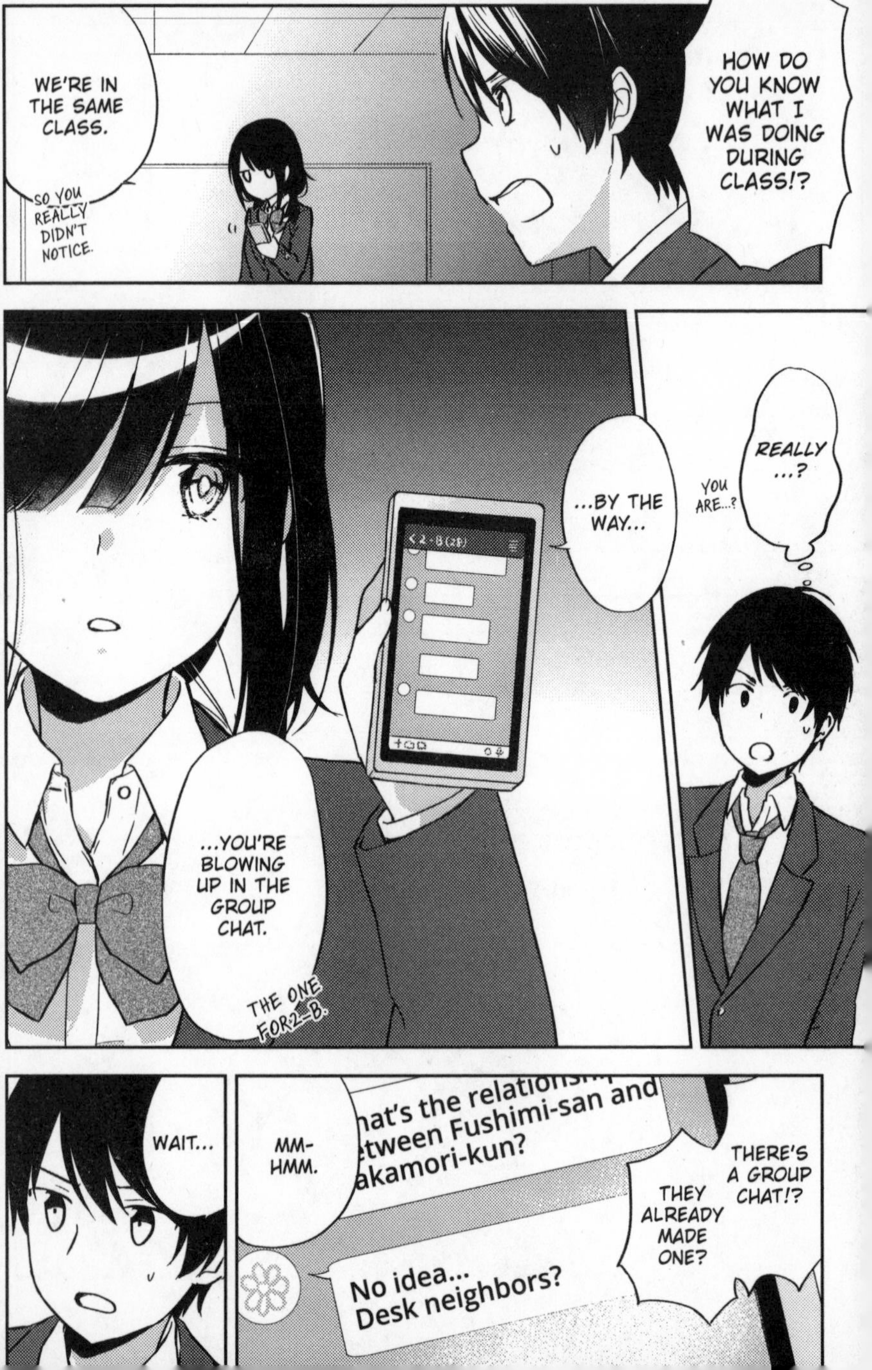
HOW DO YOU KNOW WHAT I WAS DOING DURING CLASS!?
WE'RE IN THE SAME CLASS.
SO YOU REALLY DIDN'T NOTICE.
REALLY...?
YOU ARE...?
...BY THE WAY...
2-B (28)
...YOU'RE BLOWING UP IN THE GROUP CHAT.
THE ONE FOR 2-B.
THERE'S A GROUP CHAT!?
THEY ALREADY MADE ONE?
hat's the relationsh etween Fushimi-san and akamori-kun?
MM-HMM.
No idea... Desk neighbors?
WAIT...

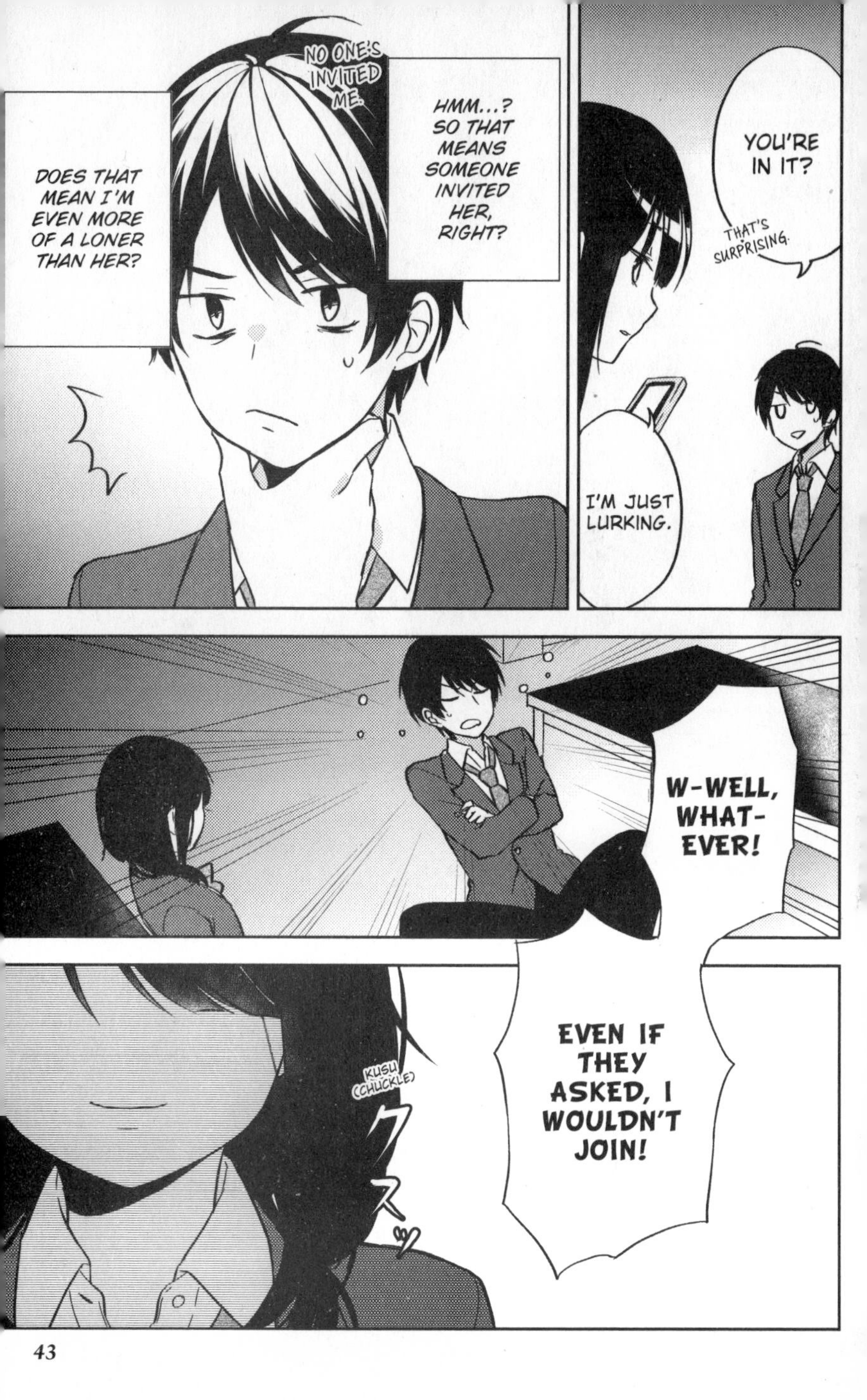
YOU'RE IN IT?
THAT'S SURPRISING.
I'M JUST LURKING.
HMM...? SO THAT MEANS SOMEONE INVITED HER, RIGHT?
NO ONE'S INVITED ME.
DOES THAT MEAN I'M EVEN MORE OF A LONER THAN HER?
W-WELL, WHAT-EVER!
EVEN IF THEY ASKED, I WOULDN'T JOIN!
KUSU (CHUCKLE)

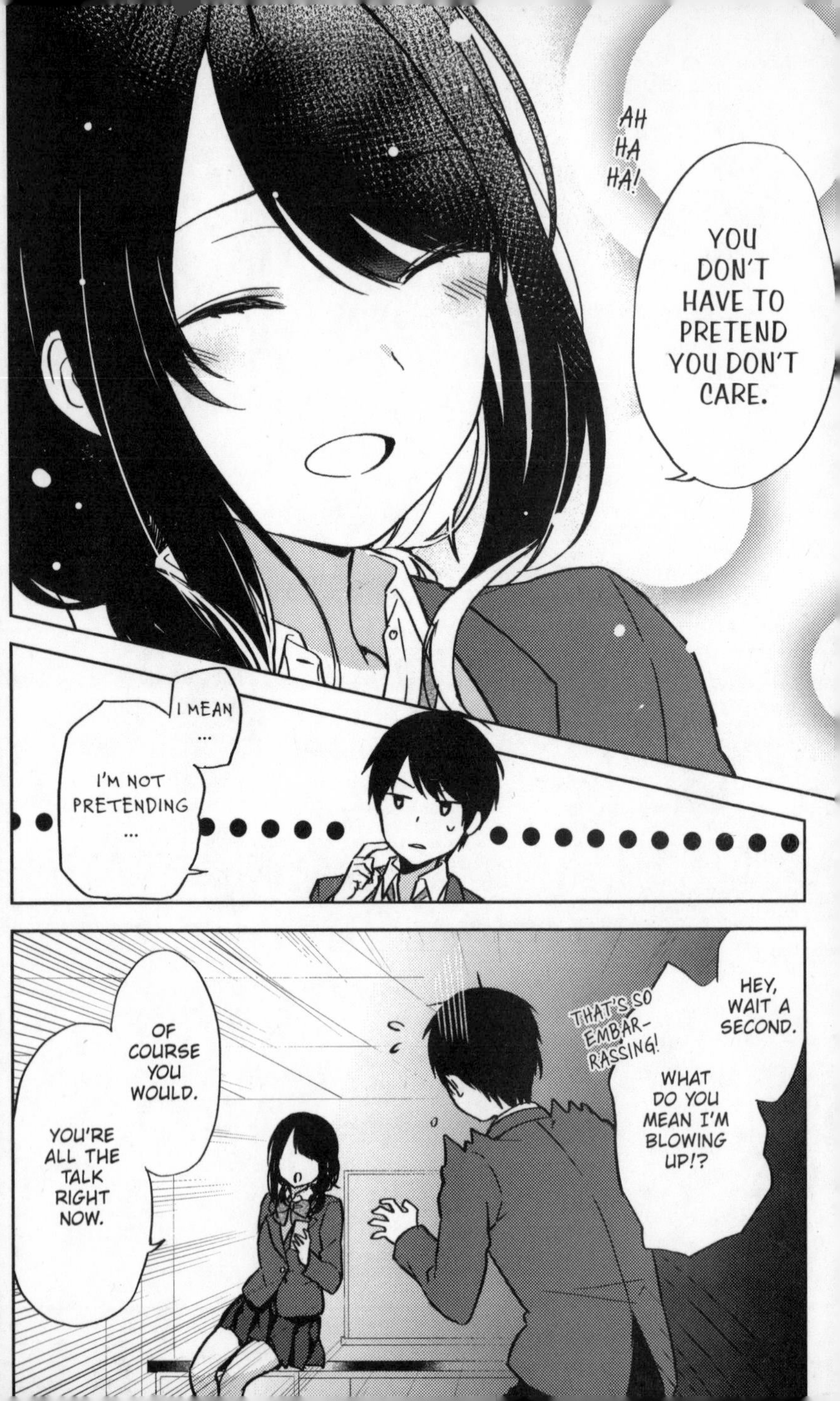
AH HA HA!
YOU DON'T HAVE TO PRETEND YOU DON'T CARE.
I MEAN ...
I'M NOT PRETENDING ...
HEY, WAIT A SECOND.
WHAT DO YOU MEAN I'M BLOWING UP!?
THAT'S SO EMBAR-RASSING!
OF COURSE YOU WOULD.
YOU'RE ALL THE TALK RIGHT NOW.

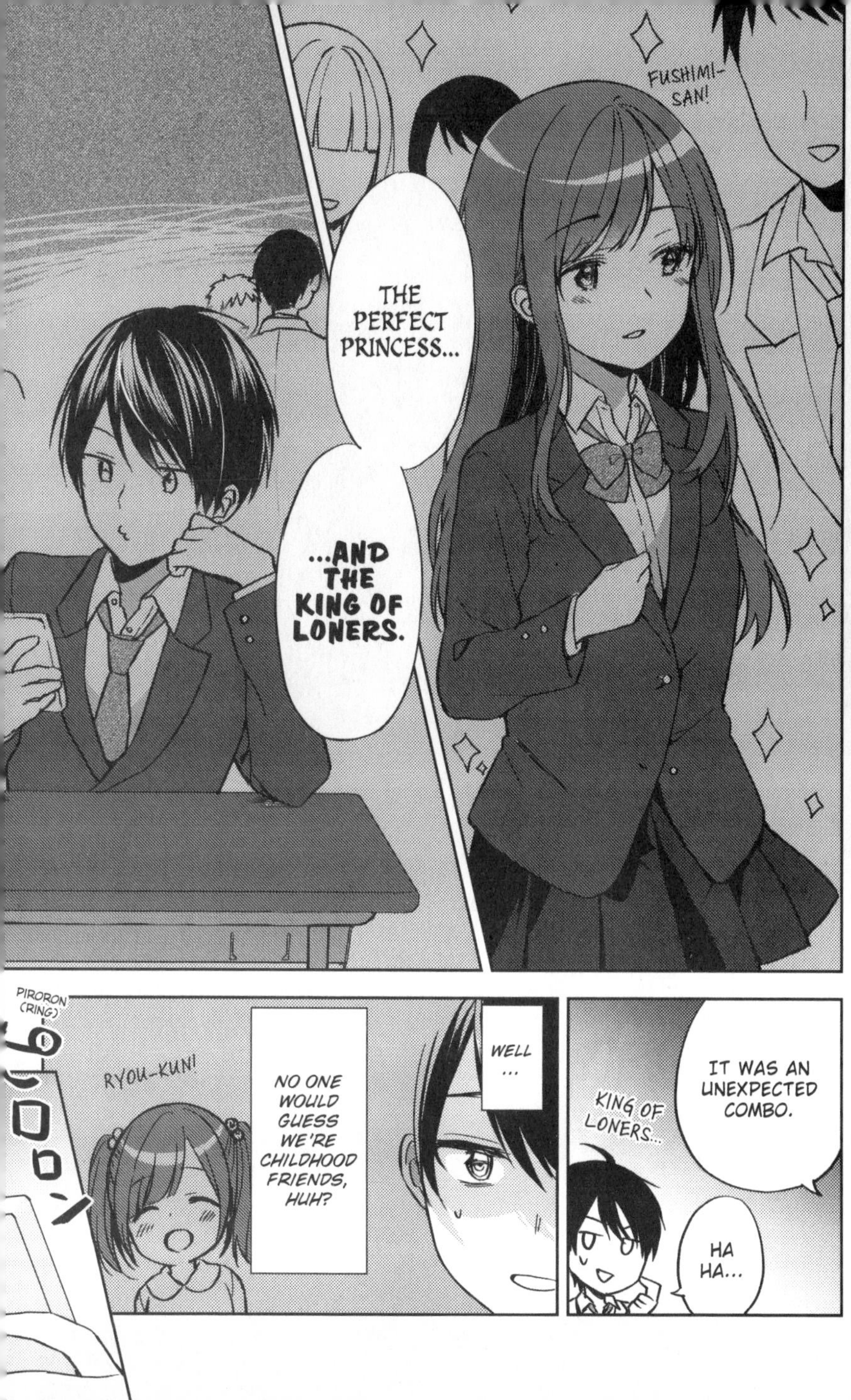
FUSHIMI-SAN!
THE PERFECT PRINCESS...
...AND THE KING OF LONERS.
IT WAS AN UNEXPECTED COMBO.
KING OF LONERS...
HA HA...
WELL ...
NO ONE WOULD GUESS WE'RE CHILDHOOD FRIENDS, HUH?
PIRORON (RING)
RYOU-KUN!

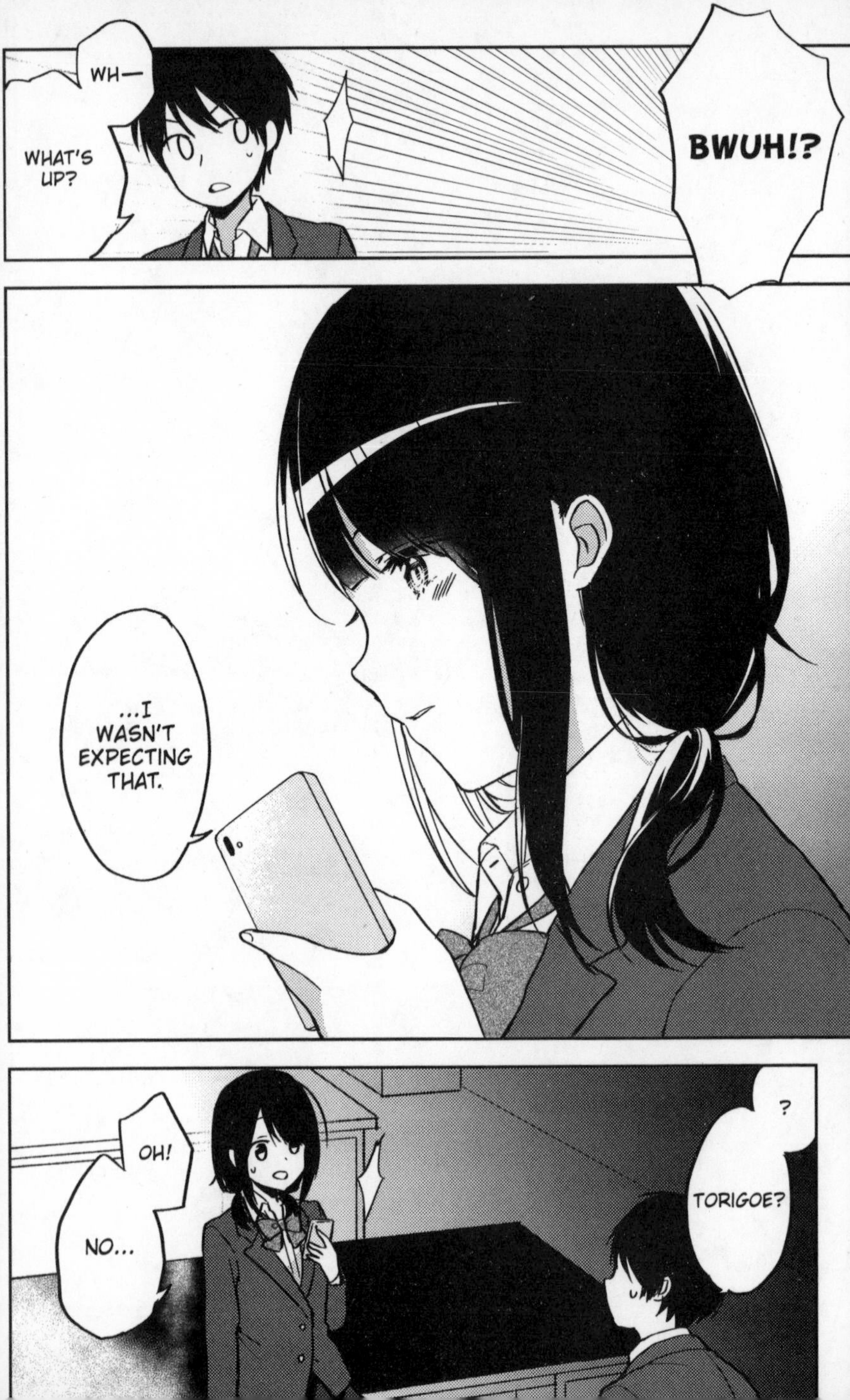
BWUH!?
WH— WHAT'S UP?
...I WASN'T EXPECTING THAT.
?
TORIGOE?
OH!
NO...

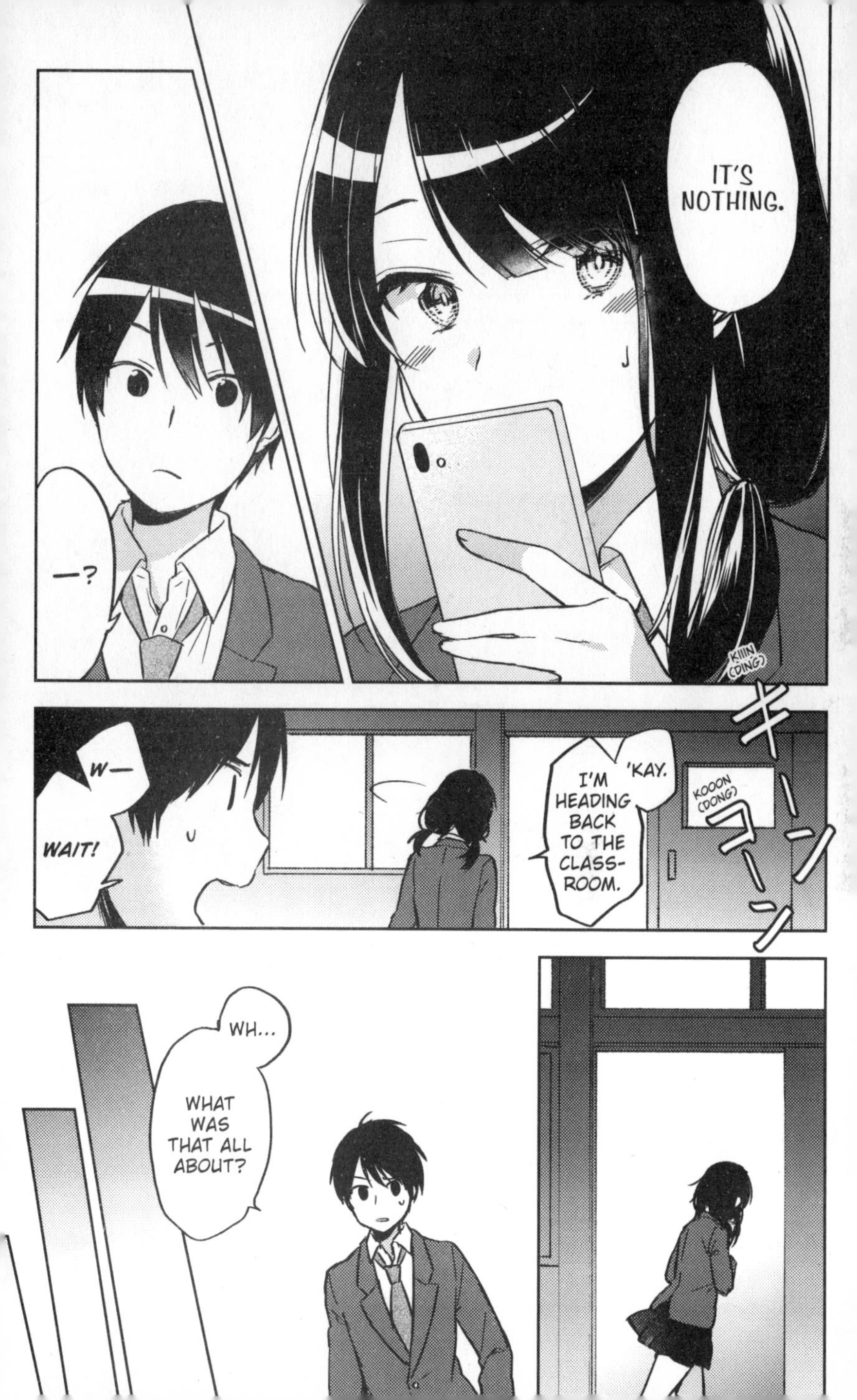

IT'S NOTHING.
KIIIN (DING)
キーン
—?
コーン
KOOON (DONG)
'KAY.
I'M HEADING BACK TO THE CLASS-ROOM.
W—
WAIT!
WH...
WHAT WAS THAT ALL ABOUT?

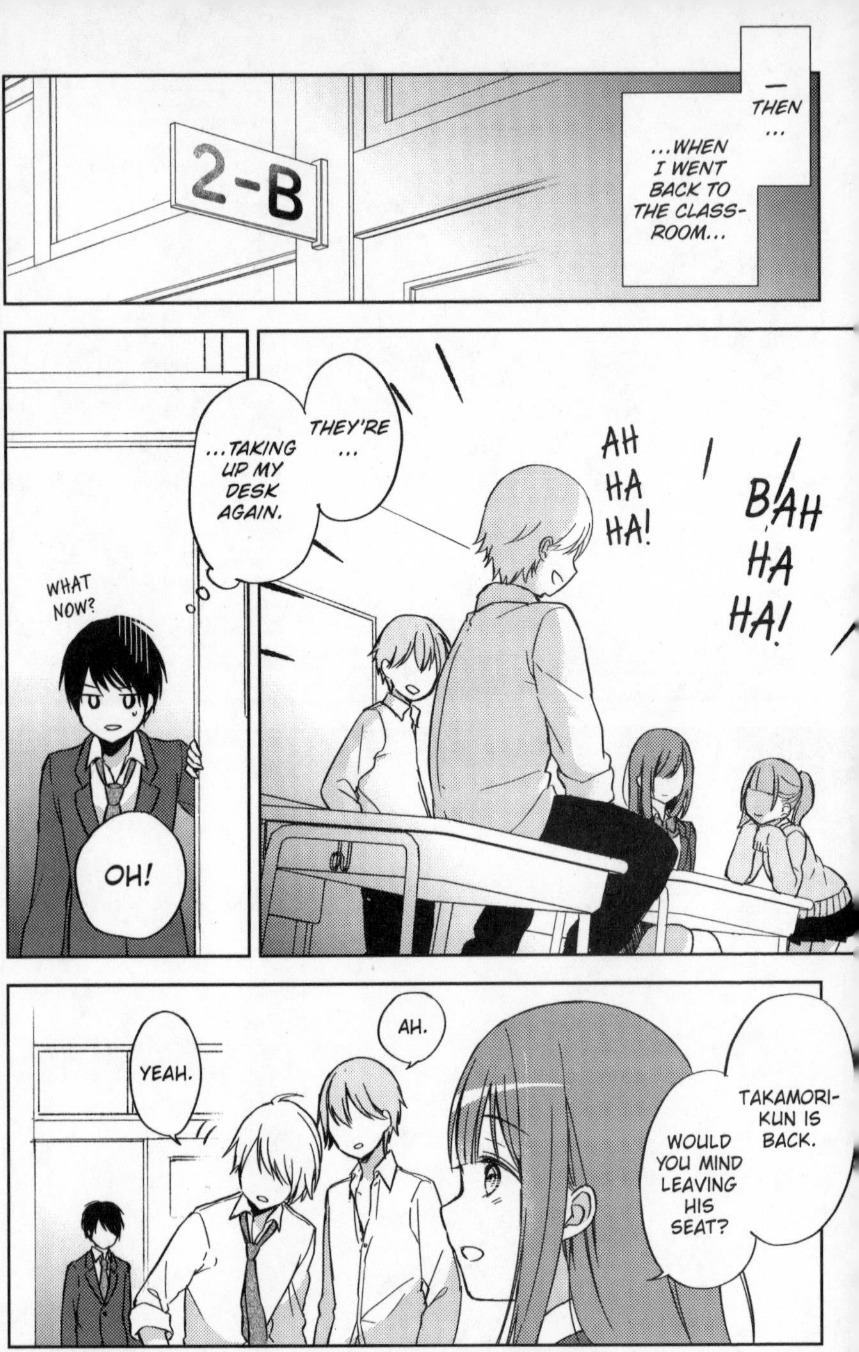
—THEN ...
...WHEN I WENT BACK TO THE CLASS-ROOM...
BAH HA HA!
AH HA HA!
THEY'RE ...
...TAKING UP MY DESK AGAIN.
WHAT NOW?
OH!
TAKAMORI-KUN IS BACK.
WOULD YOU MIND LEAVING HIS SEAT?
AH.
YEAH.

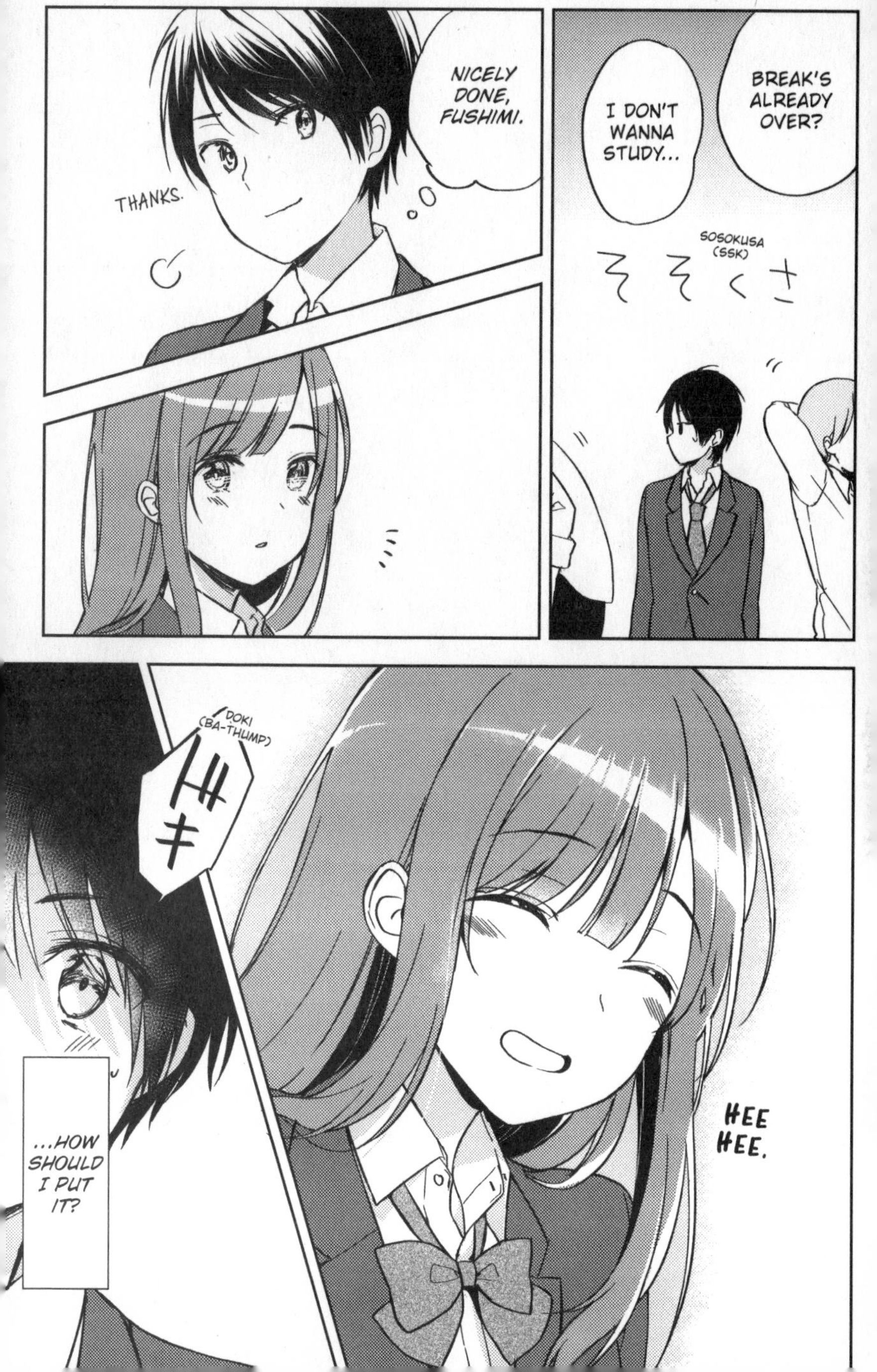
BREAK'S ALREADY OVER?
I DON'T WANNA STUDY...
SOSOKUSA (SSK)
そそくさ
NICELY DONE, FUSHIMI.
THANKS.
DOKI (BA-THUMP)
ドキ
HEE HEE.
...HOW SHOULD I PUT IT?

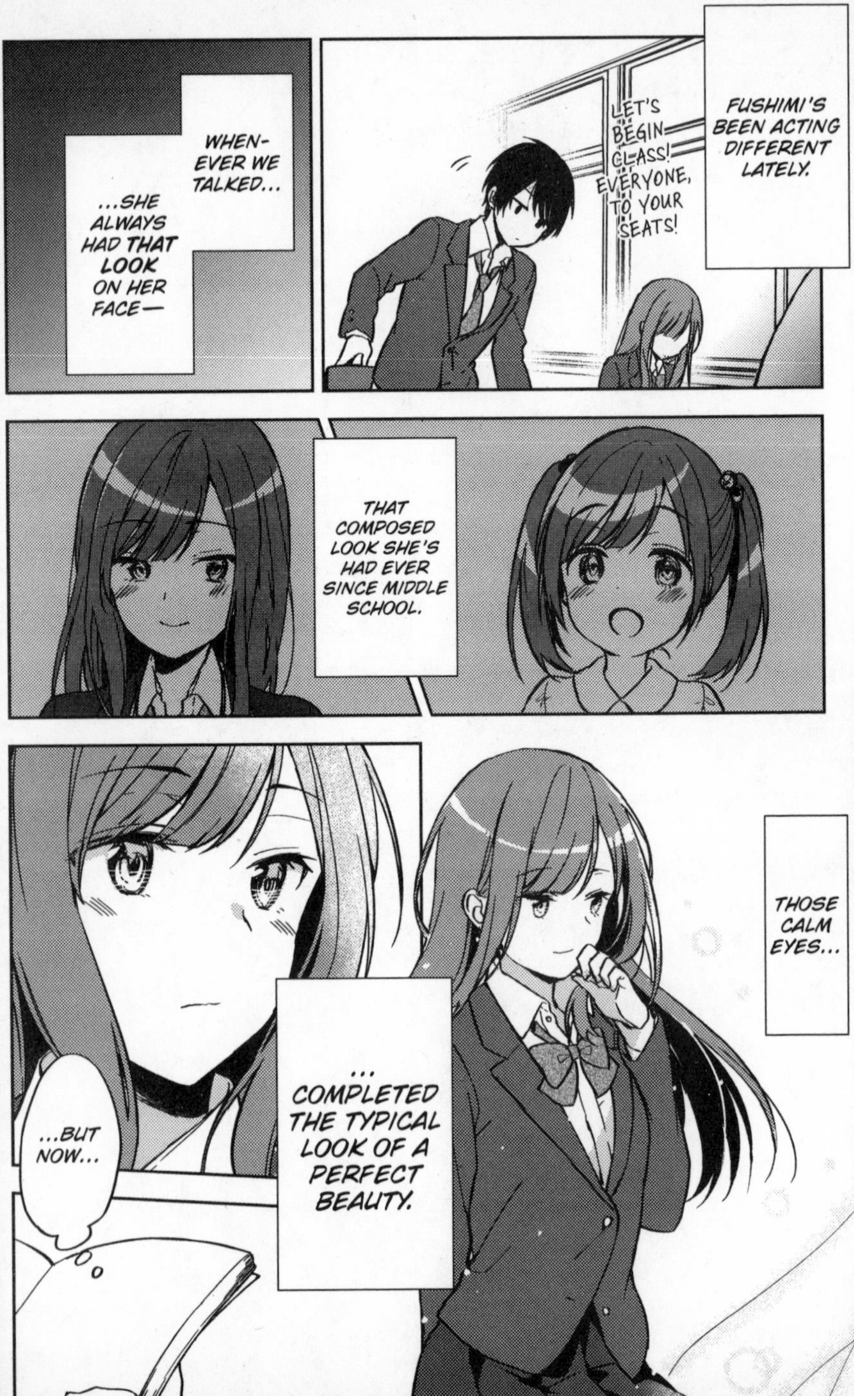

FUSHIMI'S BEEN ACTING DIFFERENT LATELY.
LET'S BEGIN CLASS! EVERYONE, TO YOUR SEATS!
WHEN-EVER WE TALKED...
...SHE ALWAYS HAD THAT LOOK ON HER FACE—
THAT COMPOSED LOOK SHE'S HAD EVER SINCE MIDDLE SCHOOL.
THOSE CALM EYES...
...COMPLETED THE TYPICAL LOOK OF A PERFECT BEAUTY.
...BUT NOW...

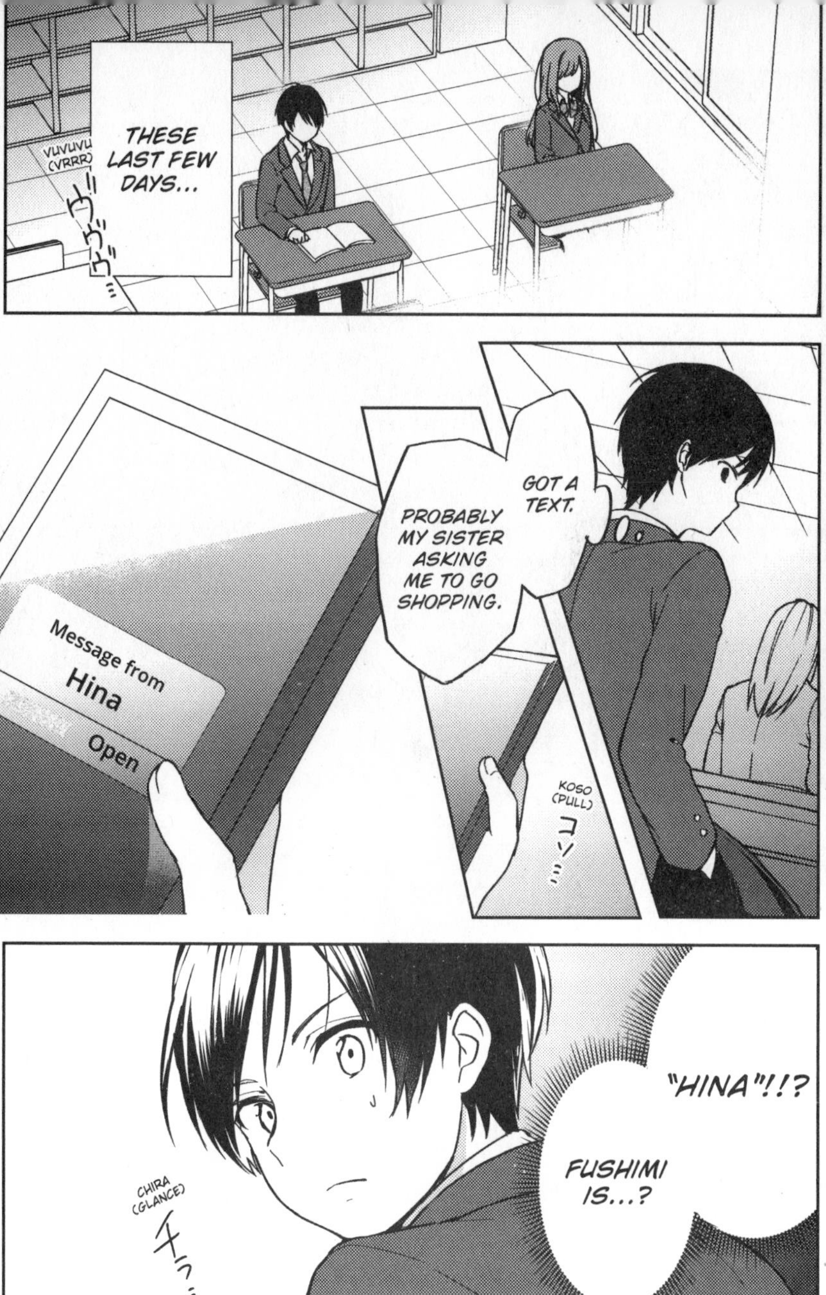
THESE LAST FEW DAYS...
VUVUVU (VRRR)
ヴヴヴ…
GOT A TEXT.
PROBABLY MY SISTER ASKING ME TO GO SHOPPING.
KOSO (PULL)
コソ…
Message from
Hina
Open
"HINA"!!?
FUSHIMI IS...?
CHIRA (GLANCE)
チラッ…

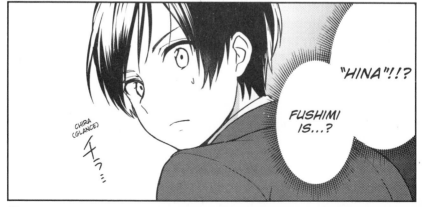

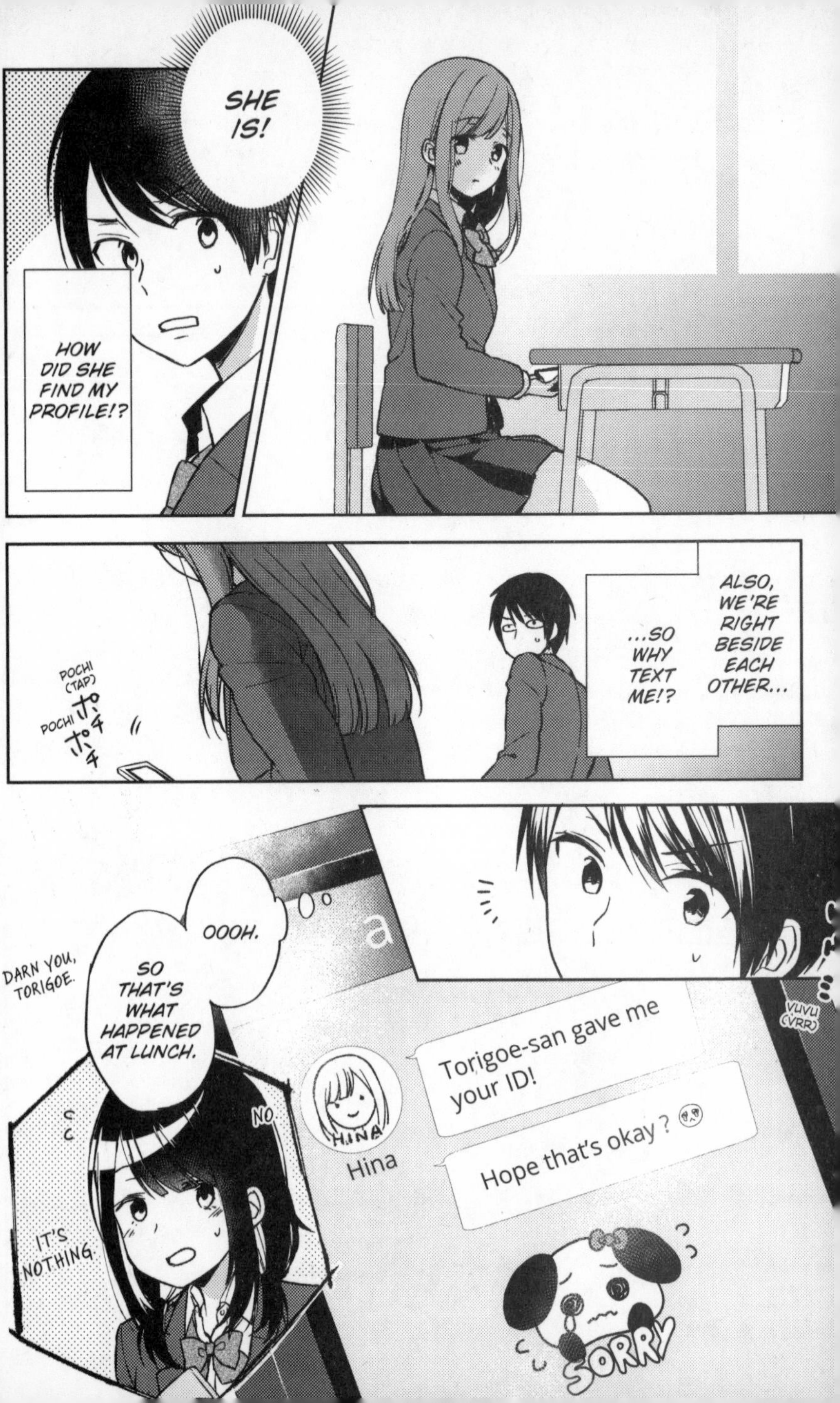
SHE IS!
HOW DID SHE FIND MY PROFILE!?
ALSO, WE'RE RIGHT BESIDE EACH OTHER...
...SO WHY TEXT ME!?
POCHI (TAP)
POCHI
VUVU (VRR)
Torigoe-san gave me your ID!
Hope that's okay?
HINA
Hina
SORRY
OOOH.
SO THAT'S WHAT HAPPENED AT LUNCH.
DARN YOU, TORIGOE.
NO
IT'S NOTHING

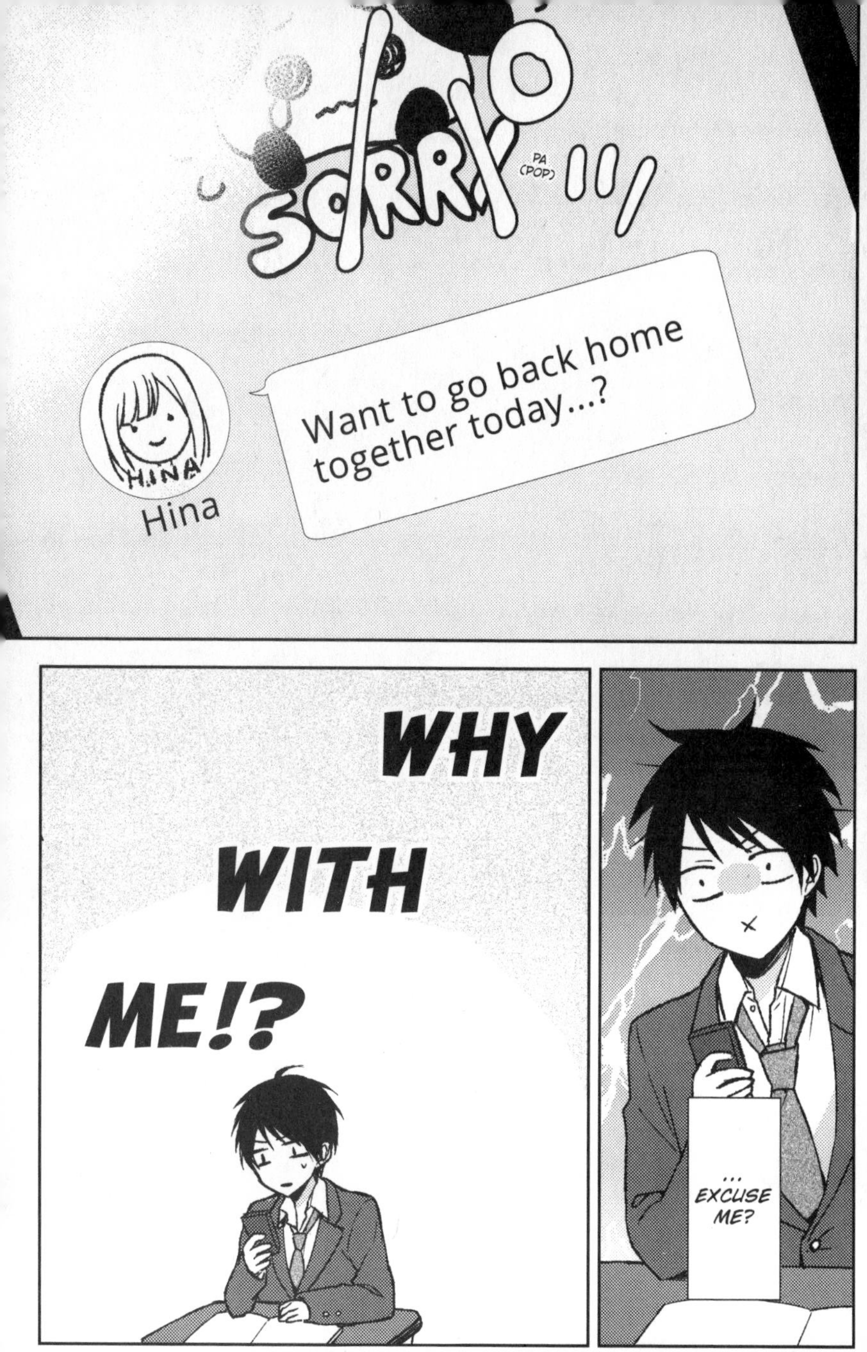
SORRY
PA (POP)
HINA
Hina
Want to go back home together today...?
... EXCUSE ME?
WHY WITH ME!?

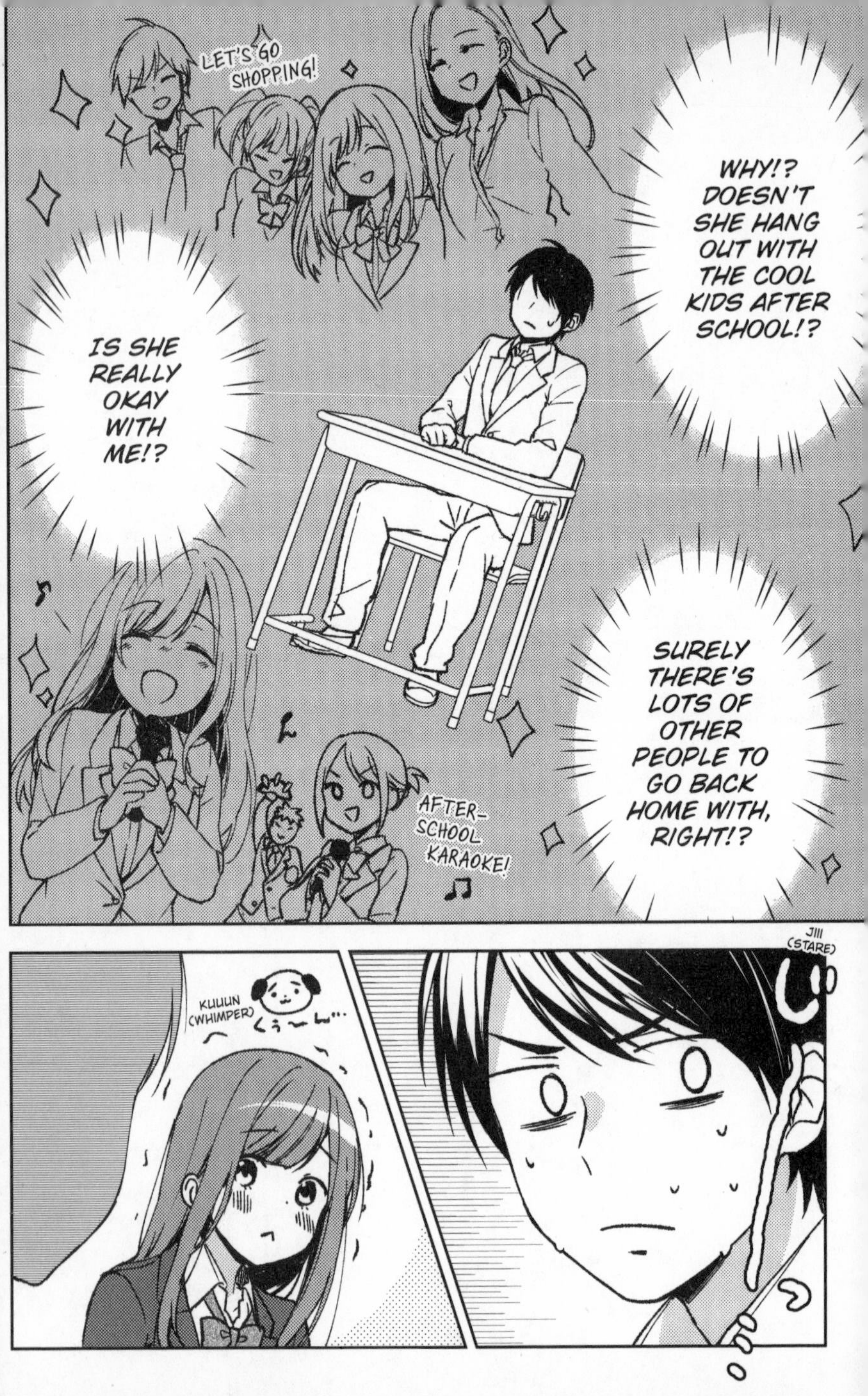
WHY!? DOESN'T SHE HANG OUT WITH THE COOL KIDS AFTER SCHOOL!?
LET'S GO SHOPPING!
IS SHE REALLY OKAY WITH ME!?
SURELY THERE'S LOTS OF OTHER PEOPLE TO GO BACK HOME WITH, RIGHT!?
AFTER-SCHOOL KARAOKE!
JIII (STARE)
KUUUN (WHIMPER)
くぅ～ん‥

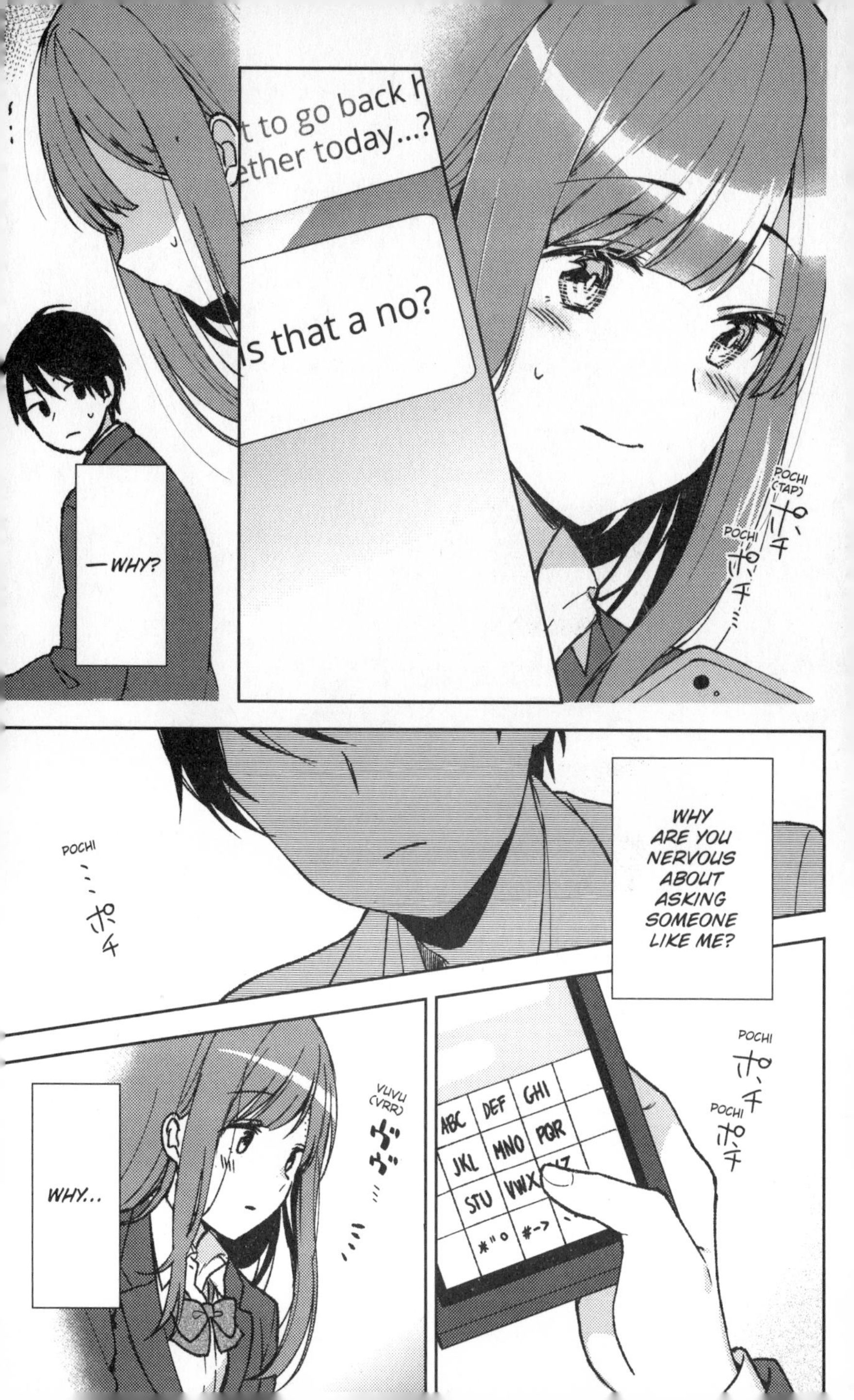
POCHI (TAP)
ポチ
POCHI
ポチ…
t to go back h
ether today…?
Is that a no?
—WHY?
WHY ARE YOU NERVOUS ABOUT ASKING SOMEONE LIKE ME?
POCHI
ポチ
POCHI
ポチ
POCHI
ポチ
ABC DEF GHI
JKL MNO PQR
STU VWX
*"° #->
VUVU (VRR)
ヴヴ…
WHY…

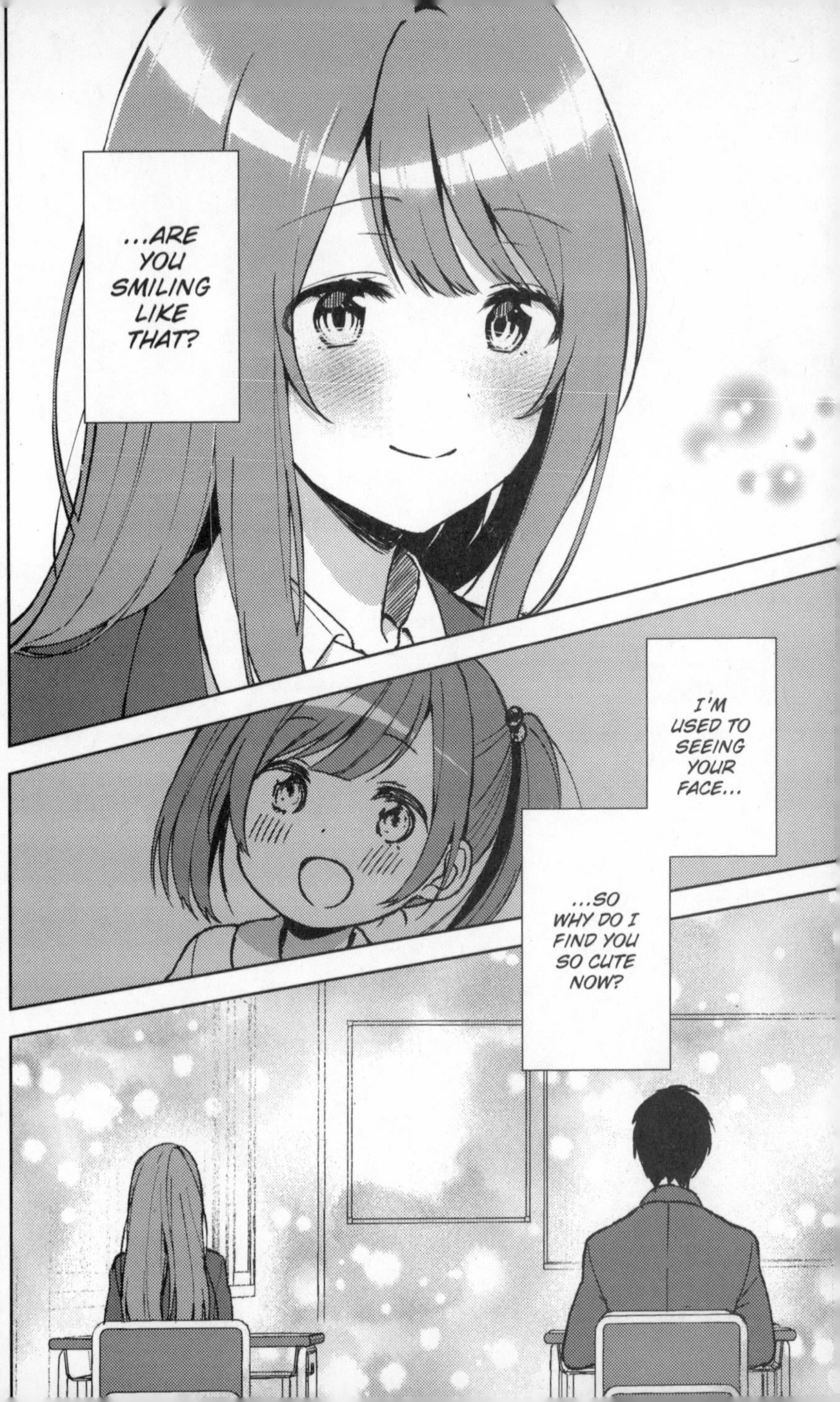
...ARE YOU SMILING LIKE THAT?
I'M USED TO SEEING YOUR FACE...
...SO WHY DO I FIND YOU SO CUTE NOW?

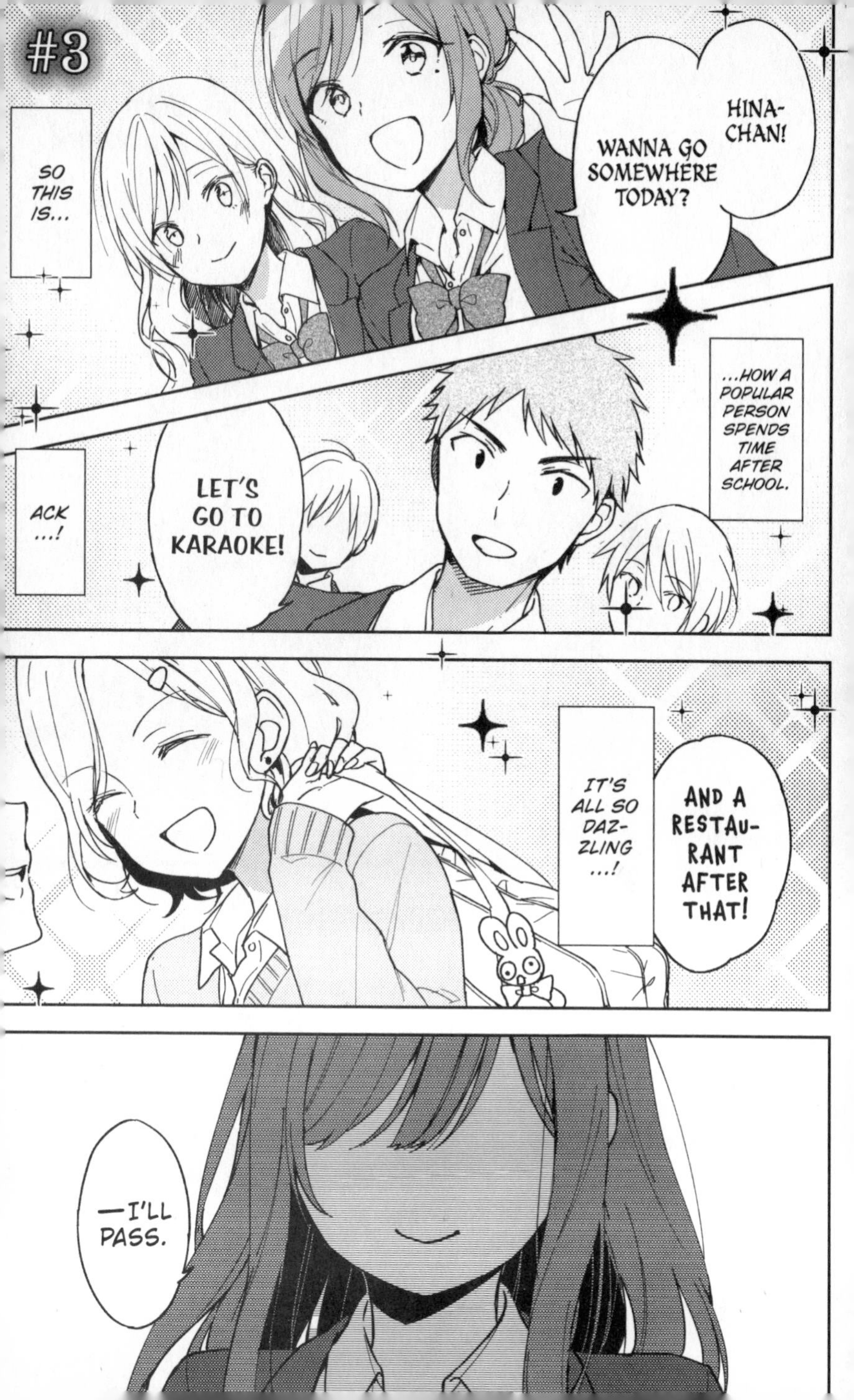
#3
HINA-CHAN!
WANNA GO SOMEWHERE TODAY?
SO THIS IS...
...HOW A POPULAR PERSON SPENDS TIME AFTER SCHOOL.
LET'S GO TO KARAOKE!
ACK ...!
AND A RESTAU-RANT AFTER THAT!
IT'S ALL SO DAZ-ZLING ...!
—I'LL PASS.

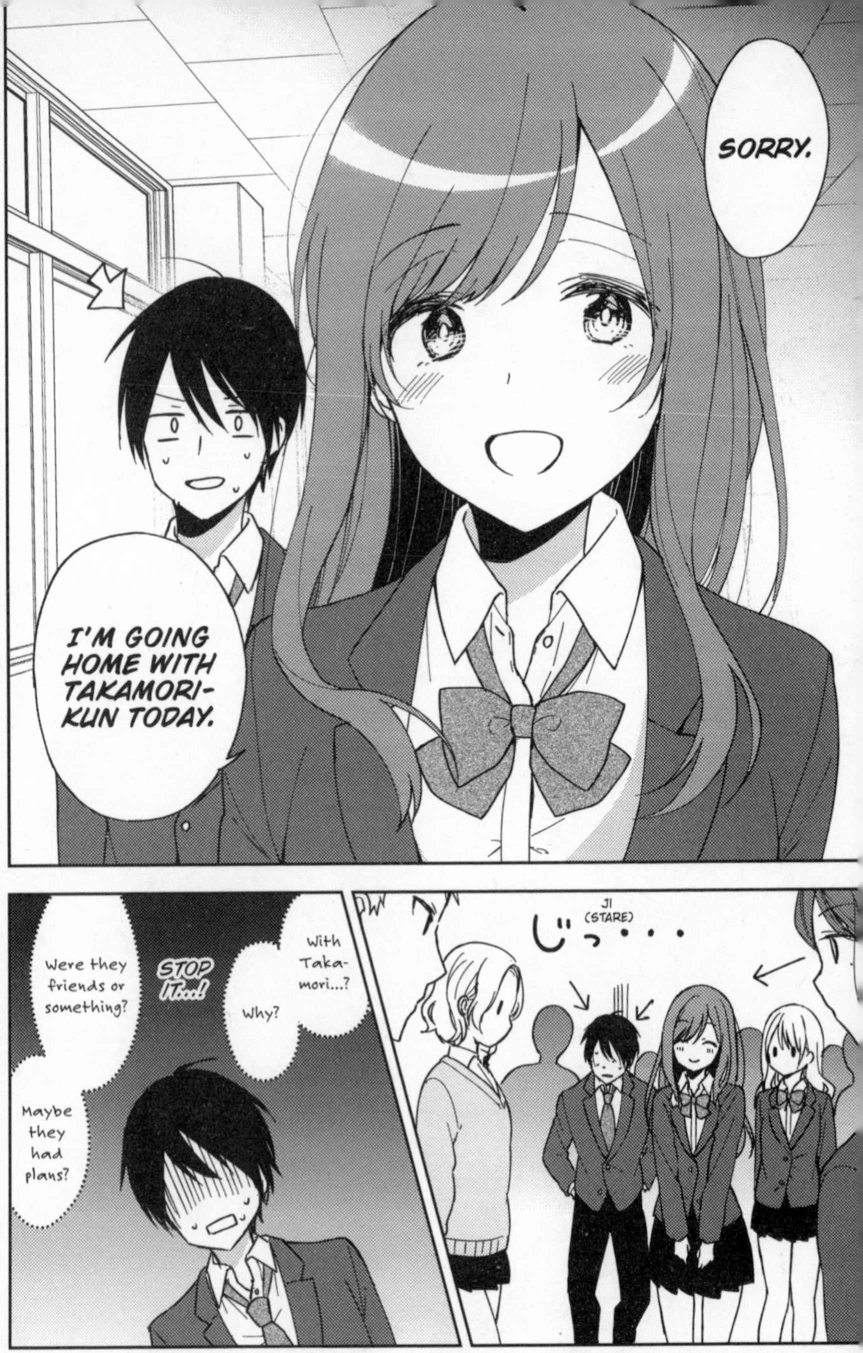
SORRY.
I'M GOING HOME WITH TAKAMORI-KUN TODAY.
JI (STARE)
じっ・・・
With Taka-mori...?
Why?
STOP IT...!
Were they friends or something?
Maybe they had plans?

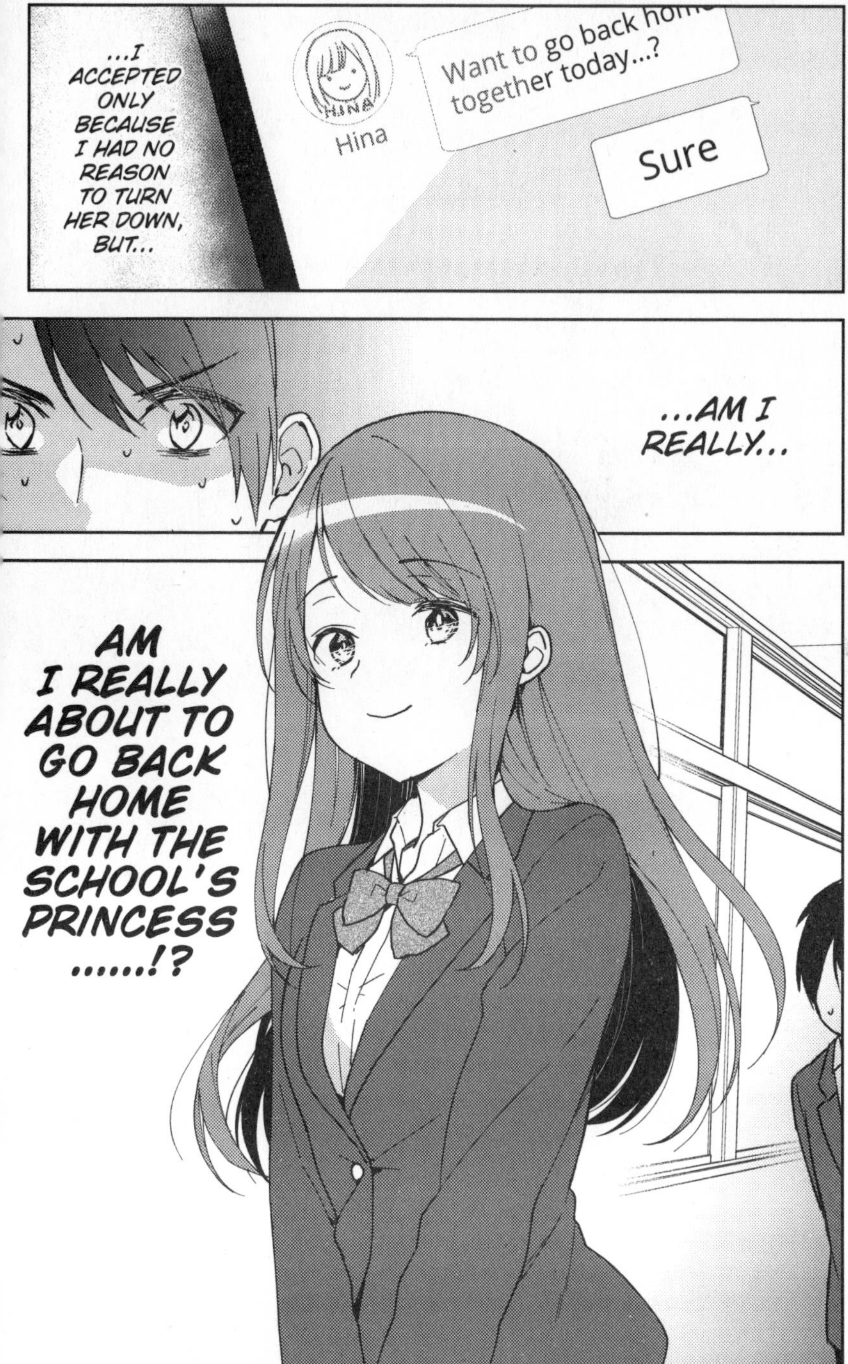
HINA
Hina
Want to go back hom
together today...?
Sure
...I ACCEPTED ONLY BECAUSE I HAD NO REASON TO TURN HER DOWN, BUT...
...AM I REALLY...
AM I REALLY ABOUT TO GO BACK HOME WITH THE SCHOOL'S PRINCESS ......!?

#3 Death (from Embarrassment)

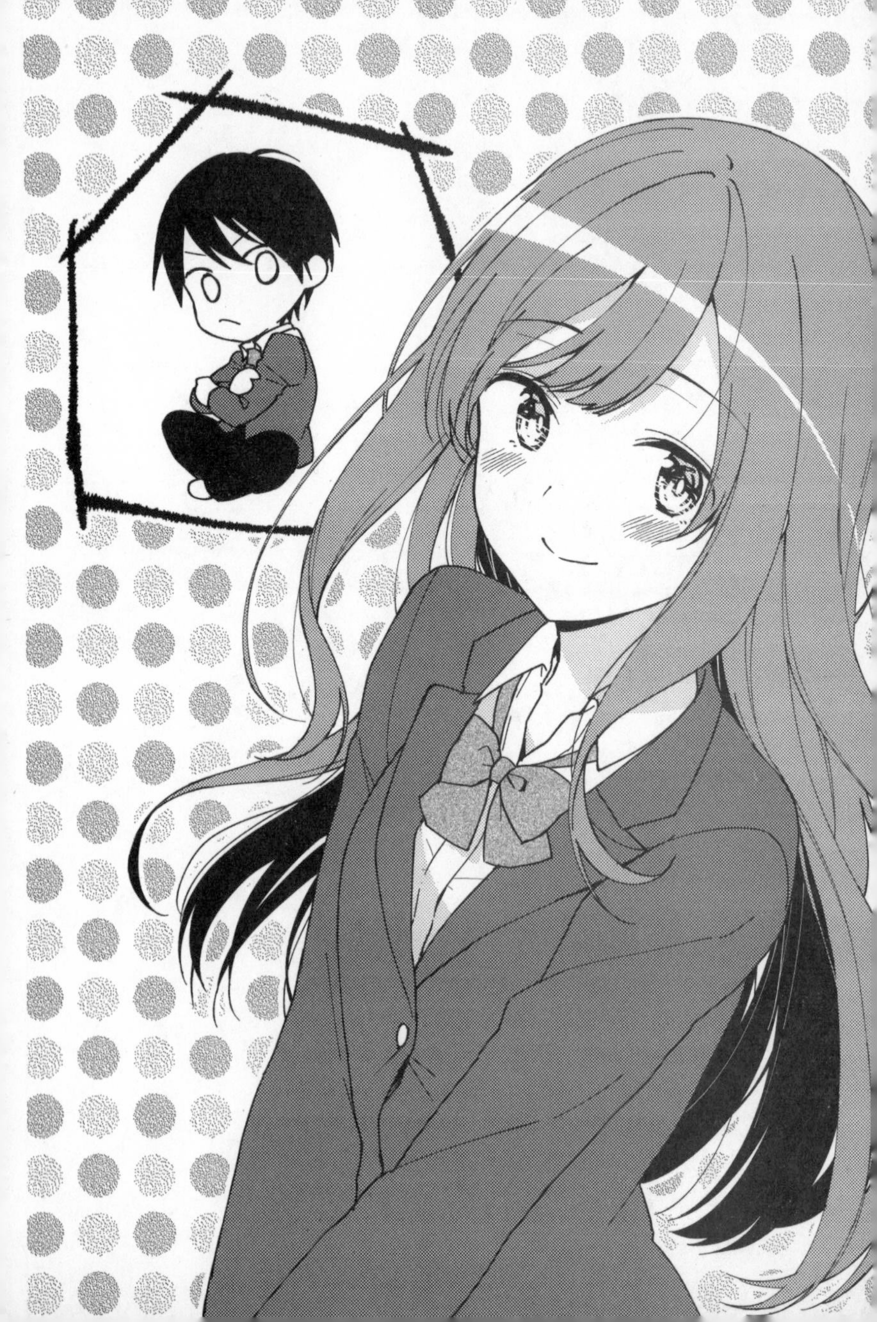

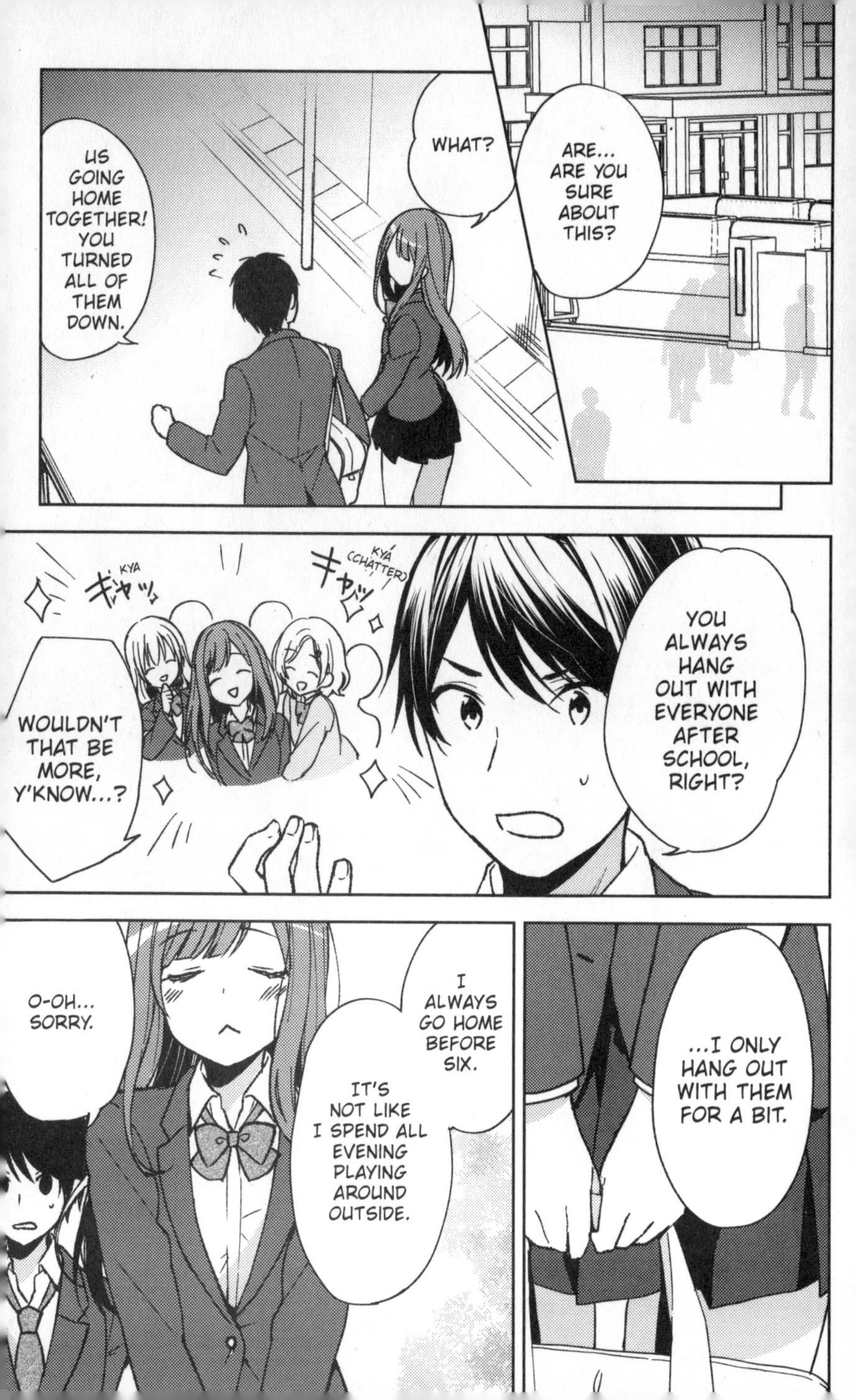

ARE... ARE YOU SURE ABOUT THIS?
WHAT?
US GOING HOME TOGETHER! YOU TURNED ALL OF THEM DOWN.
YOU ALWAYS HANG OUT WITH EVERYONE AFTER SCHOOL, RIGHT?
KYÁ (CHATTER)
KYA
WOULDN'T THAT BE MORE, Y'KNOW...?
...I ONLY HANG OUT WITH THEM FOR A BIT.
I ALWAYS GO HOME BEFORE SIX.
IT'S NOT LIKE I SPEND ALL EVENING PLAYING AROUND OUTSIDE.
O-OH... SORRY.

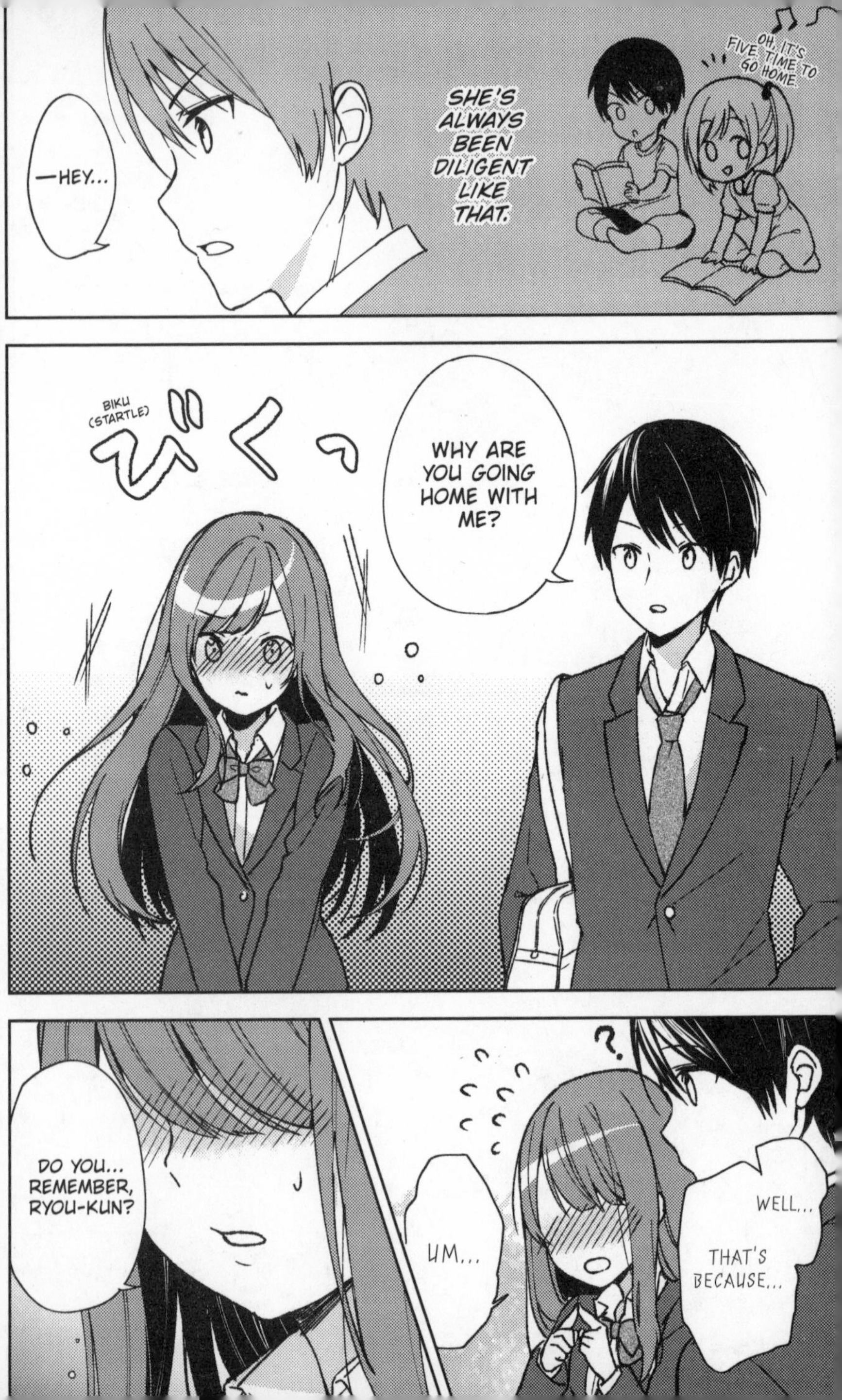
OH, IT'S FIVE, TIME TO GO HOME.
SHE'S ALWAYS BEEN DILIGENT LIKE THAT.
—HEY...
WHY ARE YOU GOING HOME WITH ME?
BIKU (STARTLE)
びくっ
WELL...
THAT'S BECAUSE...
UM...
DO YOU... REMEMBER, RYOU-KUN?

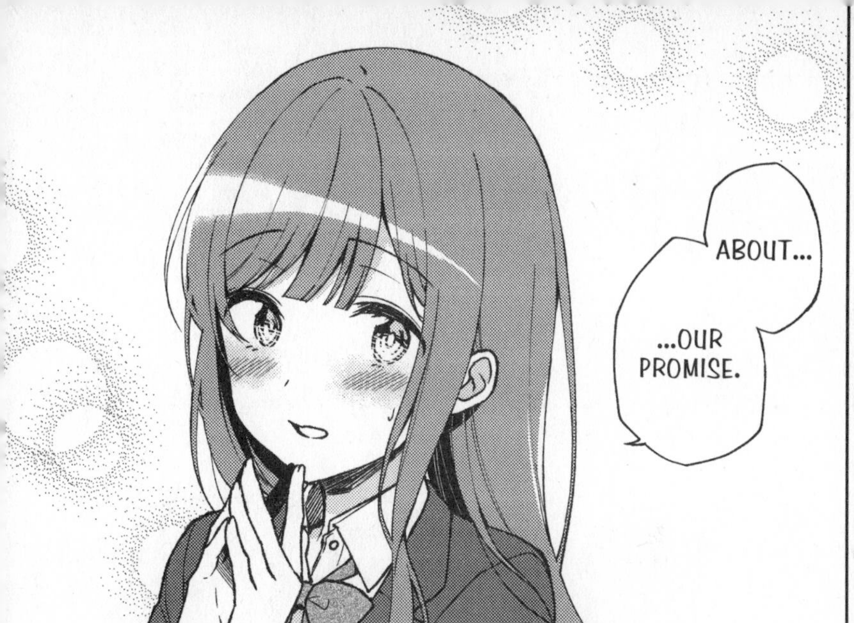
ABOUT...
...OUR PROMISE.

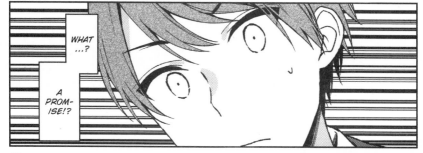

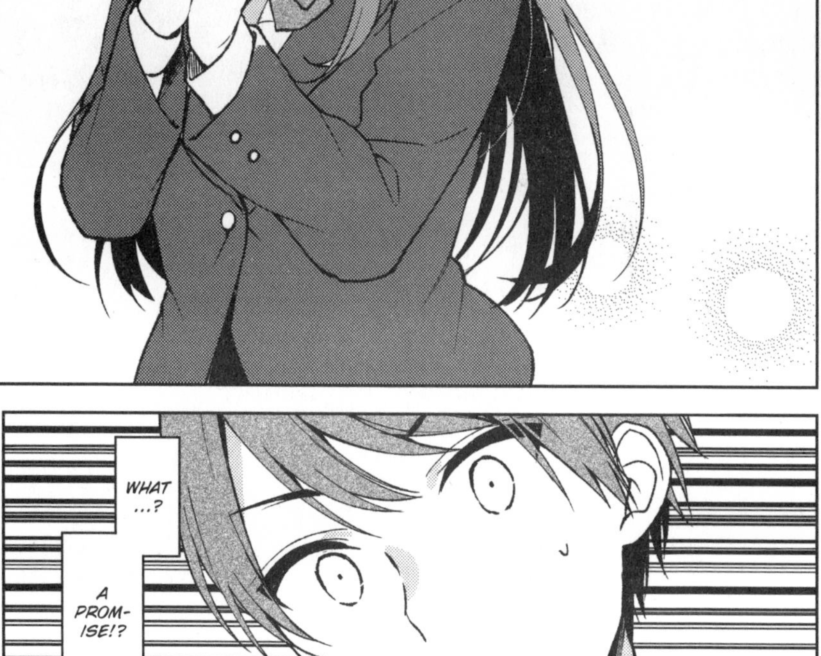
WHAT ...?
A PROM-ISE!?

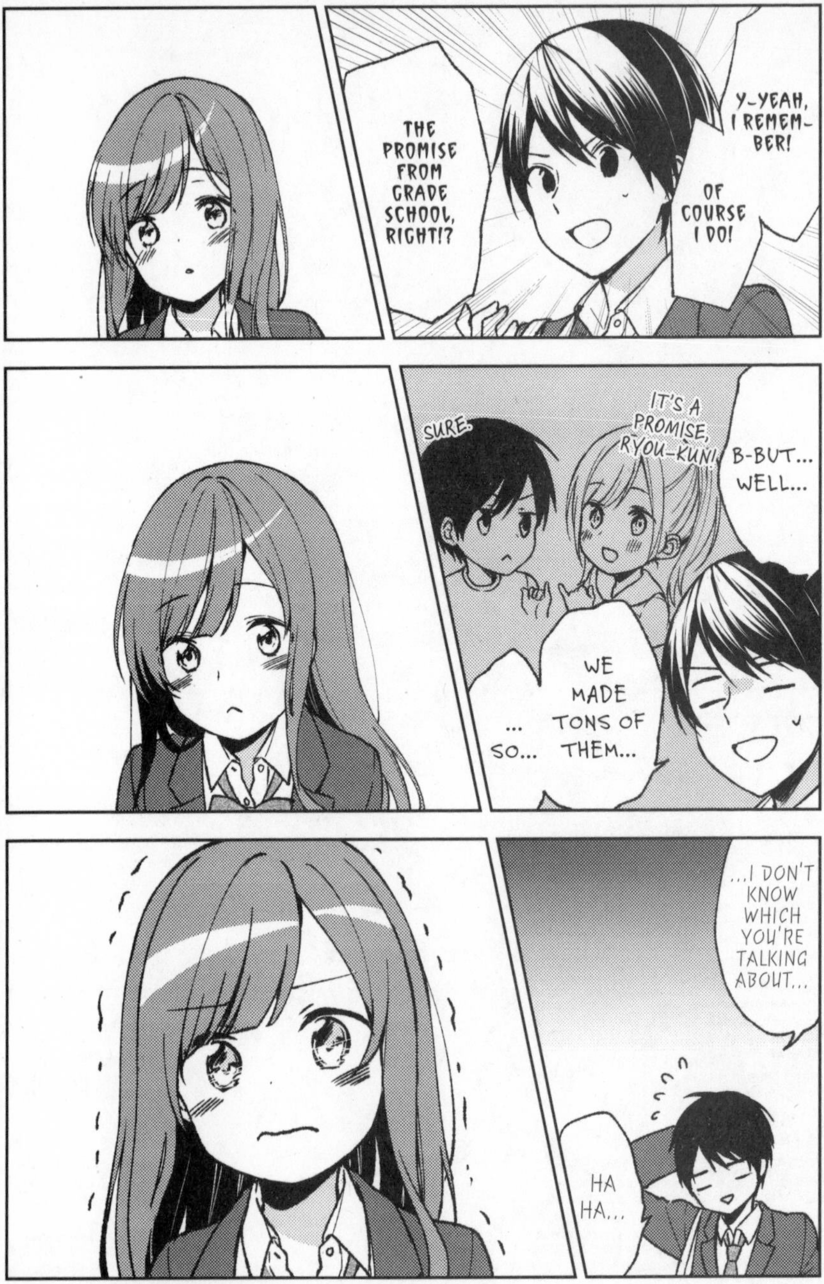
Y-YEAH, I REMEMBER!
OF COURSE I DO!
THE PROMISE FROM GRADE SCHOOL, RIGHT!?
B-BUT... WELL...
IT'S A PROMISE, RYOU-KUN!
SURE.
WE MADE TONS OF THEM...
... SO...
...I DON'T KNOW WHICH YOU'RE TALKING ABOUT...
HA HA...

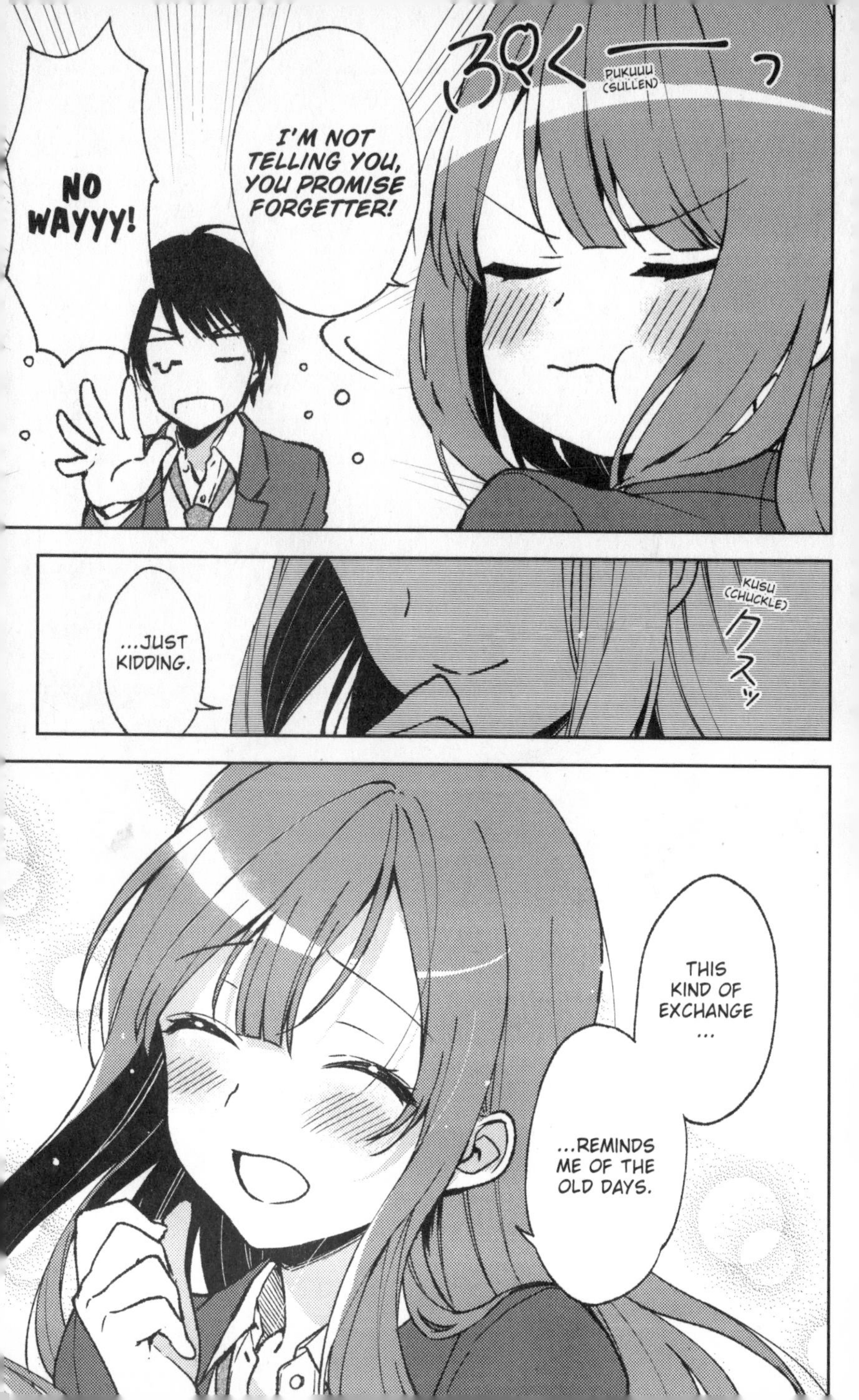
ぷくーーっ
PUKUUU (SULLEN)
I'M NOT TELLING YOU, YOU PROMISE FORGETTER!
NO WAYYY!
クスッ
KUSU (CHUCKLE)
...JUST KIDDING.
THIS KIND OF EXCHANGE ...
...REMINDS ME OF THE OLD DAYS.

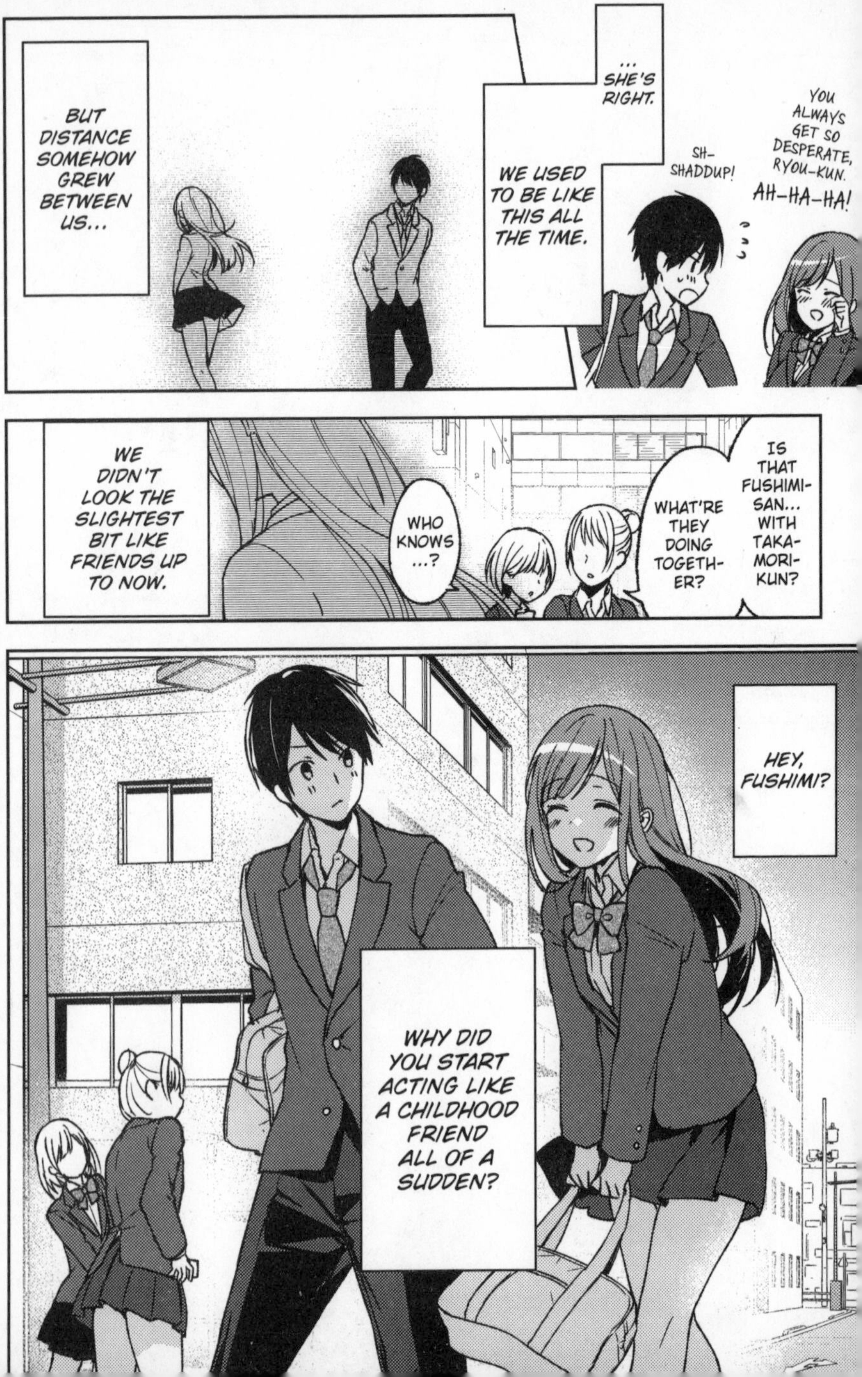
YOU ALWAYS GET SO DESPERATE, RYOU-KUN.
AH-HA-HA!
SH-SHADDUP!
... SHE'S RIGHT.
WE USED TO BE LIKE THIS ALL THE TIME.
BUT DISTANCE SOMEHOW GREW BETWEEN US...
IS THAT FUSHIMI-SAN... WITH TAKAMORI-KUN?
WHAT'RE THEY DOING TOGETHER?
WHO KNOWS ...?
WE DIDN'T LOOK THE SLIGHTEST BIT LIKE FRIENDS UP TO NOW.
HEY, FUSHIMI?
WHY DID YOU START ACTING LIKE A CHILDHOOD FRIEND ALL OF A SUDDEN?

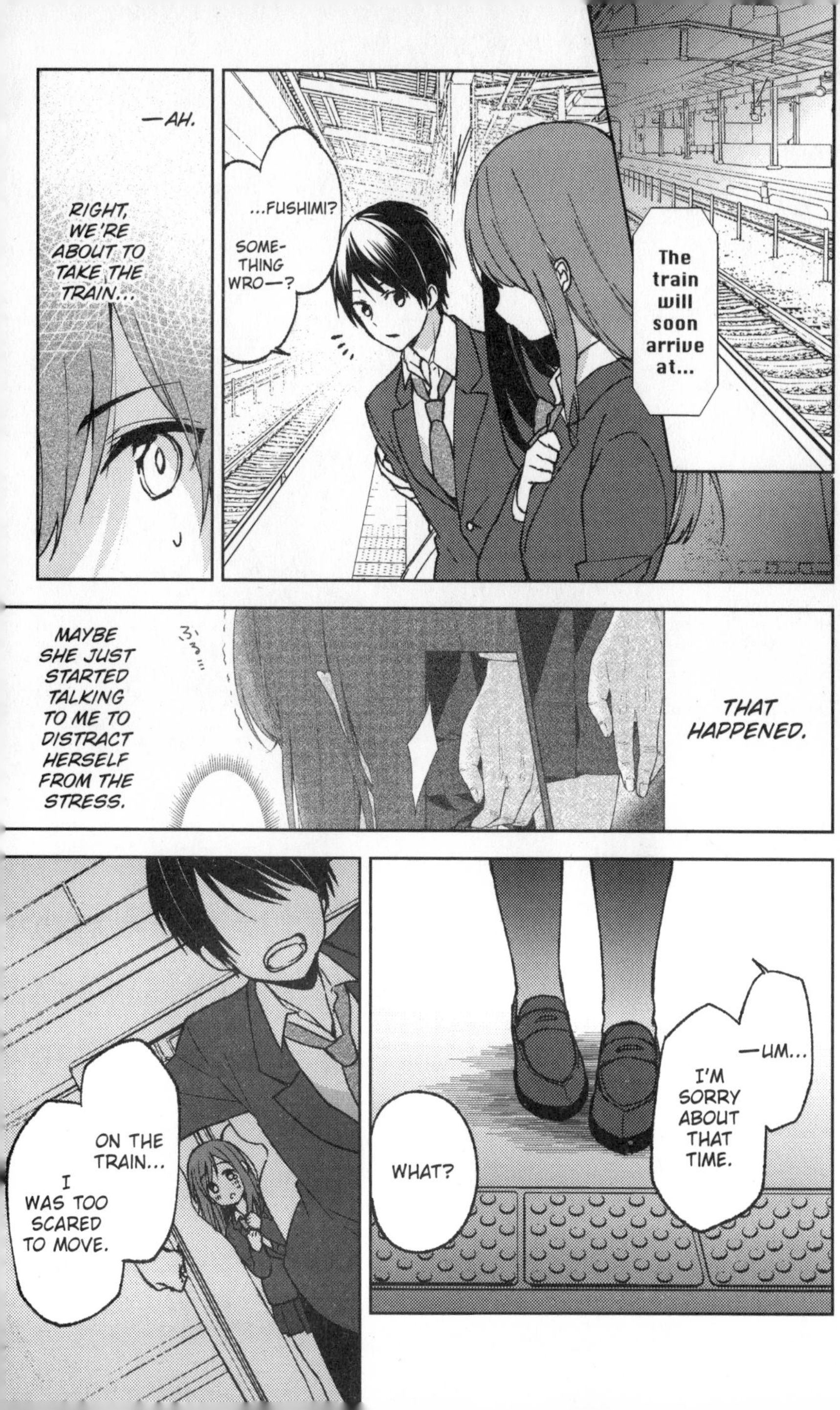
The train will soon arrive at...
...FUSHIMI?
SOMETHING WRO—?
—AH.
RIGHT, WE'RE ABOUT TO TAKE THE TRAIN...
THAT HAPPENED.
ぶる…
MAYBE SHE JUST STARTED TALKING TO ME TO DISTRACT HERSELF FROM THE STRESS.
—UM...
I'M SORRY ABOUT THAT TIME.
WHAT?
ON THE TRAIN...
I WAS TOO SCARED TO MOVE.

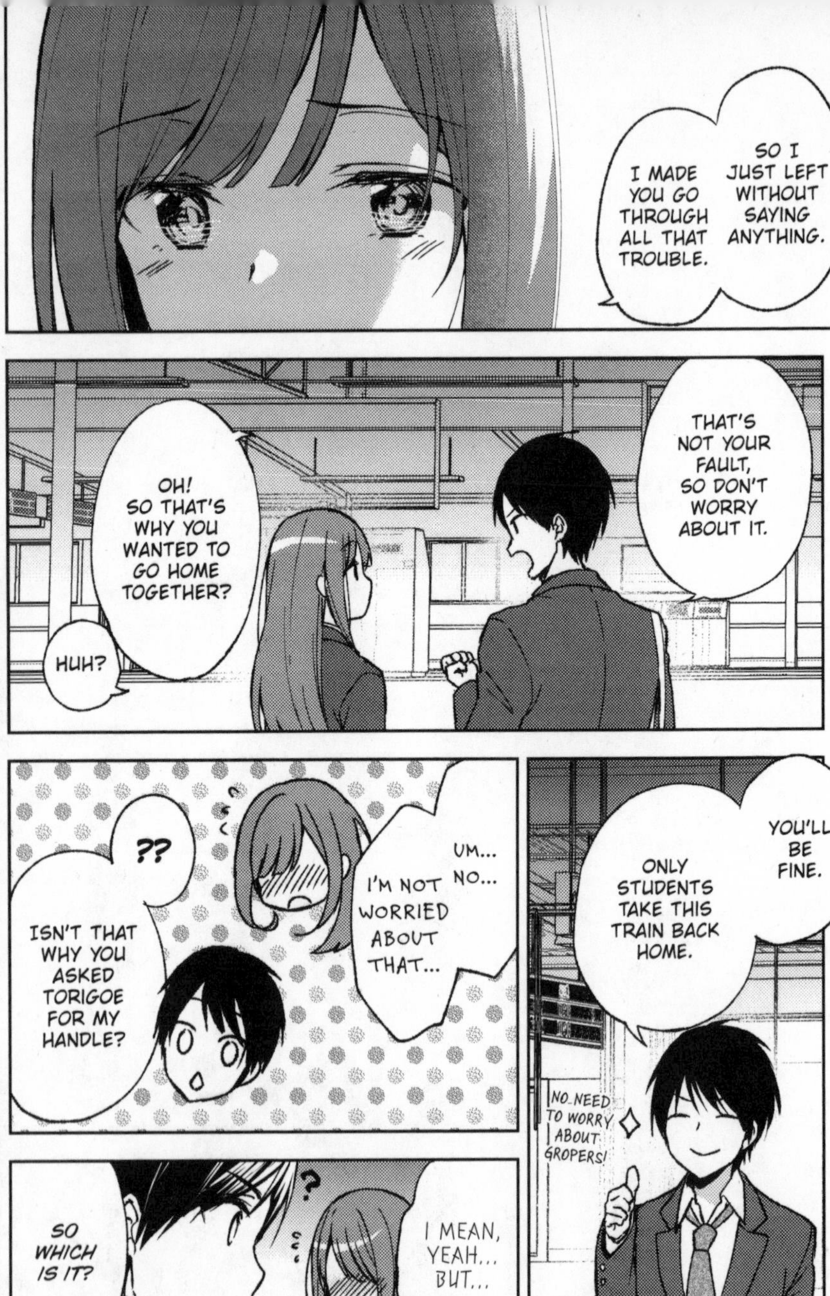
SO I JUST LEFT WITHOUT SAYING ANYTHING.
I MADE YOU GO THROUGH ALL THAT TROUBLE.
THAT'S NOT YOUR FAULT, SO DON'T WORRY ABOUT IT.
OH! SO THAT'S WHY YOU WANTED TO GO HOME TOGETHER?
HUH?
YOU'LL BE FINE.
ONLY STUDENTS TAKE THIS TRAIN BACK HOME.
NO NEED TO WORRY ABOUT GROPERS!
UM... NO...
I'M NOT WORRIED ABOUT THAT...
??
ISN'T THAT WHY YOU ASKED TORIGOE FOR MY HANDLE?
I MEAN, YEAH... BUT...
SO WHICH IS IT?

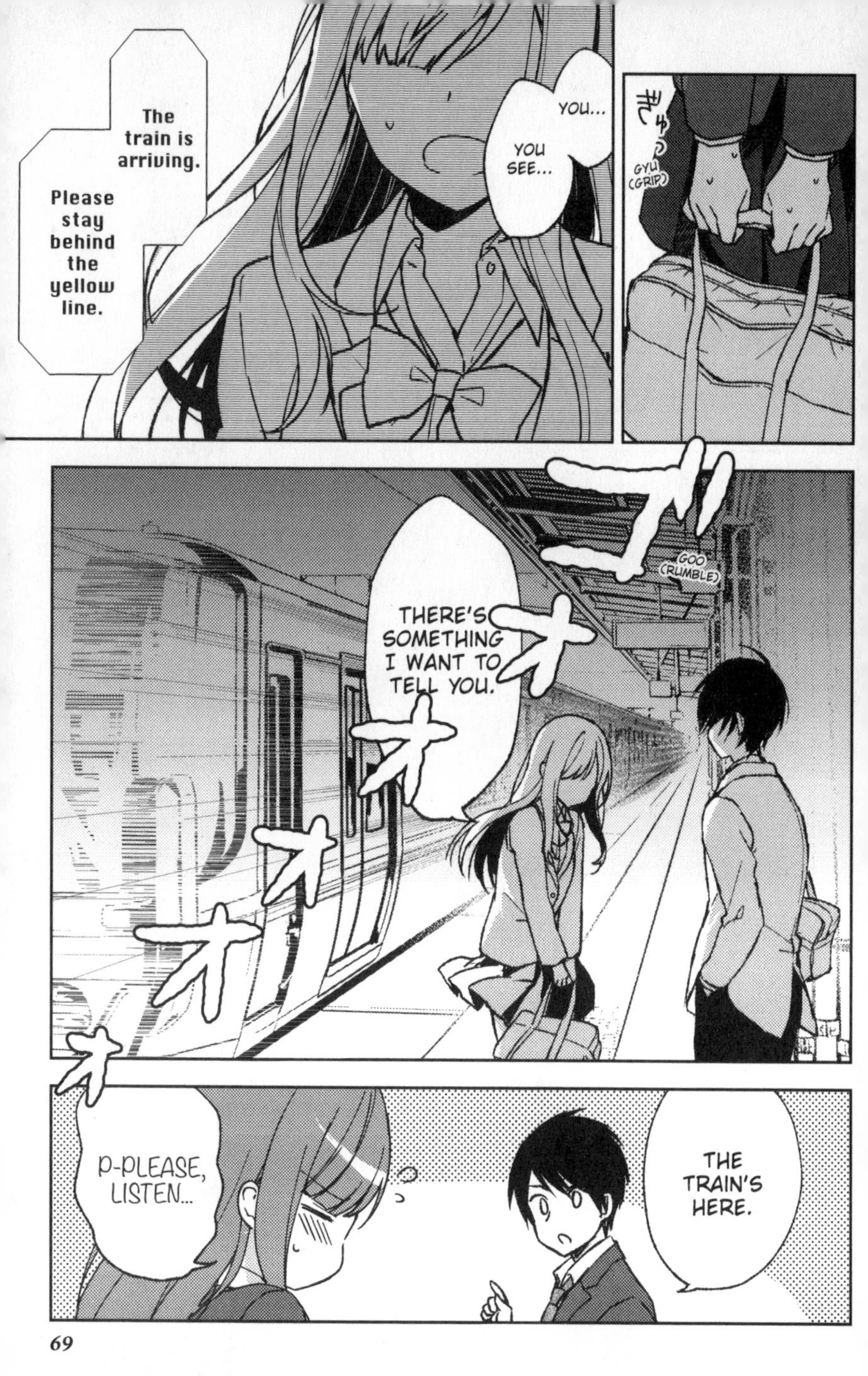
ぎゅっ
GYU (GRIP)
YOU...
YOU SEE...
The train is arriving.
Please stay behind the yellow line.
GOO (RUMBLE)
THERE'S SOMETHING I WANT TO TELL YOU.
THE TRAIN'S HERE.
P-PLEASE, LISTEN...

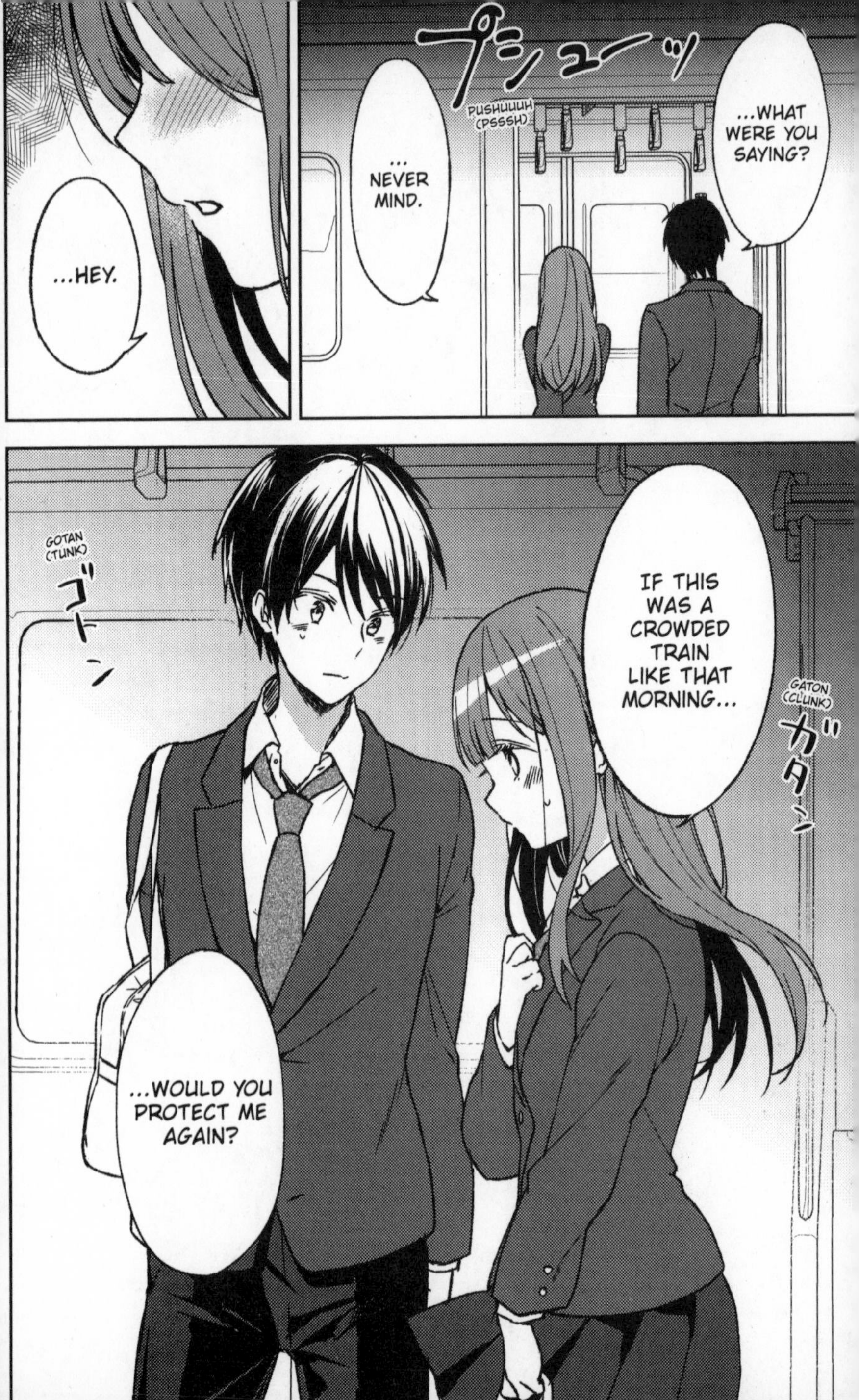
...WHAT WERE YOU SAYING?
プシューッ
PUSHUUUH (PSSSH)
... NEVER MIND.
...HEY.
ガタン
GATON (CLUNK)
IF THIS WAS A CROWDED TRAIN LIKE THAT MORNING...
ゴトン
GOTAN (TUNK)
...WOULD YOU PROTECT ME AGAIN?

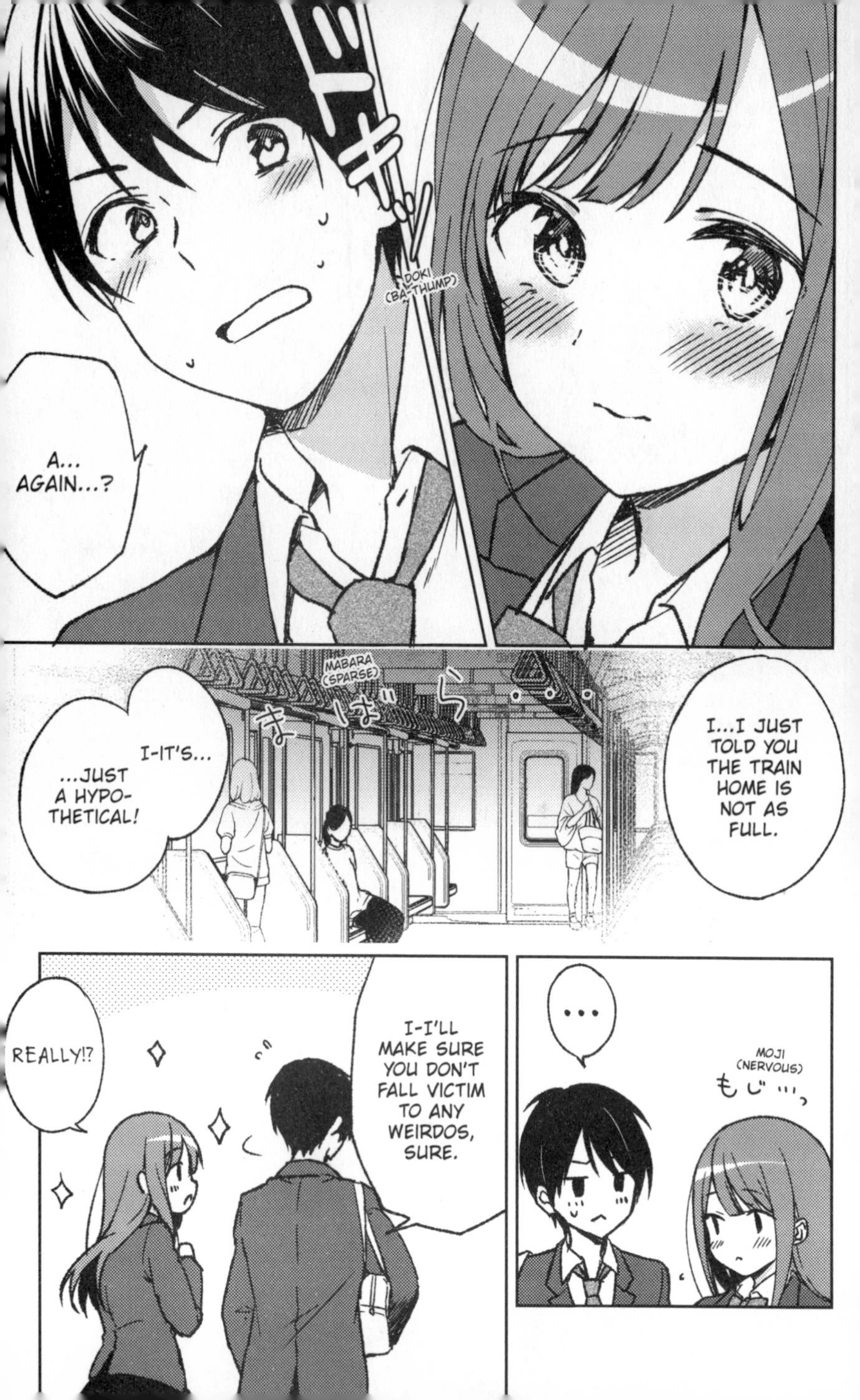
DOKI (BA-THUMP)
A... AGAIN...?
I...I JUST TOLD YOU THE TRAIN HOME IS NOT AS FULL.
MABARA (SPARSE)
I-IT'S...
...JUST A HYPOTHETICAL!
...
MOJI (NERVOUS)
I-I'LL MAKE SURE YOU DON'T FALL VICTIM TO ANY WEIRDOS, SURE.
REALLY!?

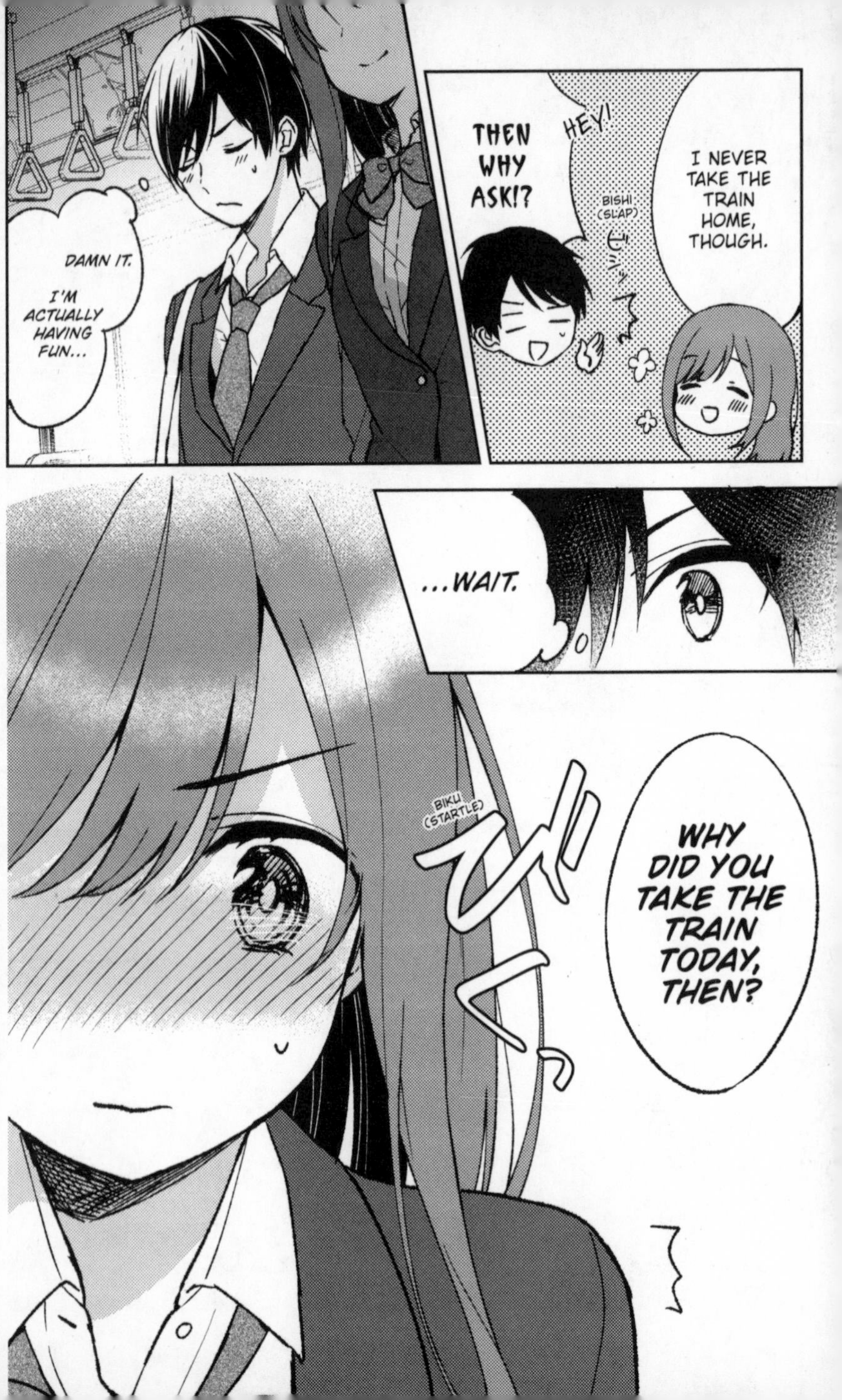
I NEVER TAKE THE TRAIN HOME, THOUGH.
HEY!
THEN WHY ASK!?
BISHI (SLAP)
DAMN IT.
I'M ACTUALLY HAVING FUN...
...WAIT.
BIKU (STARTLE)
WHY DID YOU TAKE THE TRAIN TODAY, THEN?

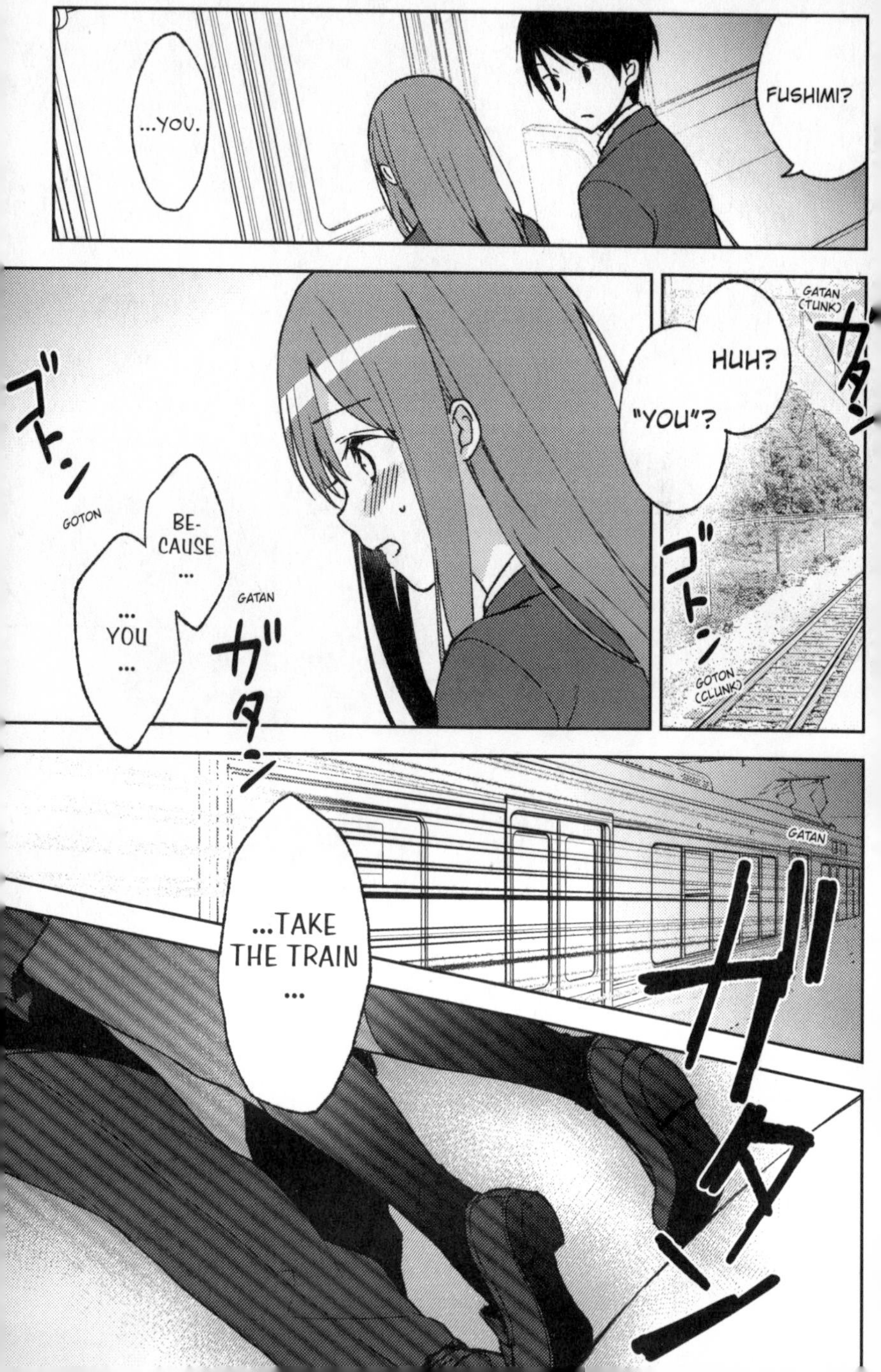
FUSHIMI?
...YOU.
ガタン
GATAN (TUNK)
HUH? "YOU"?
ゴトン
GOTON (CLUNK)
ゴトン
GOTON
BE-CAUSE... ...YOU...
ガタン
GATAN
ガタン
GATAN
...TAKE THE TRAIN...

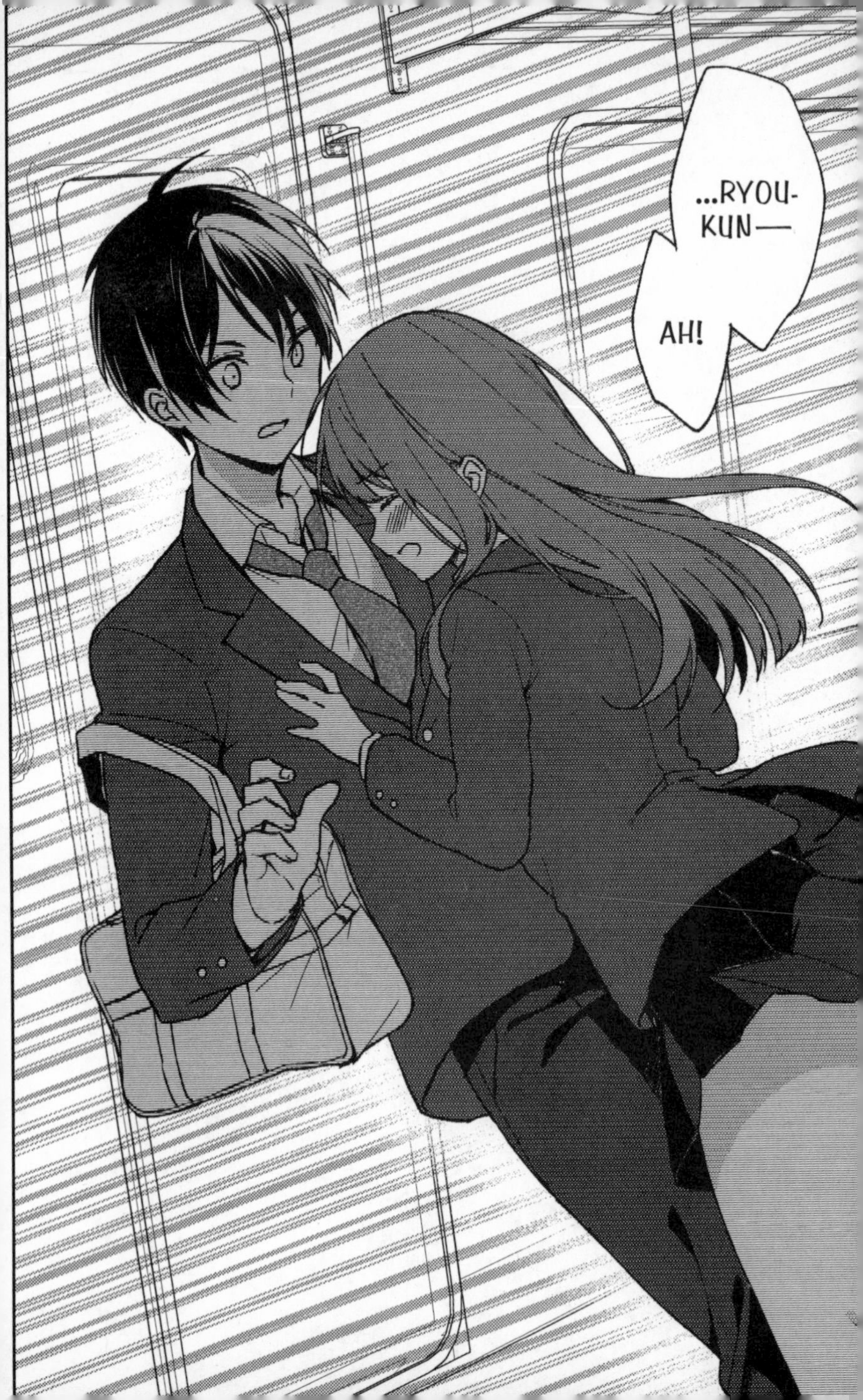
...RYOU-KUN—
AH!

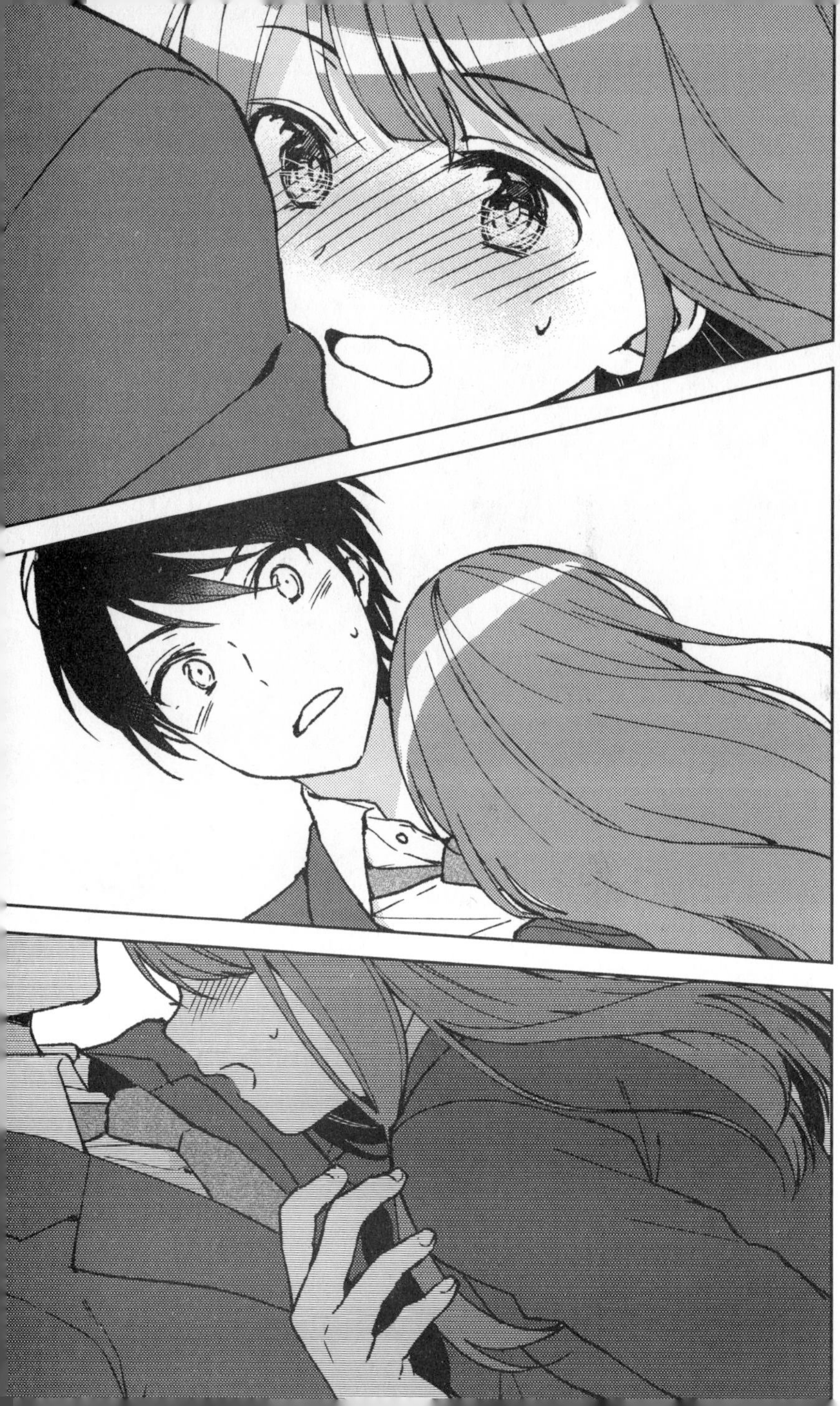

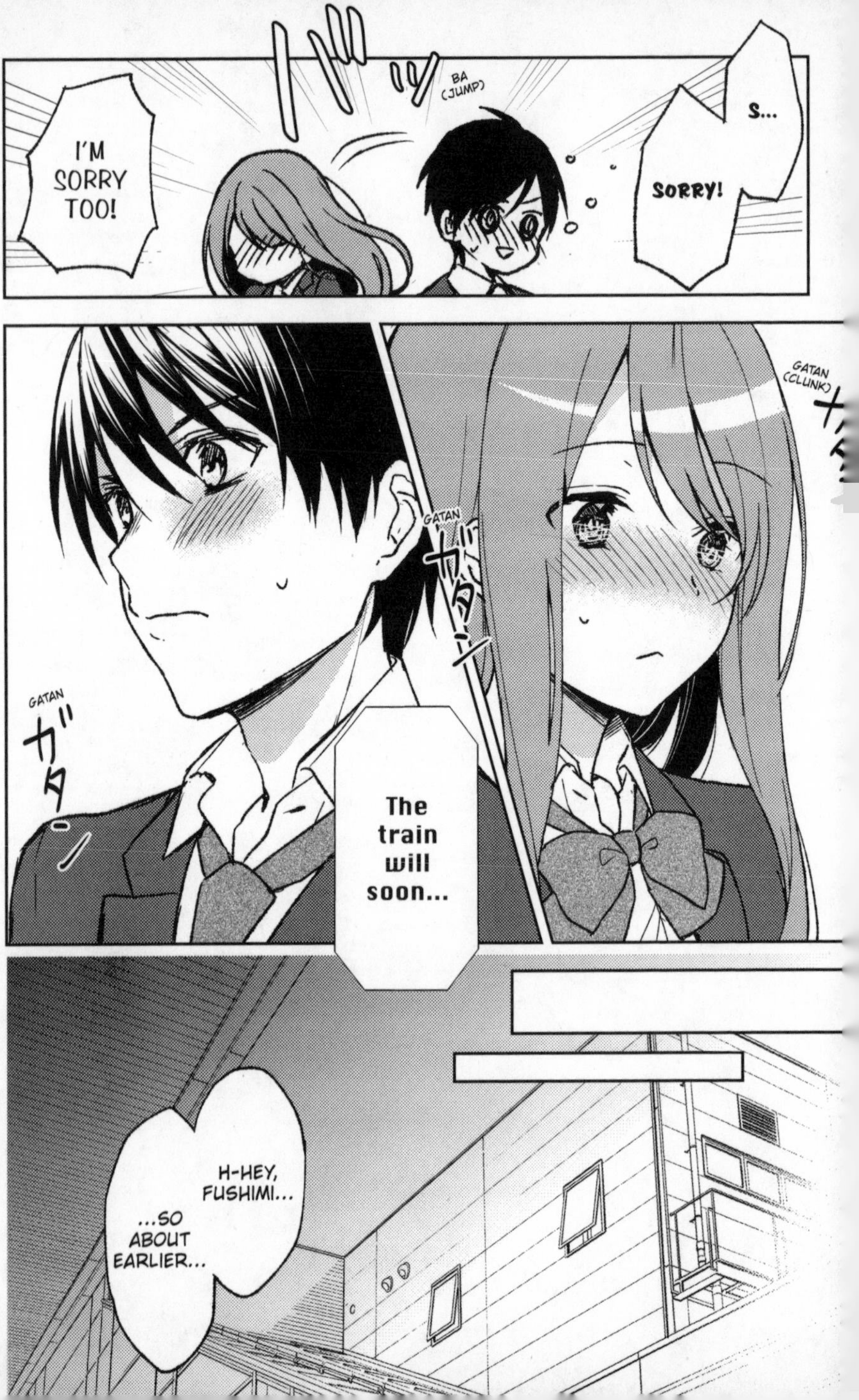
S...
SORRY!
BA (JUMP)
I'M SORRY TOO!
GATAN (CLUNK)
GATAN
GATAN
The train will soon...
H-HEY, FUSHIMI...
...SO ABOUT EARLIER...

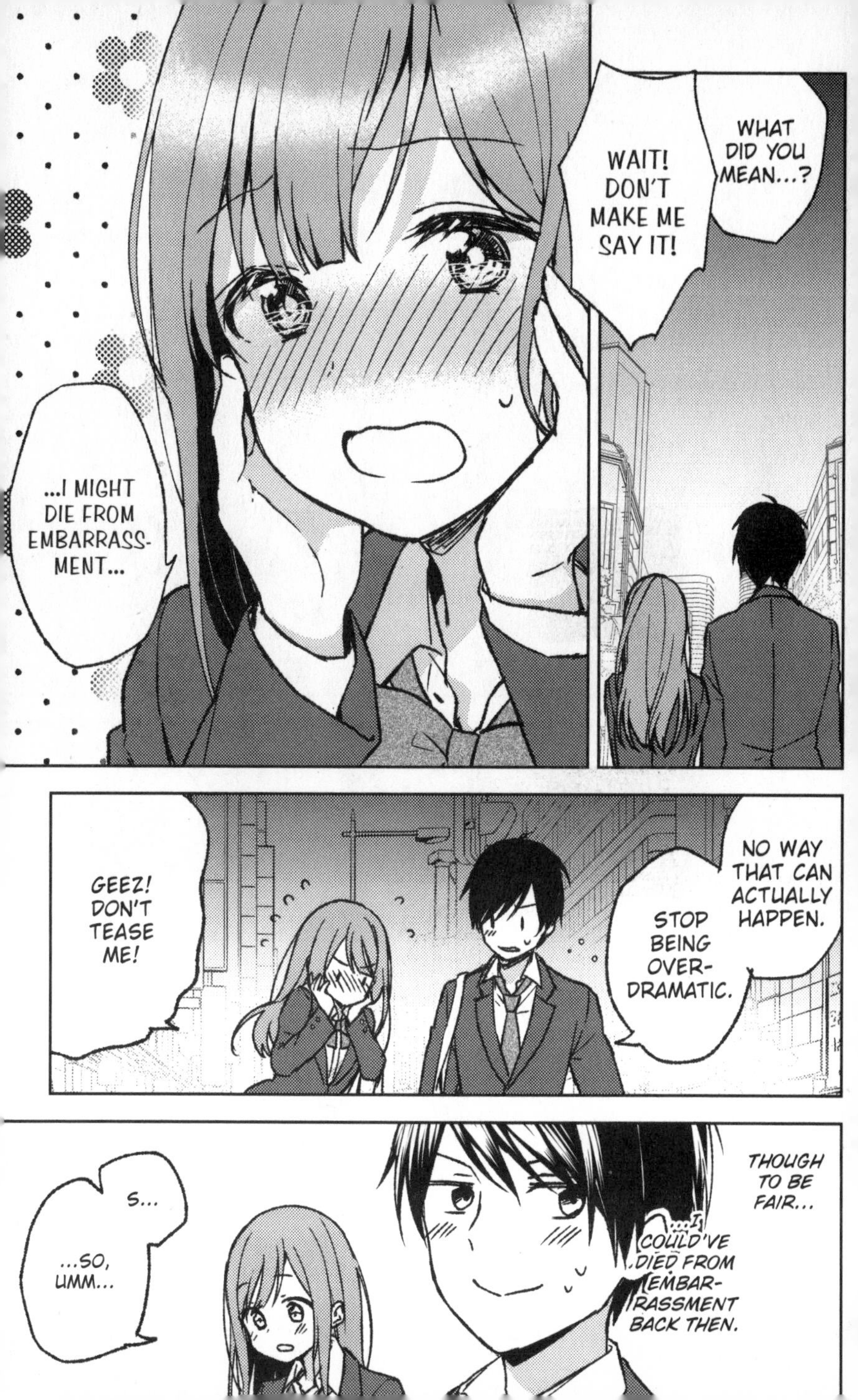
WHAT DID YOU MEAN...?
WAIT! DON'T MAKE ME SAY IT!
...I MIGHT DIE FROM EMBARRASSMENT...
NO WAY THAT CAN ACTUALLY HAPPEN.
STOP BEING OVER-DRAMATIC.
GEEZ! DON'T TEASE ME!
THOUGH TO BE FAIR...
...I COULD'VE DIED FROM EMBARRASSMENT BACK THEN.
S...
...SO, UMM...

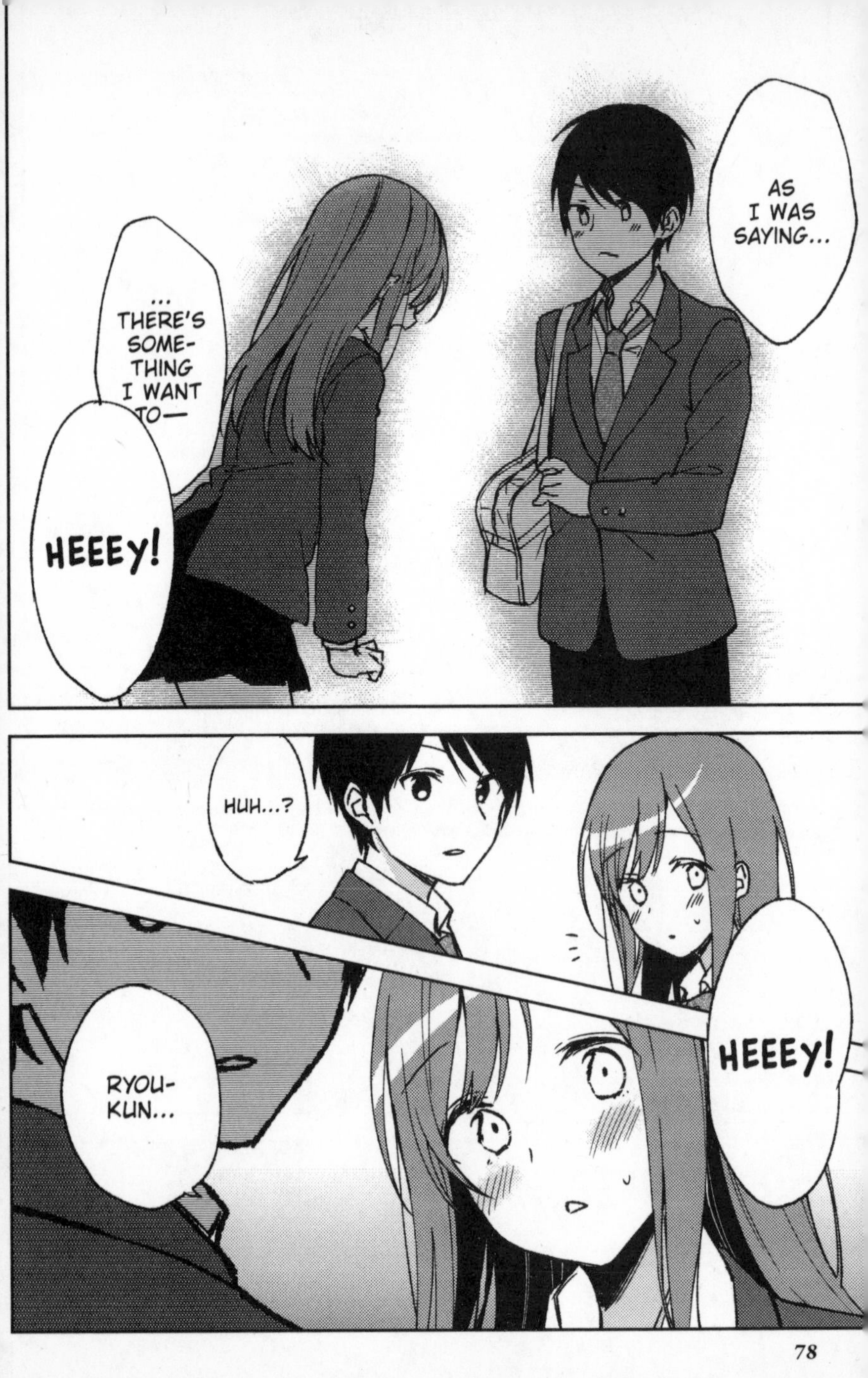
AS I WAS SAYING...
...THERE'S SOME-THING I WANT TO—
HEEEY!
HUH...?
HEEEY!
RYOU-KUN...

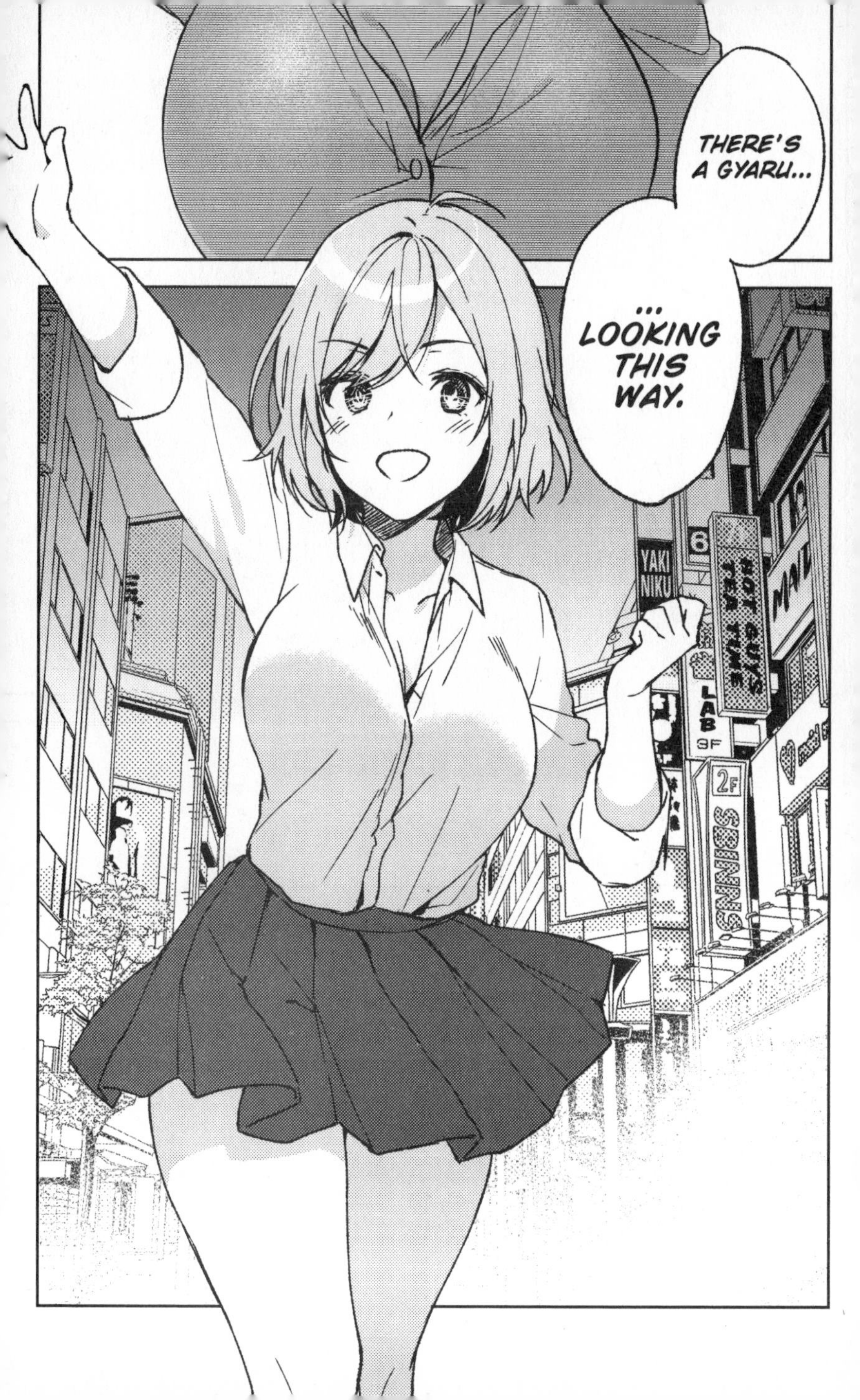
THERE'S A GYARU...
...LOOKING THIS WAY.
YAKI NIKU
HOT GUYS TEA TIME
LAB
9F
2F

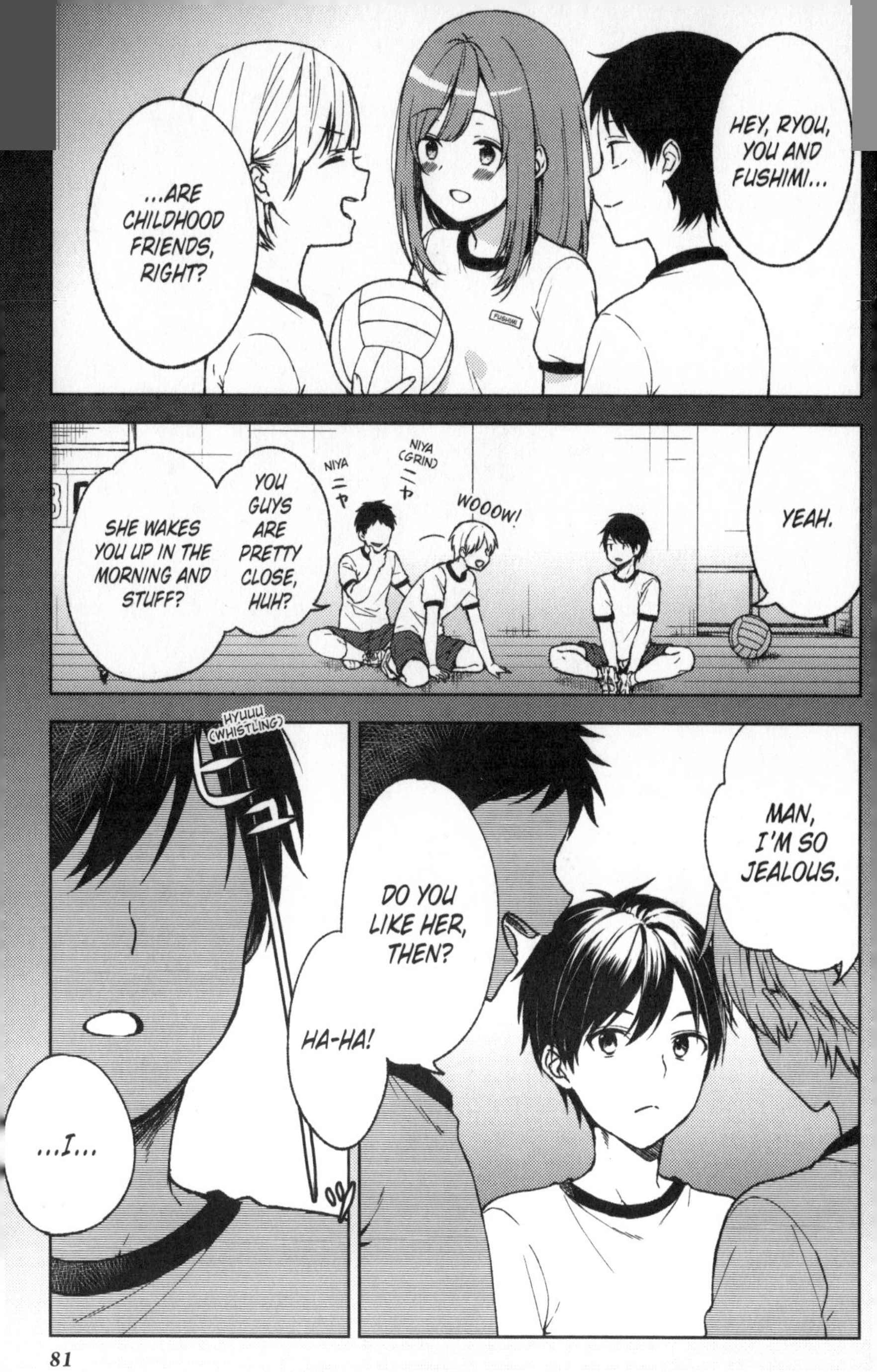
HEY, RYOU, YOU AND FUSHIMI...
...ARE CHILDHOOD FRIENDS, RIGHT?
FUSHIMI
YEAH.
WOOOW!
NIYA (GRIN)
NIYA
YOU GUYS ARE PRETTY CLOSE, HUH?
SHE WAKES YOU UP IN THE MORNING AND STUFF?
MAN, I'M SO JEALOUS.
DO YOU LIKE HER, THEN?
HA-HA!
HYUUU (WHISTLING)
...I...

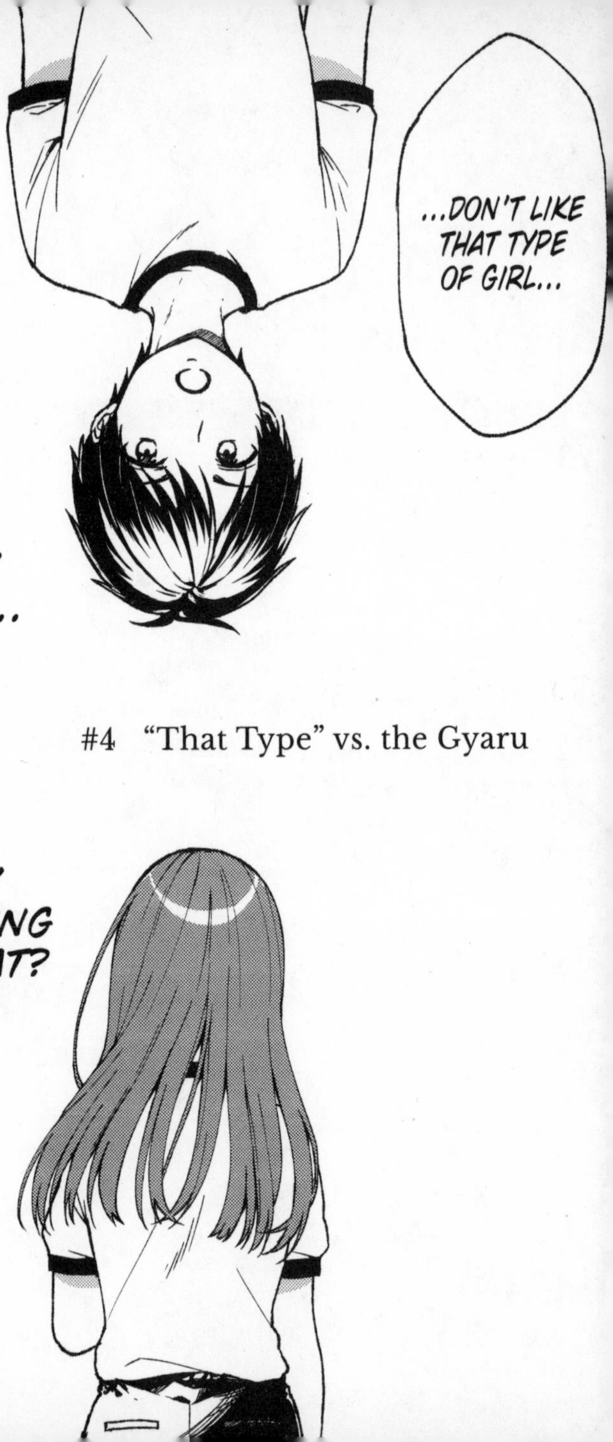
...DON'T LIKE THAT TYPE OF GIRL...
WHY DID I...
...SAY SOMETHING LIKE THAT?

#4 "That Type" vs. the Gyaru

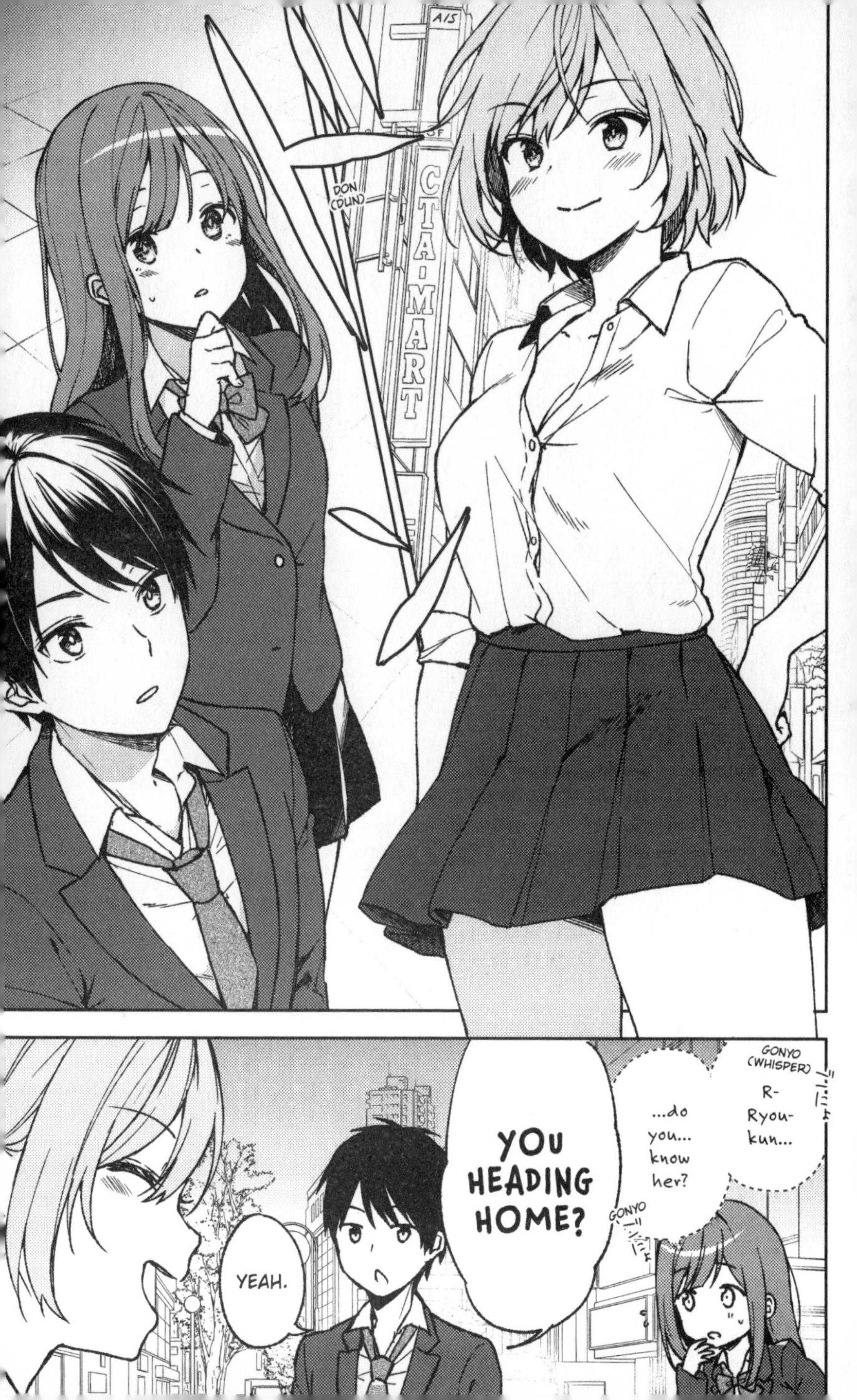
AIS
CTA-MART
DON (DUN)
GONYO (WHISPER)
R-Ryou-kun...
...do you... know her?
GONYO
YOU HEADING HOME?
YEAH.

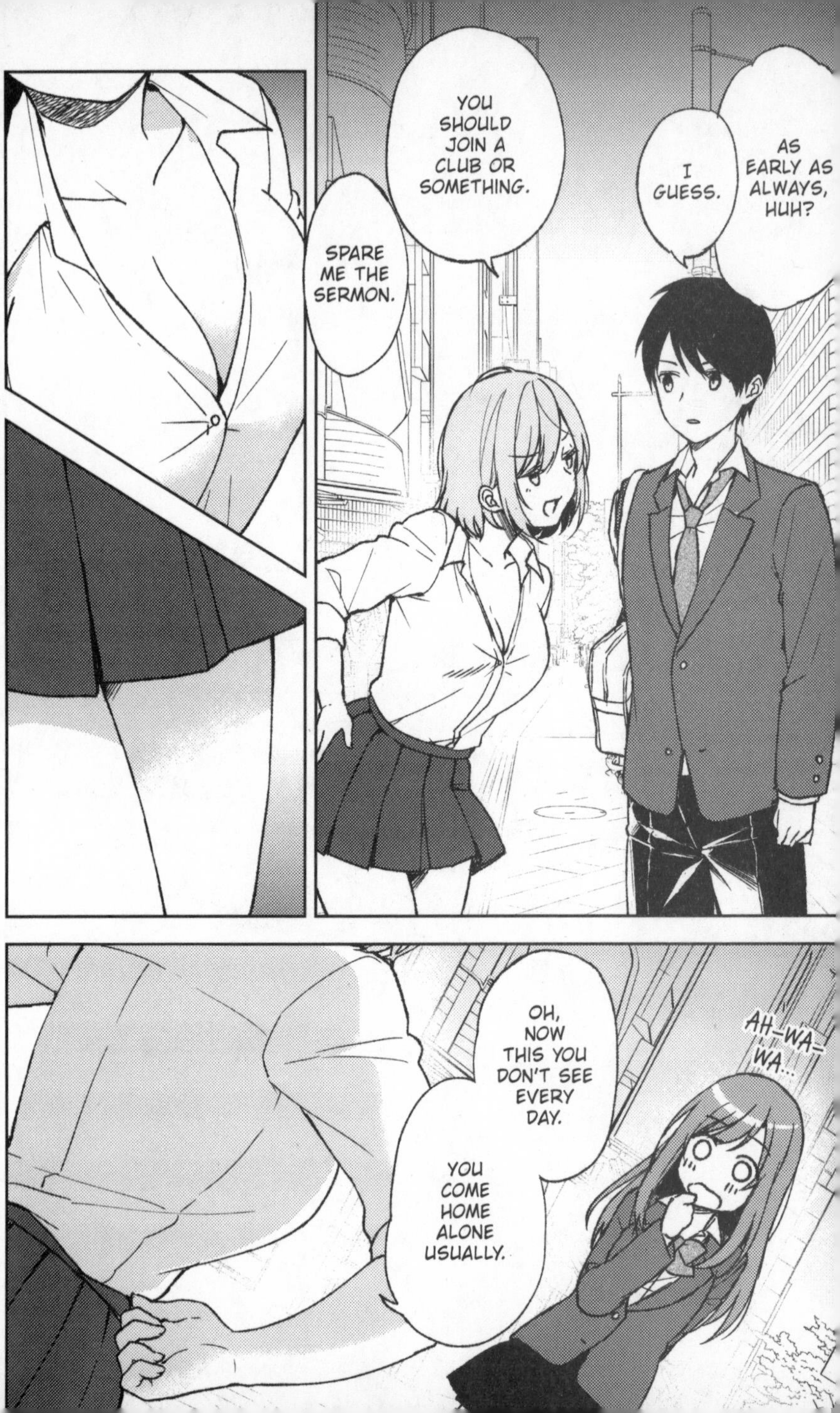
AS EARLY AS ALWAYS, HUH?
I GUESS.
YOU SHOULD JOIN A CLUB OR SOMETHING.
SPARE ME THE SERMON.
AH-WA-WA...
OH, NOW THIS YOU DON'T SEE EVERY DAY.
YOU COME HOME ALONE USUALLY.

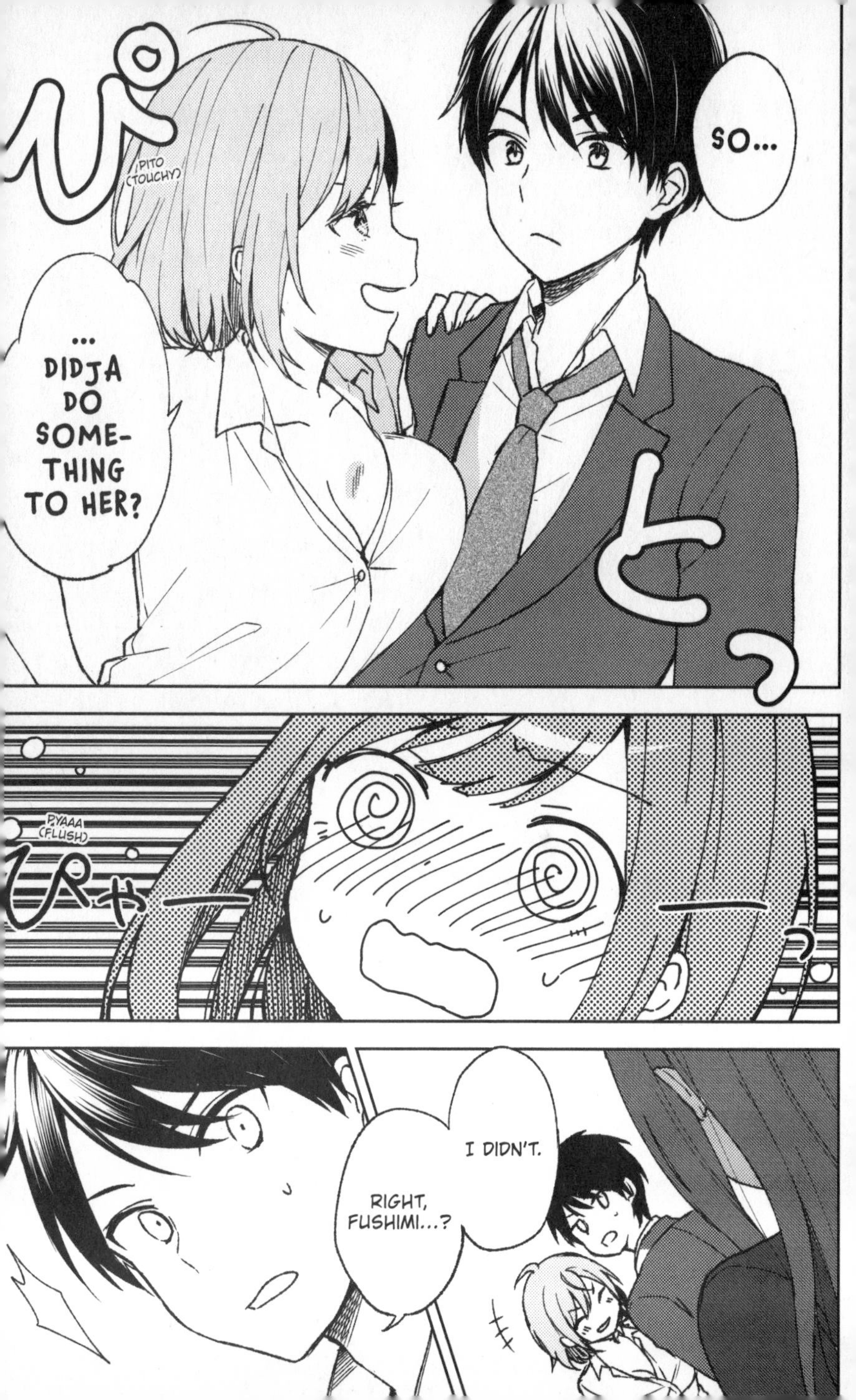
SO...
ぴとっ
PITO (TOUCHY)
... DIDJA DO SOME-THING TO HER?
ぴゃーーーっ
PYAAA (FLUSH)
I DIDN'T.
RIGHT, FUSHIMI...?

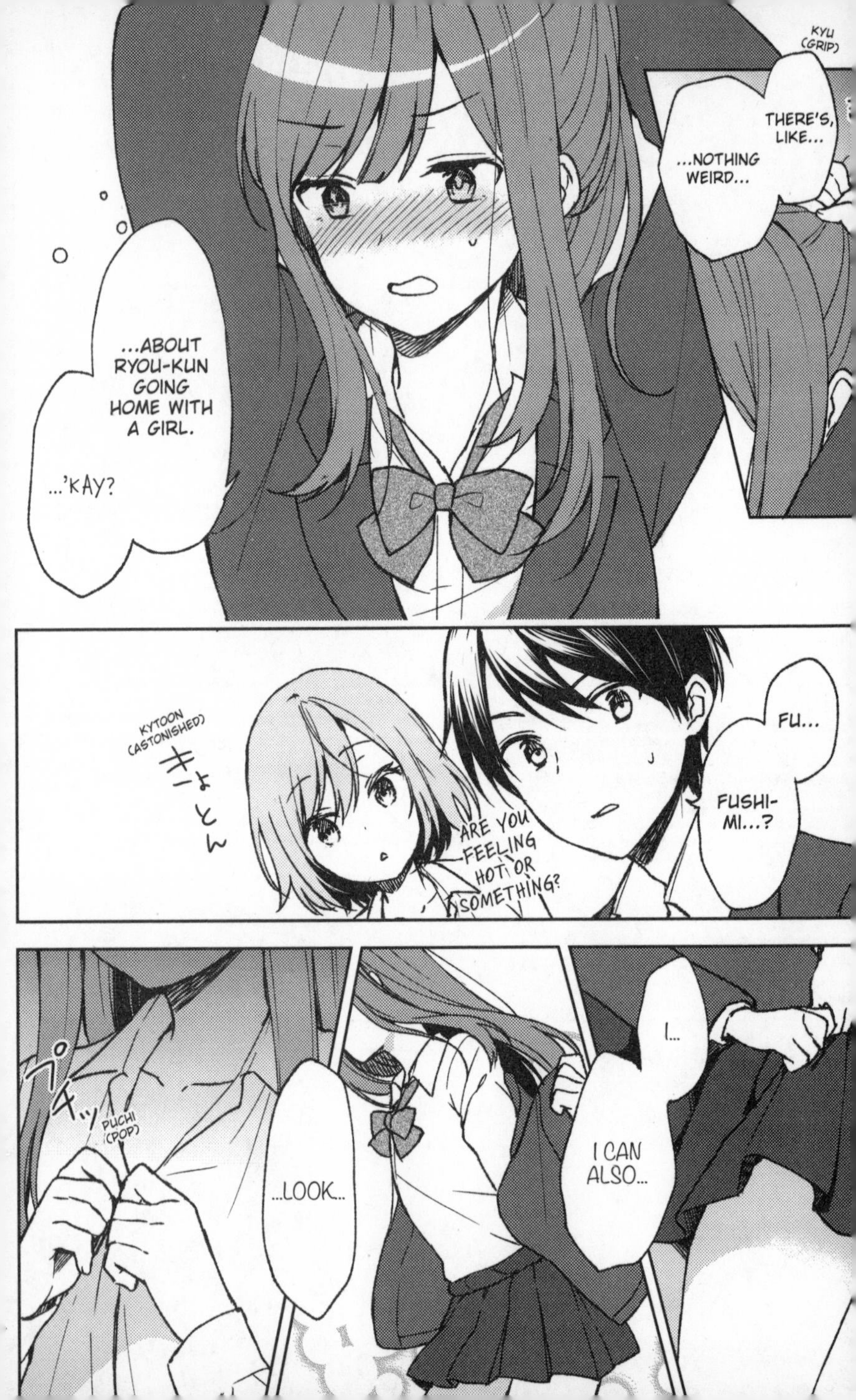
KYU (GRIP)
THERE'S, LIKE...
...NOTHING WEIRD...
...ABOUT RYOU-KUN GOING HOME WITH A GIRL.
...'KAY?
FU...
FUSHI-MI...?
ARE YOU FEELING HOT OR SOMETHING?
KYTOON (ASTONISHED)
I...
I CAN ALSO...
...LOOK...
PUCHI (POP)

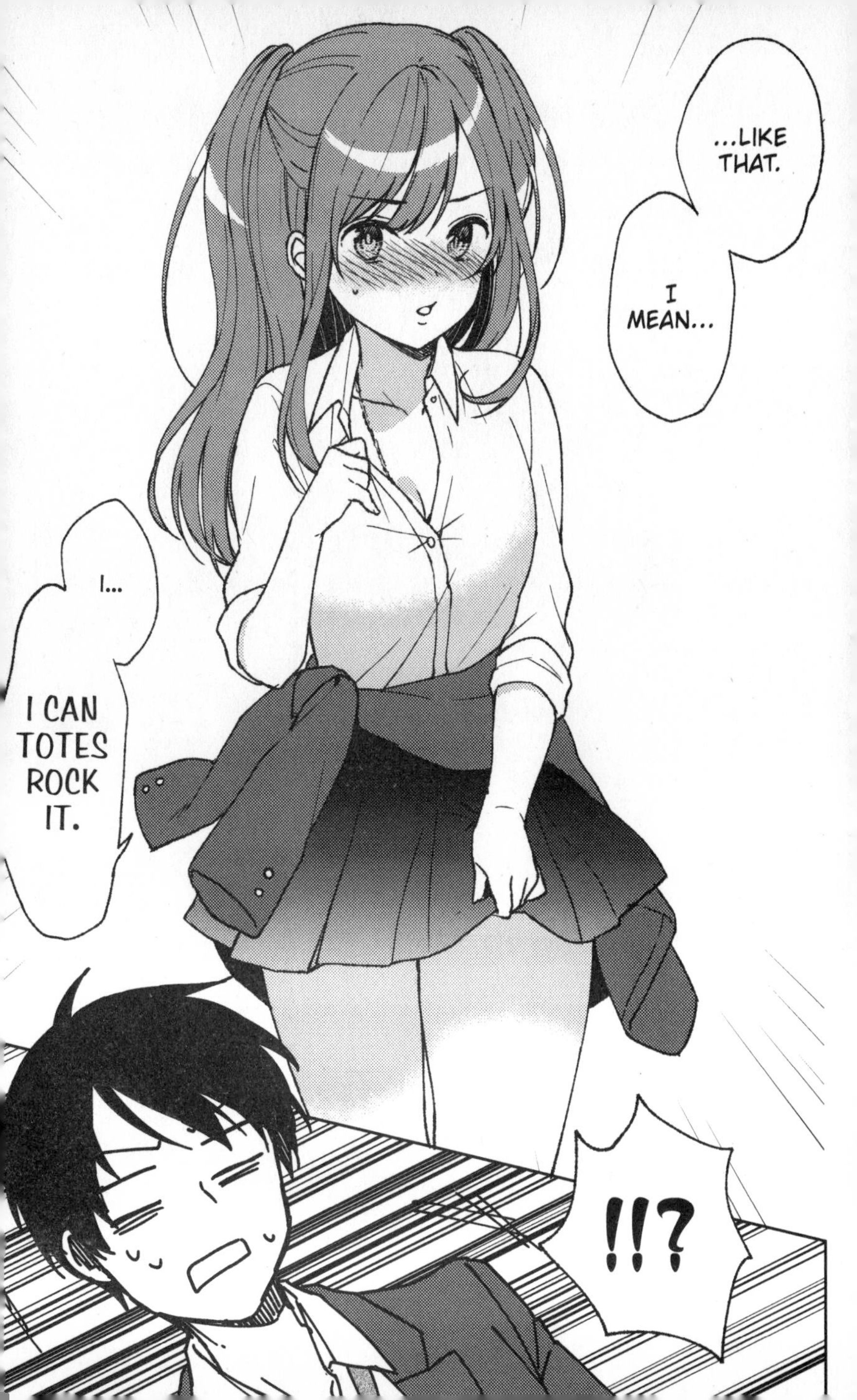
...LIKE THAT.
I MEAN...
I...
I CAN TOTES ROCK IT.
!!?

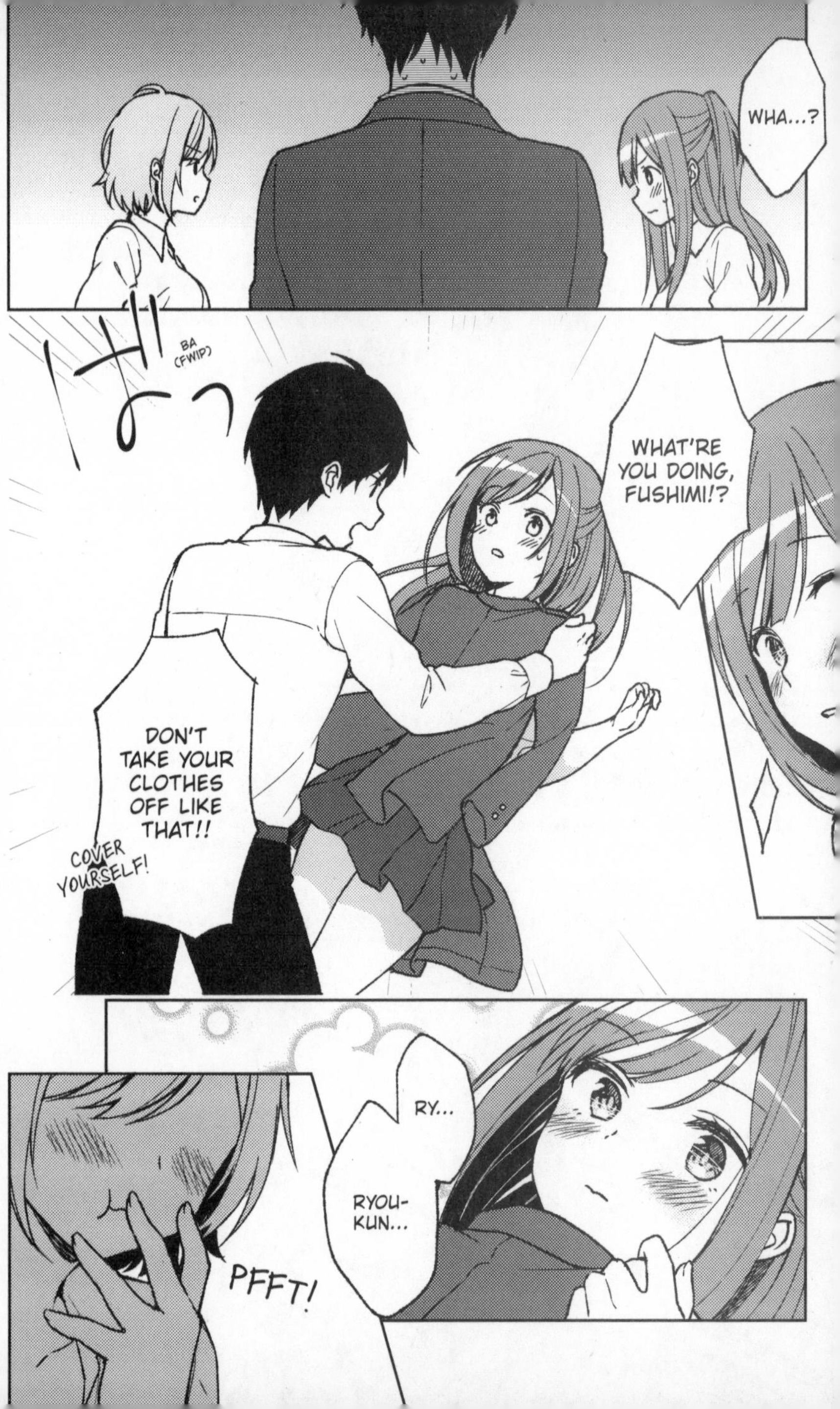

WHA...?
WHAT'RE YOU DOING, FUSHIMI!?
ばっ
BA (FWIP)
DON'T TAKE YOUR CLOTHES OFF LIKE THAT!!
COVER YOURSELF!
RY...
RYOU-KUN...
PFFT!

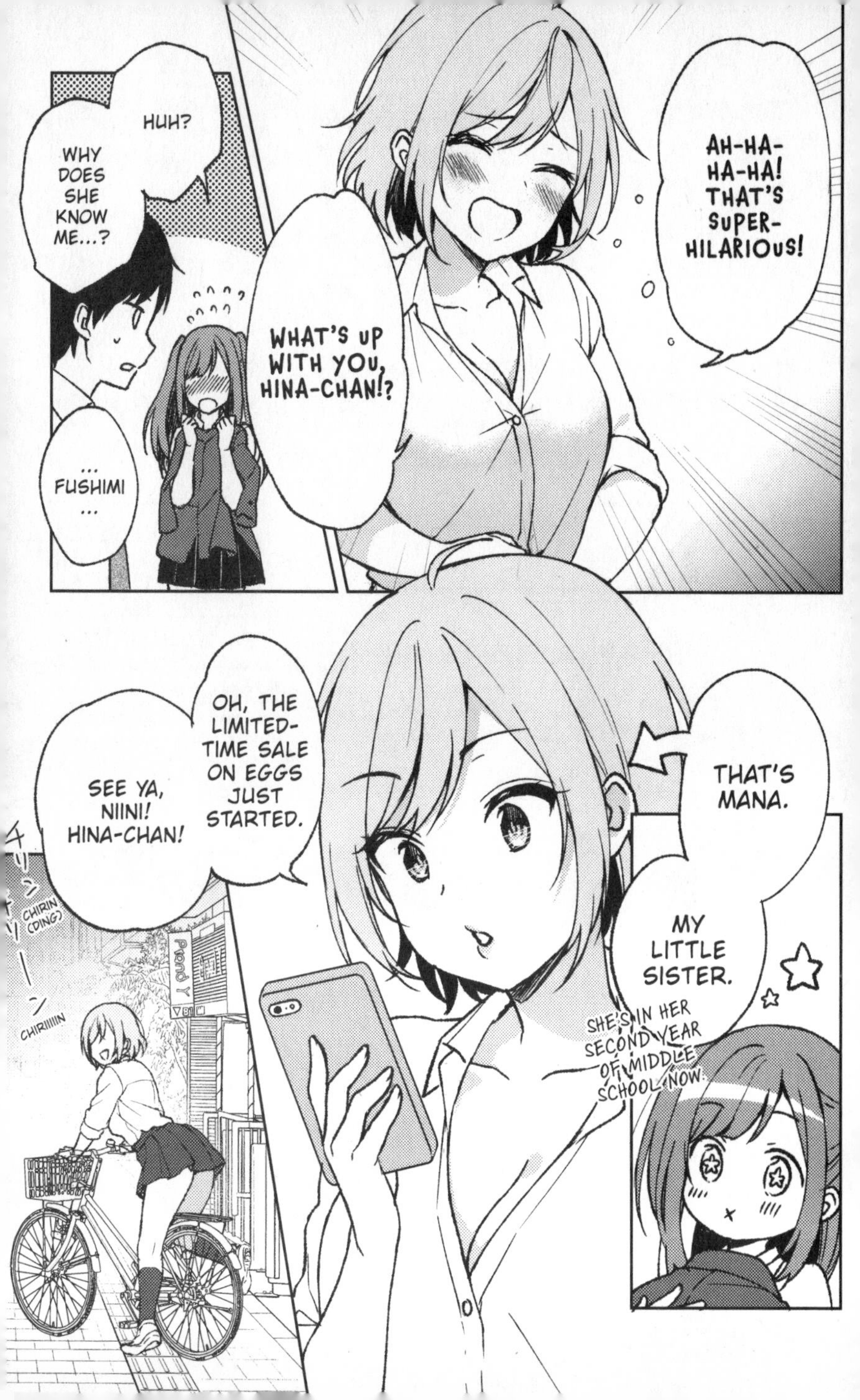
AH-HA-HA-HA! THAT'S SUPER-HILARIOUS!
WHAT'S UP WITH YOU, HINA-CHAN!?
HUH?
WHY DOES SHE KNOW ME...?
... FUSHIMI ...
THAT'S MANA.
MY LITTLE SISTER.
SHE'S IN HER SECOND YEAR OF MIDDLE SCHOOL NOW.
OH, THE LIMITED-TIME SALE ON EGGS JUST STARTED.
SEE YA, NIINI! HINA-CHAN!
CHIRIN (DING)
CHIRIIIIIN

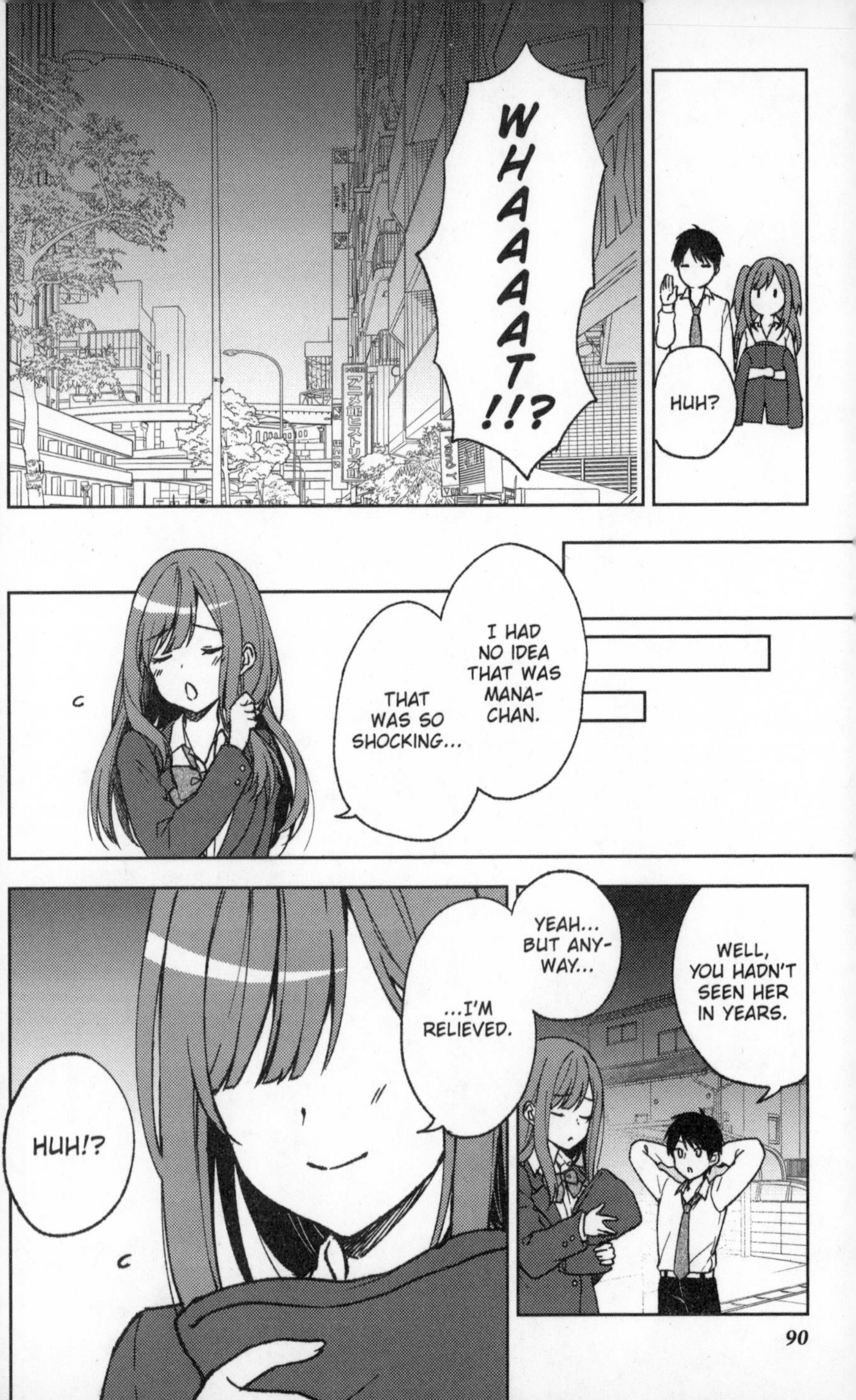
HUH?
WHAAAAAT!!?
I HAD NO IDEA THAT WAS MANA-CHAN.
THAT WAS SO SHOCKING...
WELL, YOU HADN'T SEEN HER IN YEARS.
YEAH... BUT ANY-WAY...
...I'M RELIEVED.
HUH!?

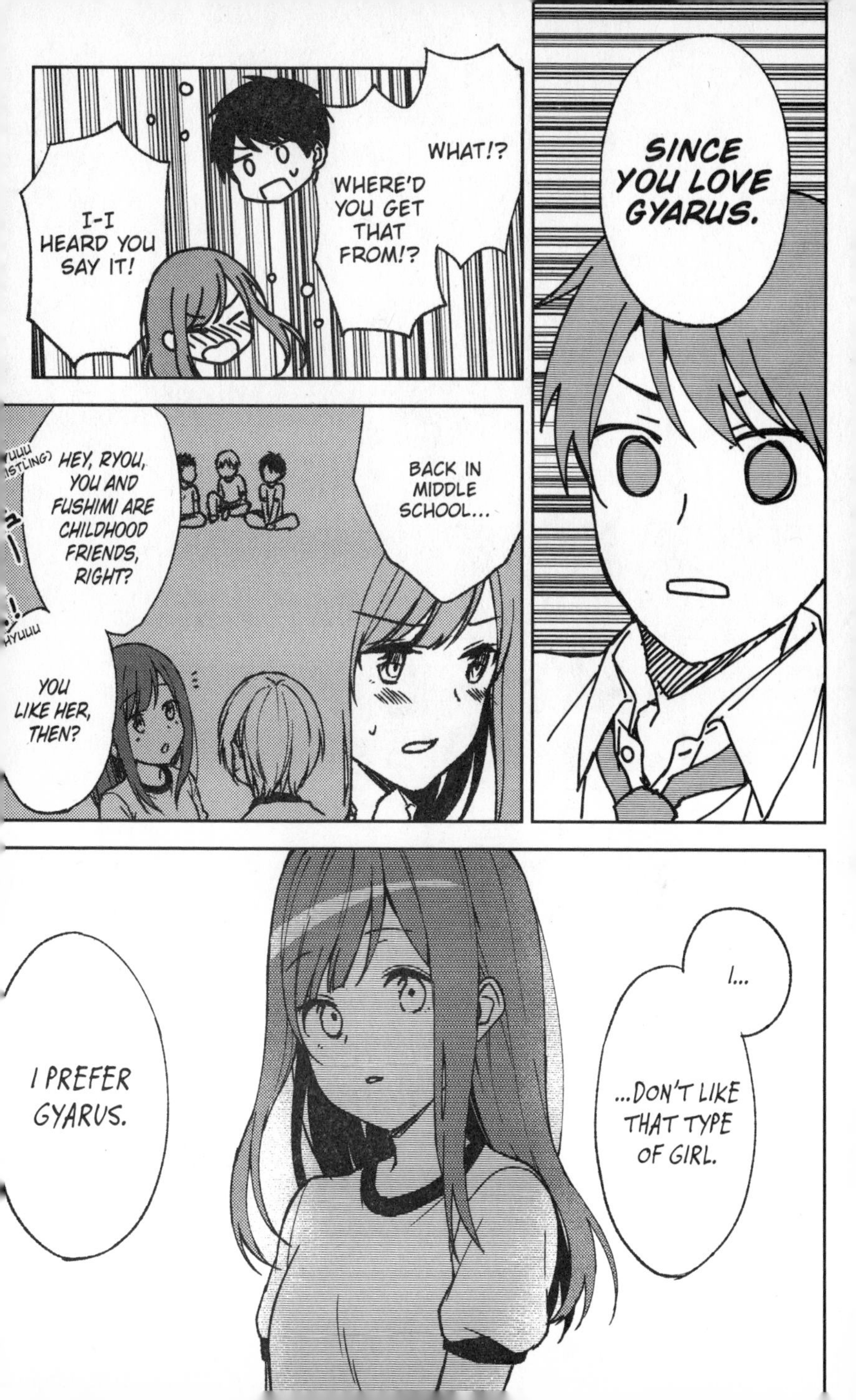
SINCE YOU LOVE GYARUS.
WHAT!?
WHERE'D YOU GET THAT FROM!?
I-I HEARD YOU SAY IT!
BACK IN MIDDLE SCHOOL...
HEY, RYOU, YOU AND FUSHIMI ARE CHILDHOOD FRIENDS, RIGHT?
YOU LIKE HER, THEN?
I...
...DON'T LIKE THAT TYPE OF GIRL.
I PREFER GYARUS.

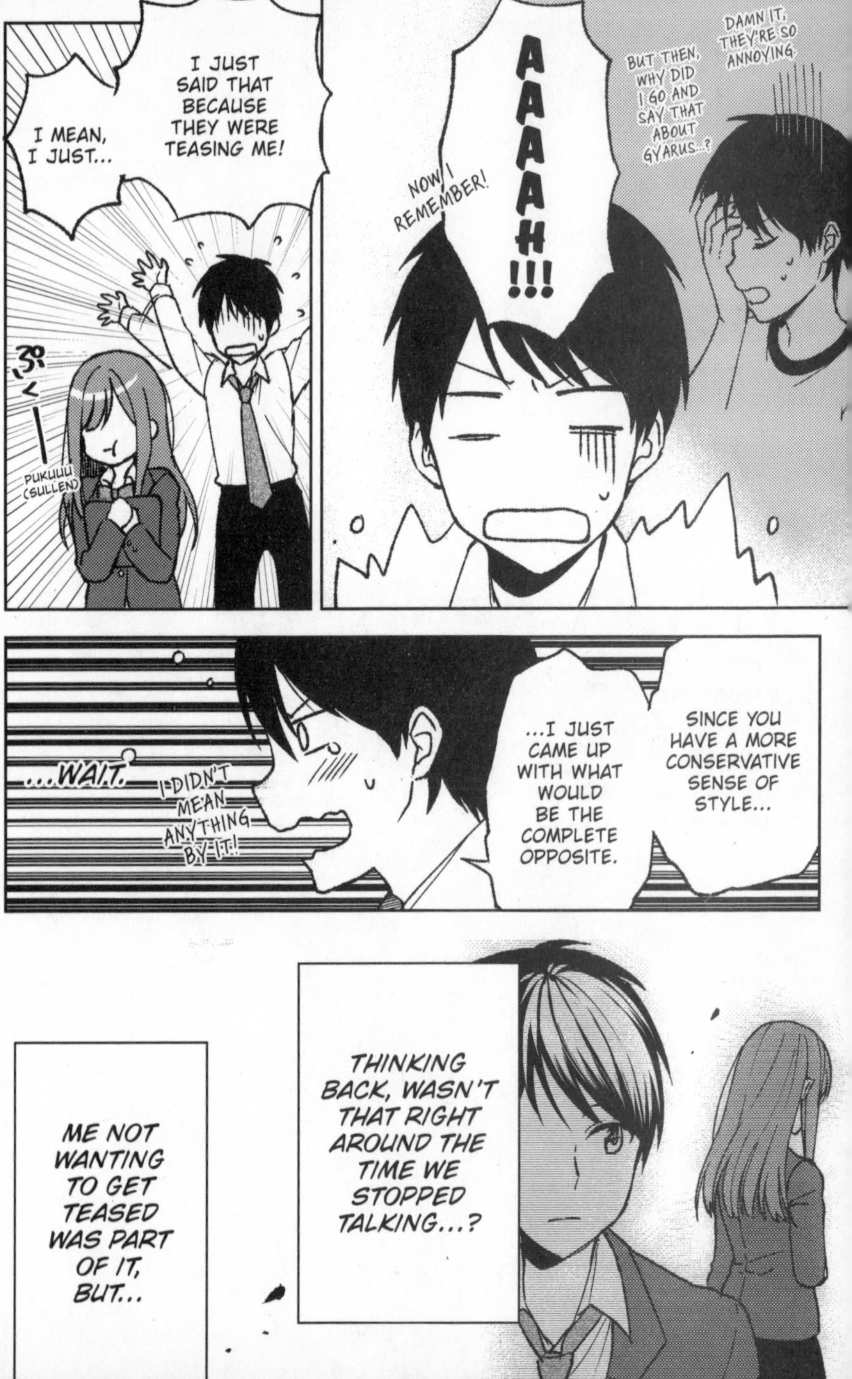
DAMN IT, THEY'RE SO ANNOYING.
BUT THEN, WHY DID I GO AND SAY THAT ABOUT GYARUS...?
AAAAAH!!!
NOW I REMEMBER!
I JUST SAID THAT BECAUSE THEY WERE TEASING ME!
I MEAN, I JUST...
ぷくー
PUKUUU (SULLEN)
SINCE YOU HAVE A MORE CONSERVATIVE SENSE OF STYLE...
...I JUST CAME UP WITH WHAT WOULD BE THE COMPLETE OPPOSITE.
I DIDN'T MEAN ANYTHING BY IT!
...WAIT.
THINKING BACK, WASN'T THAT RIGHT AROUND THE TIME WE STOPPED TALKING...?
ME NOT WANTING TO GET TEASED WAS PART OF IT, BUT...

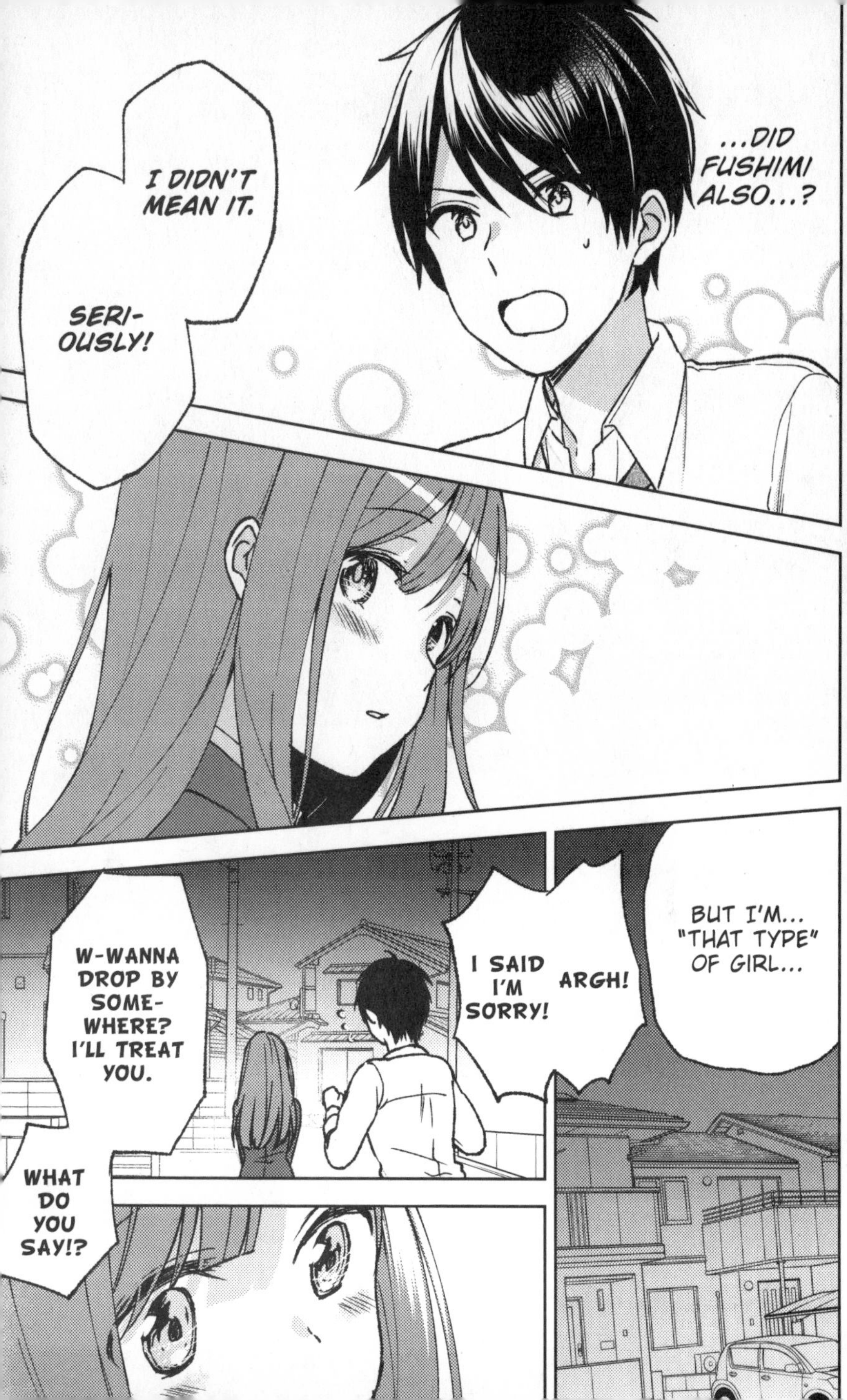
...DID FUSHIMI ALSO...?
I DIDN'T MEAN IT.
SERI-OUSLY!
BUT I'M... "THAT TYPE" OF GIRL...
ARGH!
I SAID I'M SORRY!
W-WANNA DROP BY SOME-WHERE? I'LL TREAT YOU.
WHAT DO YOU SAY!?

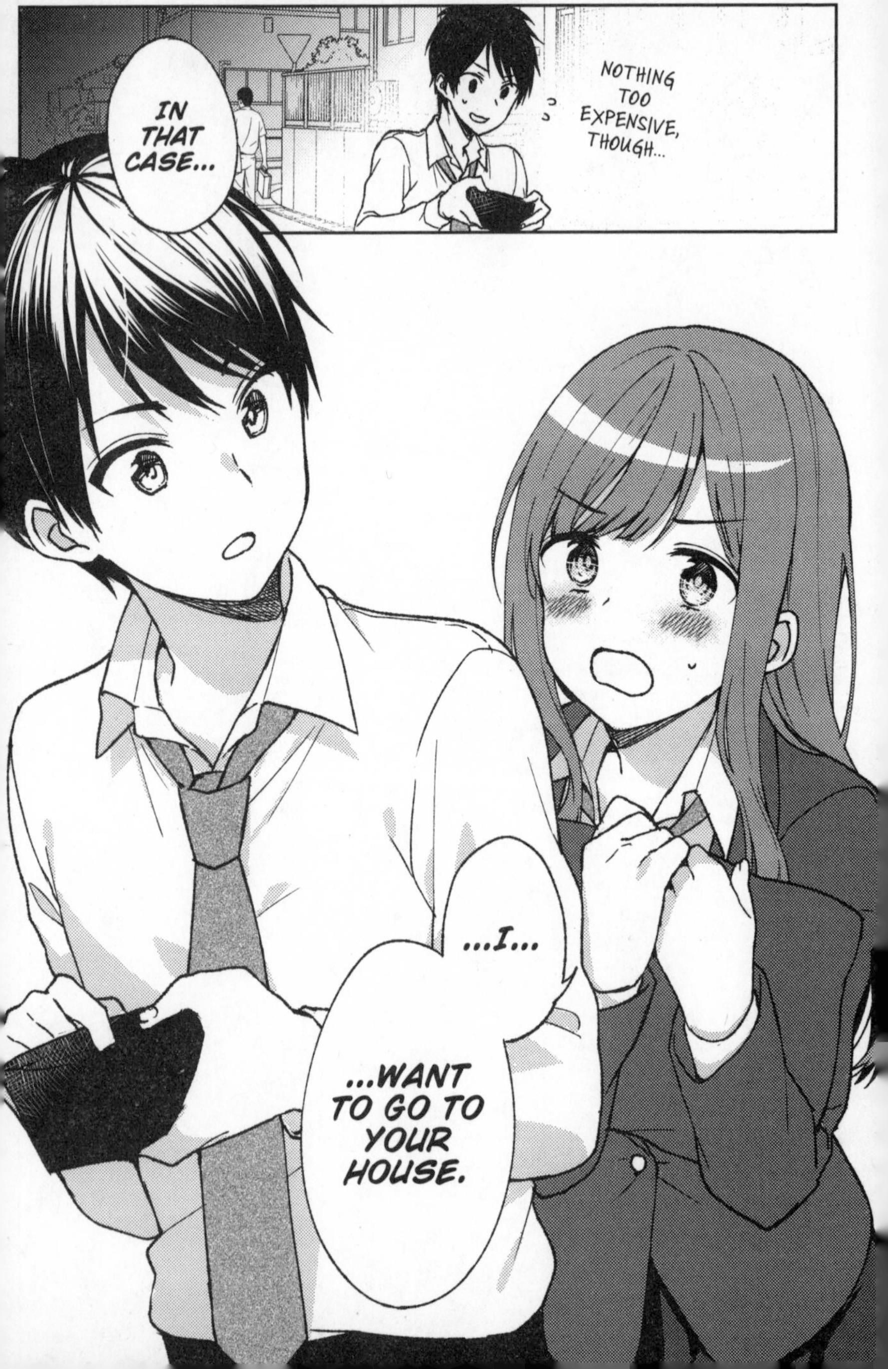
NOTHING TOO EXPENSIVE, THOUGH...
IN THAT CASE...
...I...
...WANT TO GO TO YOUR HOUSE.

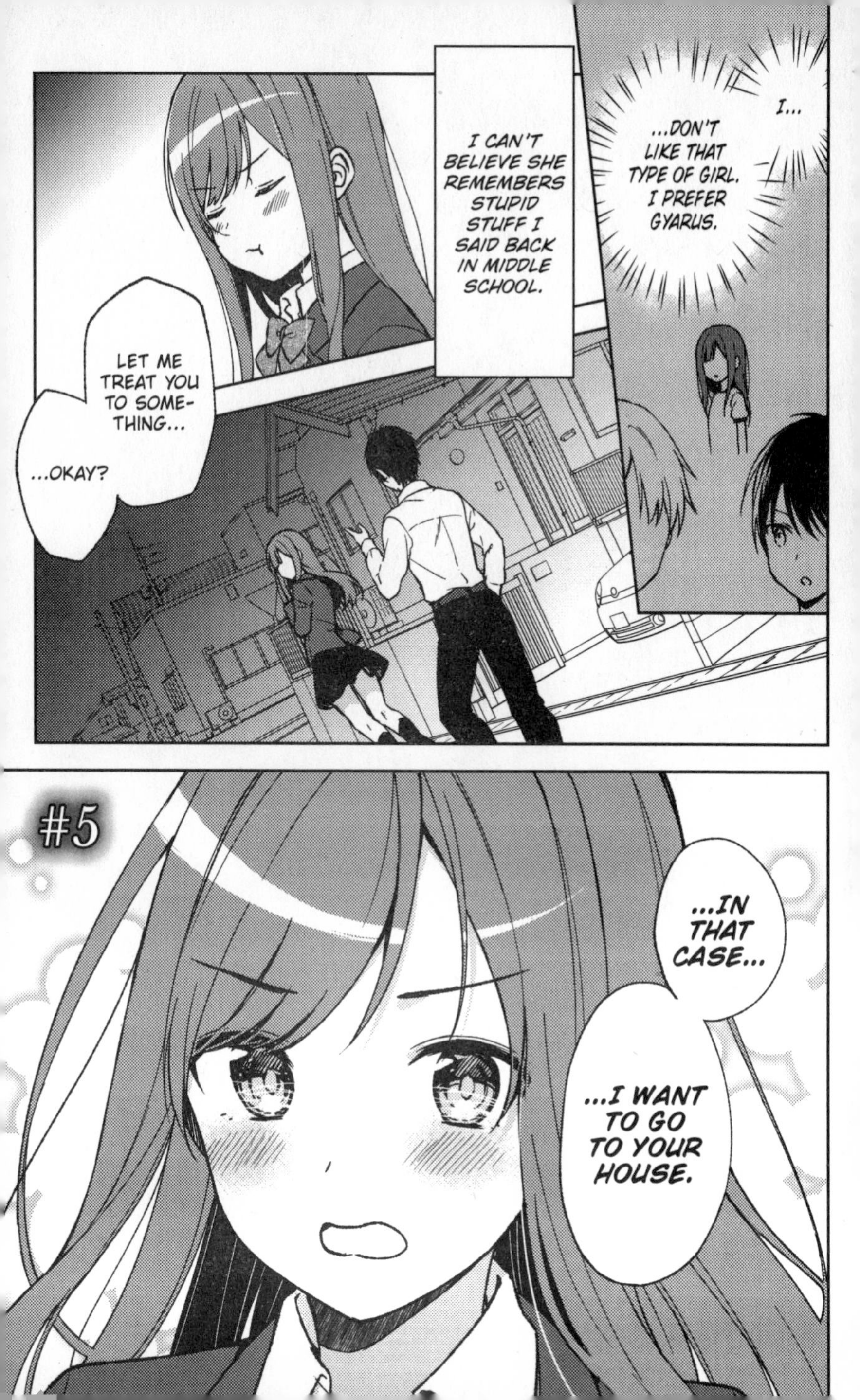
I...
...DON'T LIKE THAT TYPE OF GIRL. I PREFER GYARUS.
I CAN'T BELIEVE SHE REMEMBERS STUPID STUFF I SAID BACK IN MIDDLE SCHOOL.
LET ME TREAT YOU TO SOME-THING...
...OKAY?
#5
...IN THAT CASE...
...I WANT TO GO TO YOUR HOUSE.

#5 First Visit in Four Years

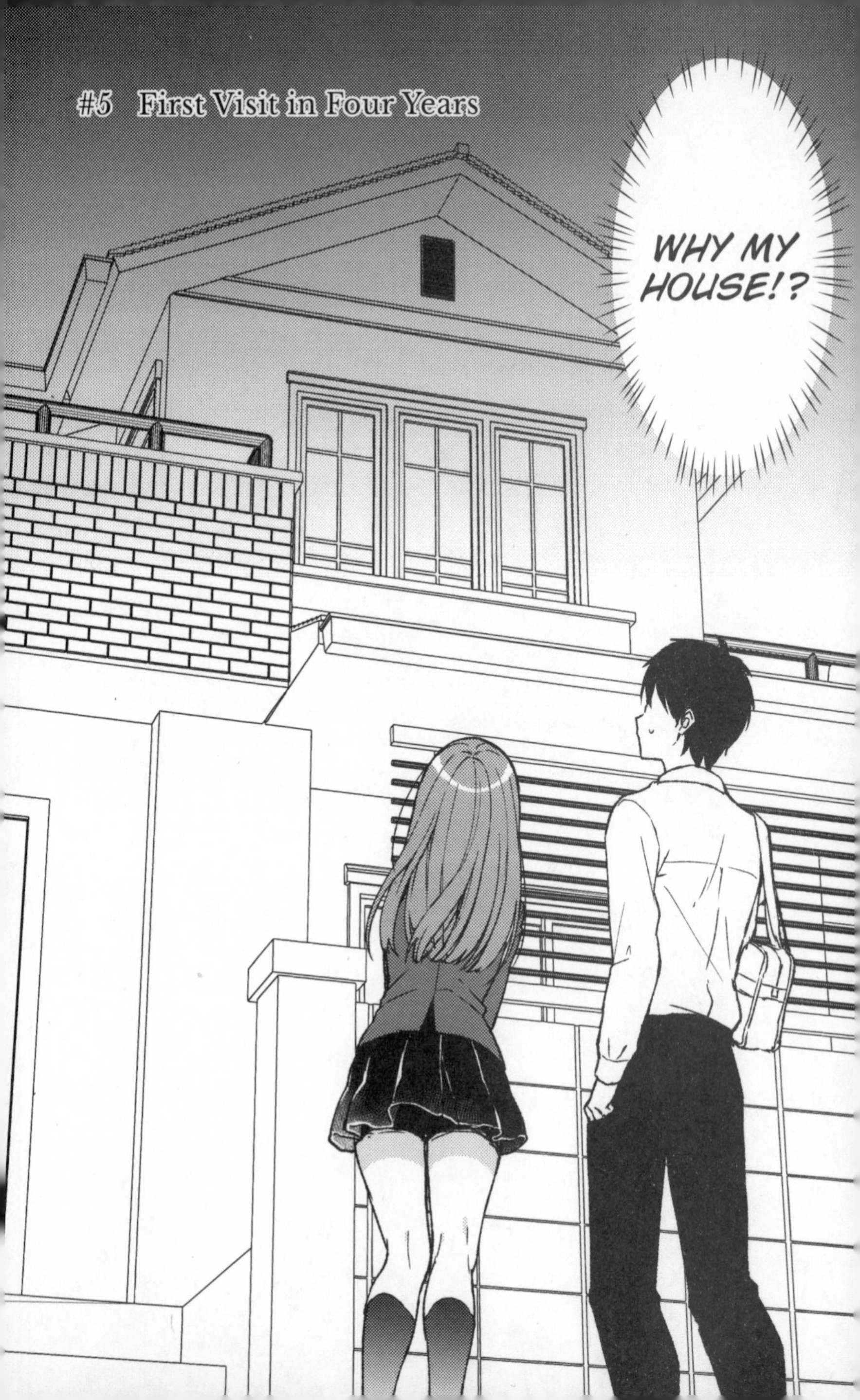
WHY MY HOUSE!?

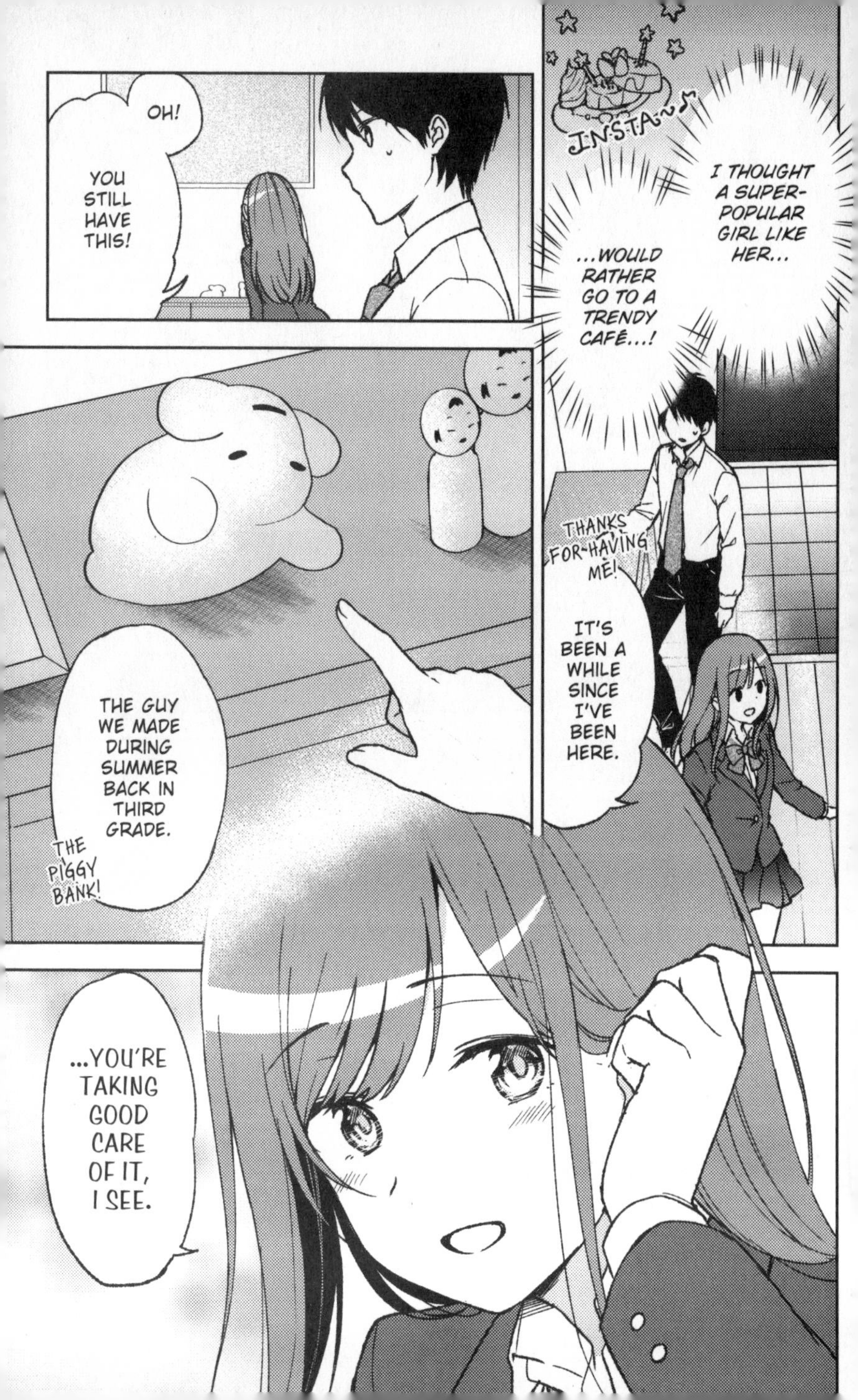
INSTA~♪
I THOUGHT A SUPER-POPULAR GIRL LIKE HER...
...WOULD RATHER GO TO A TRENDY CAFÉ...!
THANKS FOR HAVING ME!
IT'S BEEN A WHILE SINCE I'VE BEEN HERE.
OH!
YOU STILL HAVE THIS!
THE GUY WE MADE DURING SUMMER BACK IN THIRD GRADE.
THE PIGGY BANK!
...YOU'RE TAKING GOOD CARE OF IT, I SEE.

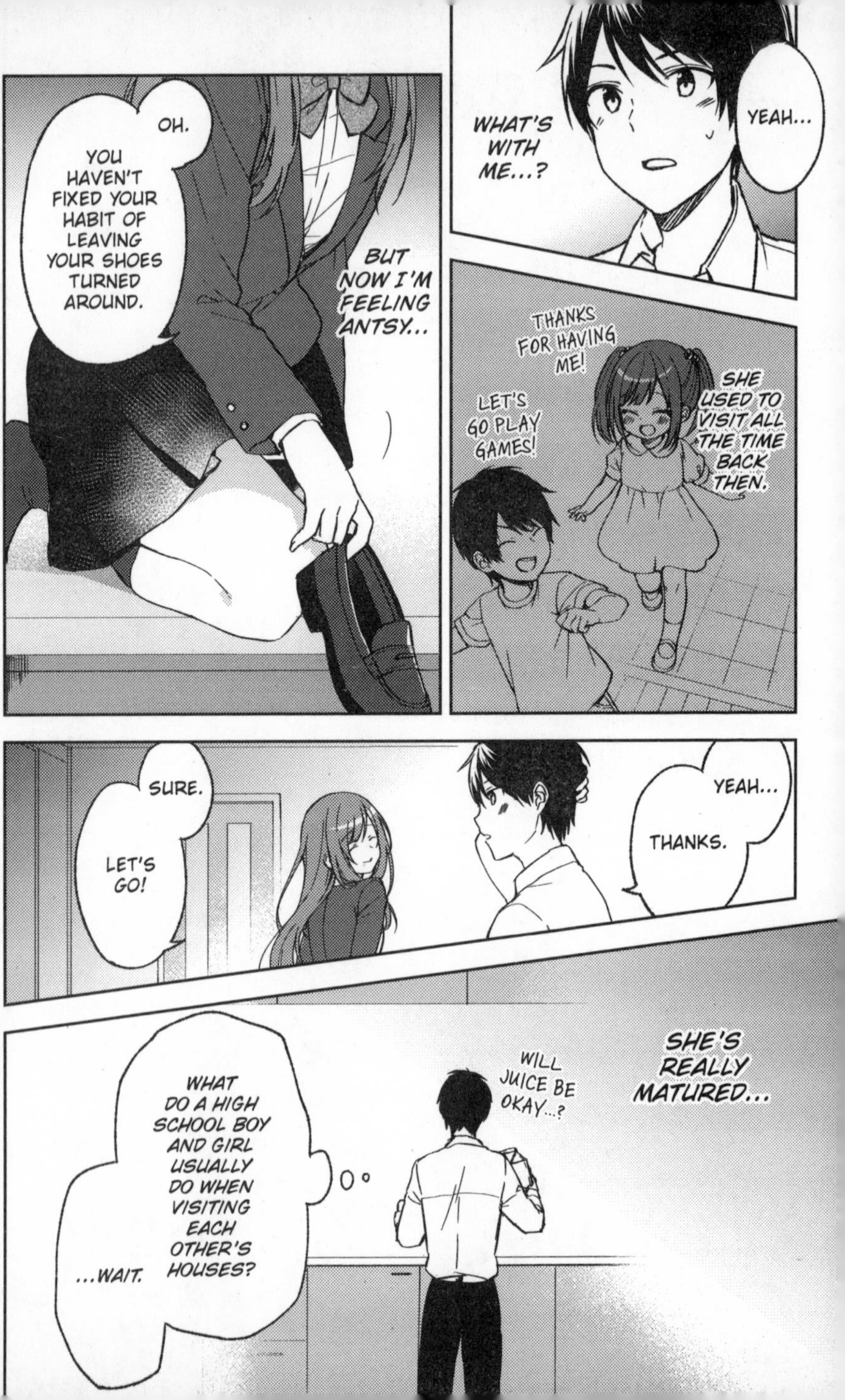
YEAH...
WHAT'S WITH ME...?
THANKS FOR HAVING ME!
LET'S GO PLAY GAMES!
SHE USED TO VISIT ALL THE TIME BACK THEN.
OH. YOU HAVEN'T FIXED YOUR HABIT OF LEAVING YOUR SHOES TURNED AROUND.
BUT NOW I'M FEELING ANTSY...
YEAH... THANKS.
SURE. LET'S GO!
SHE'S REALLY MATURED...
WILL JUICE BE OKAY...?
WHAT DO A HIGH SCHOOL BOY AND GIRL USUALLY DO WHEN VISITING EACH OTHER'S HOUSES?
...WAIT.

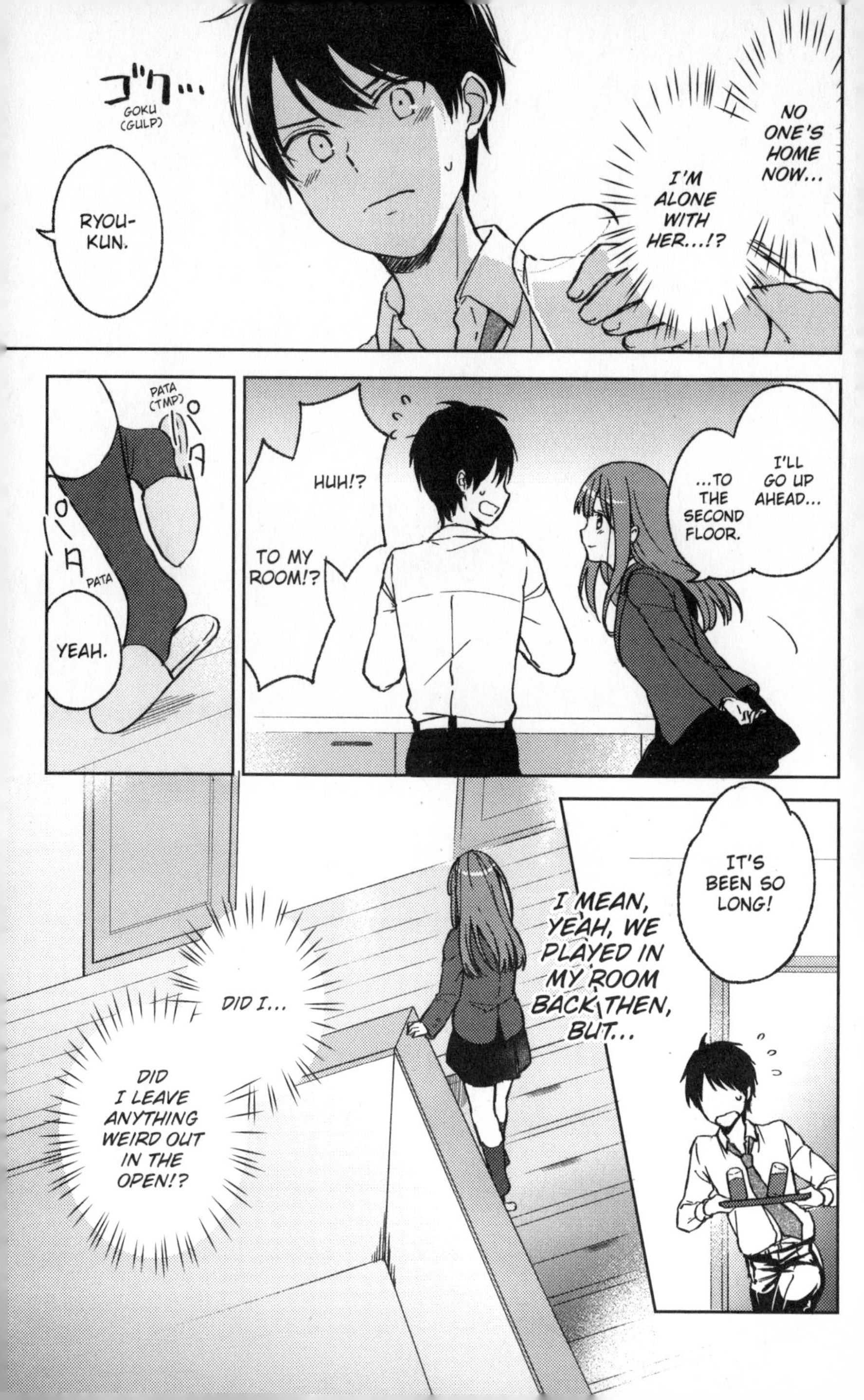
NO ONE'S HOME NOW...
I'M ALONE WITH HER...!?
ゴク...
GOKU (GULP)
RYOU-KUN.
I'LL GO UP AHEAD...
...TO THE SECOND FLOOR.
HUH!?
TO MY ROOM!?
パタ
PATA (TMP)
パタ
PATA
YEAH.
IT'S BEEN SO LONG!
I MEAN, YEAH, WE PLAYED IN MY ROOM BACK THEN, BUT...
DID I...
DID I LEAVE ANYTHING WEIRD OUT IN THE OPEN!?

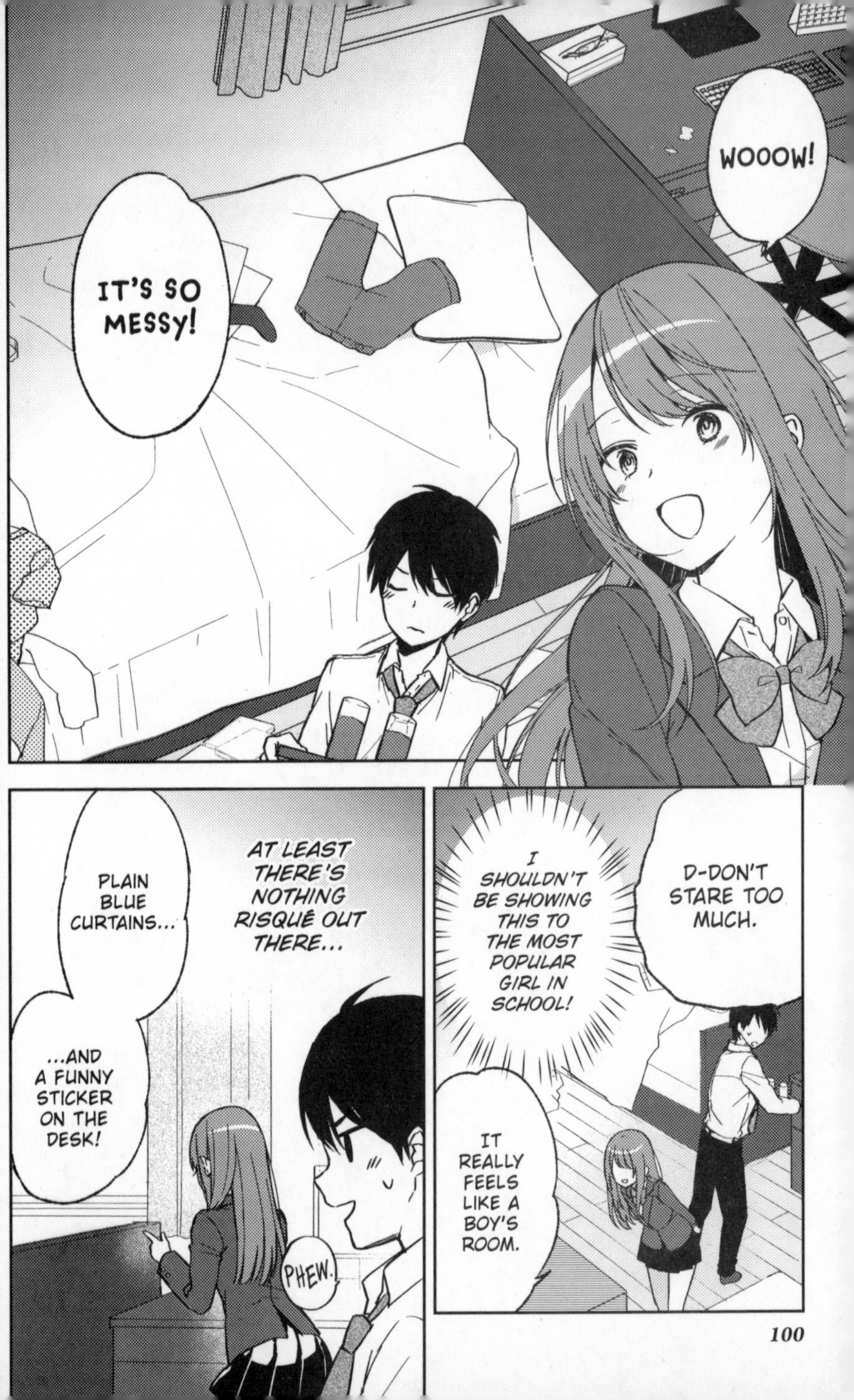
WOOOW!
IT'S SO MESSY!
D-DON'T STARE TOO MUCH.
I SHOULDN'T BE SHOWING THIS TO THE MOST POPULAR GIRL IN SCHOOL!
IT REALLY FEELS LIKE A BOY'S ROOM.
AT LEAST THERE'S NOTHING RISQUÉ OUT THERE...
PLAIN BLUE CURTAINS...
...AND A FUNNY STICKER ON THE DESK!
PHEW.

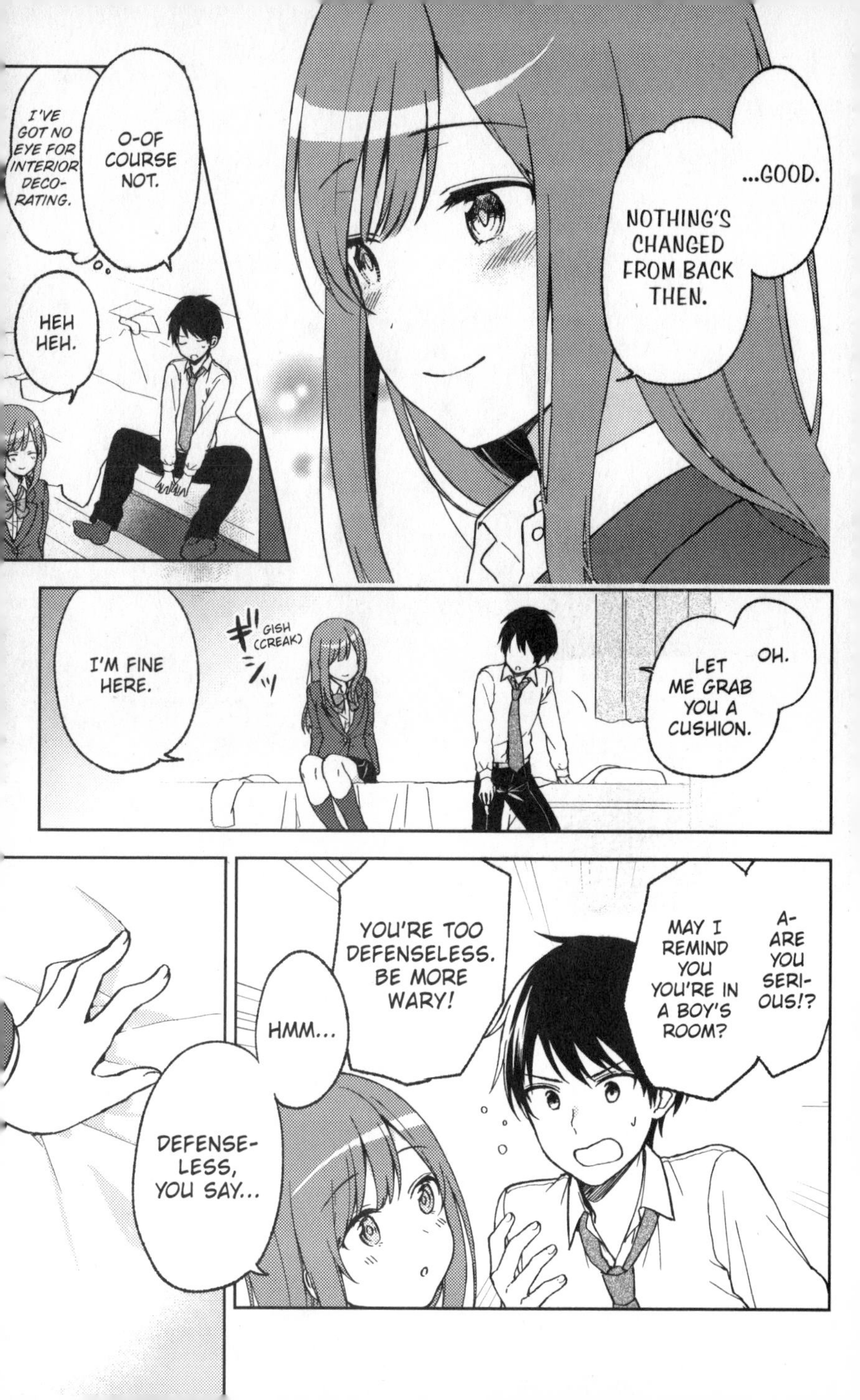
...GOOD.
NOTHING'S CHANGED FROM BACK THEN.
O-OF COURSE NOT.
I'VE GOT NO EYE FOR INTERIOR DECO-RATING.
HEH HEH.
OH.
LET ME GRAB YOU A CUSHION.
GISH (CREAK)
I'M FINE HERE.
A-ARE YOU SERI-OUS!?
MAY I REMIND YOU YOU'RE IN A BOY'S ROOM?
YOU'RE TOO DEFENSELESS. BE MORE WARY!
HMM...
DEFENSE-LESS, YOU SAY...

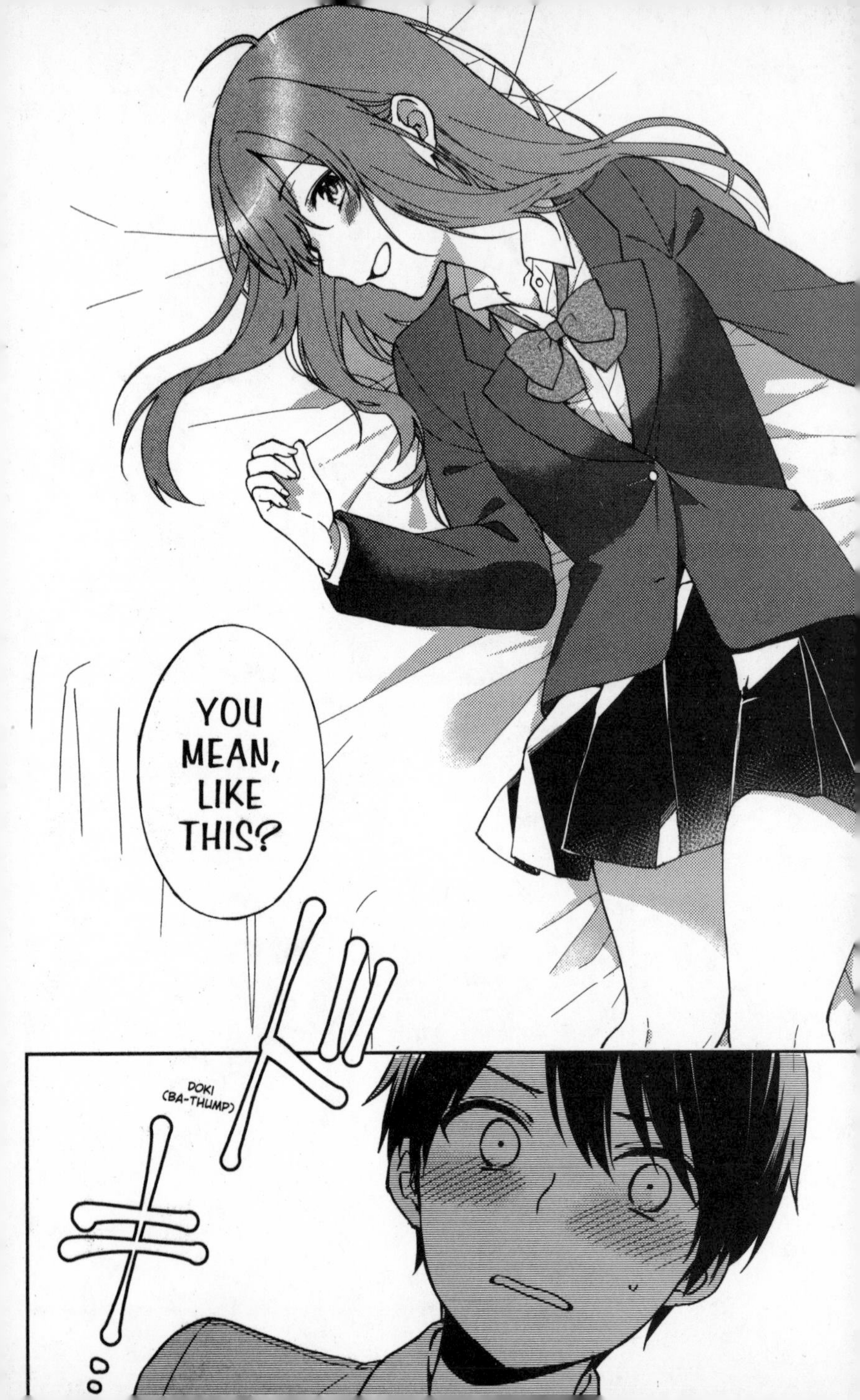
YOU MEAN, LIKE THIS?
DOKI (BA-THUMP)

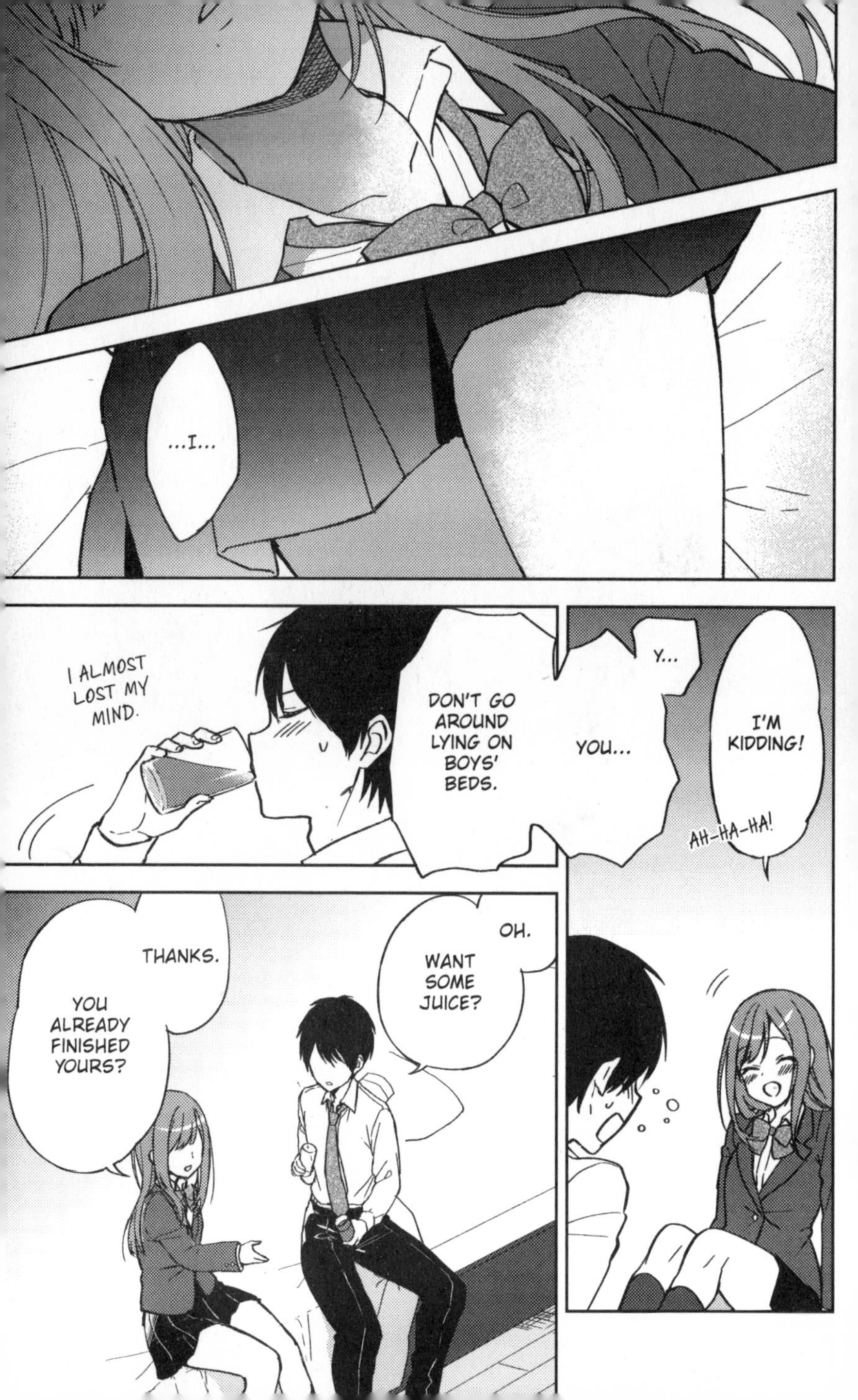
...I...
I'M KIDDING!
AH-HA-HA!
Y...
YOU...
DON'T GO AROUND LYING ON BOYS' BEDS.
I ALMOST LOST MY MIND.
OH.
WANT SOME JUICE?
THANKS.
YOU ALREADY FINISHED YOURS?

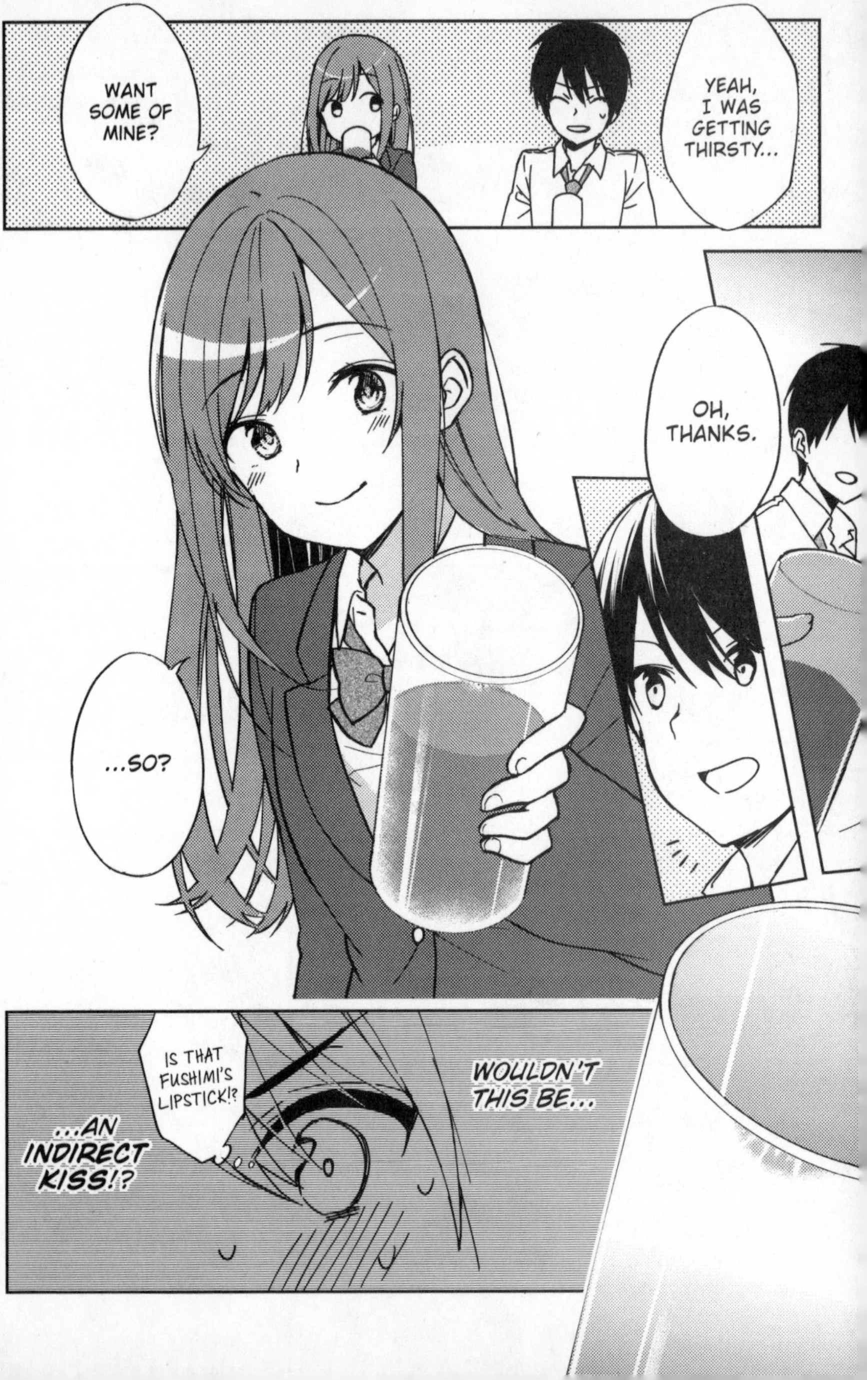
YEAH, I WAS GETTING THIRSTY...
WANT SOME OF MINE?
OH, THANKS.
...SO?
WOULDN'T THIS BE...
IS THAT FUSHIMI'S LIPSTICK!?
...AN INDIRECT KISS!?

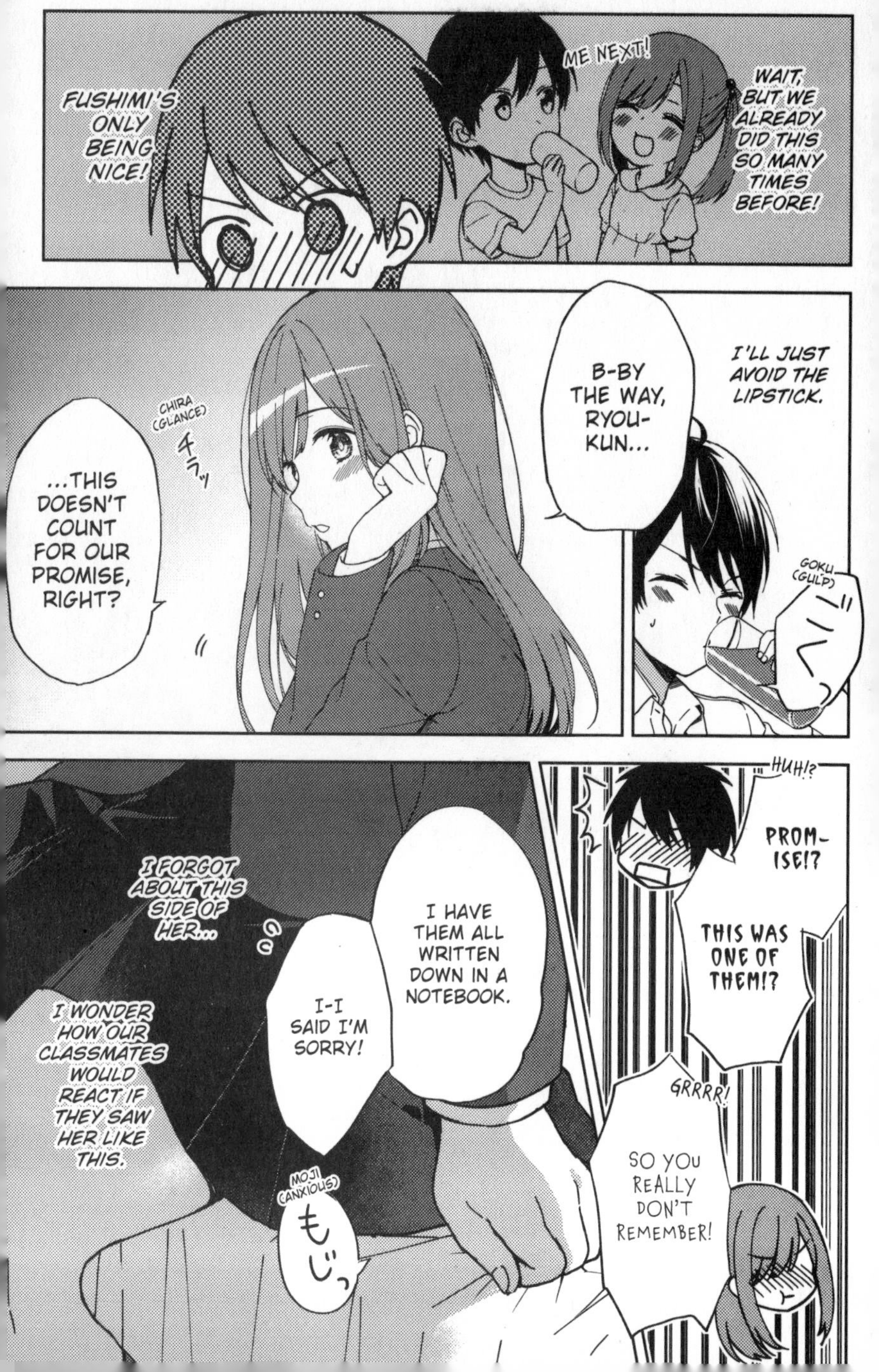
WAIT, BUT WE ALREADY DID THIS SO MANY TIMES BEFORE!
ME NEXT!
FUSHIMI'S ONLY BEING NICE!
I'LL JUST AVOID THE LIPSTICK.
GOKU (GULP)
B-BY THE WAY, RYOU-KUN...
CHIRA (GLANCE)
チラッ
...THIS DOESN'T COUNT FOR OUR PROMISE, RIGHT?
HUH!?
PROMISE!?
THIS WAS ONE OF THEM!?
GRRRR!
SO YOU REALLY DON'T REMEMBER!
I HAVE THEM ALL WRITTEN DOWN IN A NOTEBOOK.
I-I SAID I'M SORRY!
I FORGOT ABOUT THIS SIDE OF HER...
MOJI (ANXIOUS)
もじっ
I WONDER HOW OUR CLASSMATES WOULD REACT IF THEY SAW HER LIKE THIS.

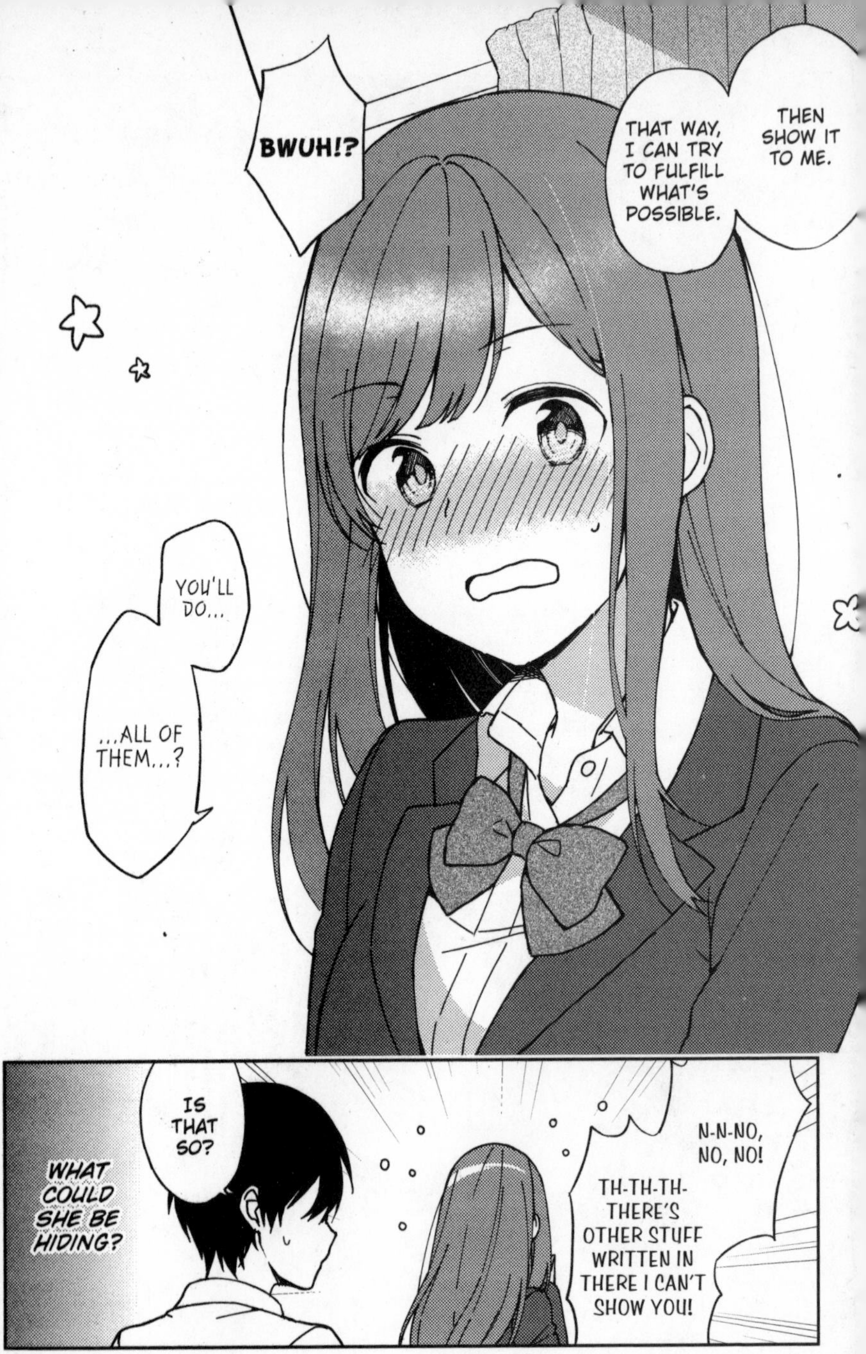
THEN SHOW IT TO ME.
THAT WAY, I CAN TRY TO FULFILL WHAT'S POSSIBLE.
BWUH!?
YOU'LL DO...
...ALL OF THEM...?
N-N-NO, NO, NO!
TH-TH-TH-THERE'S OTHER STUFF WRITTEN IN THERE I CAN'T SHOW YOU!
IS THAT SO?
WHAT COULD SHE BE HIDING?

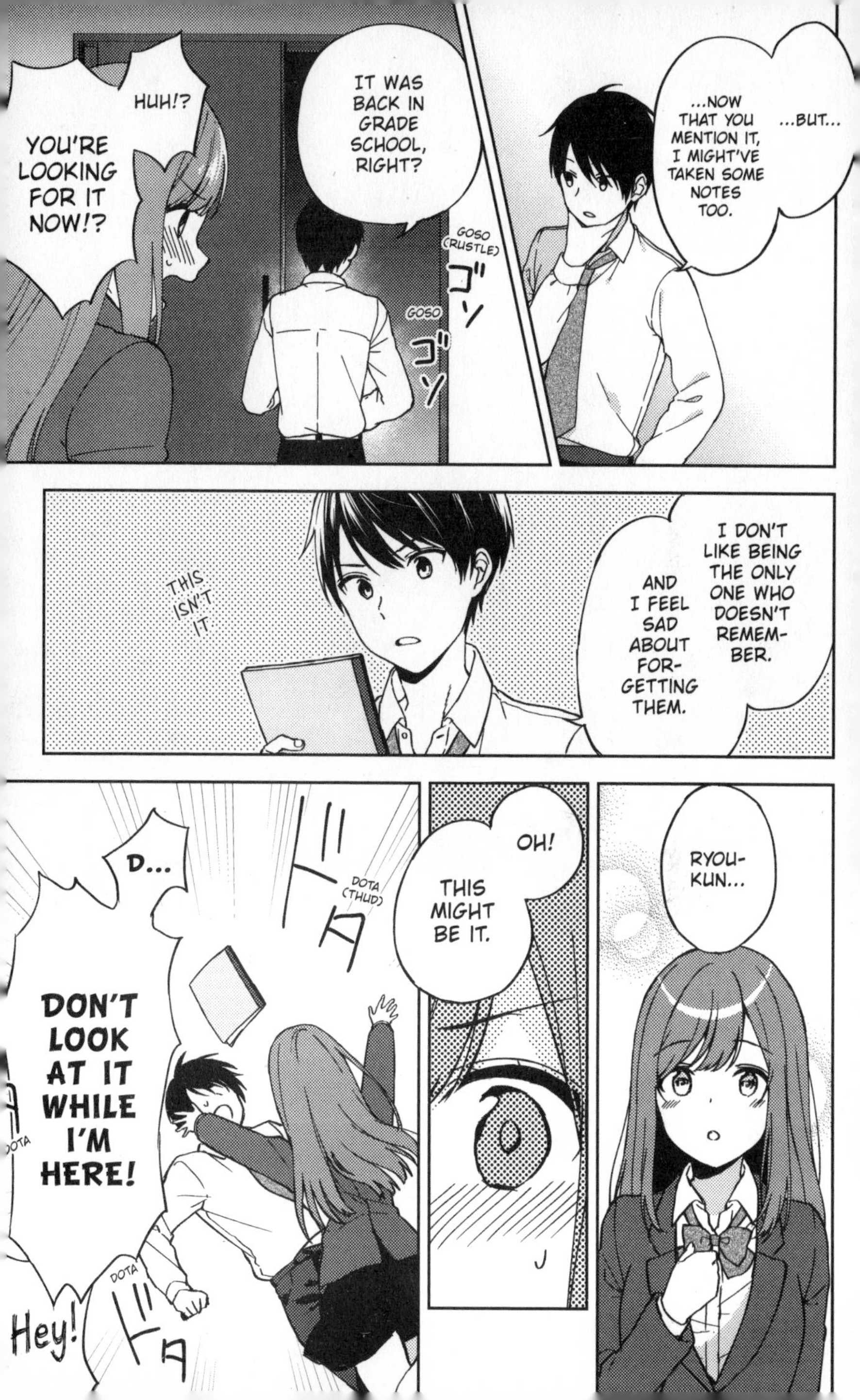
...NOW THAT YOU MENTION IT, I MIGHT'VE TAKEN SOME NOTES TOO.
...BUT...
IT WAS BACK IN GRADE SCHOOL, RIGHT?
GOSO (RUSTLE)
GOSO
HUH!?
YOU'RE LOOKING FOR IT NOW!?
I DON'T LIKE BEING THE ONLY ONE WHO DOESN'T REMEMBER.
AND I FEEL SAD ABOUT FORGETTING THEM.
THIS ISN'T IT
RYOU-KUN...
OH!
THIS MIGHT BE IT.
D...
DOTA (THUD)
DON'T LOOK AT IT WHILE I'M HERE!
DOTA
DOTA
Hey!

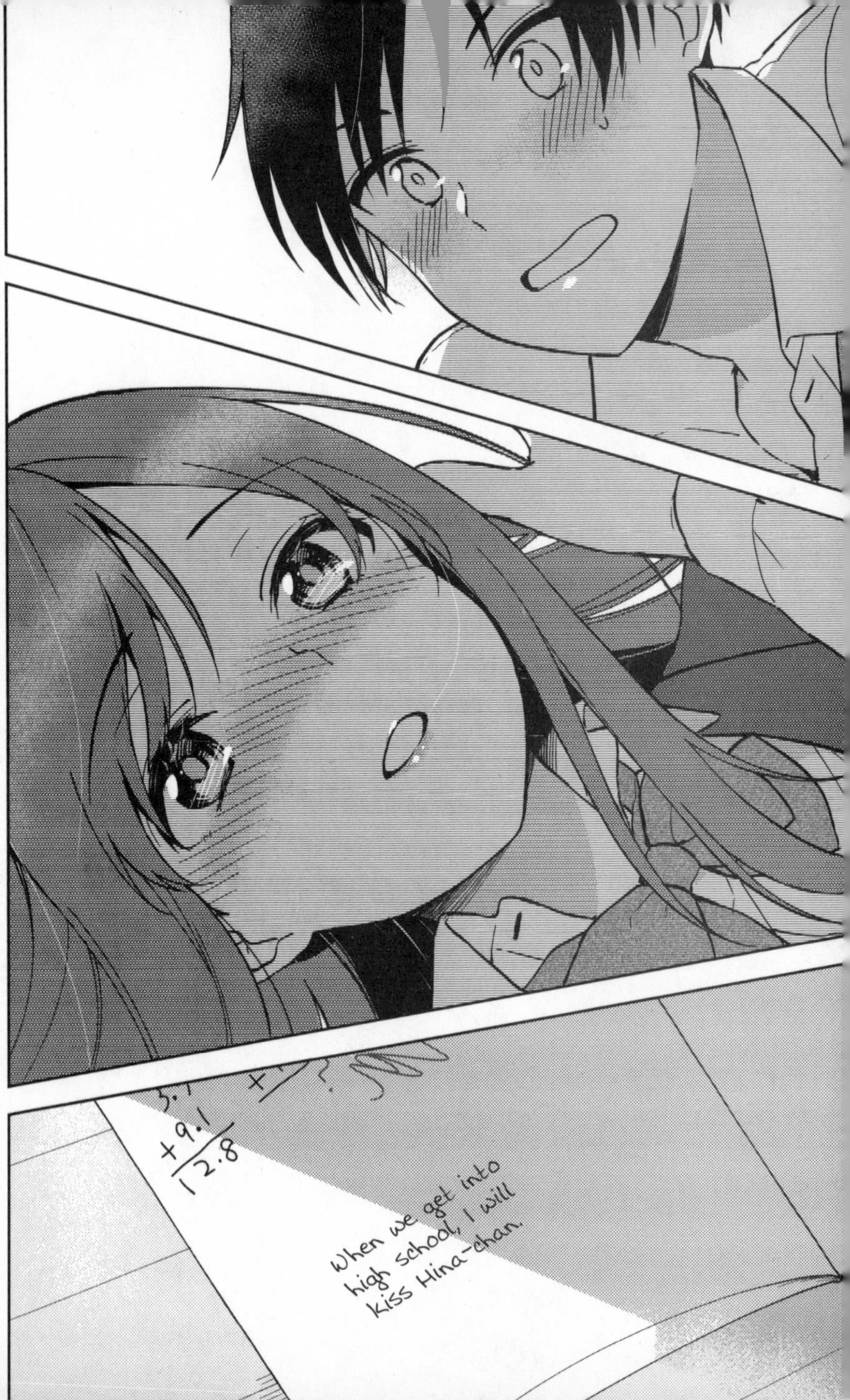
3.7
+9.1
12.8
When we get into high school, I will kiss Hina-chan.

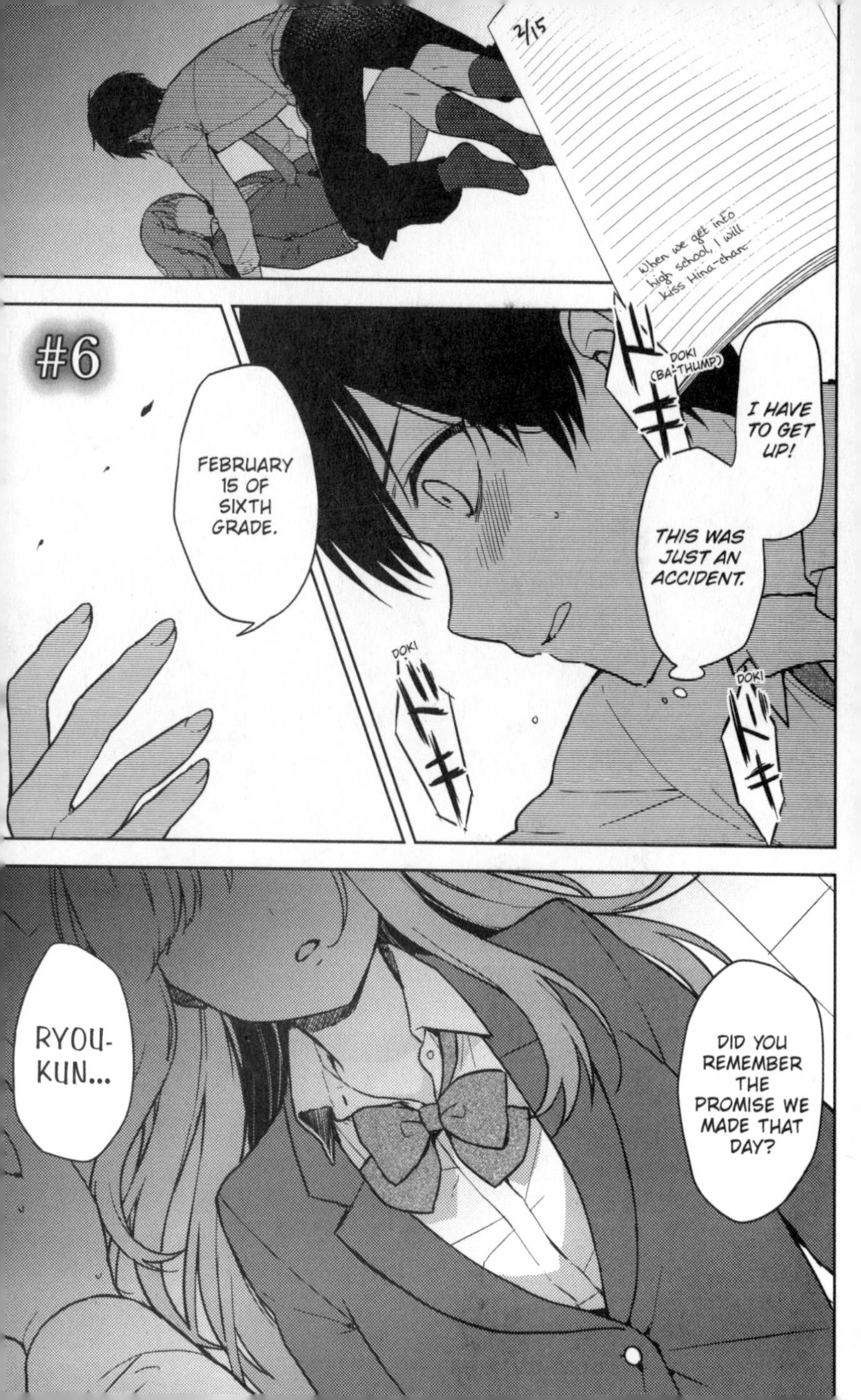
2/15
When we get into high school, I will kiss Hina-chan.
DOKI (BA-THUMP)
I HAVE TO GET UP!
THIS WAS JUST AN ACCIDENT.
DOKI
DOKI
#6
FEBRUARY 15 OF SIXTH GRADE.
DID YOU REMEMBER THE PROMISE WE MADE THAT DAY?
RYOU-KUN...

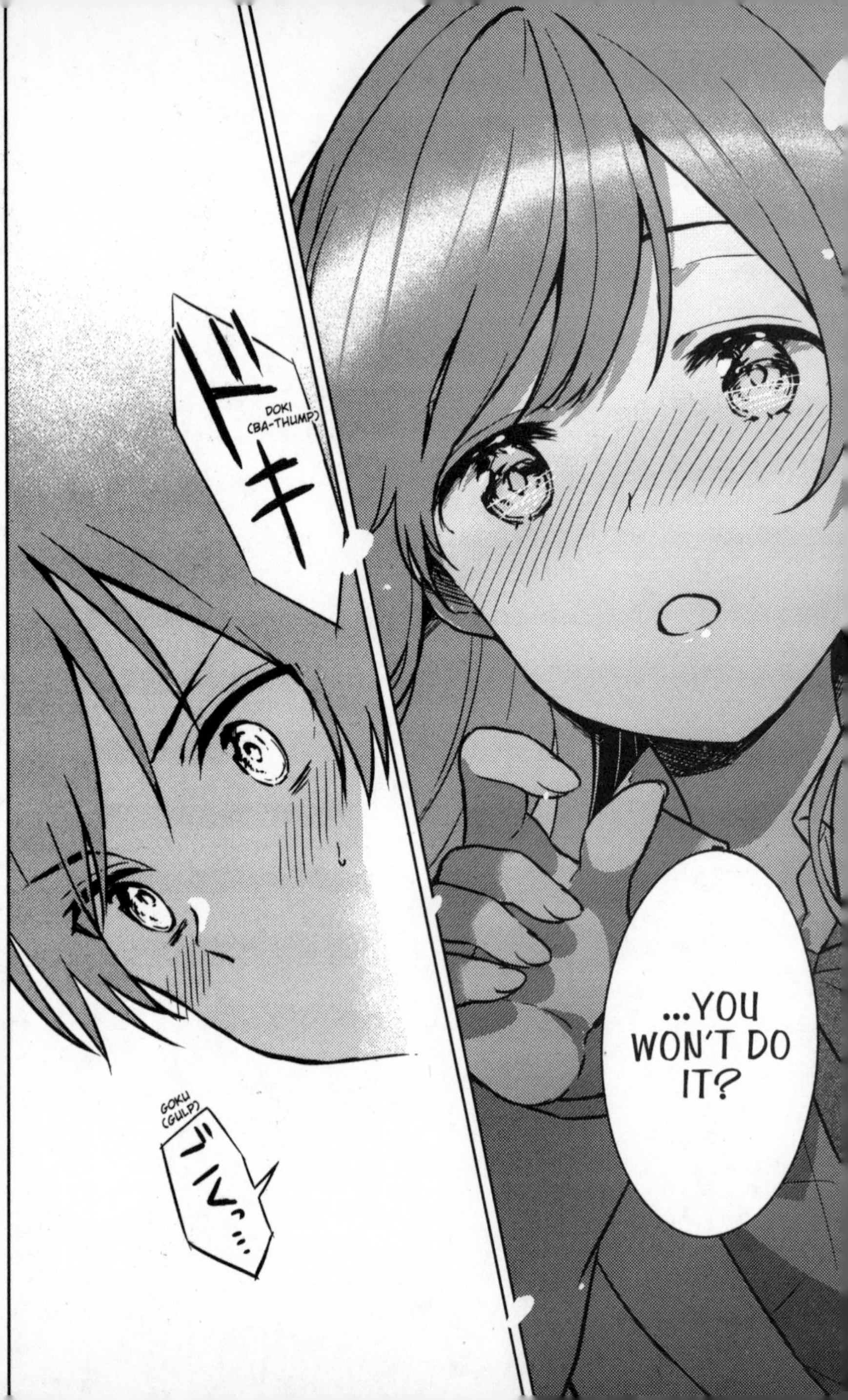
...YOU WON'T DO IT?
ドキ
DOKI (BA-THUMP)
ゴクッ…
GOKU (GULP)

#6 A Piece of Our Promises

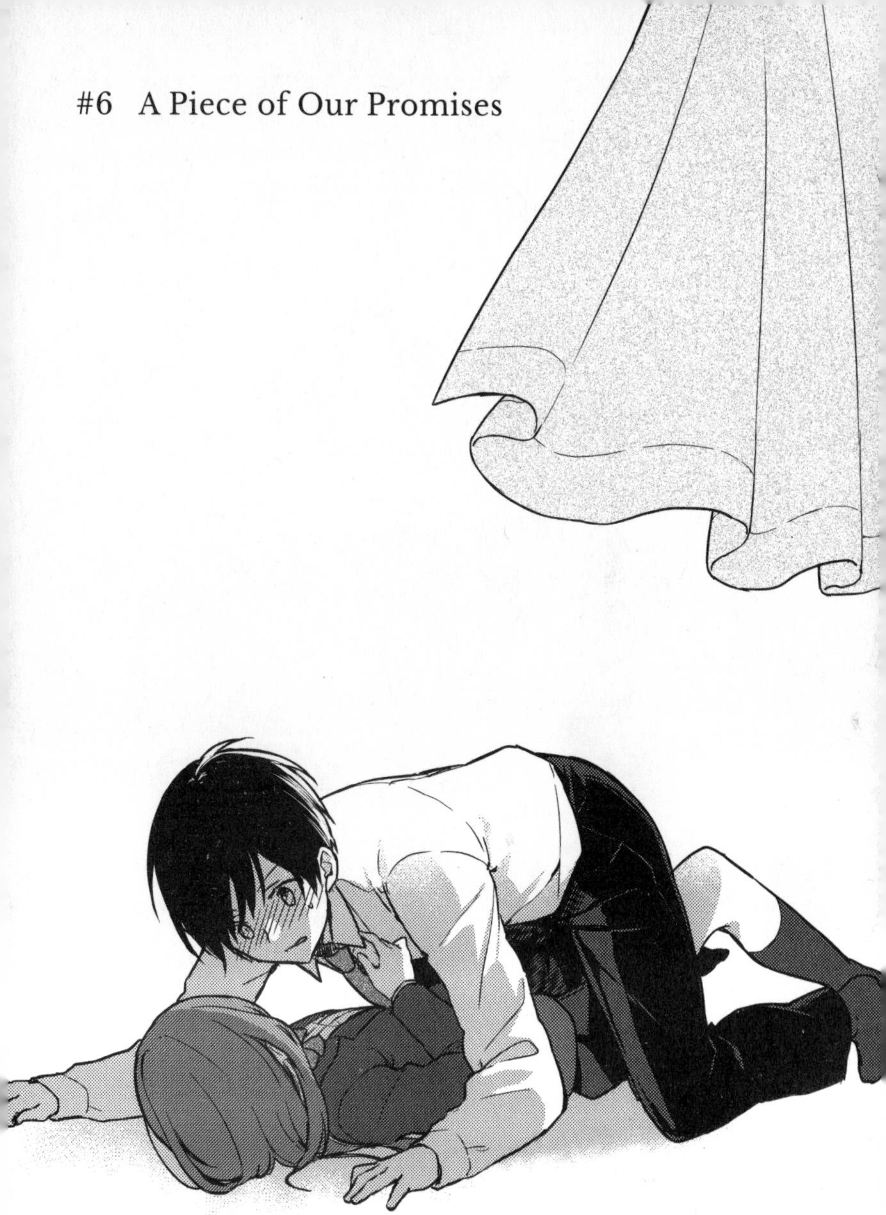

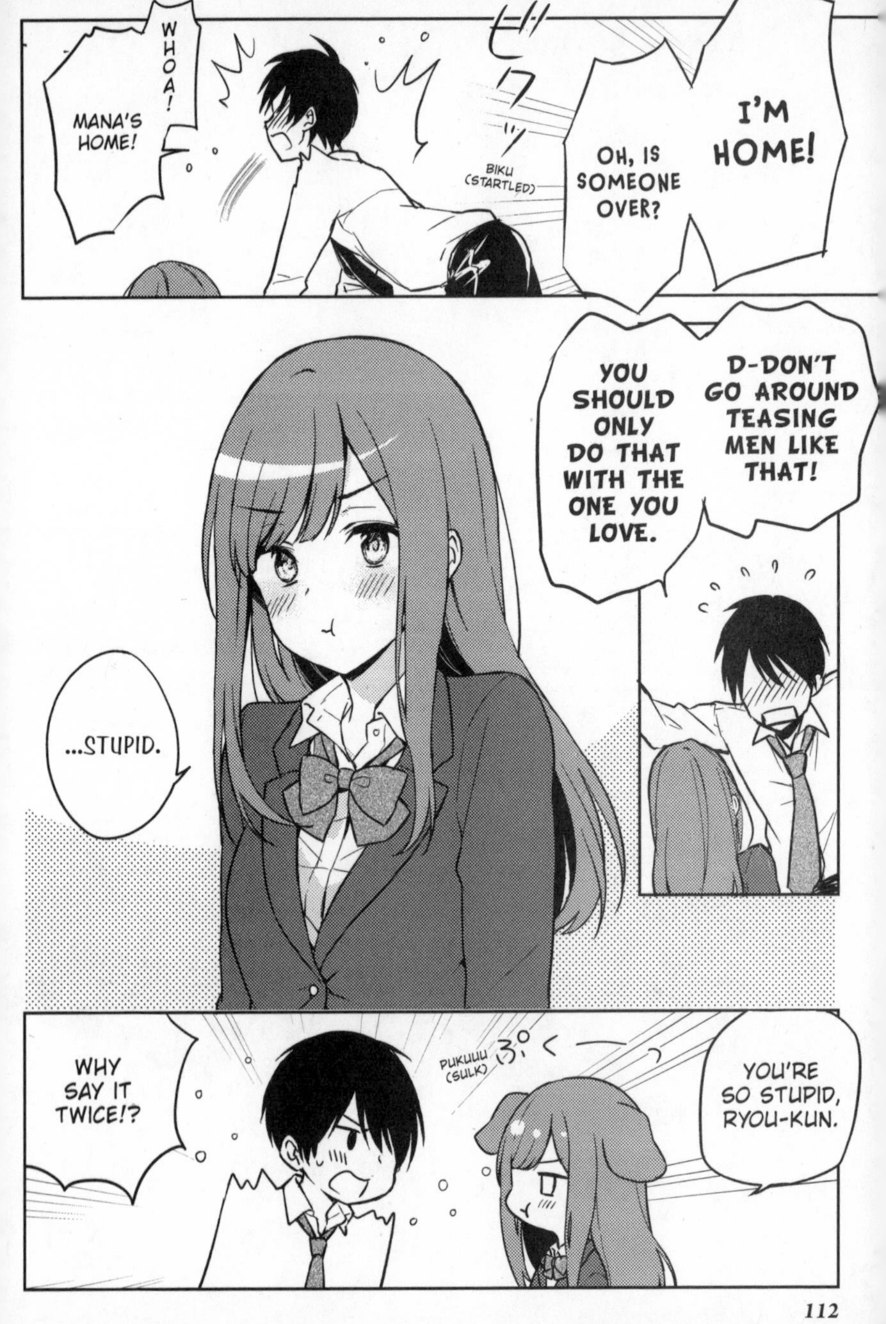
I'M HOME!
OH, IS SOMEONE OVER?
ビクッ
BIKU (STARTLED)
WHOA! MANA'S HOME!
D-DON'T GO AROUND TEASING MEN LIKE THAT!
YOU SHOULD ONLY DO THAT WITH THE ONE YOU LOVE.
...STUPID.
YOU'RE SO STUPID, RYOU-KUN.
ぷくーっ
PUKUUU (SULK)
WHY SAY IT TWICE!?

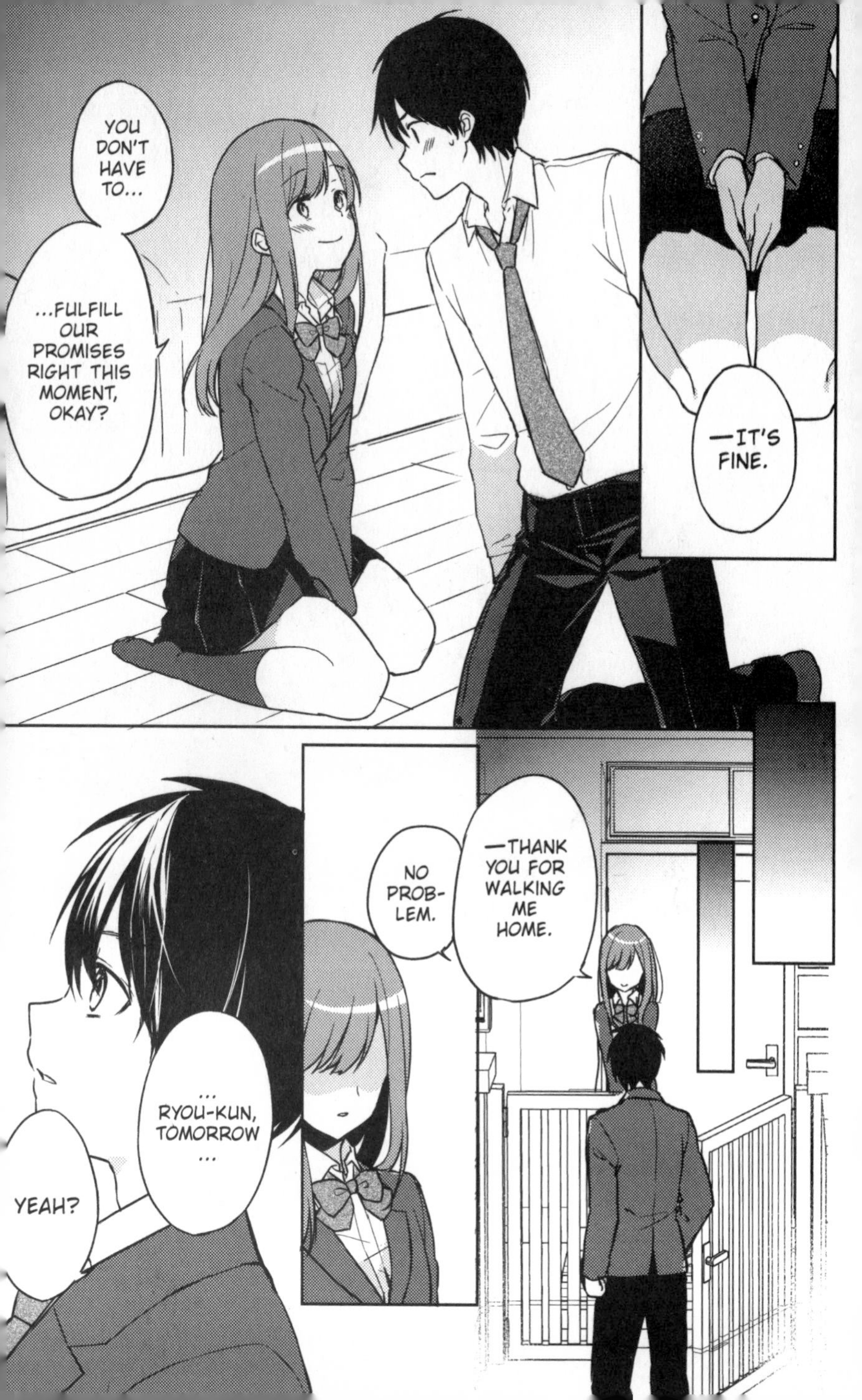
—IT'S FINE.
YOU DON'T HAVE TO...
...FULFILL OUR PROMISES RIGHT THIS MOMENT, OKAY?
—THANK YOU FOR WALKING ME HOME.
NO PROB-LEM.
...RYOU-KUN, TOMORROW...
YEAH?

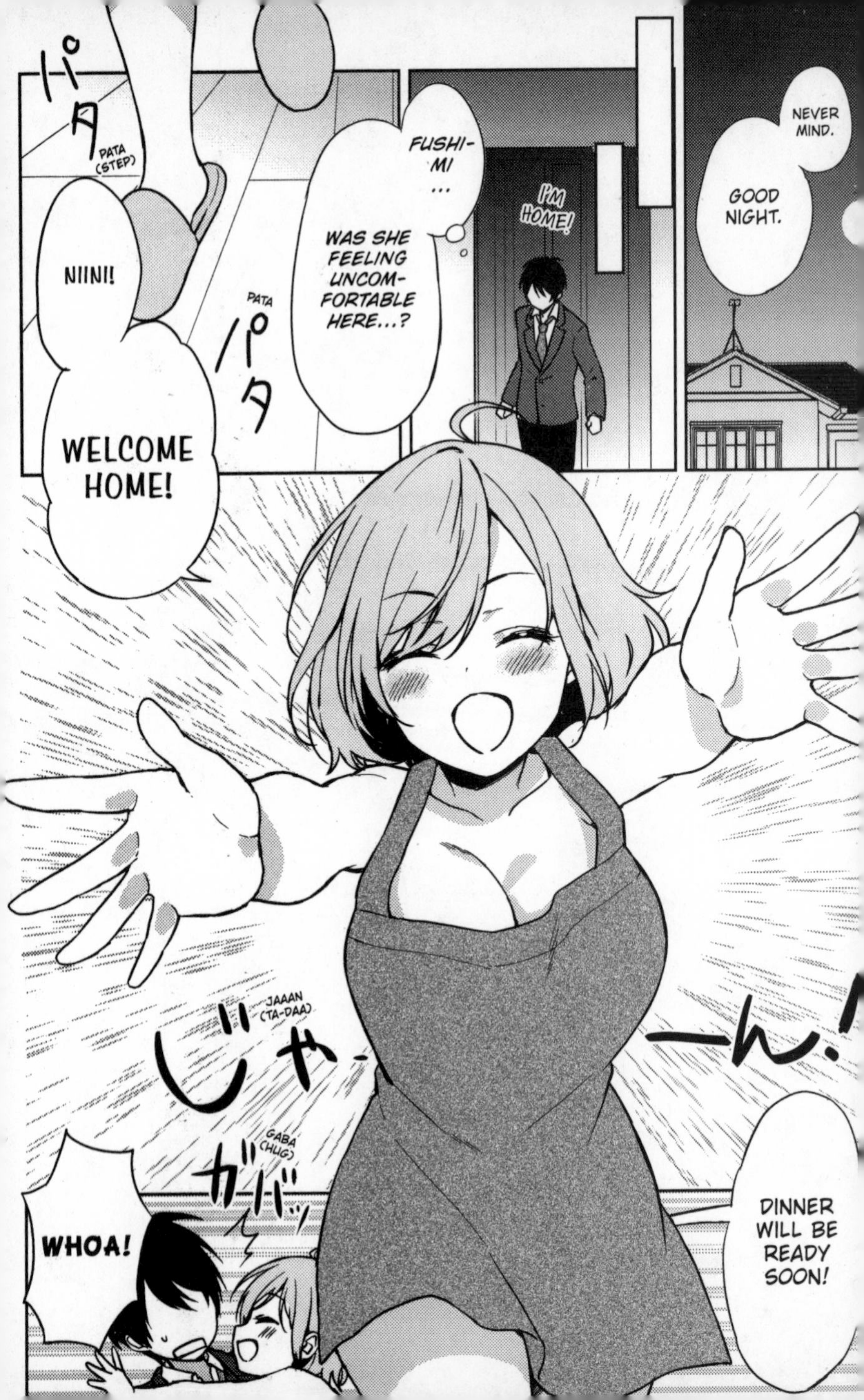
NEVER MIND.
GOOD NIGHT.
FUSHI-MI... WAS SHE FEELING UNCOM-FORTABLE HERE...?
I'M HOME!
パタ
PATA (STEP)
NIINI!
パタ
PATA
WELCOME HOME!
じゃーーん!
JAAAN (TA-DAA)
DINNER WILL BE READY SOON!
ガバッ
GABA (HUG)
WHOA!

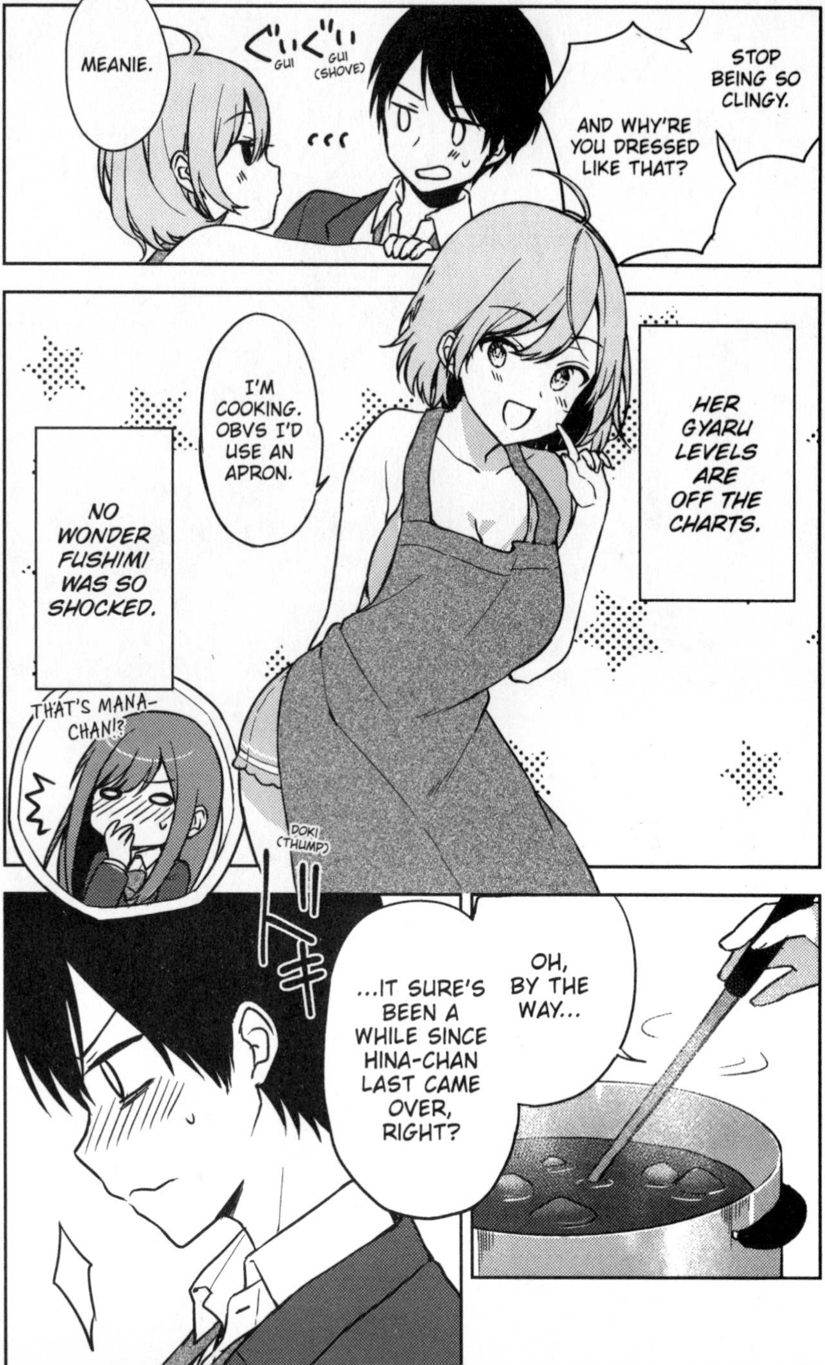
STOP BEING SO CLINGY.
AND WHY'RE YOU DRESSED LIKE THAT?
...
ぐいぐい
GUI GUI (SHOVE)
MEANIE.
HER GYARU LEVELS ARE OFF THE CHARTS.
I'M COOKING. OBVS I'D USE AN APRON.
NO WONDER FUSHIMI WAS SO SHOCKED.
THAT'S MANA-CHAN!?
OH, BY THE WAY...
...IT SURE'S BEEN A WHILE SINCE HINA-CHAN LAST CAME OVER, RIGHT?
ドキ
DOKI (THUMP)

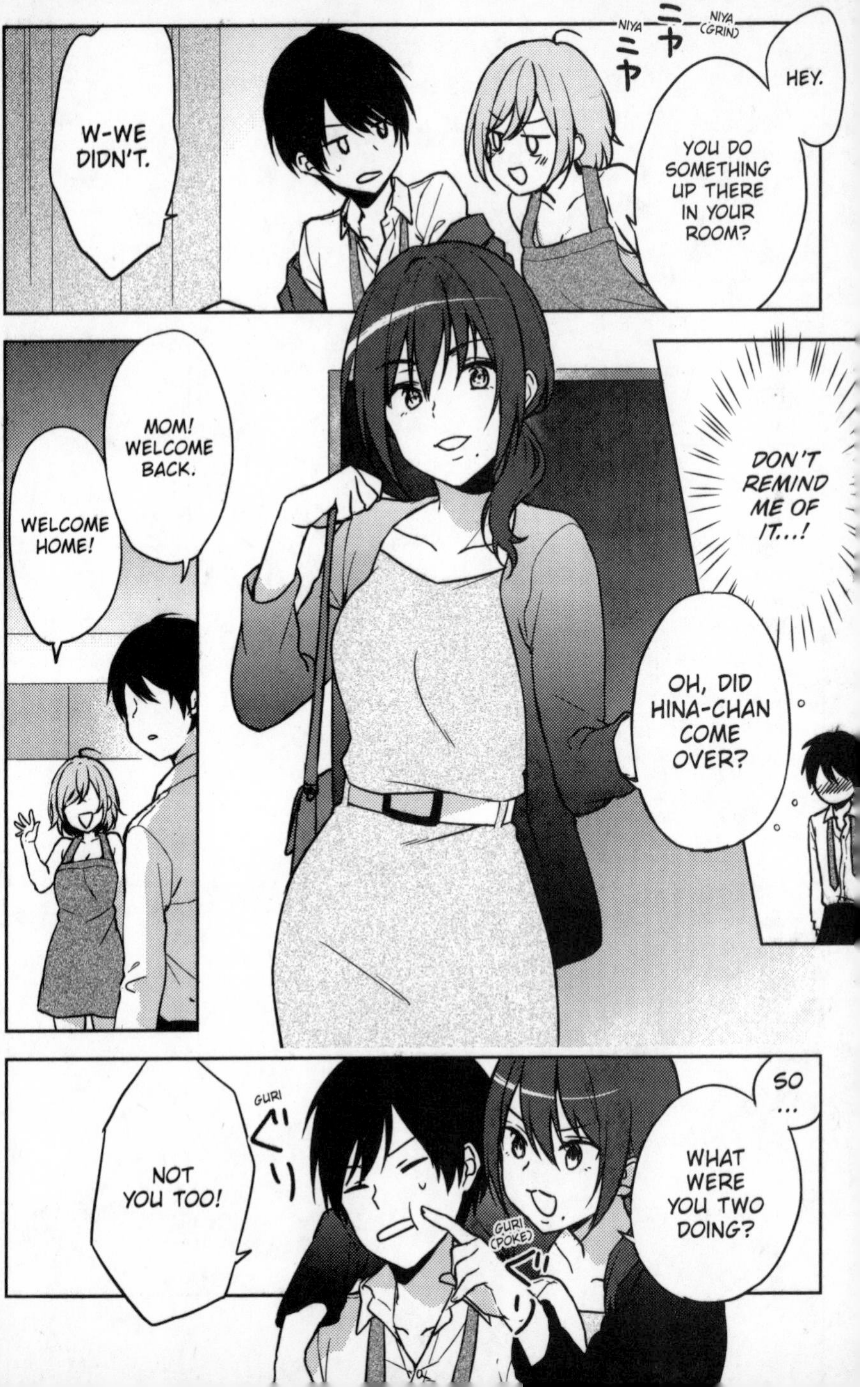
NIYA ニヤ NIYA (GRIN) ニヤ
HEY.
YOU DO SOMETHING UP THERE IN YOUR ROOM?
W-WE DIDN'T.
DON'T REMIND ME OF IT...!
OH, DID HINA-CHAN COME OVER?
MOM! WELCOME BACK.
WELCOME HOME!
SO...
WHAT WERE YOU TWO DOING?
GURI (POKE) ぐり
GURI ぐり
NOT YOU TOO!

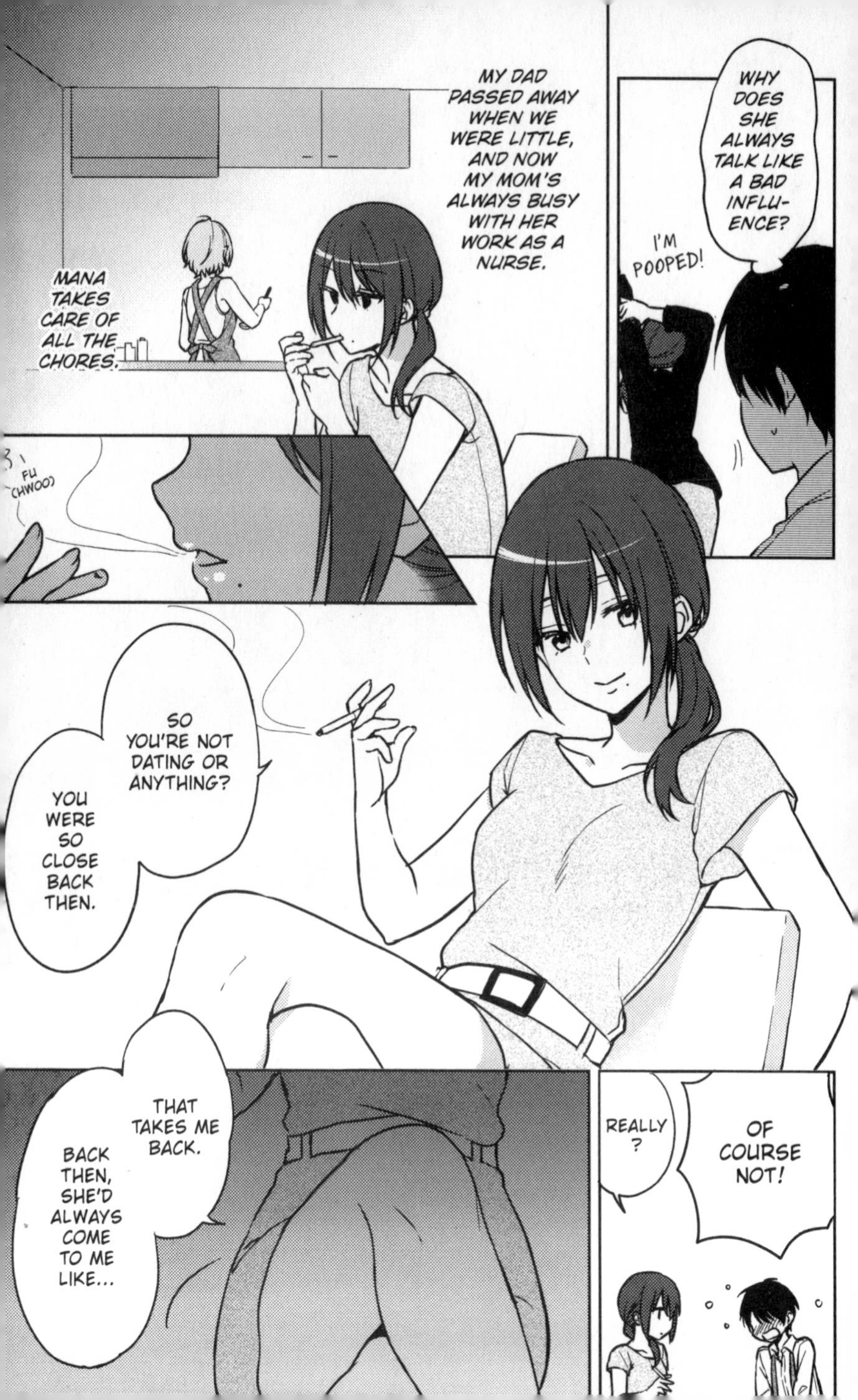
WHY DOES SHE ALWAYS TALK LIKE A BAD INFLU-ENCE?
I'M POOPED!
MY DAD PASSED AWAY WHEN WE WERE LITTLE, AND NOW MY MOM'S ALWAYS BUSY WITH HER WORK AS A NURSE.
MANA TAKES CARE OF ALL THE CHORES.
FU CHWOO
SO YOU'RE NOT DATING OR ANYTHING?
YOU WERE SO CLOSE BACK THEN.
OF COURSE NOT!
REALLY?
THAT TAKES ME BACK.
BACK THEN, SHE'D ALWAYS COME TO ME LIKE...

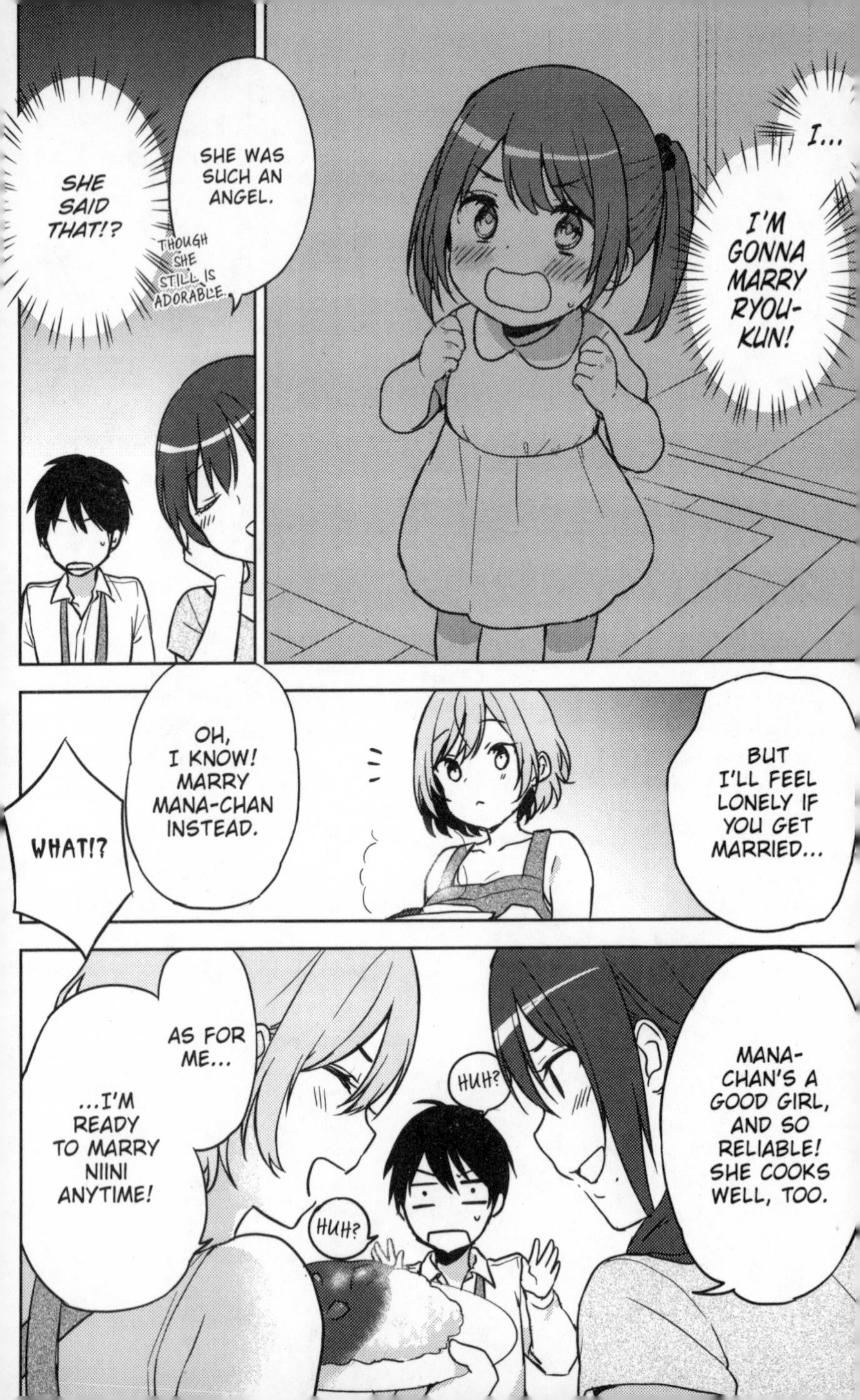
I...
I'M GONNA MARRY RYOU-KUN!
SHE WAS SUCH AN ANGEL.
THOUGH SHE STILL IS ADORABLE.
SHE SAID THAT!?
BUT I'LL FEEL LONELY IF YOU GET MARRIED...
OH, I KNOW! MARRY MANA-CHAN INSTEAD.
WHAT!?
MANA-CHAN'S A GOOD GIRL, AND SO RELIABLE! SHE COOKS WELL, TOO.
HUH?
AS FOR ME...
...I'M READY TO MARRY NIINI ANYTIME!
HUH?

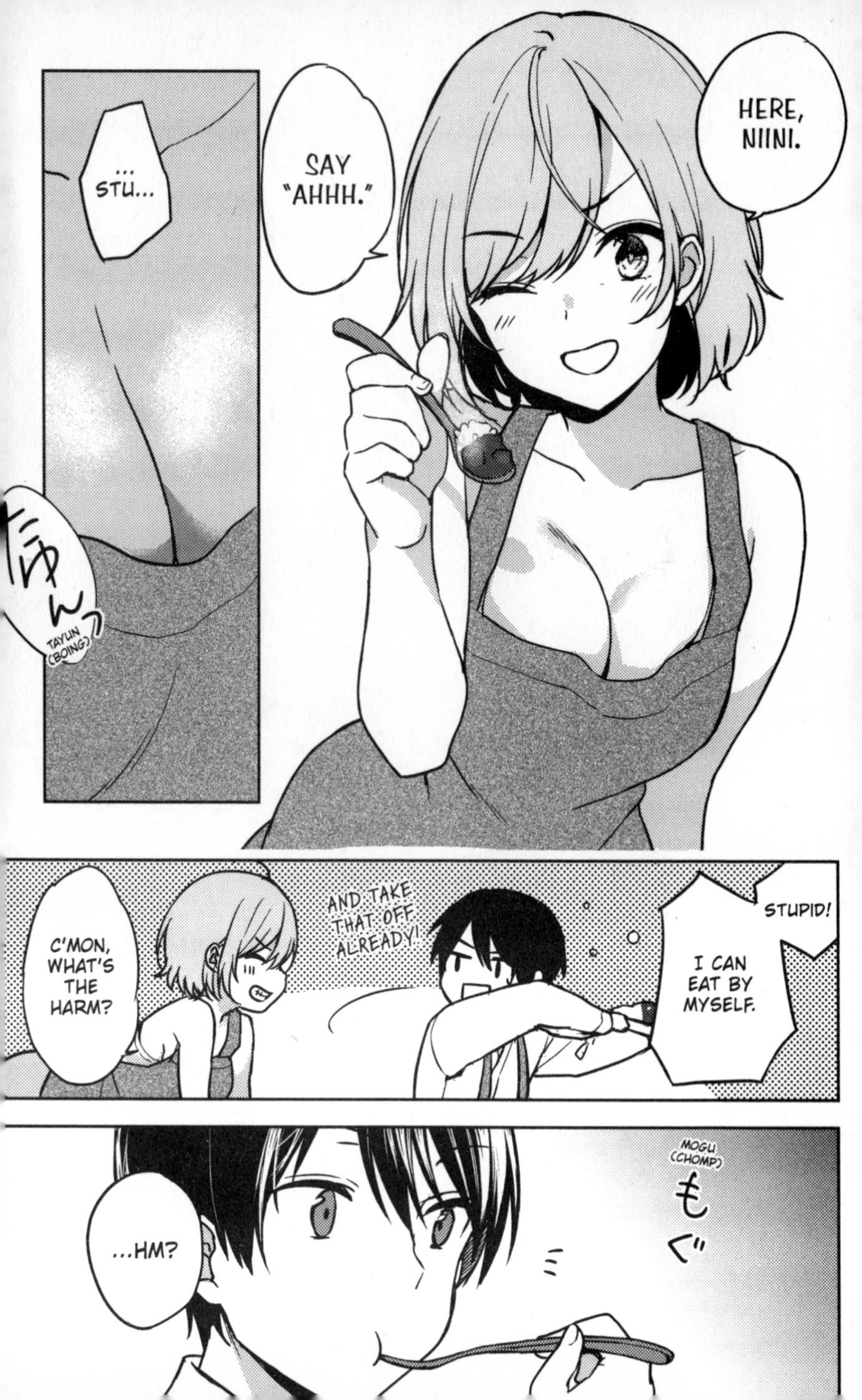
HERE, NIINI.
SAY "AHHH."
...STU...
たゆん
TAYUN (BOING)
STUPID!
I CAN EAT BY MYSELF.
AND TAKE THAT OFF ALREADY!
C'MON, WHAT'S THE HARM?
もぐ
MOGU (CHOMP)
...HM?

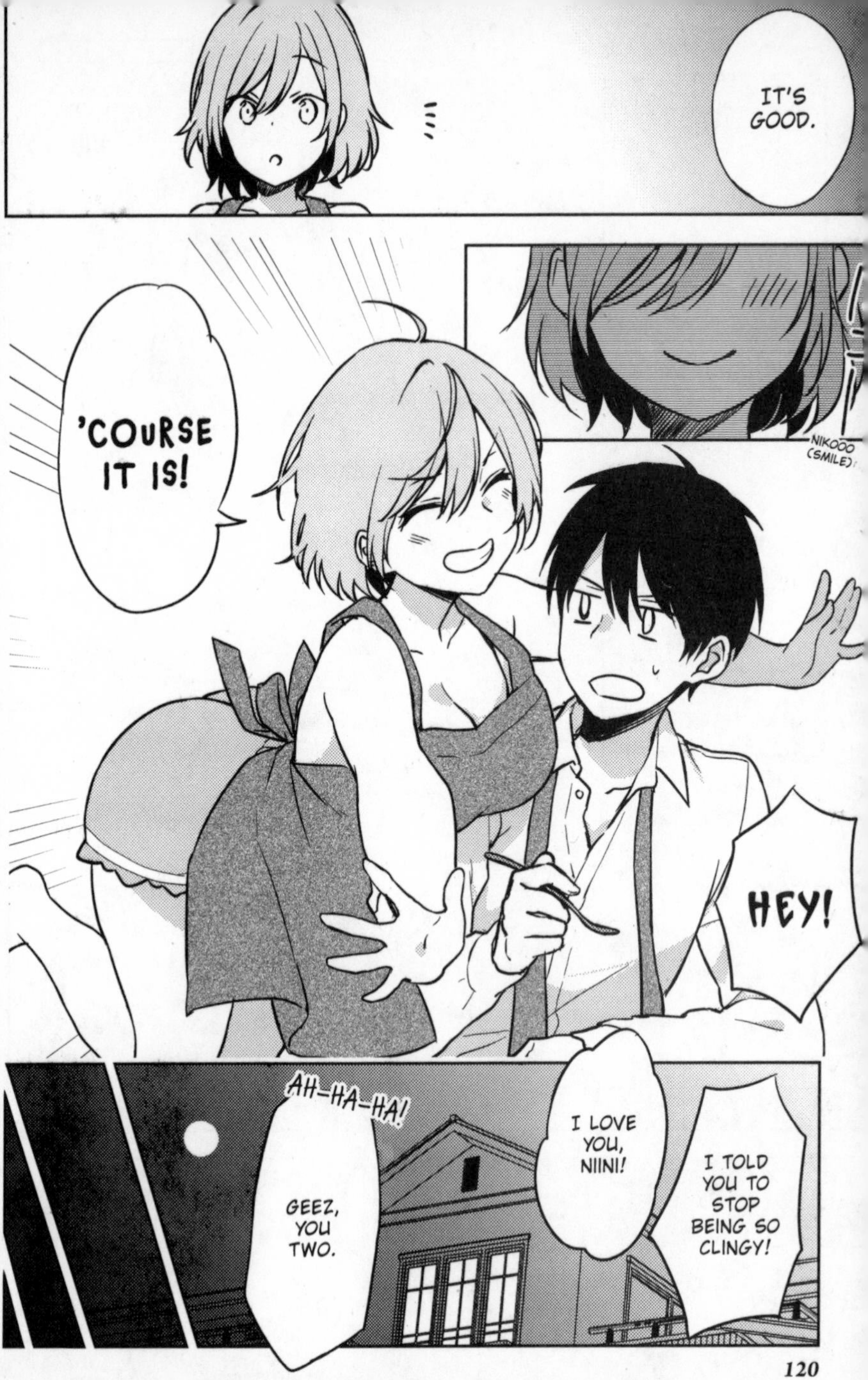
IT'S GOOD.
NIKOOO (SMILE)
'COURSE IT IS!
HEY!
I TOLD YOU TO STOP BEING SO CLINGY!
I LOVE YOU, NIINI!
AH-HA-HA!
GEEZ, YOU TWO.

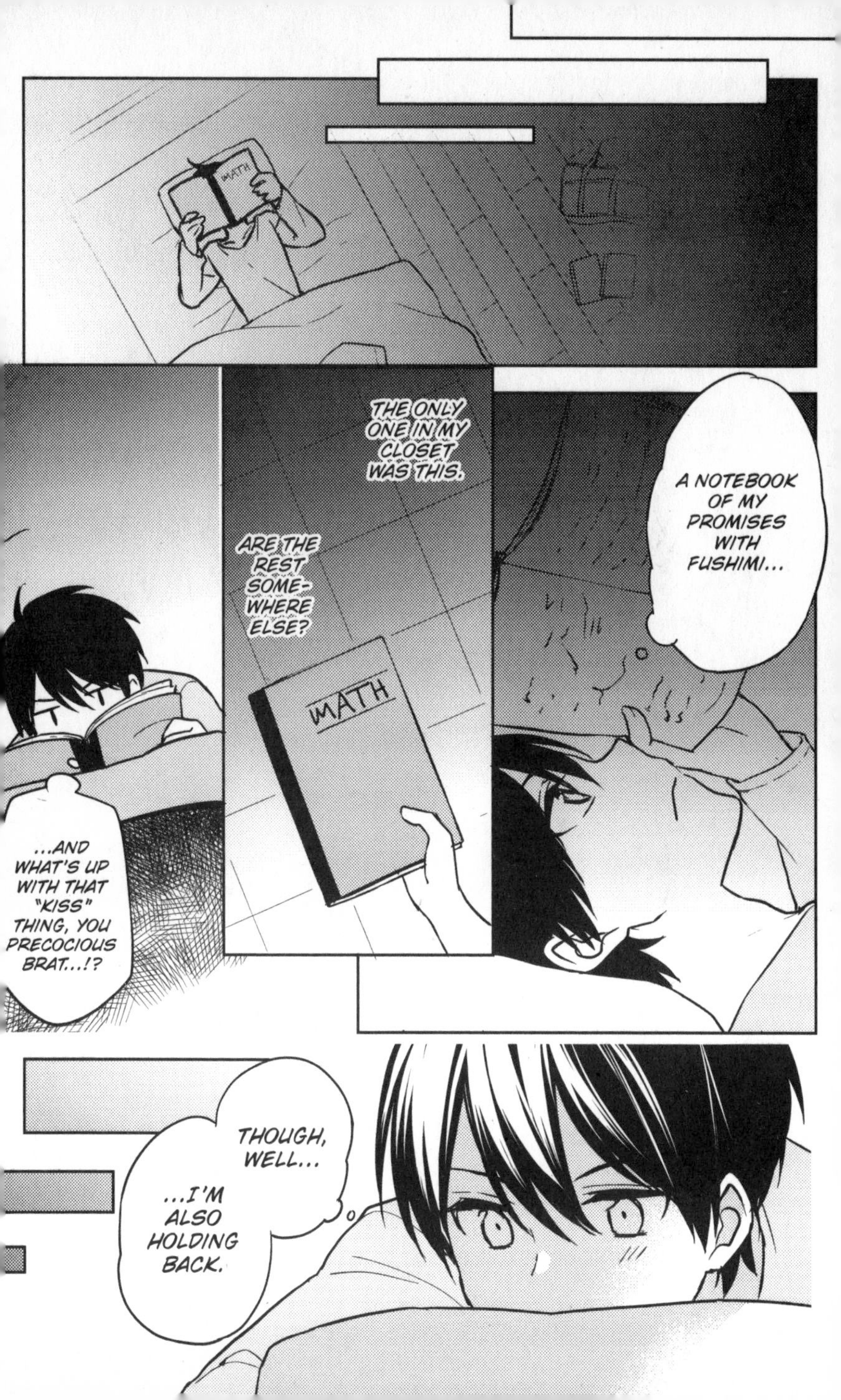
MATH
A NOTEBOOK OF MY PROMISES WITH FUSHIMI...
THE ONLY ONE IN MY CLOSET WAS THIS.
ARE THE REST SOME-WHERE ELSE?
MATH
...AND WHAT'S UP WITH THAT "KISS" THING, YOU PRECOCIOUS BRAT...!?
THOUGH, WELL...
...I'M ALSO HOLDING BACK.

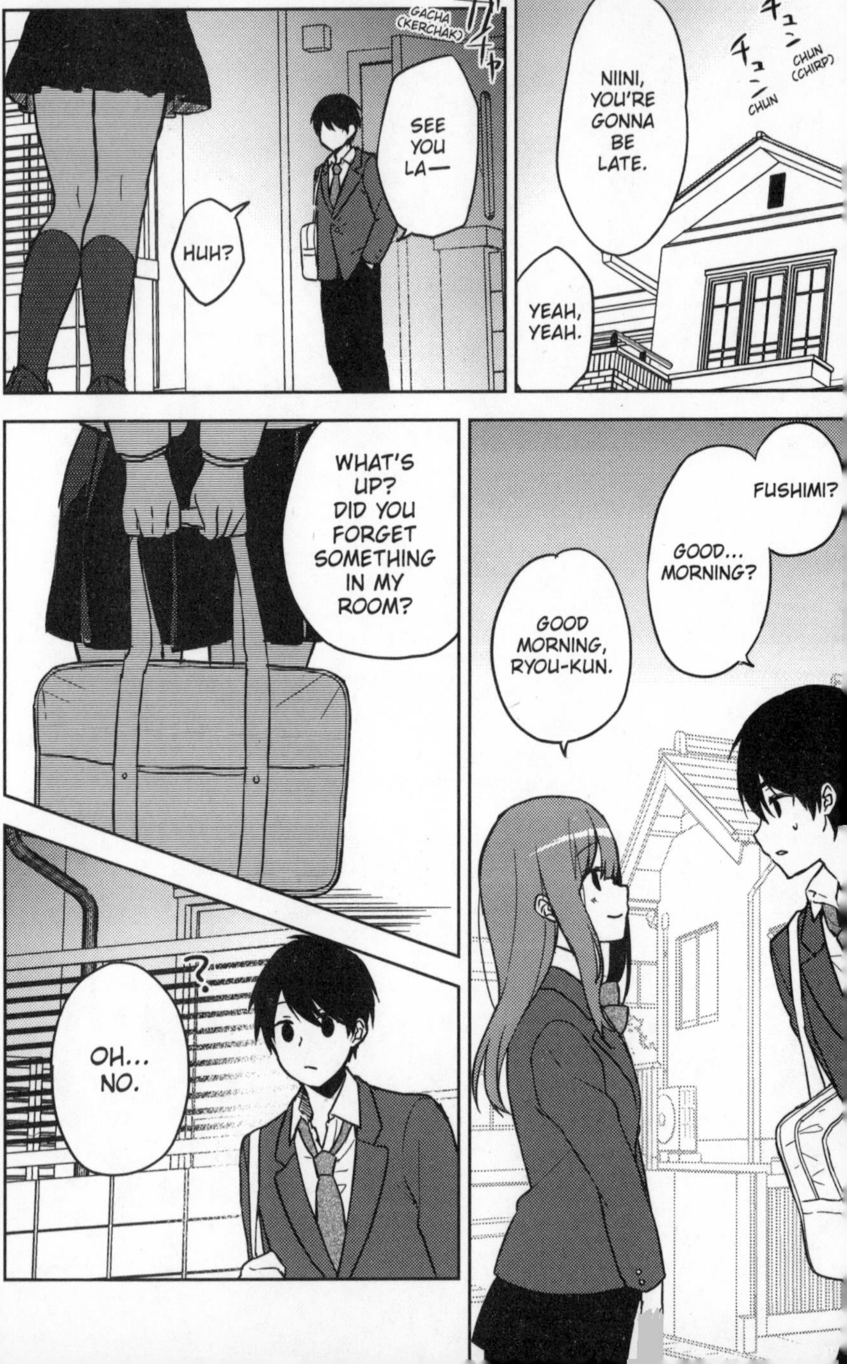
チュン
チュン
CHUN (CHIRP)
CHUN
NIINI, YOU'RE GONNA BE LATE.
YEAH, YEAH.
ガチャ
GACHA (KERCHAK)
SEE YOU LA—
HUH?
FUSHIMI?
GOOD... MORNING?
GOOD MORNING, RYOU-KUN.
WHAT'S UP? DID YOU FORGET SOMETHING IN MY ROOM?
?
OH... NO.

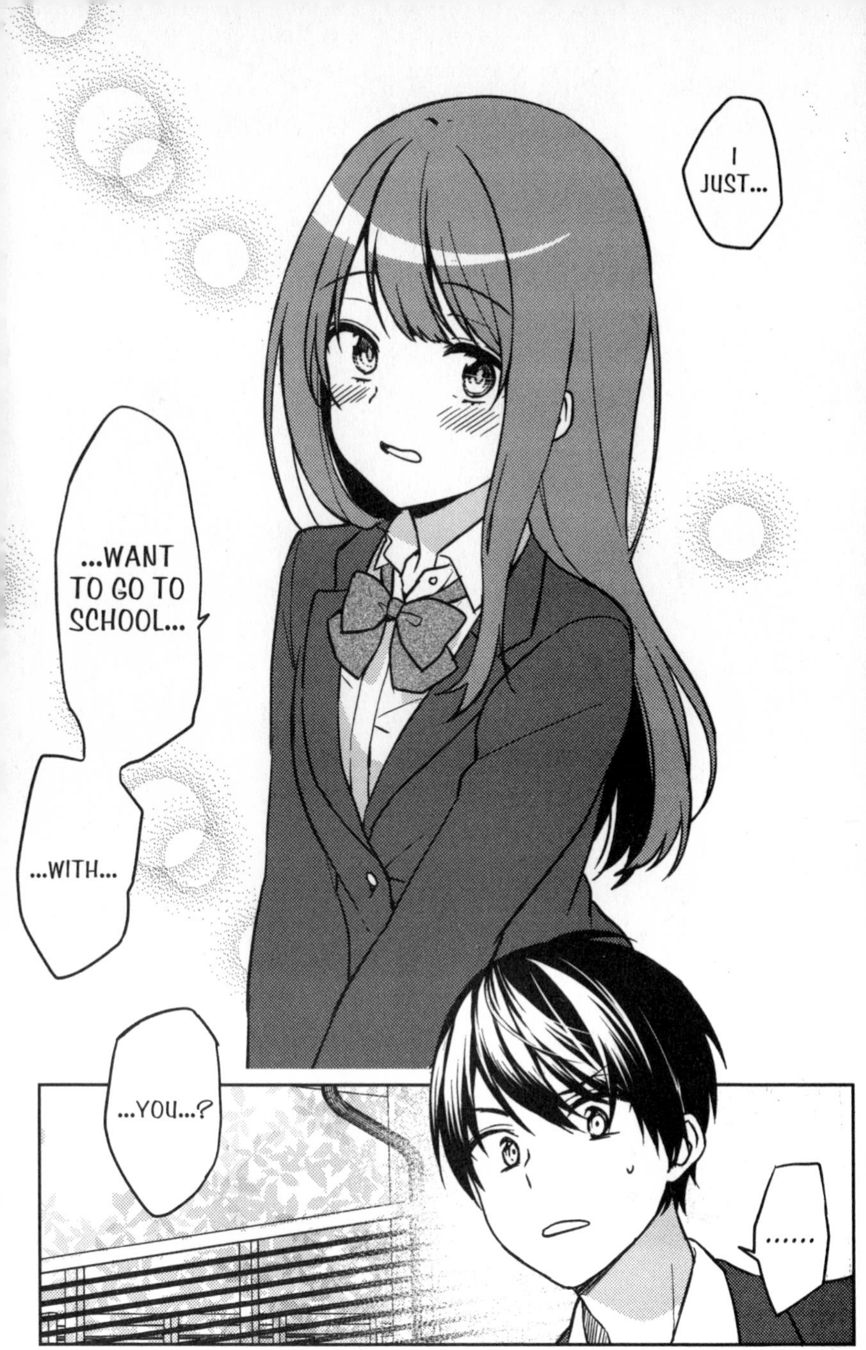
I JUST...
...WANT TO GO TO SCHOOL...
...WITH...
...YOU...?
......

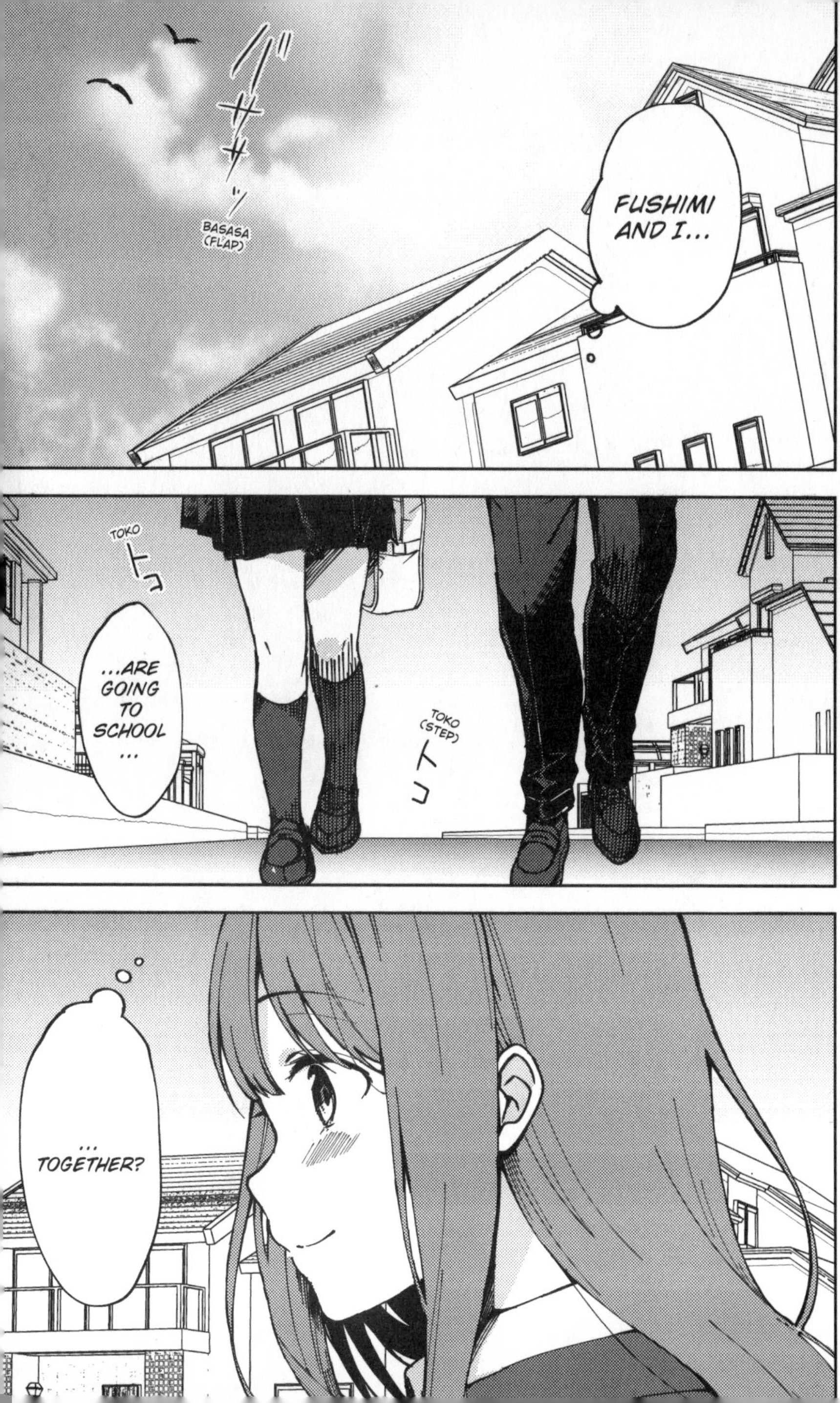
FUSHIMI AND I...
グサザッ
BASASA (FLAP)
TOKO (STEP)
トコ
...ARE GOING TO SCHOOL...
トコ
TOKO
...TOGETHER?

#7 Accident

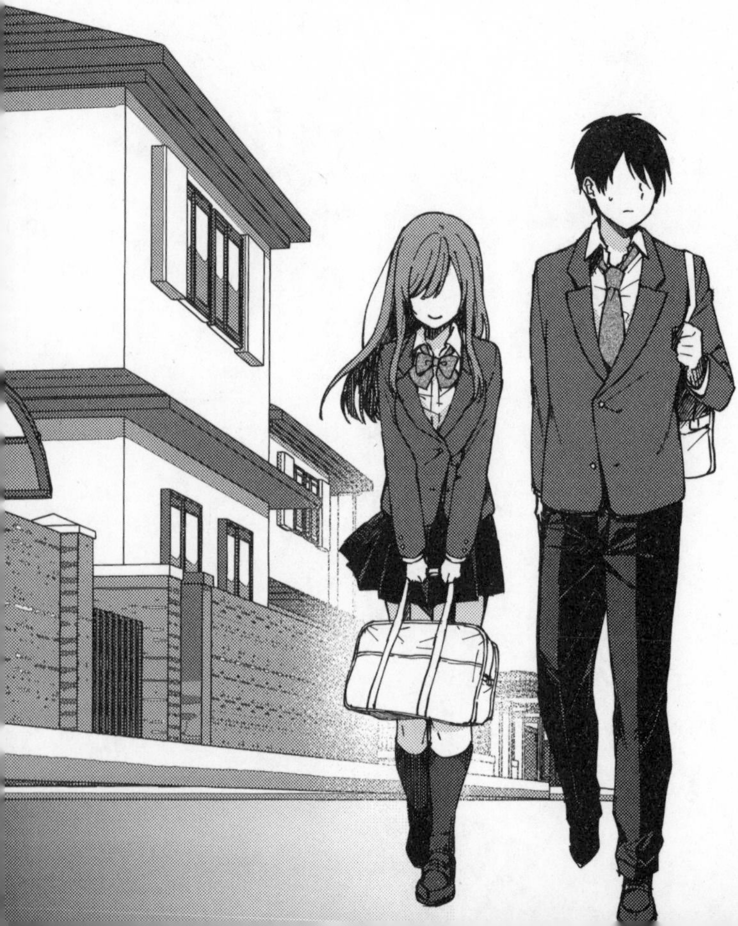

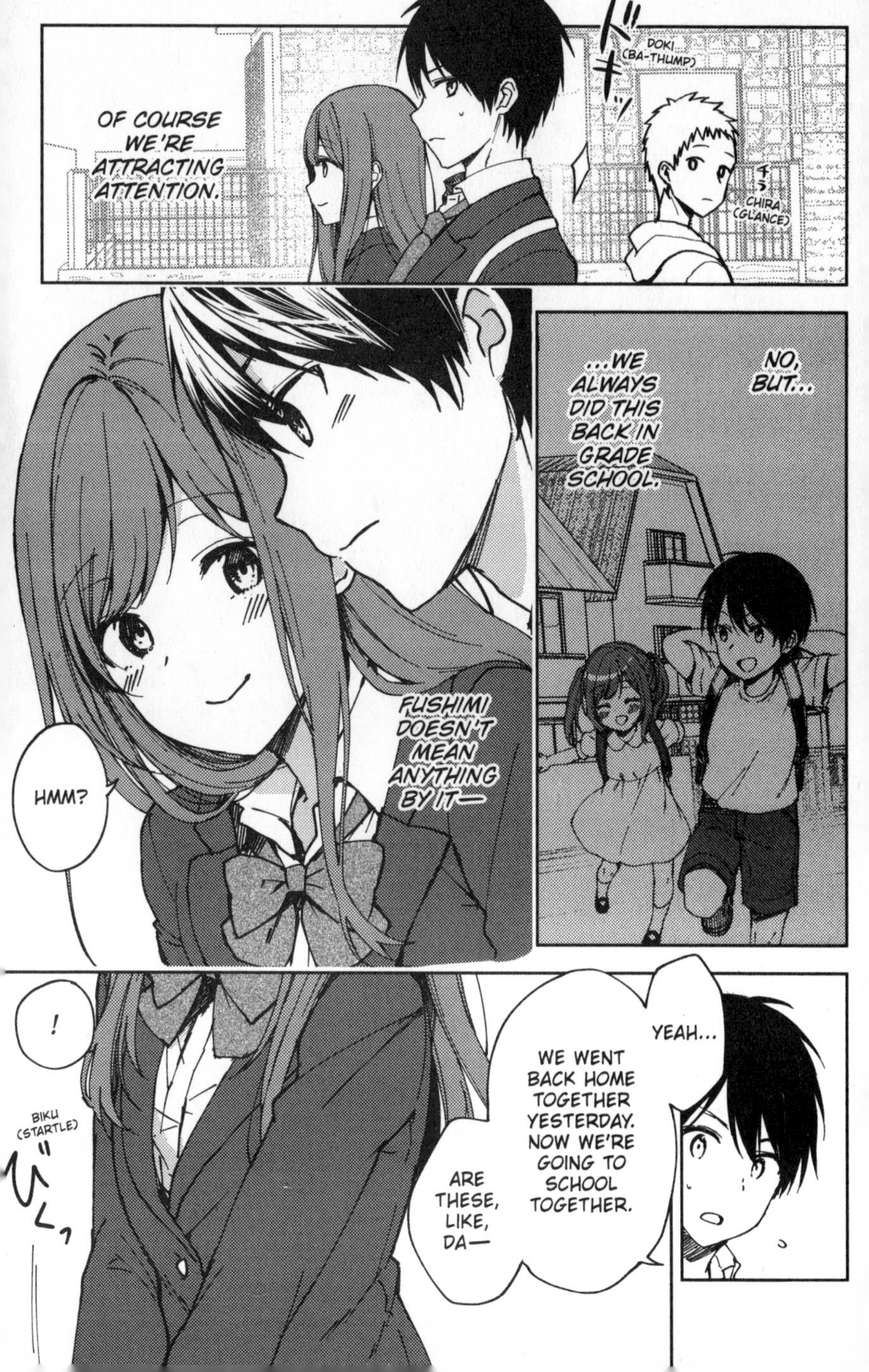
DOKI (BA-THUMP)
CHIRA (GLANCE)
OF COURSE WE'RE ATTRACTING ATTENTION.
NO, BUT...
...WE ALWAYS DID THIS BACK IN GRADE SCHOOL.
FUSHIMI DOESN'T MEAN ANYTHING BY IT—
HMM?
YEAH...
WE WENT BACK HOME TOGETHER YESTERDAY. NOW WE'RE GOING TO SCHOOL TOGETHER.
ARE THESE, LIKE, DA—
!
BIKU (STARTLE)

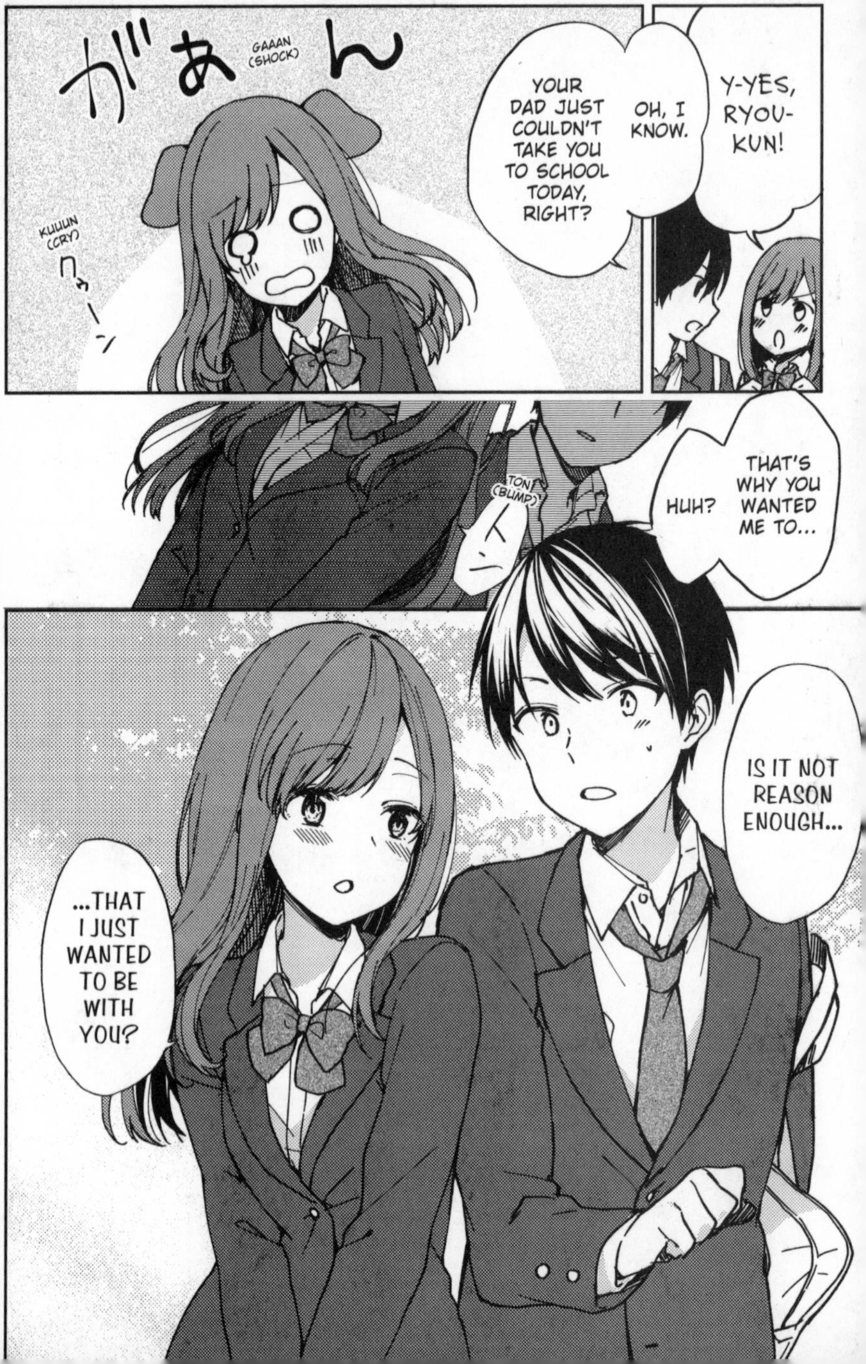
Y-YES, RYOU-KUN!
OH, I KNOW.
YOUR DAD JUST COULDN'T TAKE YOU TO SCHOOL TODAY, RIGHT?
がぁん
GAAAN (SHOCK)
KUUUN (CRY)
THAT'S WHY YOU WANTED ME TO...
HUH?
TON (BUMP)
IS IT NOT REASON ENOUGH...
...THAT I JUST WANTED TO BE WITH YOU?

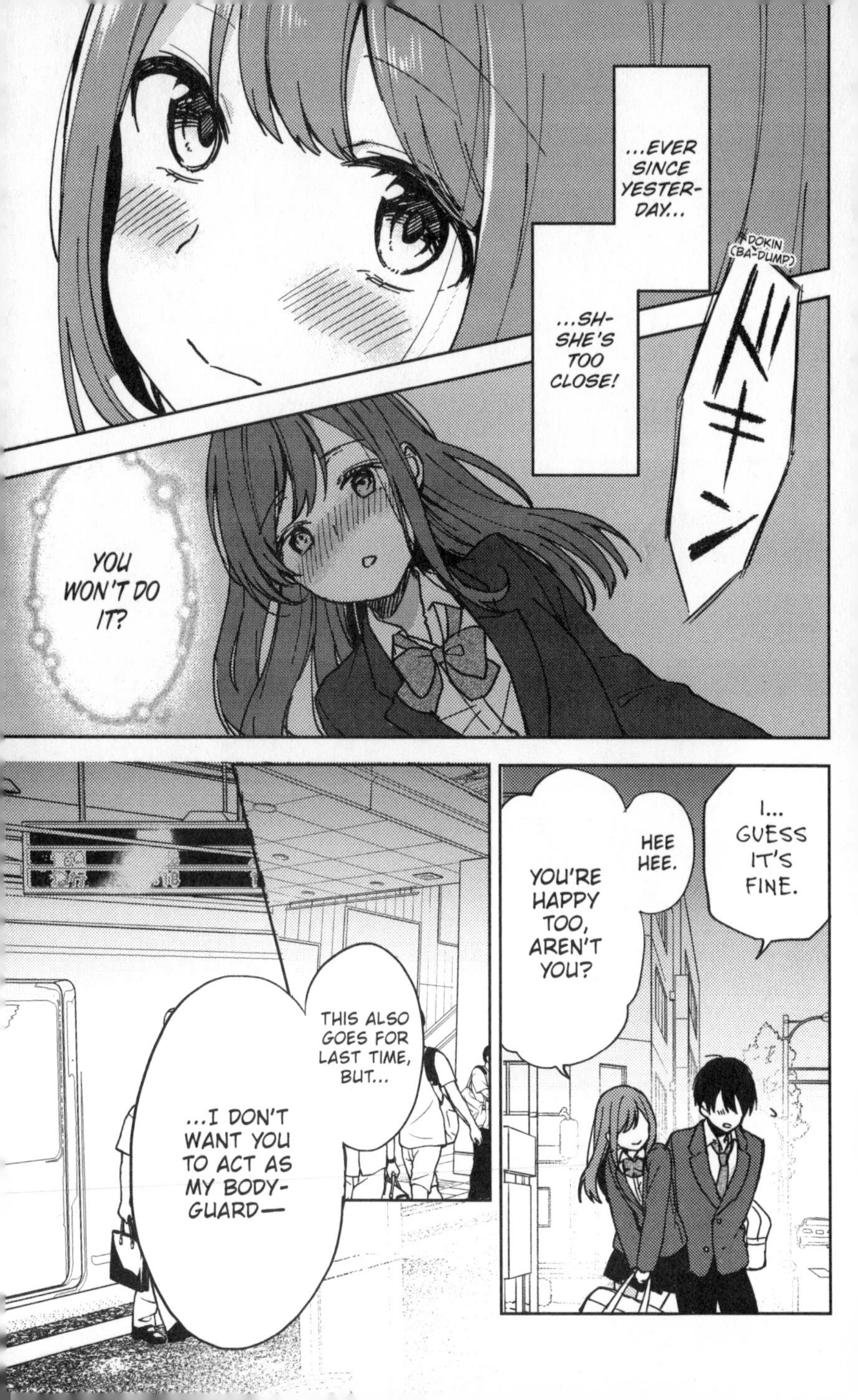
...EVER SINCE YESTER-DAY...
...SH-SHE'S TOO CLOSE!
DOKIN (BA-DUMP)
YOU WON'T DO IT?
I... GUESS IT'S FINE.
HEE HEE.
YOU'RE HAPPY TOO, AREN'T YOU?
THIS ALSO GOES FOR LAST TIME, BUT...
...I DON'T WANT YOU TO ACT AS MY BODY-GUARD—

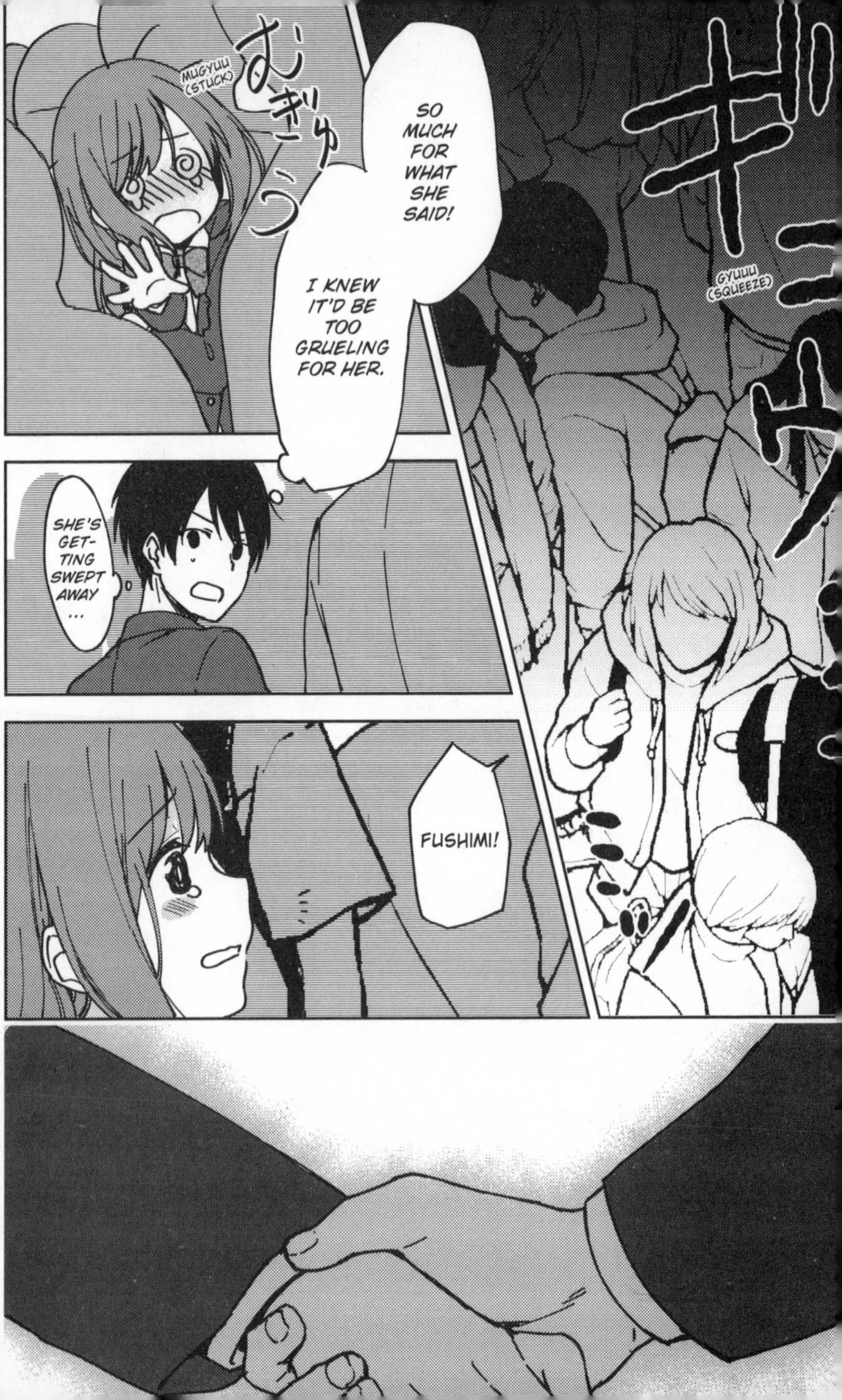
GYUUU (SQUEEZE)
MUGYUU (STUCK)
SO MUCH FOR WHAT SHE SAID!
I KNEW IT'D BE TOO GRUELING FOR HER.
SHE'S GET-TING SWEPT AWAY ...
FUSHIMI!

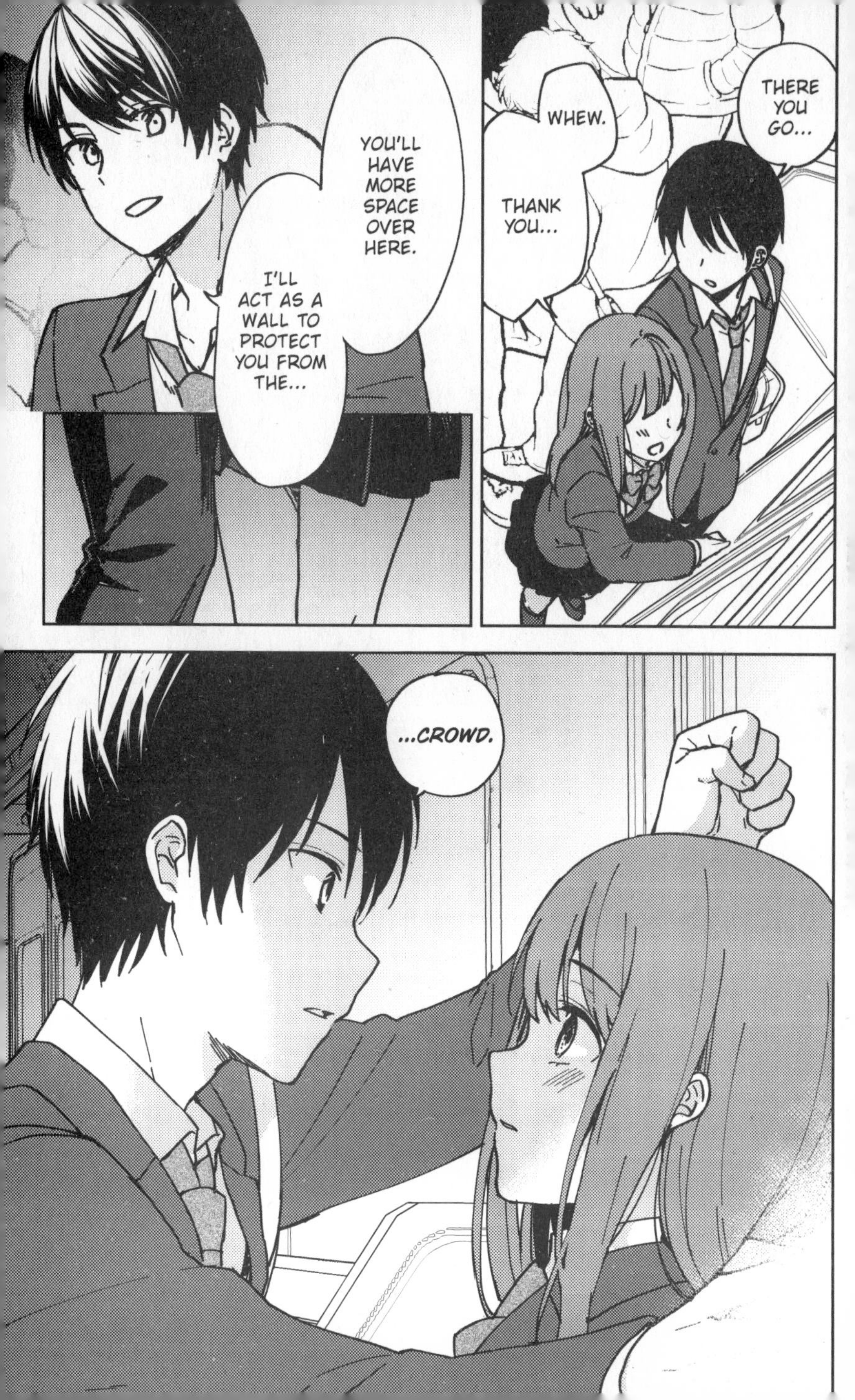
THERE YOU GO...
WHEW.
THANK YOU...
YOU'LL HAVE MORE SPACE OVER HERE.
I'LL ACT AS A WALL TO PROTECT YOU FROM THE...
...CROWD.

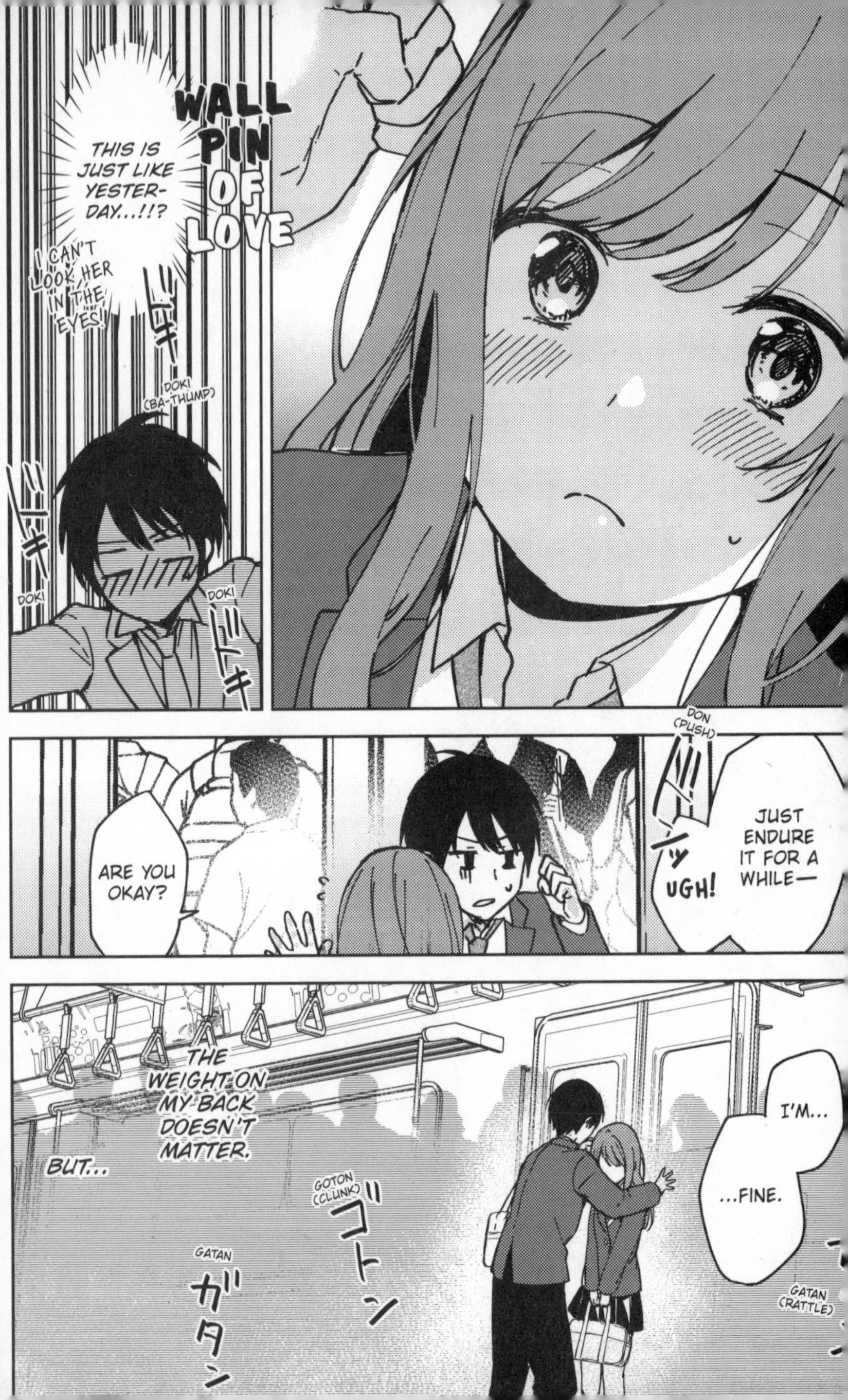
WALL PIN OF LOVE
THIS IS JUST LIKE YESTER-DAY...!!?
I CAN'T LOOK HER IN THE EYES!
DOKI (BA-THUMP)
DOKI
DOKI
DON (PUSH)
UGH!
JUST ENDURE IT FOR A WHILE—
ARE YOU OKAY?
I'M...
...FINE.
GATAN (RATTLE)
GOTON (CLUNK)
GATAN
THE WEIGHT ON MY BACK DOESN'T MATTER.
BUT...

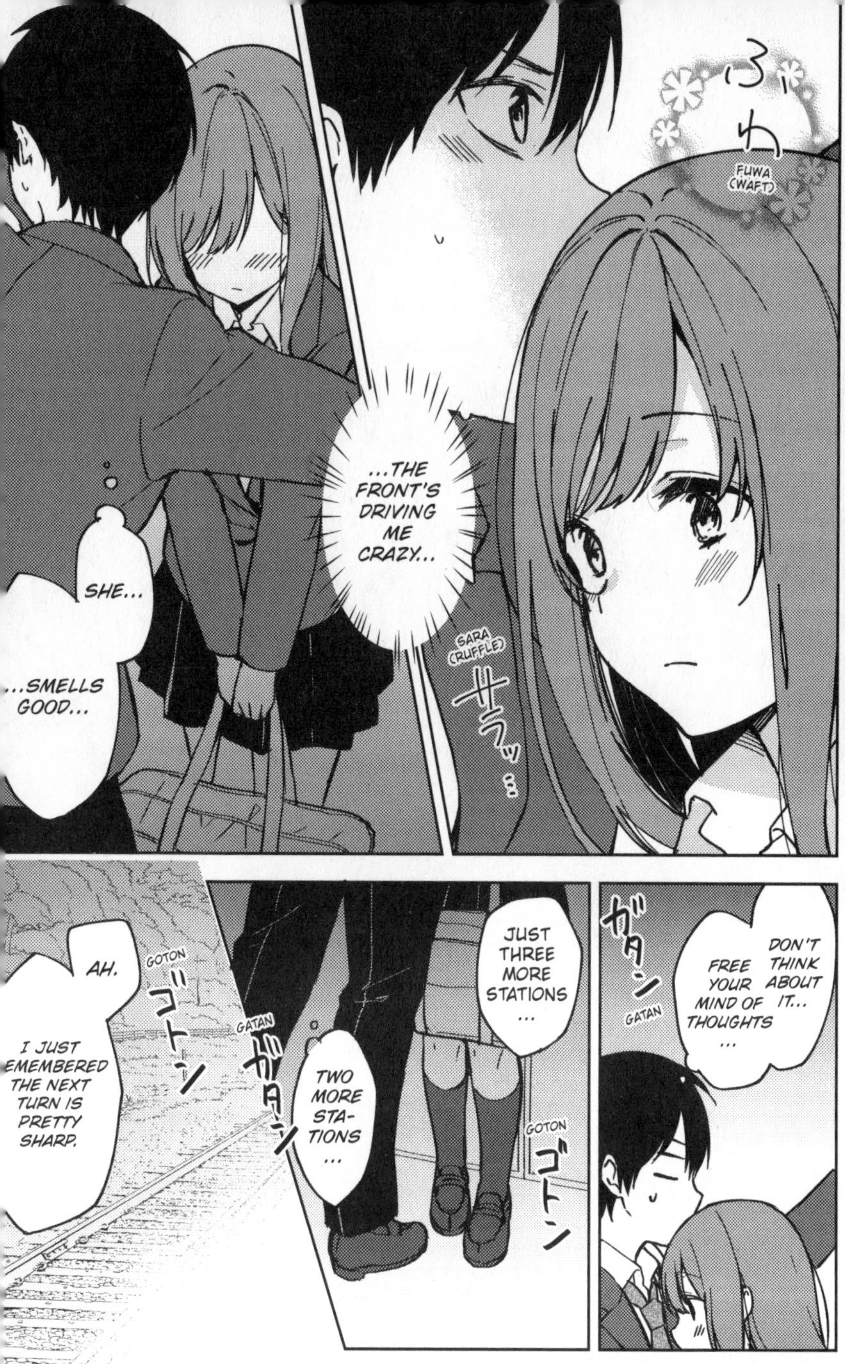

ふわ
FUWA (WAFT)
SARA (RUFFLE)
サラッ
...THE FRONT'S DRIVING ME CRAZY...
SHE...
...SMELLS GOOD...
ガタン
GATAN
DON'T THINK ABOUT IT...
FREE YOUR MIND OF THOUGHTS...
JUST THREE MORE STATIONS...
GOTON
ゴトン
TWO MORE STATIONS...
GATAN
ガタン
GOTON
ゴトン
AH.
I JUST EMEMBERED THE NEXT TURN IS PRETTY SHARP.

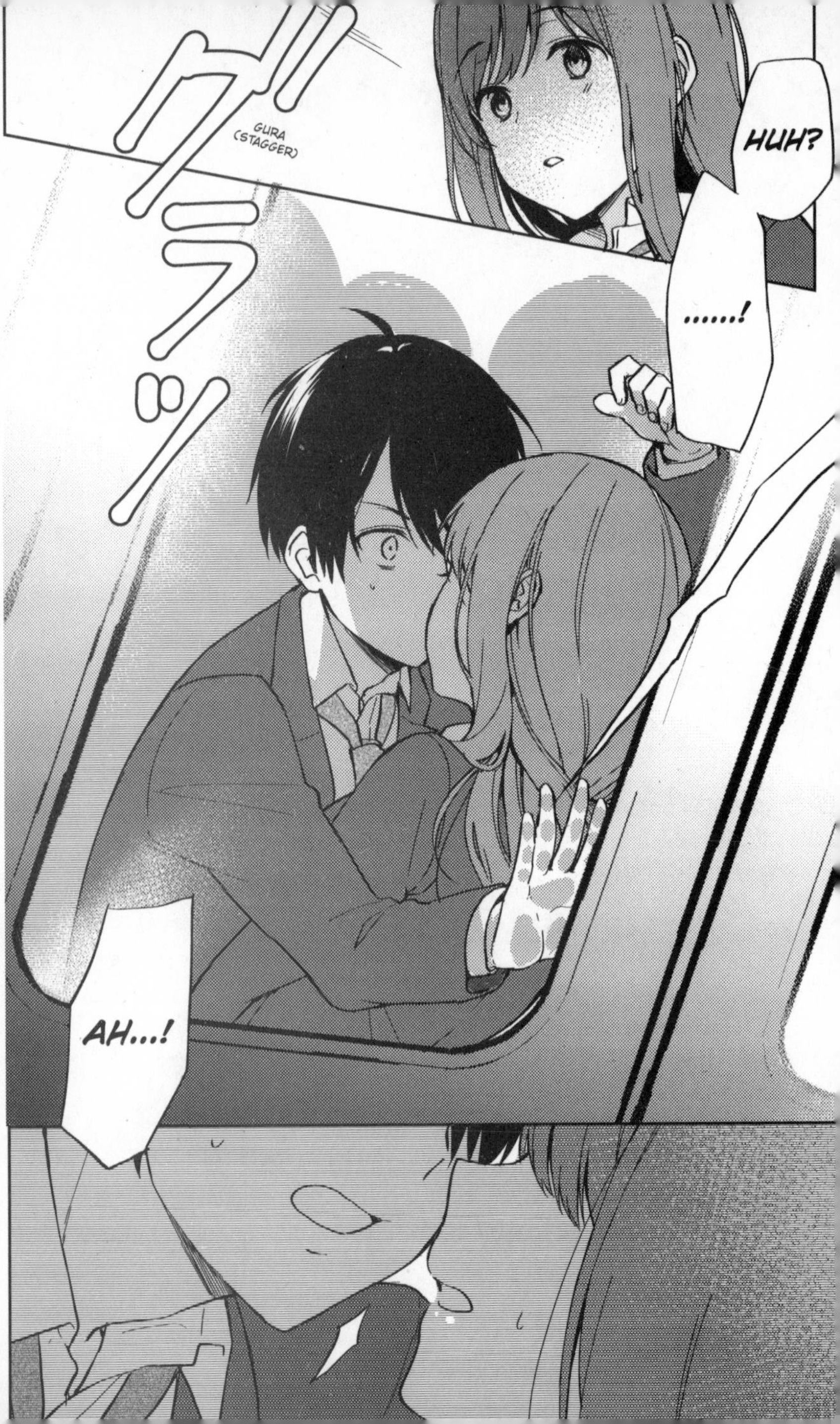
HUH?
......!
グラッ
GURA (STAGGER)
AH...!

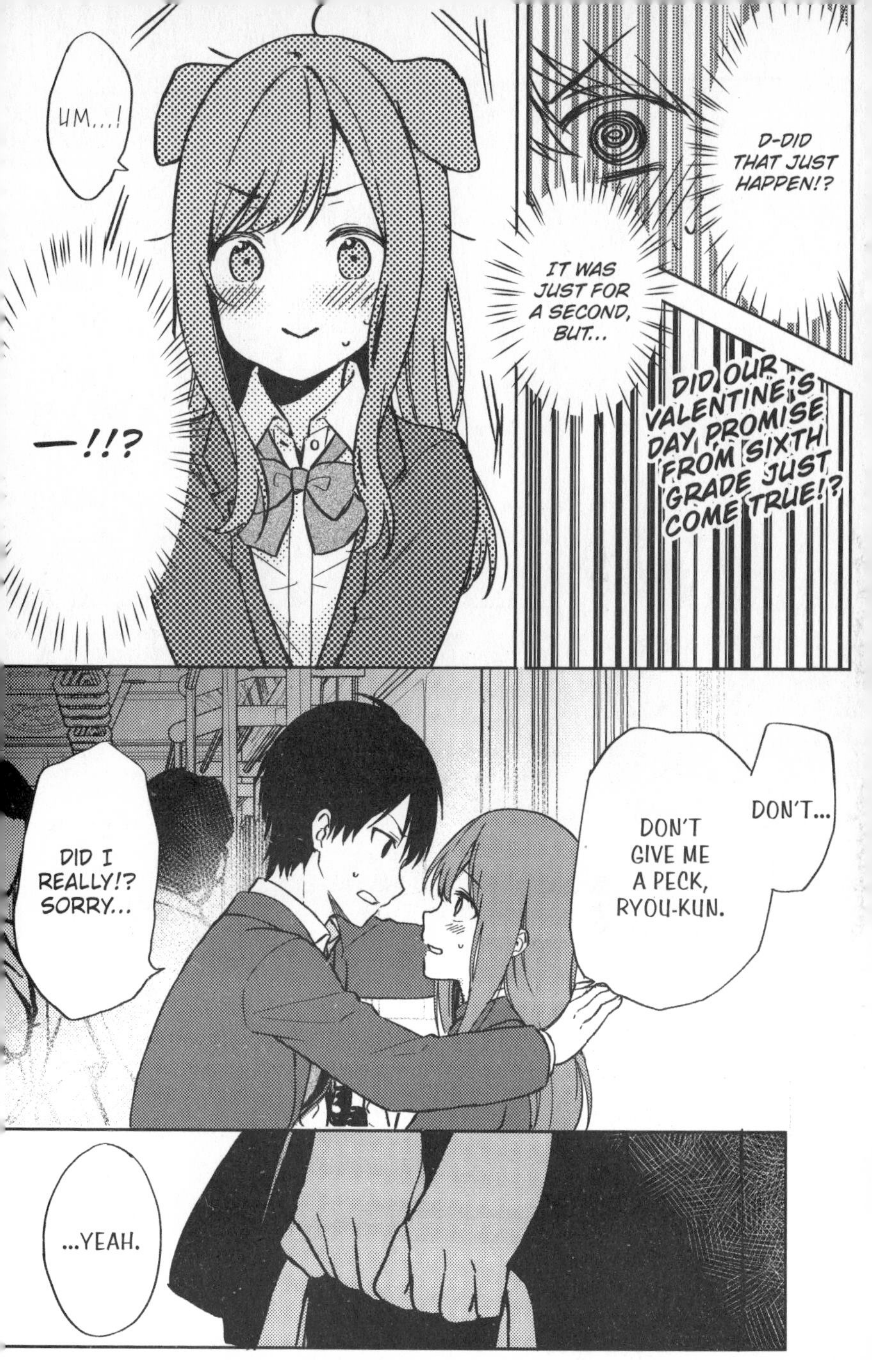
D-DID THAT JUST HAPPEN!?
IT WAS JUST FOR A SECOND, BUT...
DID OUR VALENTINE'S DAY PROMISE FROM SIXTH GRADE JUST COME TRUE!?
UM...!
—!!?
DON'T...
DON'T GIVE ME A PECK, RYOU-KUN.
DID I REALLY!? SORRY...
...YEAH.

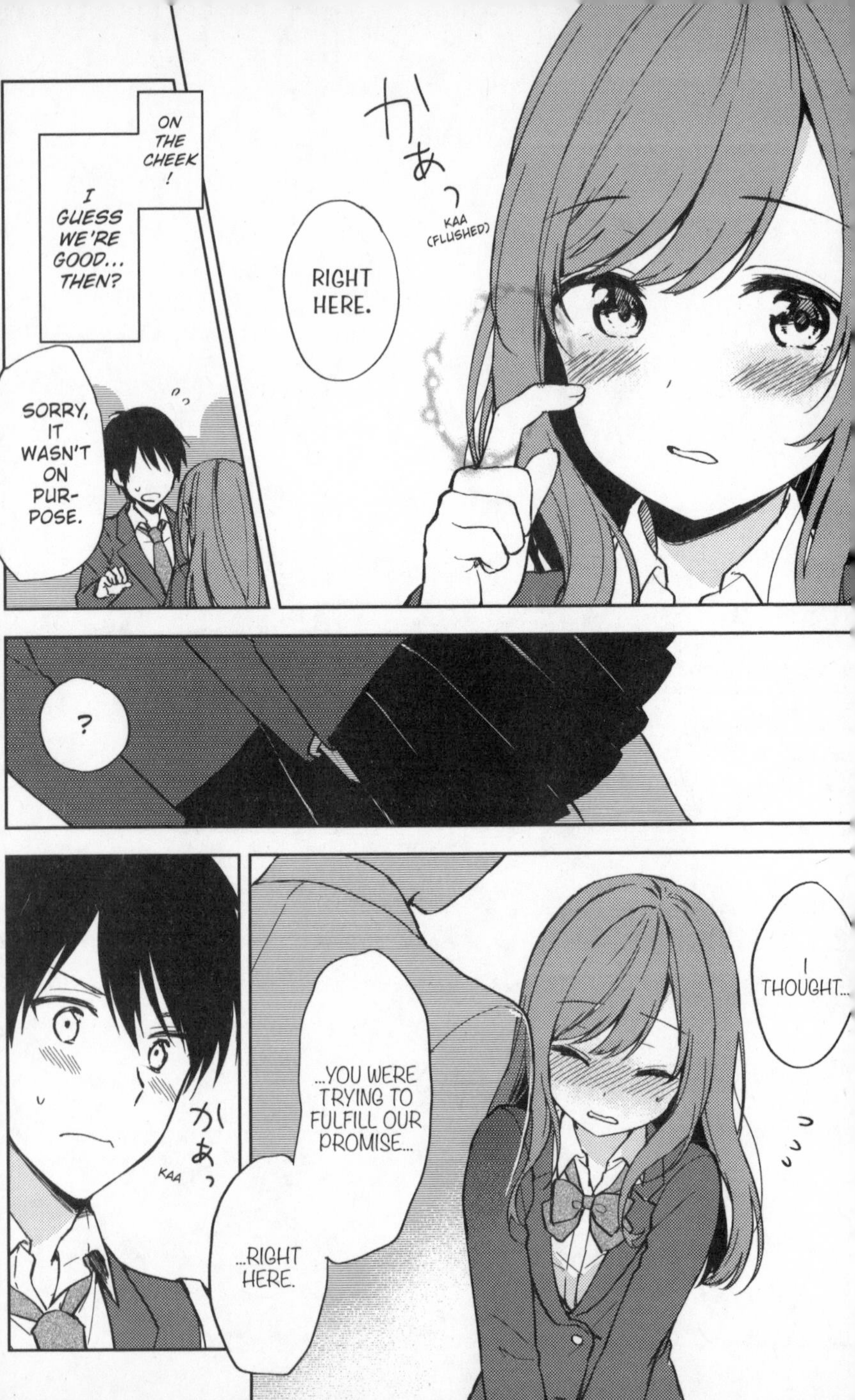
かあっ
KAA (FLUSHED)
RIGHT HERE.
ON THE CHEEK!
I GUESS WE'RE GOOD... THEN?
SORRY, IT WASN'T ON PURPOSE.
?
I THOUGHT...
...YOU WERE TRYING TO FULFILL OUR PROMISE...
...RIGHT HERE.
かあっ
KAA

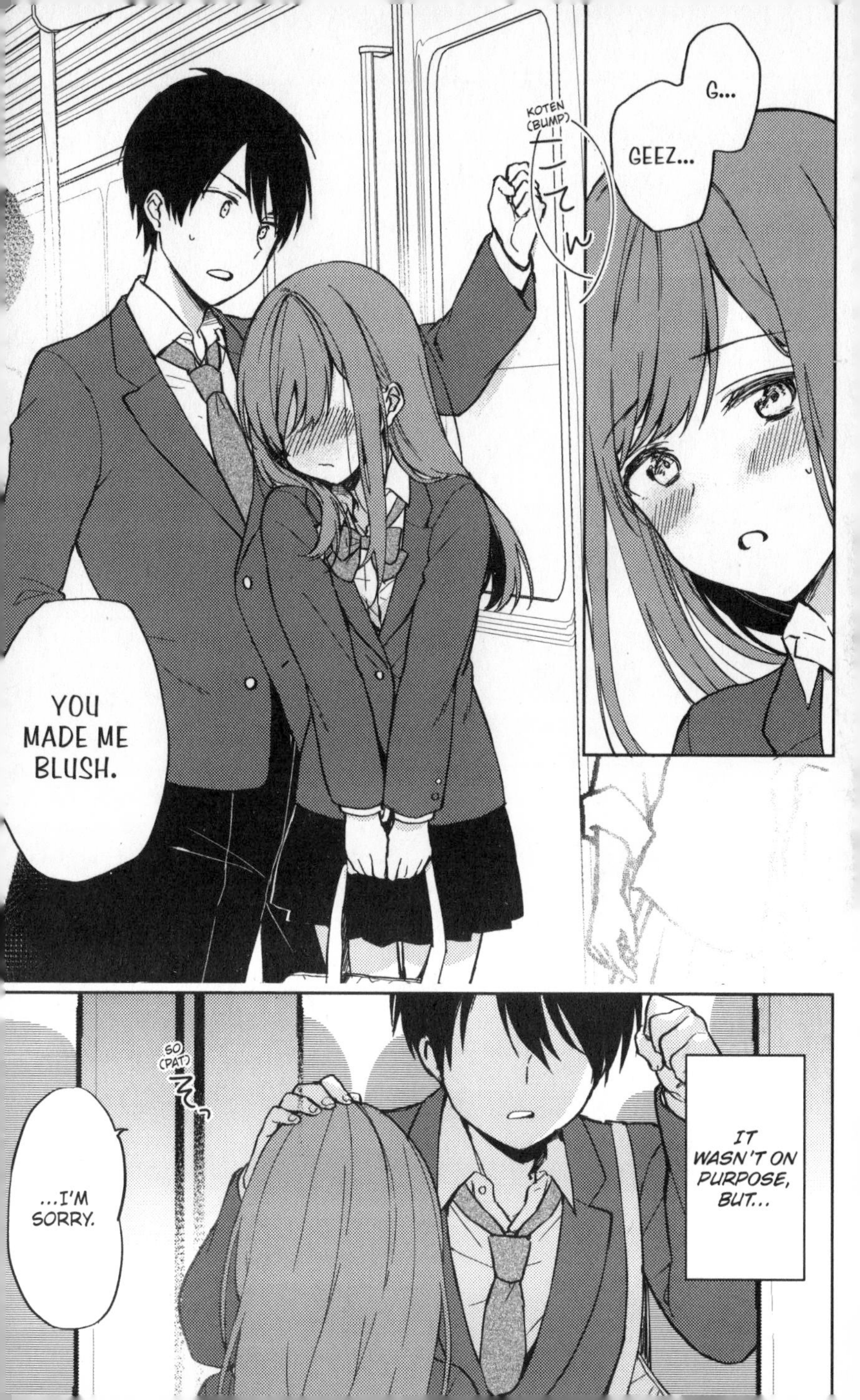
G...
GEEZ...
KOTEN (BUMP)
YOU MADE ME BLUSH.
IT WASN'T ON PURPOSE, BUT...
SO (PAT)
...I'M SORRY.

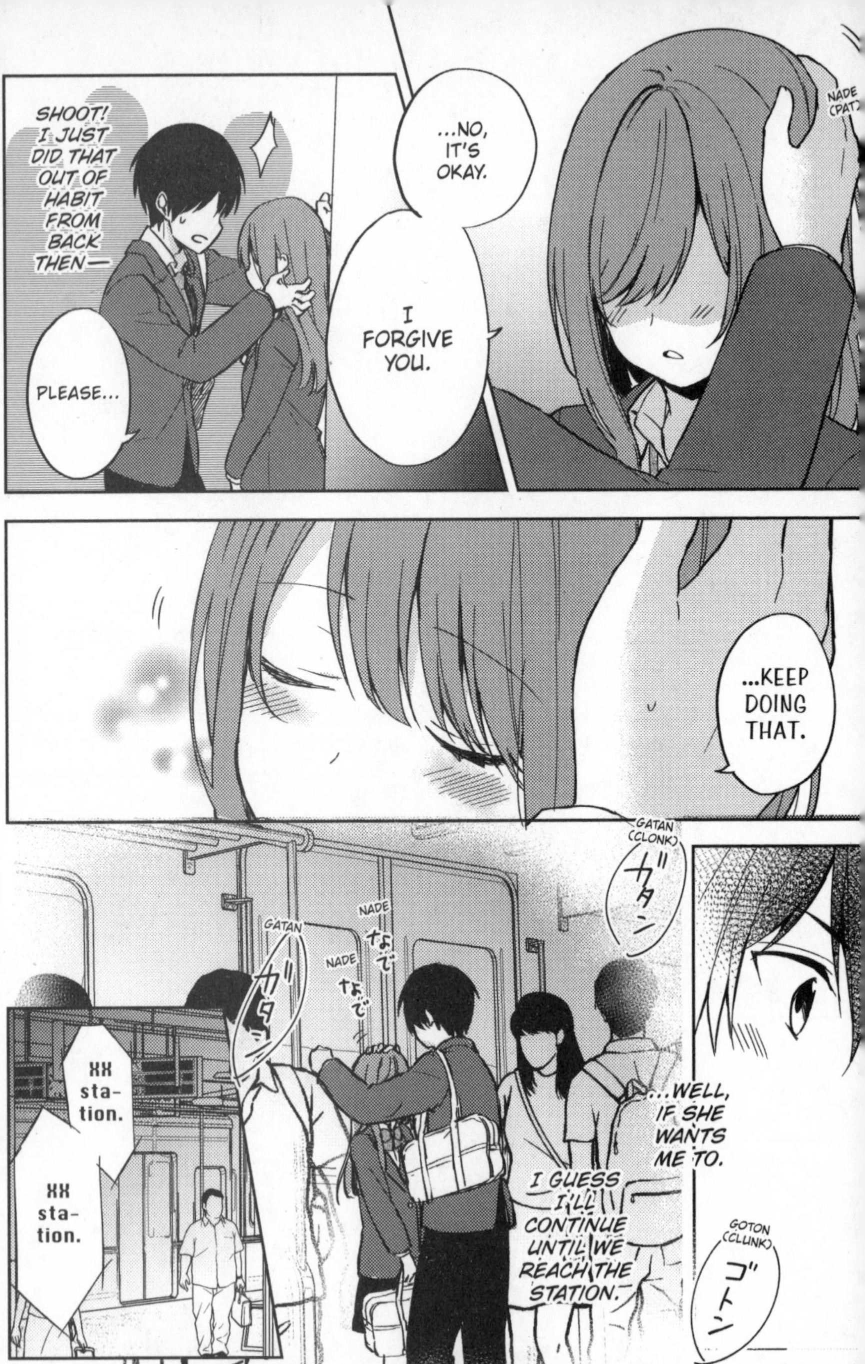
NADE (PAT)
...NO, IT'S OKAY.
I FORGIVE YOU.
SHOOT! I JUST DID THAT OUT OF HABIT FROM BACK THEN—
PLEASE...
...KEEP DOING THAT.
GATAN (CLONK)
ガタン
...WELL, IF SHE WANTS ME TO.
GOTON (CLUNK)
ゴトン
NADE
なで
NADE
なで
GATAN
ガタン
I GUESS I'LL CONTINUE UNTIL WE REACH THE STATION.
XX station.
XX station.

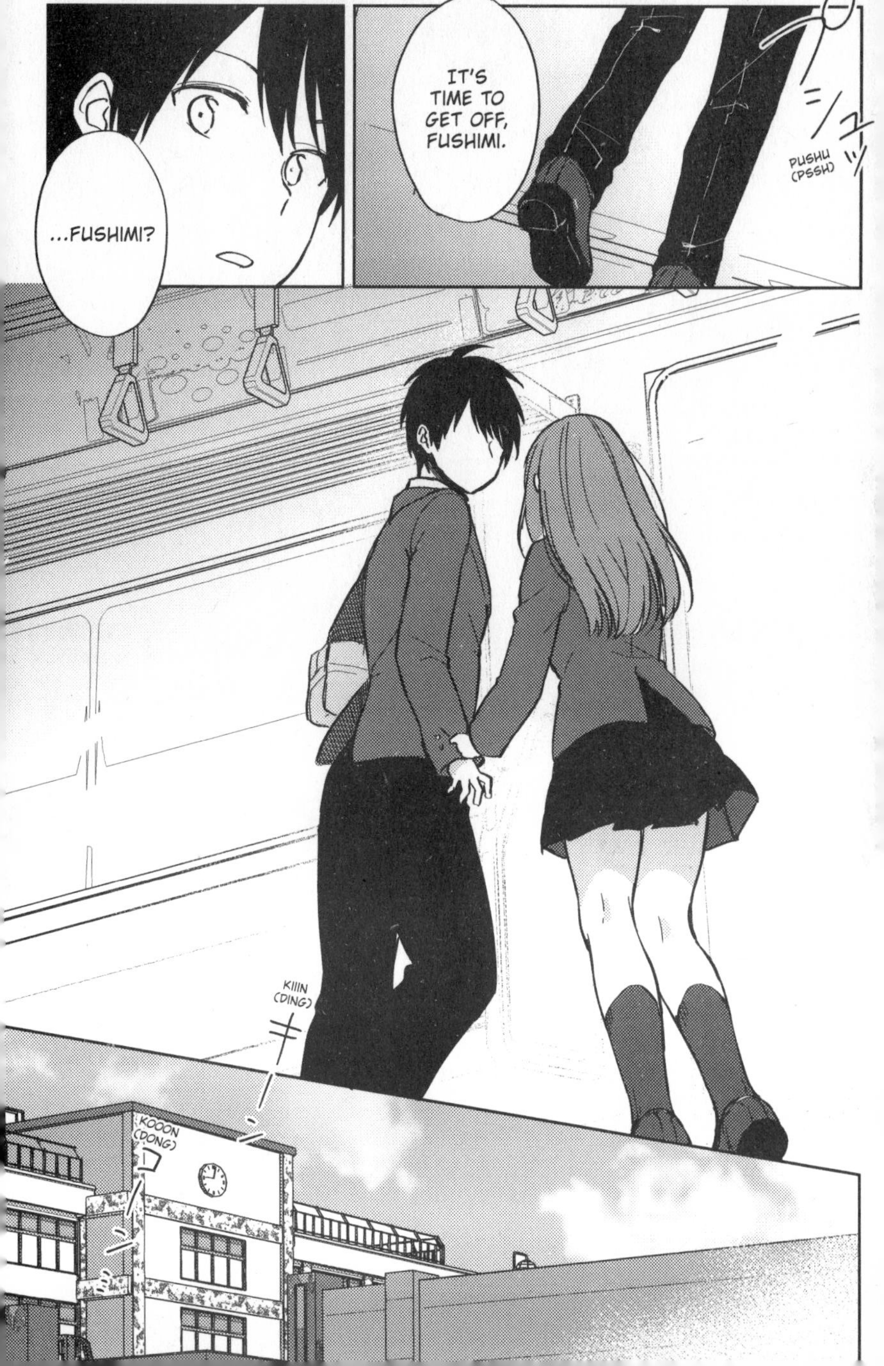
IT'S TIME TO GET OFF, FUSHIMI.
PUSHU (PSSH)
...FUSHIMI?
KIIIN (DING)
KOOON (DONG)

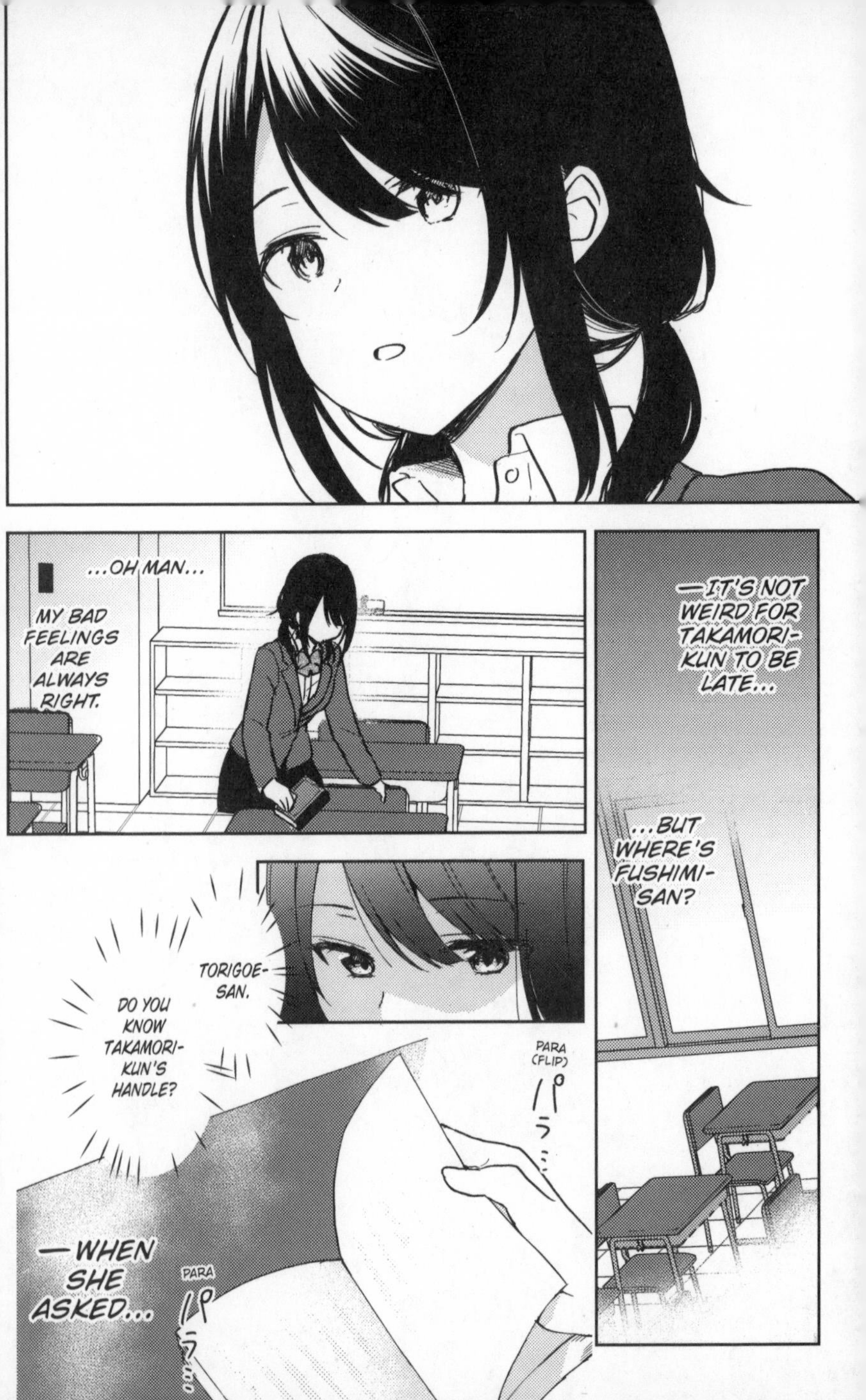
—IT'S NOT WEIRD FOR TAKAMORI-KUN TO BE LATE...
...BUT WHERE'S FUSHIMI-SAN?
...OH MAN...
MY BAD FEELINGS ARE ALWAYS RIGHT.
TORIGOE-SAN.
DO YOU KNOW TAKAMORI-KUN'S HANDLE?
PARA (FLIP)
パラ…
—WHEN SHE ASKED...
PARA
パラ…

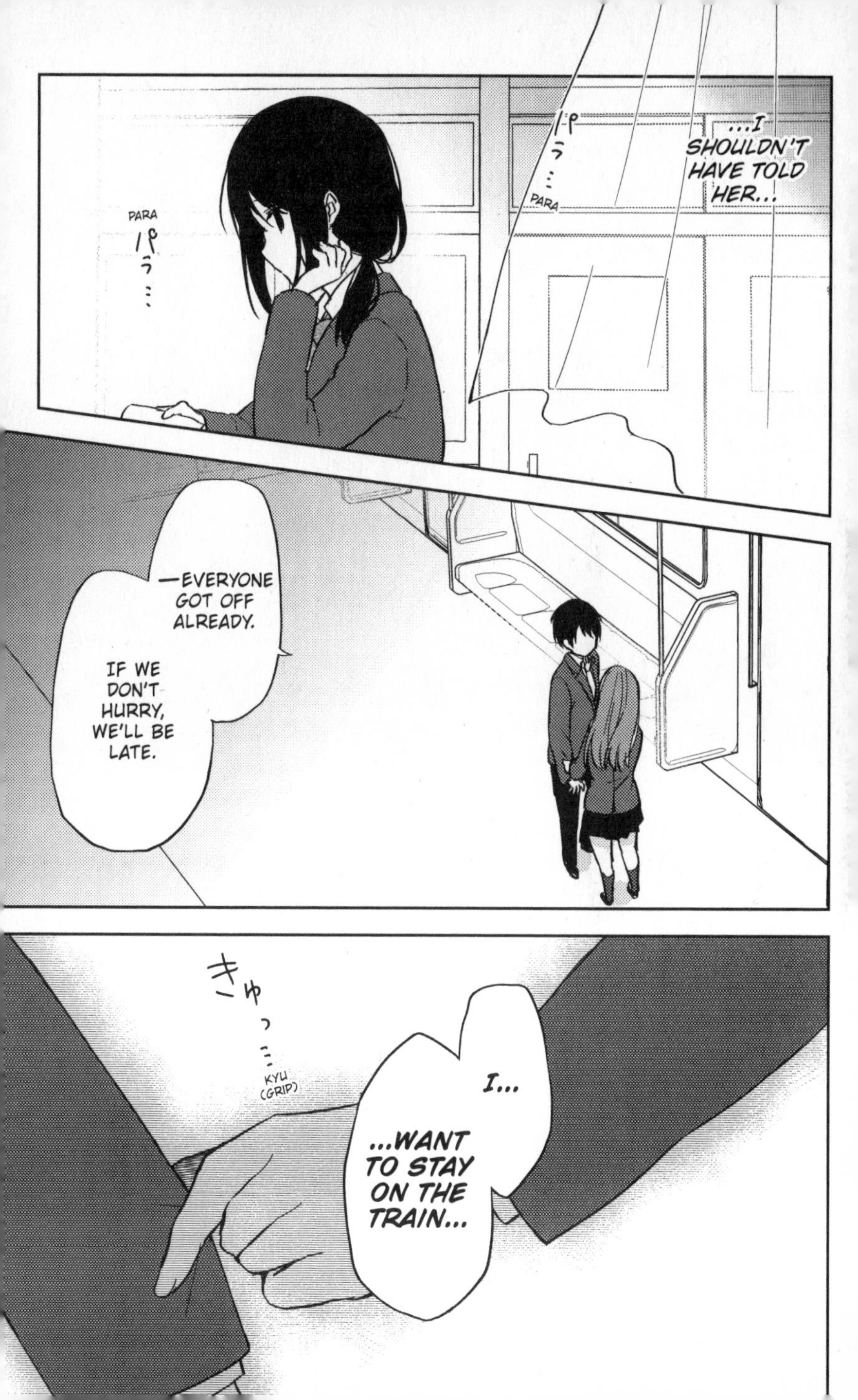
...I SHOULDN'T HAVE TOLD HER...
パラ…
PARA
パラ…
PARA
—EVERYONE GOT OFF ALREADY.
IF WE DON'T HURRY, WE'LL BE LATE.
きゅっ…
KYU (GRIP)
I...
...WANT TO STAY ON THE TRAIN...

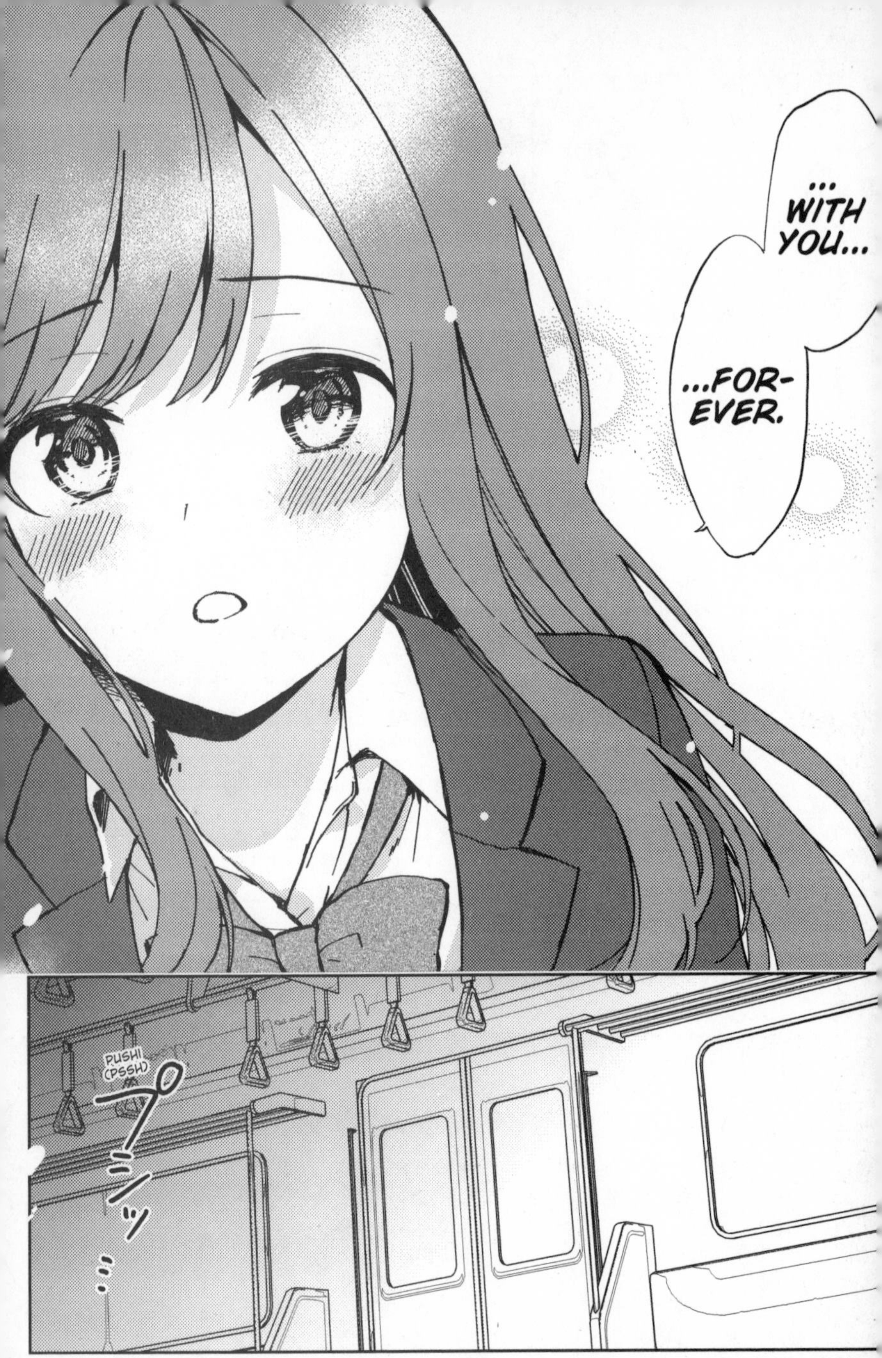
...WITH YOU...
...FOR-EVER.
PUSHI (PSSH)
プシッ…

#8

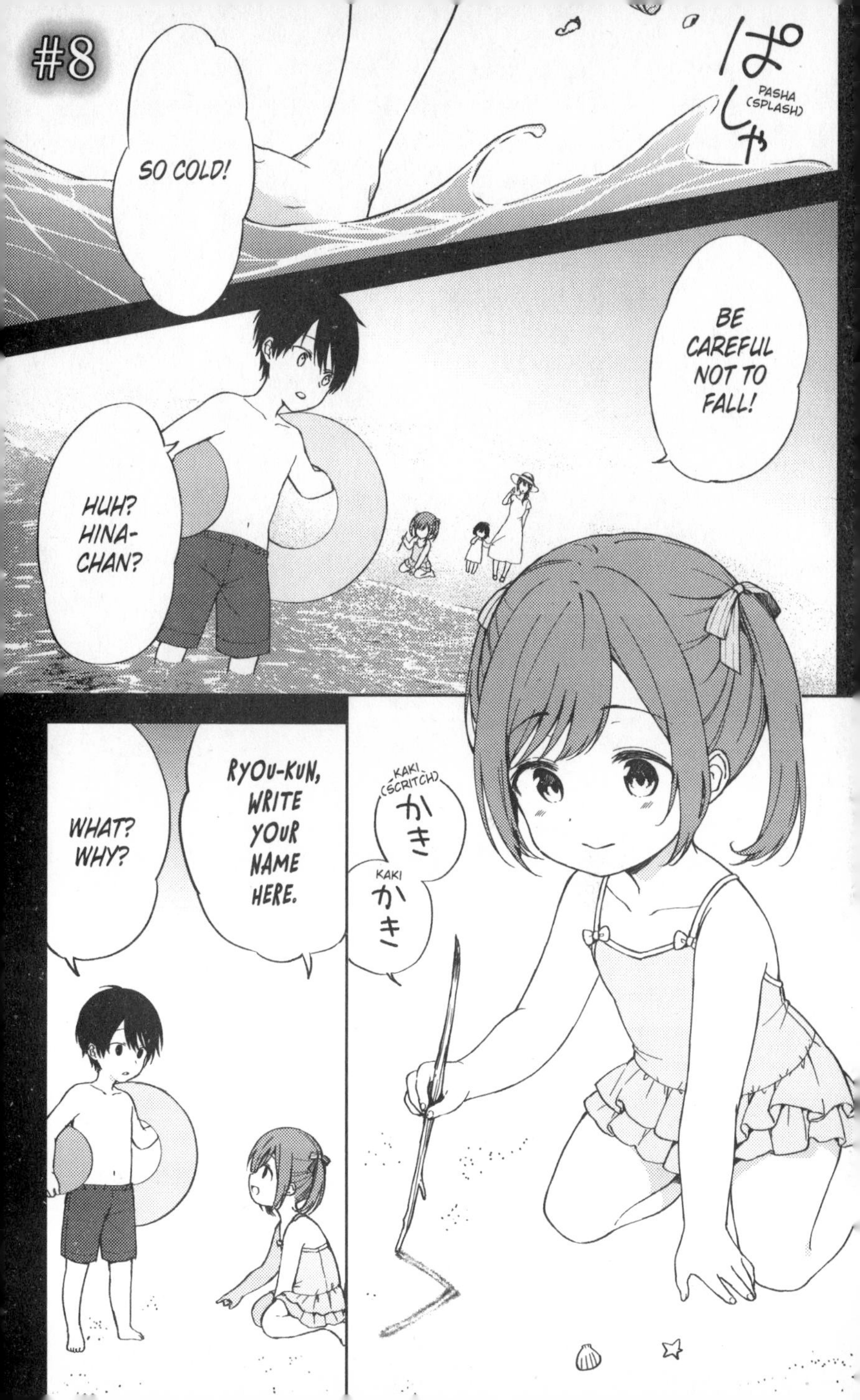
ぱしゃ
PASHA (SPLASH)
SO COLD!
BE CAREFUL NOT TO FALL!
HUH? HINA-CHAN?
KAKI (SCRITCH)
かき
KAKI
かき
RYOU-KUN, WRITE YOUR NAME HERE.
WHAT? WHY?

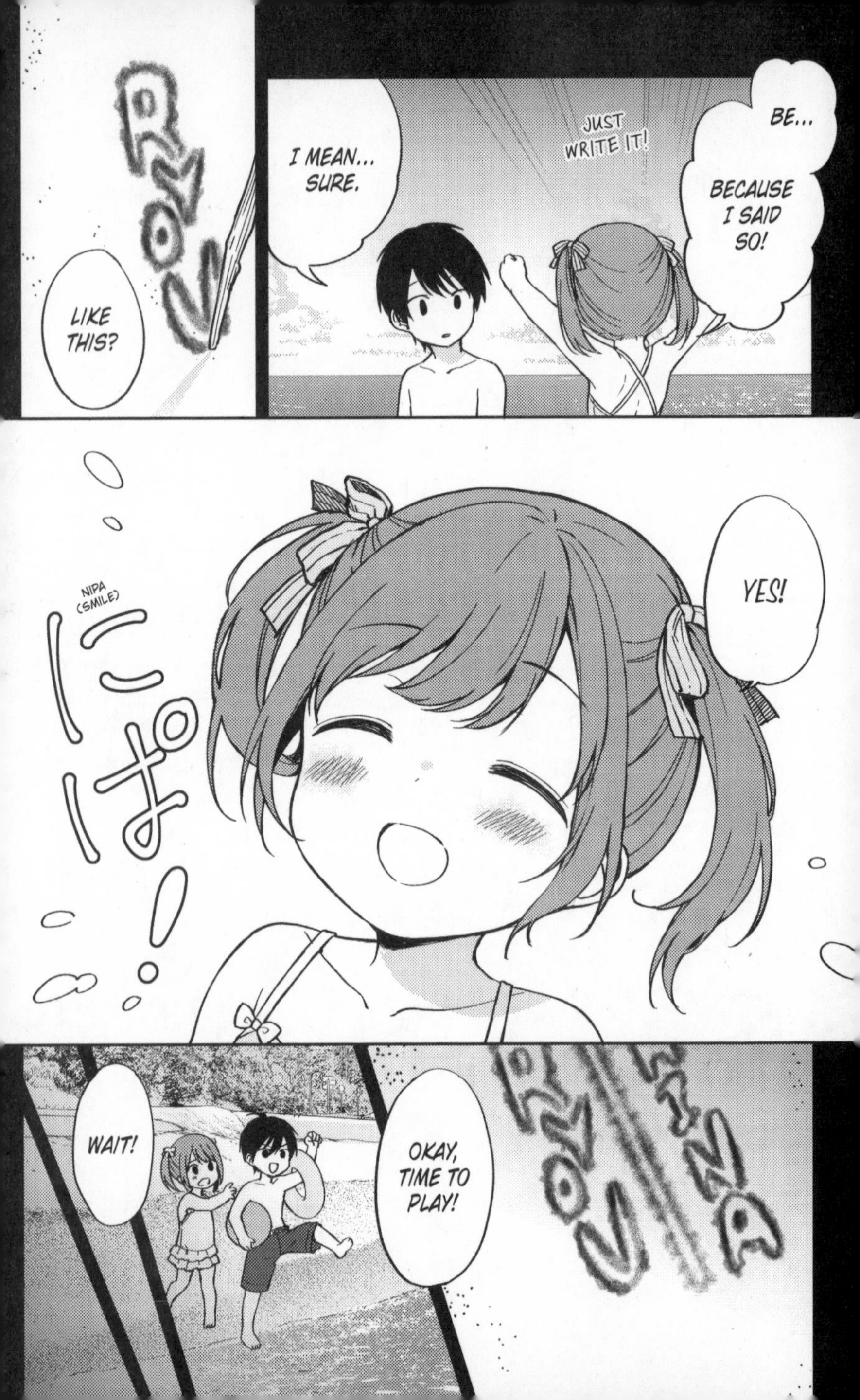
BE...
BECAUSE I SAID SO!
JUST WRITE IT!
I MEAN... SURE.
LIKE THIS?
YES!
NIPA (SMILE)
にぱー!
OKAY, TIME TO PLAY!
WAIT!

#8 Mr. Reoffender and Ms. Diligent

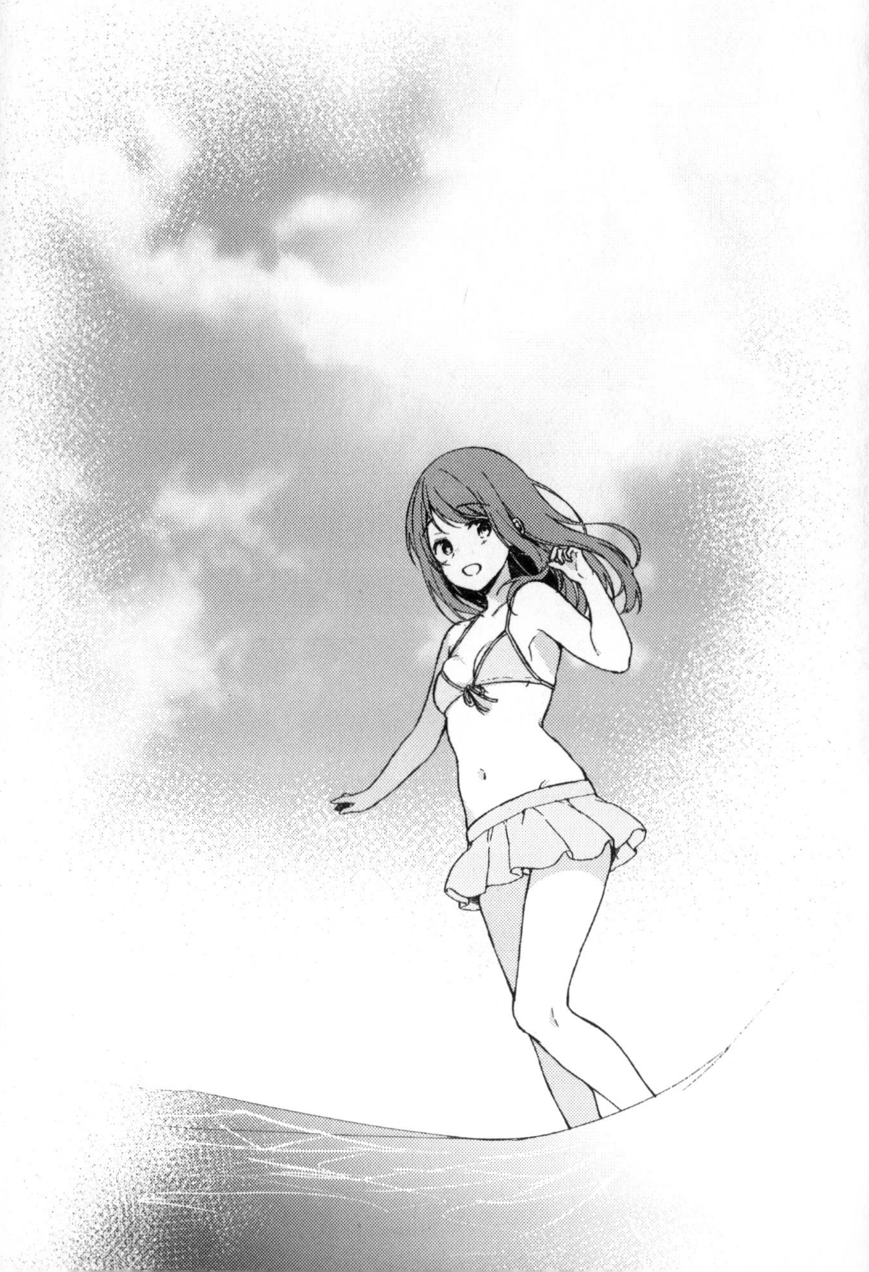

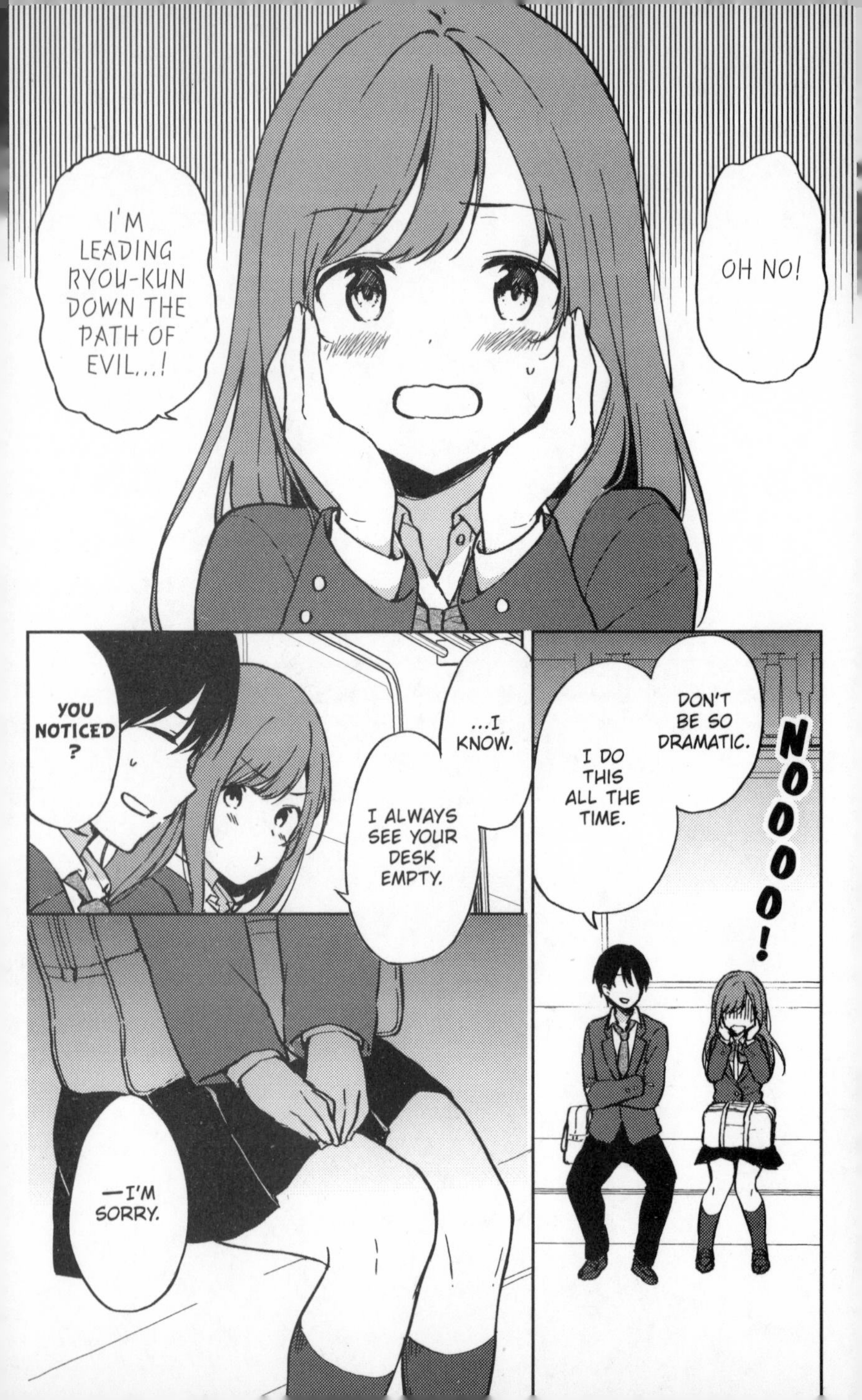
OH NO!
I'M LEADING RYOU-KUN DOWN THE PATH OF EVIL...!
DON'T BE SO DRAMATIC.
I DO THIS ALL THE TIME.
NOOOO!
...I KNOW.
I ALWAYS SEE YOUR DESK EMPTY.
YOU NOTICED?
—I'M SORRY.

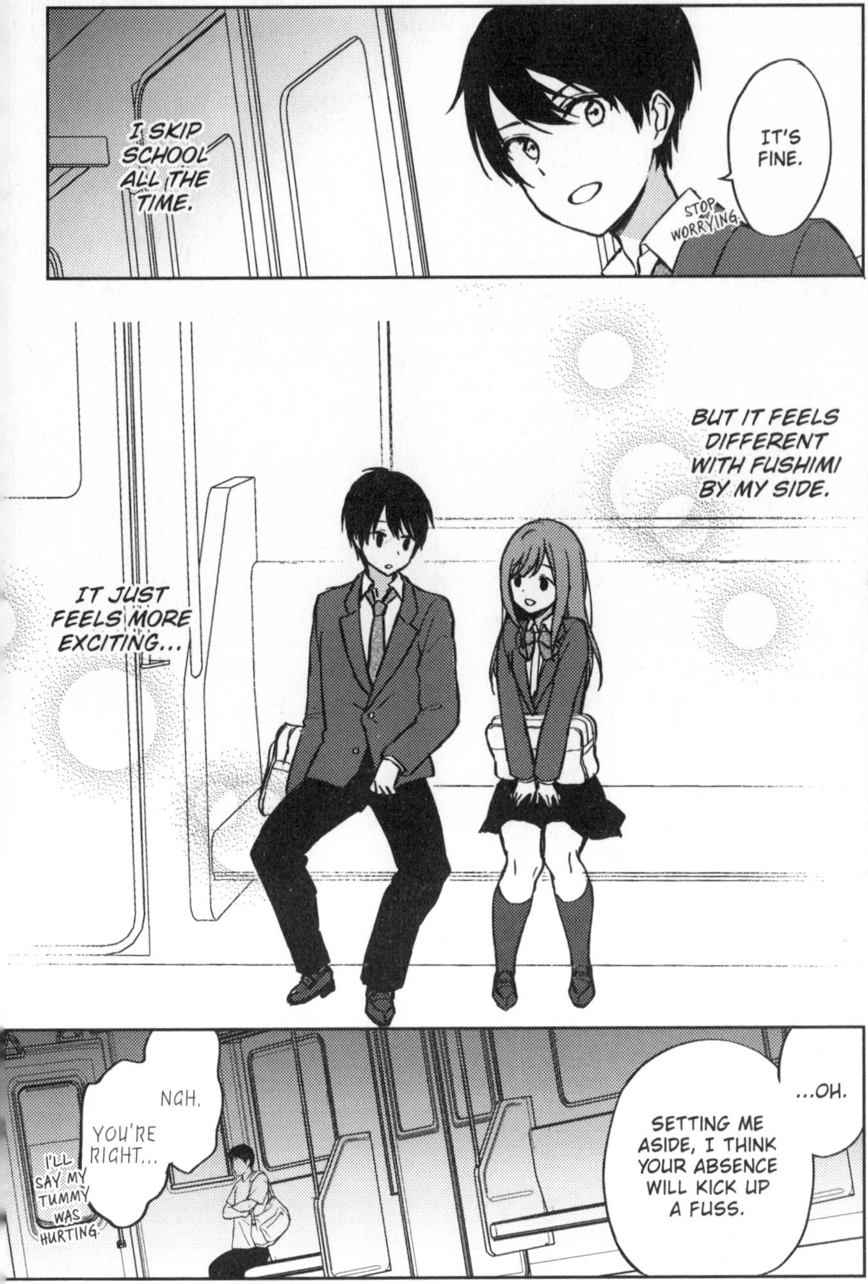
IT'S FINE.
STOP WORRYING.
I SKIP SCHOOL ALL THE TIME.
BUT IT FEELS DIFFERENT WITH FUSHIMI BY MY SIDE.
IT JUST FEELS MORE EXCITING...
...OH.
SETTING ME ASIDE, I THINK YOUR ABSENCE WILL KICK UP A FUSS.
NGH.
YOU'RE RIGHT...
I'LL SAY MY TUMMY WAS HURTING.

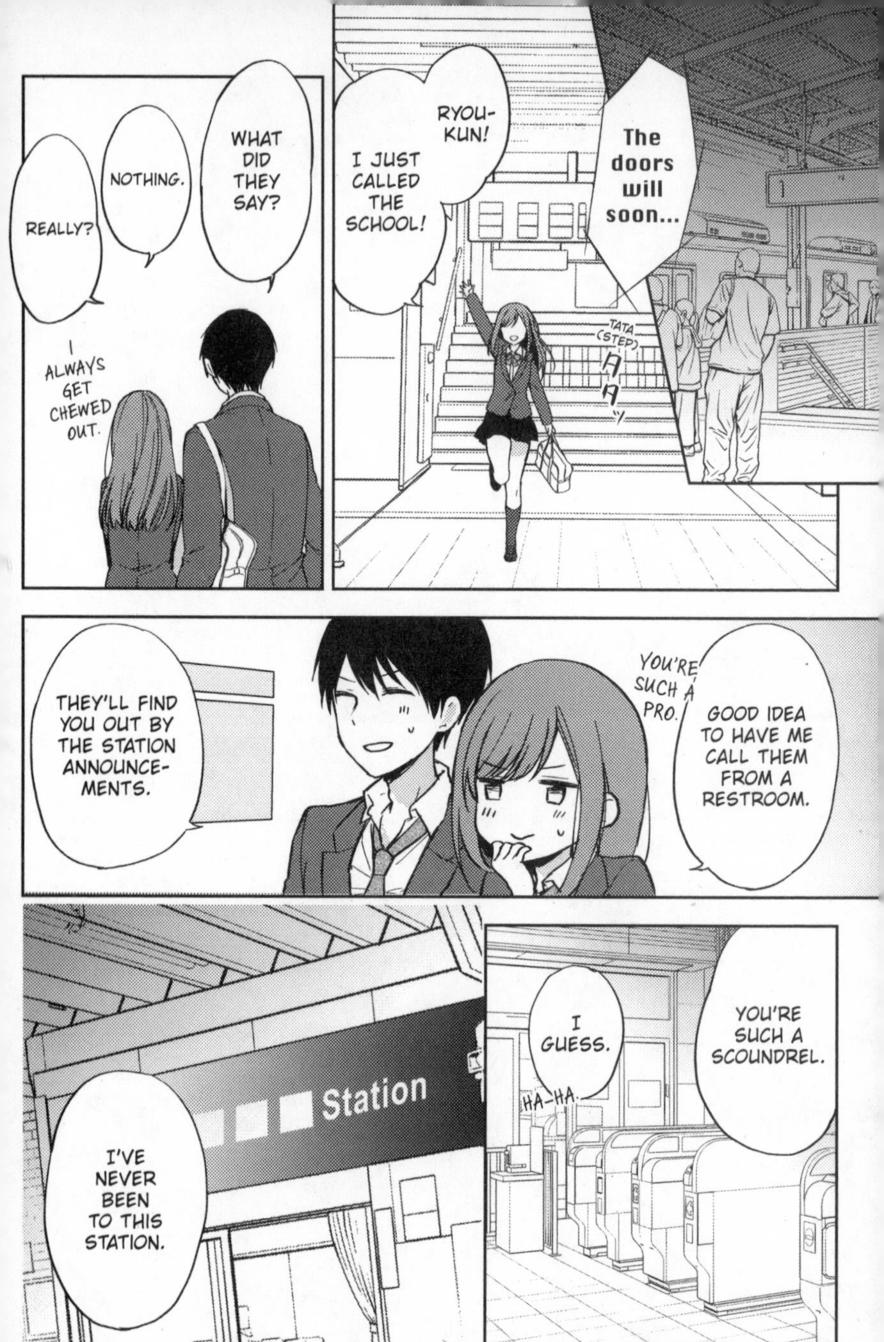
The doors will soon...
RYOU-KUN!
I JUST CALLED THE SCHOOL!
TATA (STEP)
WHAT DID THEY SAY?
NOTHING.
REALLY?
I ALWAYS GET CHEWED OUT.
GOOD IDEA TO HAVE ME CALL THEM FROM A RESTROOM.
YOU'RE SUCH A PRO.
THEY'LL FIND YOU OUT BY THE STATION ANNOUNCEMENTS.
YOU'RE SUCH A SCOUNDREL.
I GUESS.
HA-HA.
Station
I'VE NEVER BEEN TO THIS STATION.

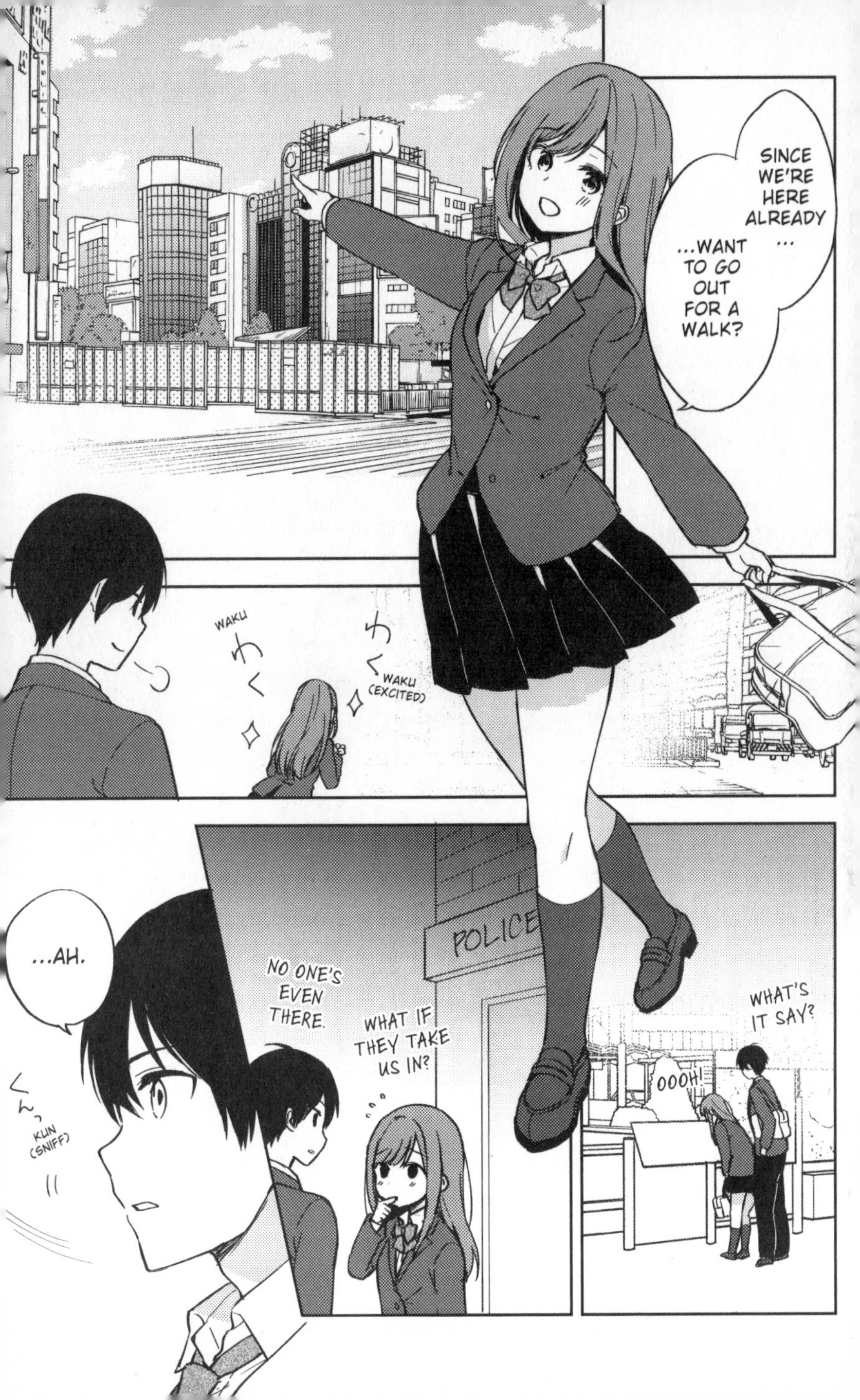
SINCE WE'RE HERE ALREADY...
...WANT TO GO OUT FOR A WALK?
わく
WAKU (EXCITED)
WAKU
わく
WHAT'S IT SAY?
OOOH!
POLICE
NO ONE'S EVEN THERE.
WHAT IF THEY TAKE US IN?
...AH.
くん、
KUN (SNIFF)

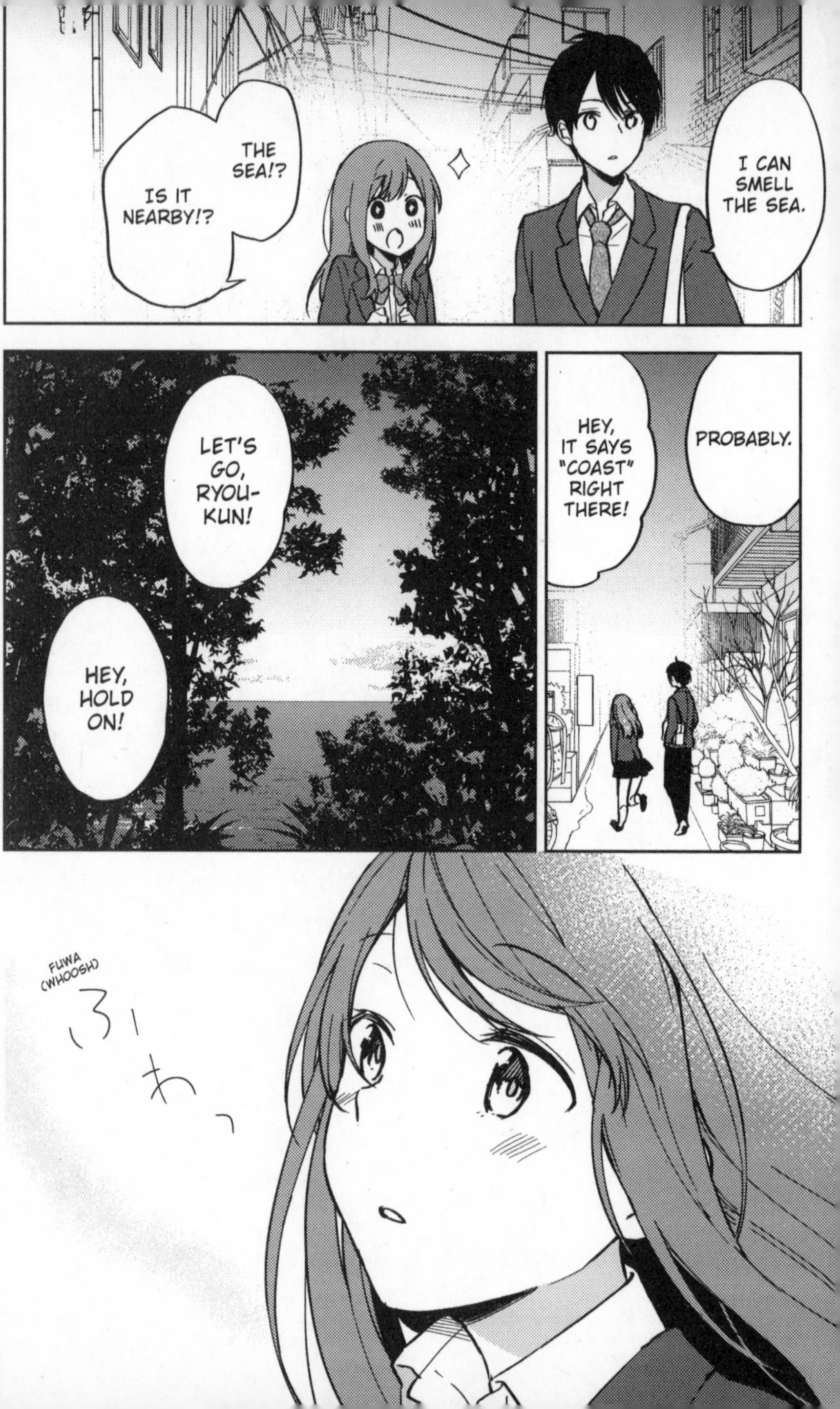
I CAN SMELL THE SEA.
THE SEA!? IS IT NEARBY!?
PROBABLY.
HEY, IT SAYS "COAST" RIGHT THERE!
LET'S GO, RYOU-KUN!
HEY, HOLD ON!
FUWA (WHOOSH)
ふわっ

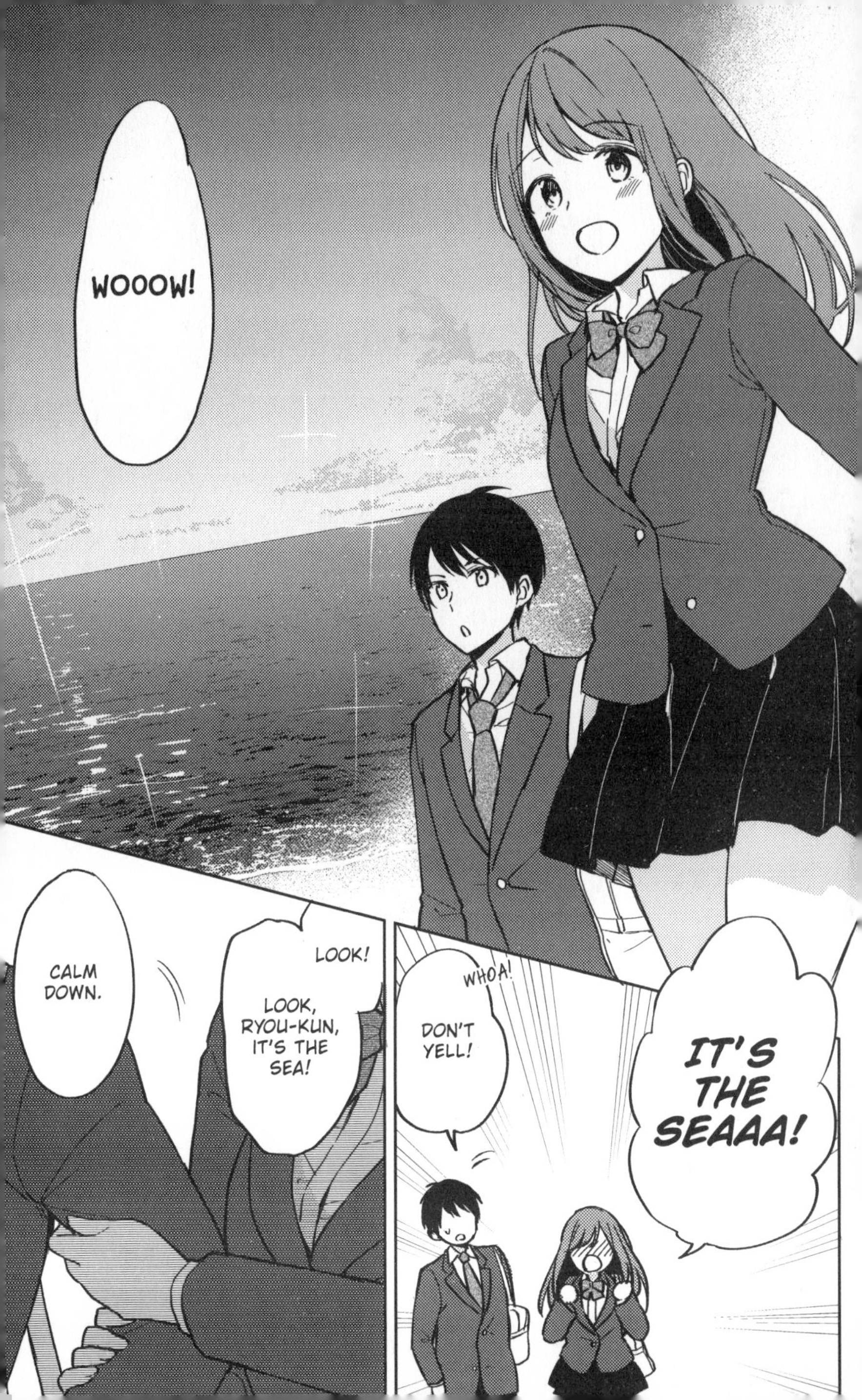
WOOOW!
IT'S THE SEAAA!
WHOA!
DON'T YELL!
LOOK!
LOOK, RYOU-KUN, IT'S THE SEA!
CALM DOWN.

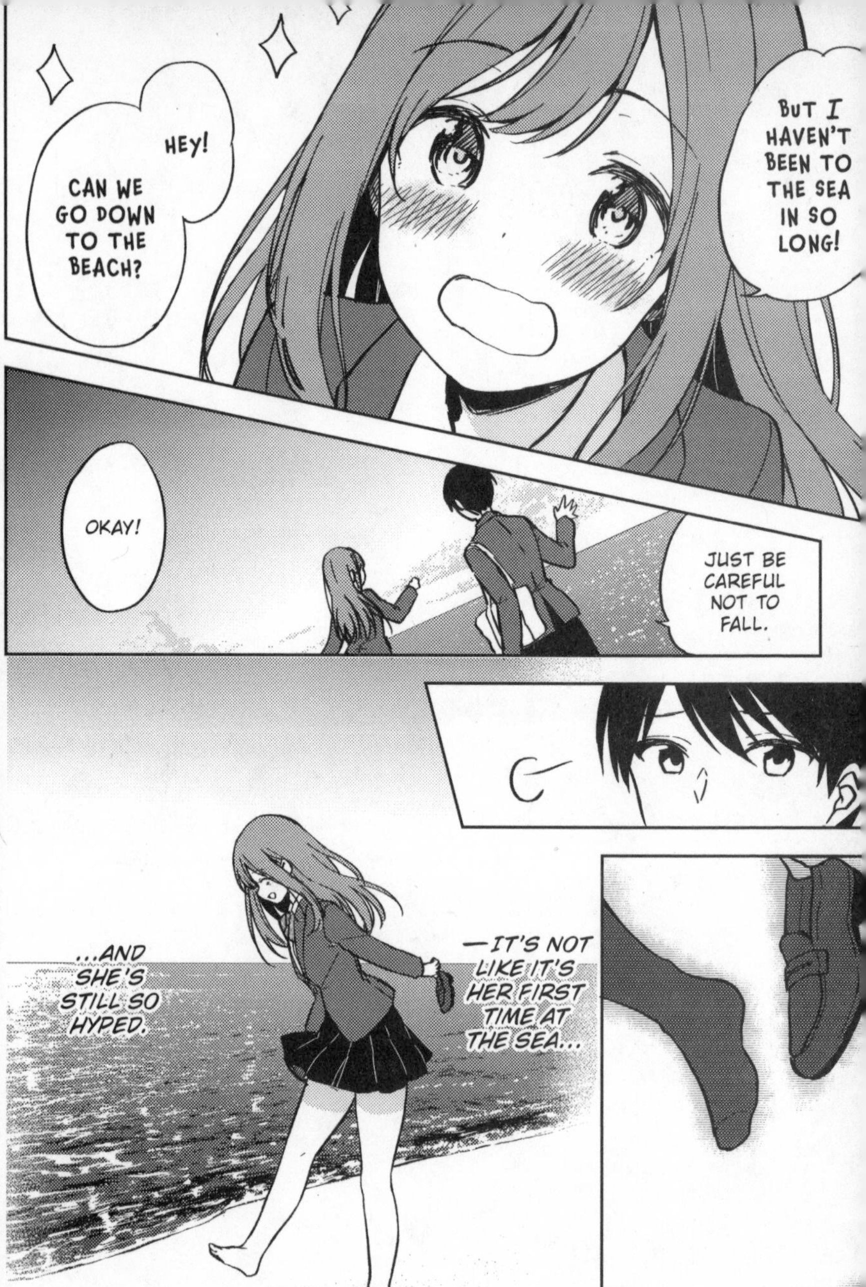
BUT I HAVEN'T BEEN TO THE SEA IN SO LONG!
HEY!
CAN WE GO DOWN TO THE BEACH?
JUST BE CAREFUL NOT TO FALL.
OKAY!
—IT'S NOT LIKE IT'S HER FIRST TIME AT THE SEA...
...AND SHE'S STILL SO HYPED.

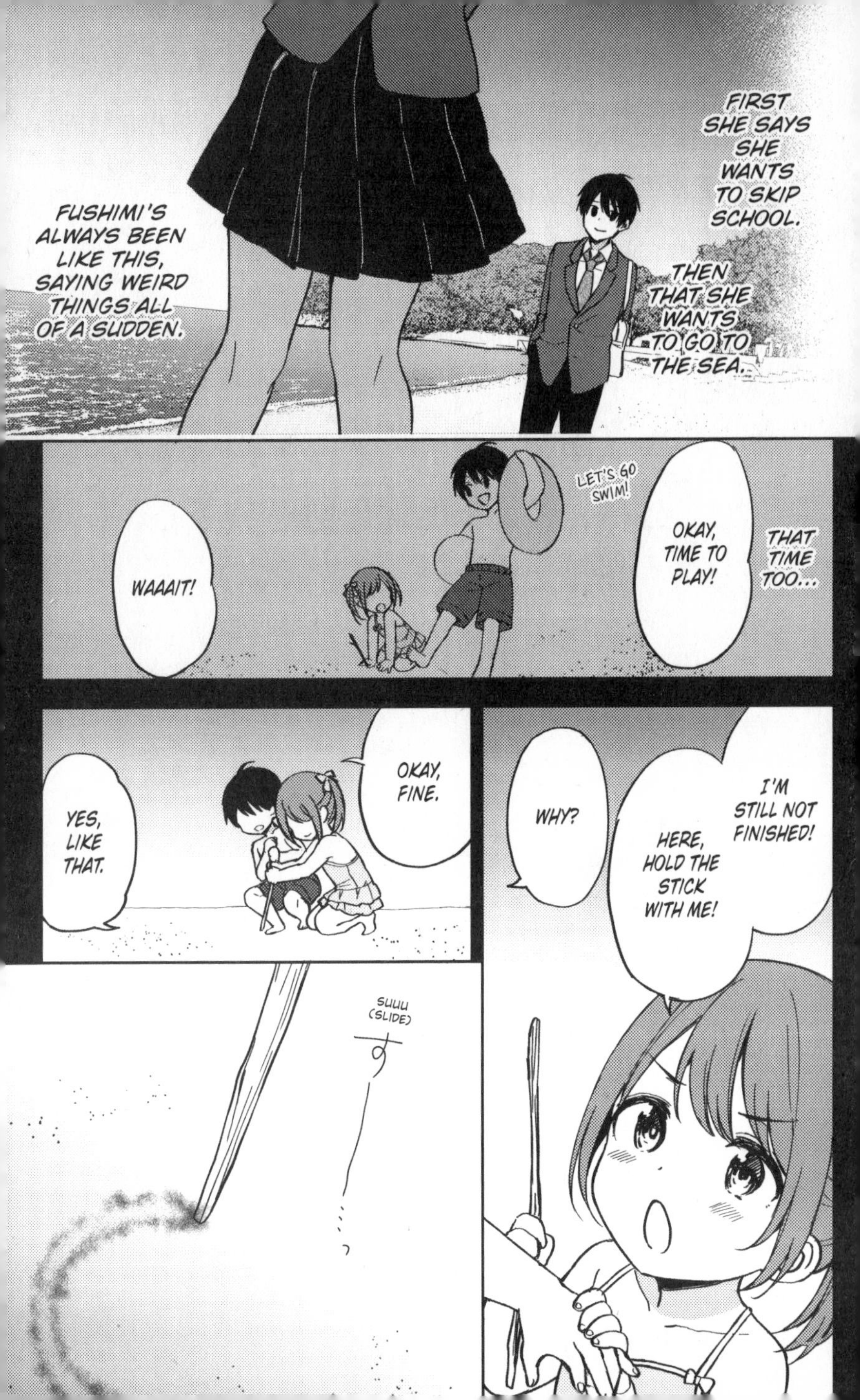
FIRST SHE SAYS SHE WANTS TO SKIP SCHOOL.
THEN THAT SHE WANTS TO GO TO THE SEA.
FUSHIMI'S ALWAYS BEEN LIKE THIS, SAYING WEIRD THINGS ALL OF A SUDDEN.
THAT TIME TOO...
OKAY, TIME TO PLAY!
LET'S GO SWIM!
WAAAIT!
I'M STILL NOT FINISHED!
HERE, HOLD THE STICK WITH ME!
WHY?
OKAY, FINE.
YES, LIKE THAT.
SUUU (SLIDE)
す

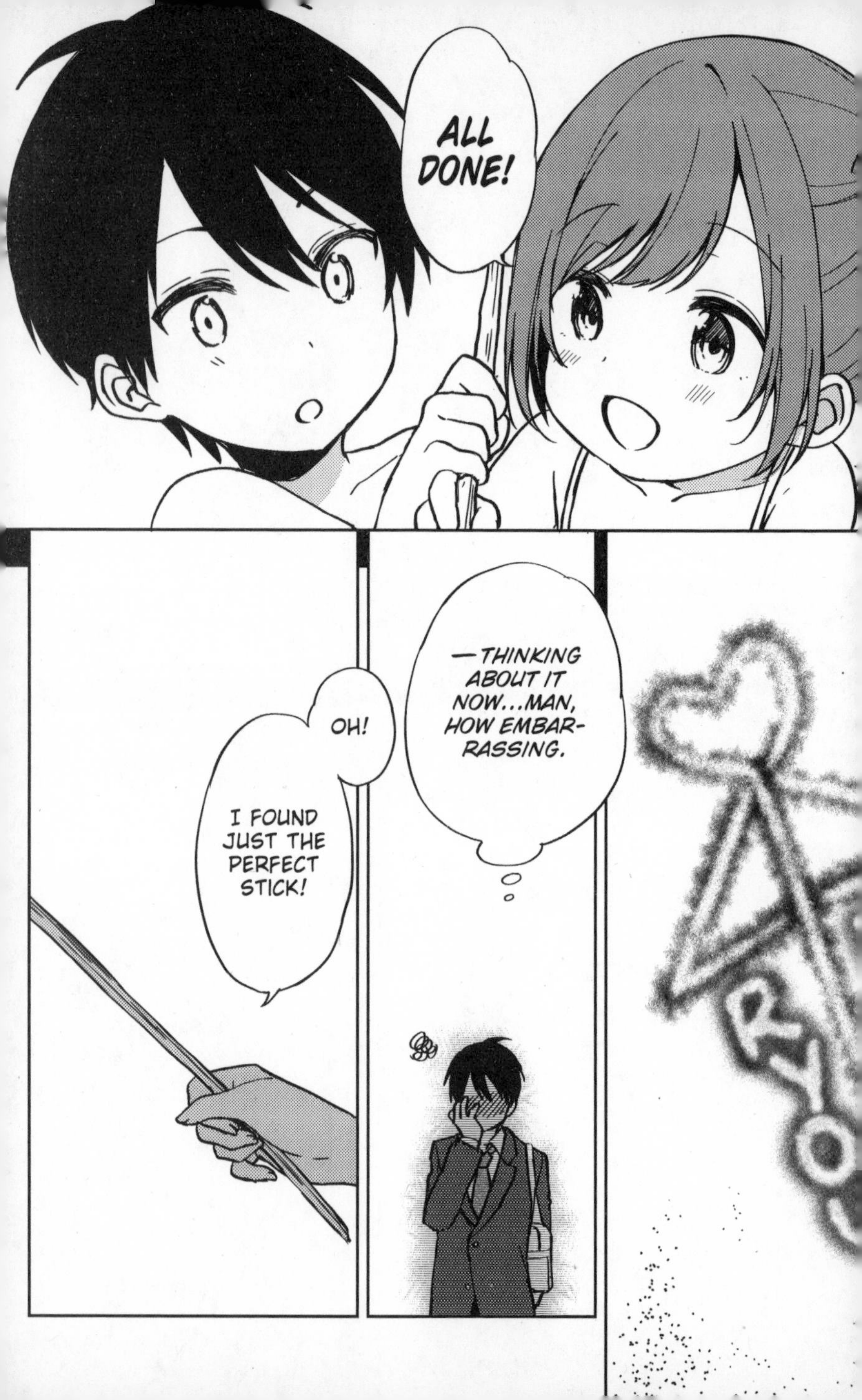
ALL DONE!
—THINKING ABOUT IT NOW...MAN, HOW EMBARRASSING.
OH!
I FOUND JUST THE PERFECT STICK!

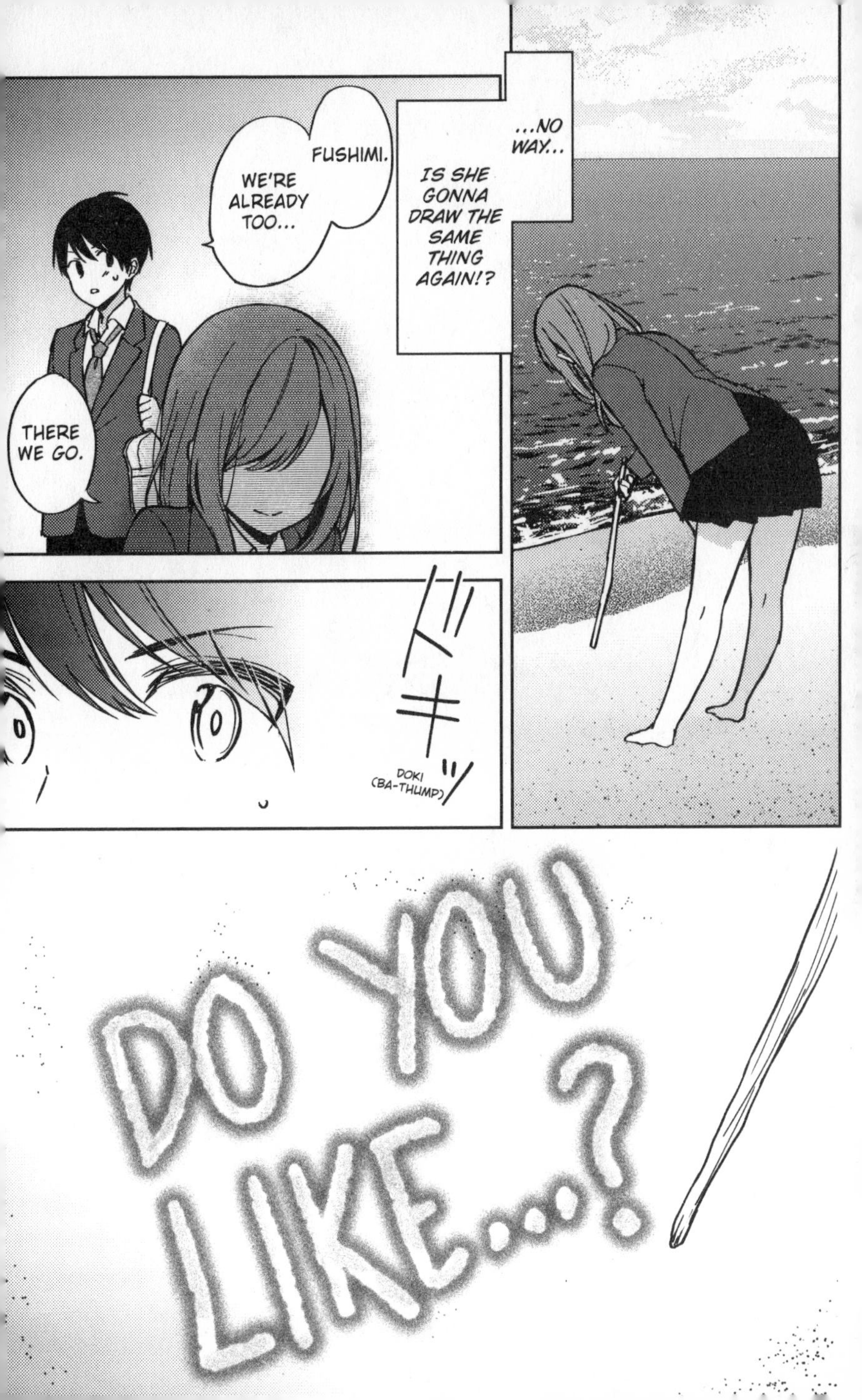
...NO WAY...
IS SHE GONNA DRAW THE SAME THING AGAIN!?
FUSHIMI.
WE'RE ALREADY TOO...
THERE WE GO.
DOKI (BA-THUMP)
DO YOU LIKE...?

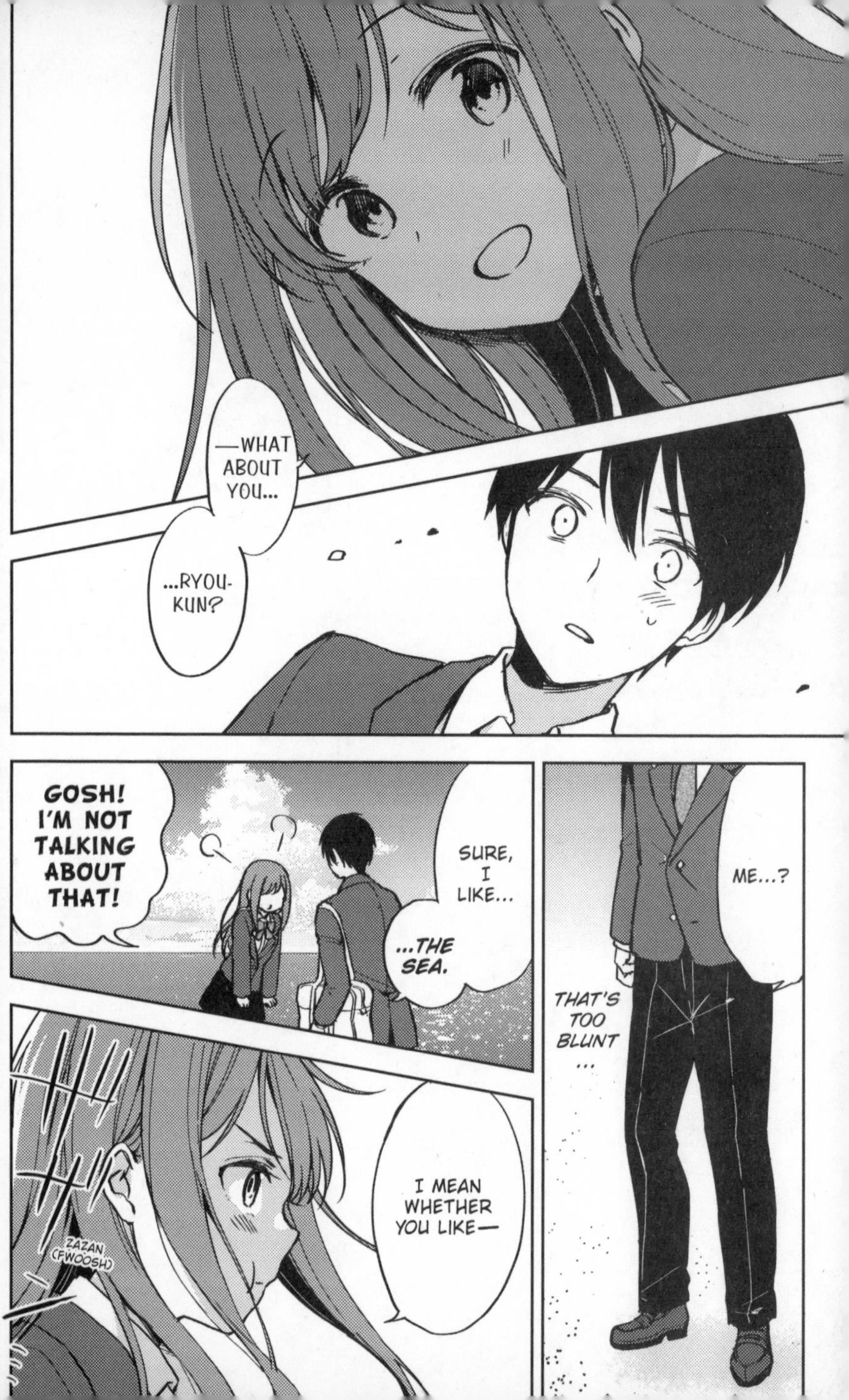
—WHAT ABOUT YOU...
...RYOU-KUN?
ME...?
THAT'S TOO BLUNT ...
SURE, I LIKE...
...THE SEA.
GOSH! I'M NOT TALKING ABOUT THAT!
I MEAN WHETHER YOU LIKE—
ZAZAN (FWOOSH)

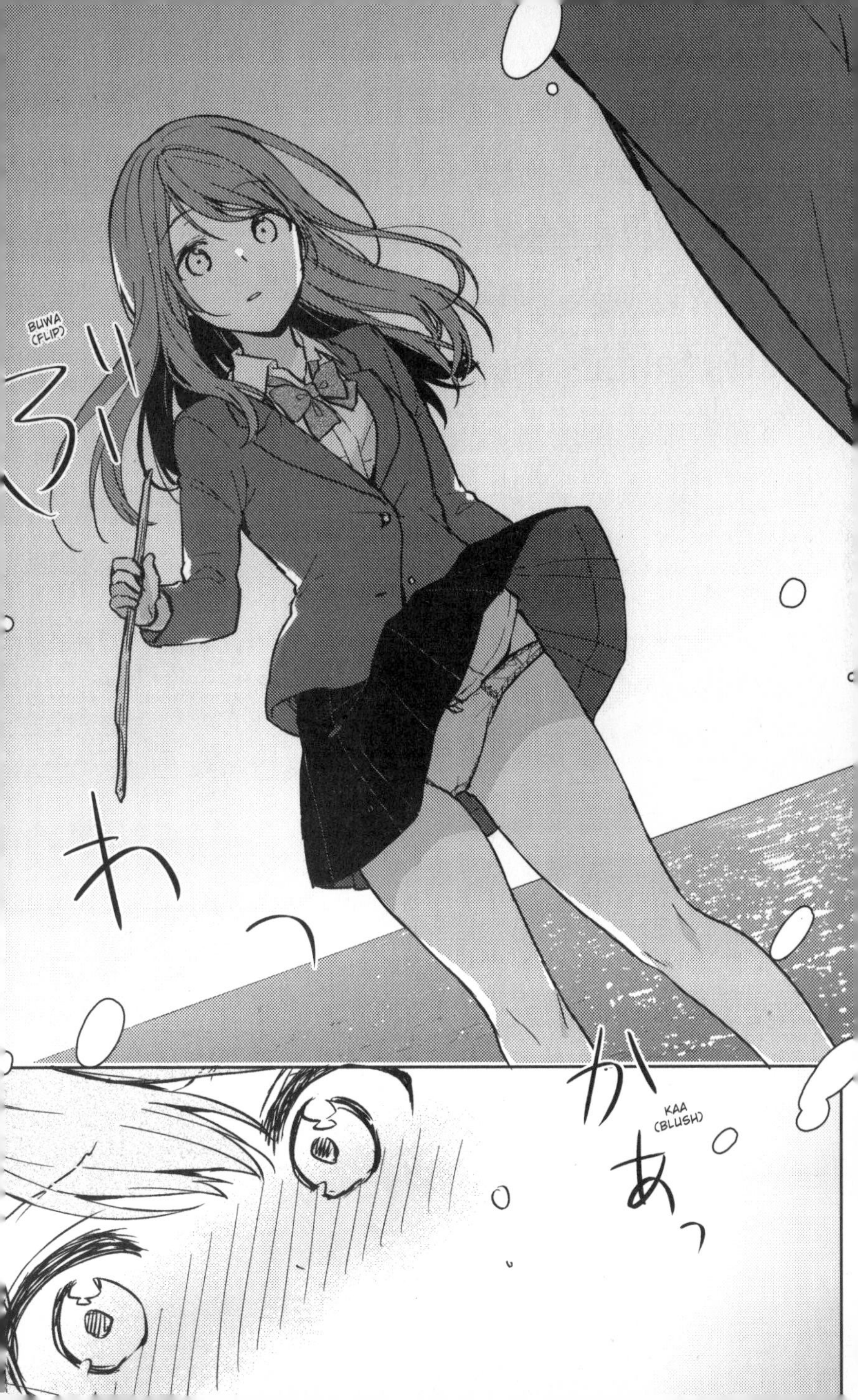
BUWA (FLIP)
ふわっ
KAA (BLUSH)
かあっ

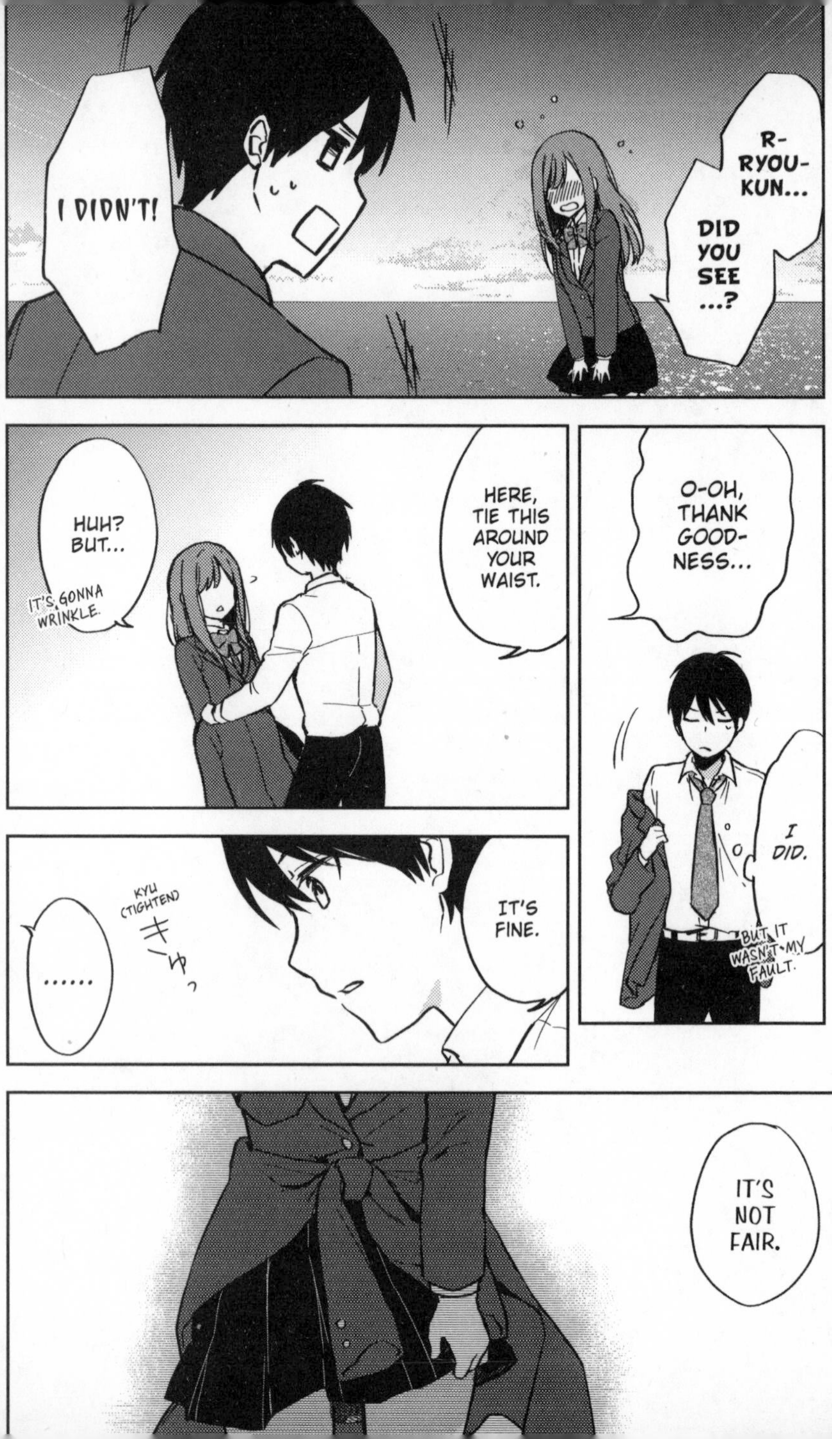
R-RYOU-KUN... DID YOU SEE ...?
I DIDN'T!
O-OH, THANK GOOD-NESS...
I DID.
BUT IT WASN'T MY FAULT.
HERE, TIE THIS AROUND YOUR WAIST.
HUH? BUT...
IT'S GONNA WRINKLE.
IT'S FINE.
KYU (TIGHTEN)
きゅっ
......
IT'S NOT FAIR.

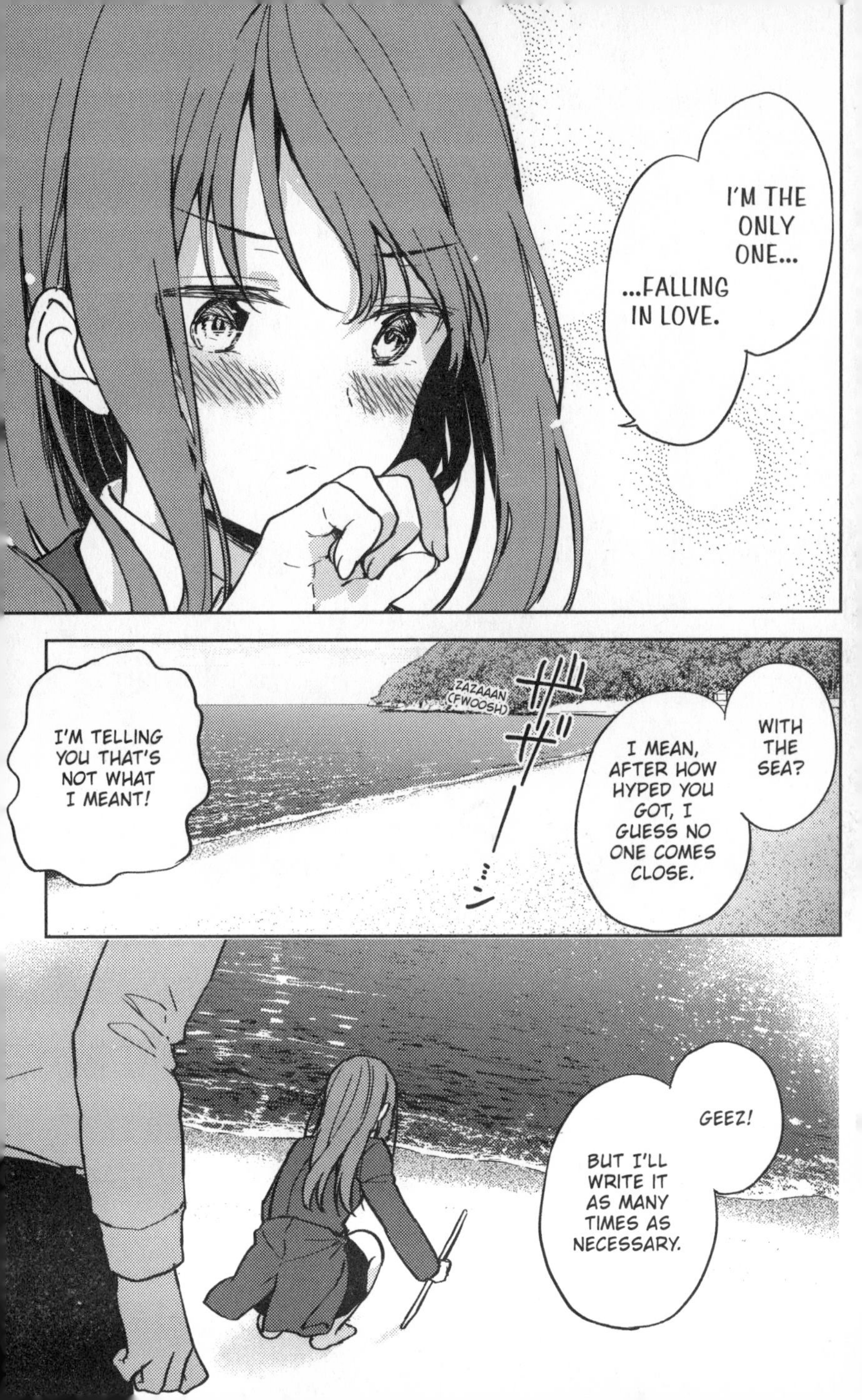
I'M THE ONLY ONE...
...FALLING IN LOVE.
WITH THE SEA?
I MEAN, AFTER HOW HYPED YOU GOT, I GUESS NO ONE COMES CLOSE.
ZAZAAAN (FWOOSH)
I'M TELLING YOU THAT'S NOT WHAT I MEANT!
GEEZ!
BUT I'LL WRITE IT AS MANY TIMES AS NECESSARY.

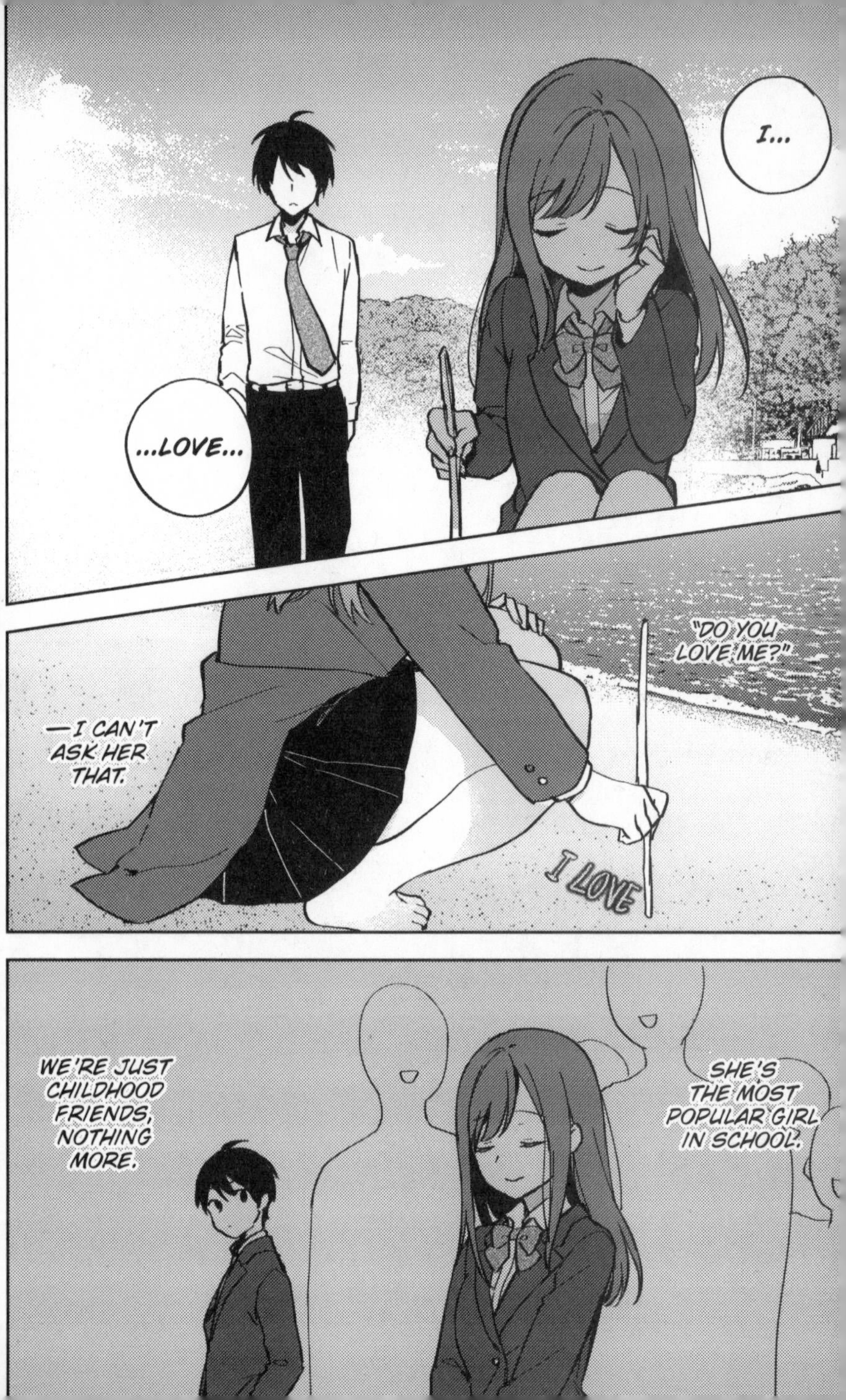
I...
...LOVE...
"DO YOU LOVE ME?"
—I CAN'T ASK HER THAT.
I LOVE
SHE'S THE MOST POPULAR GIRL IN SCHOOL.
WE'RE JUST CHILDHOOD FRIENDS, NOTHING MORE.

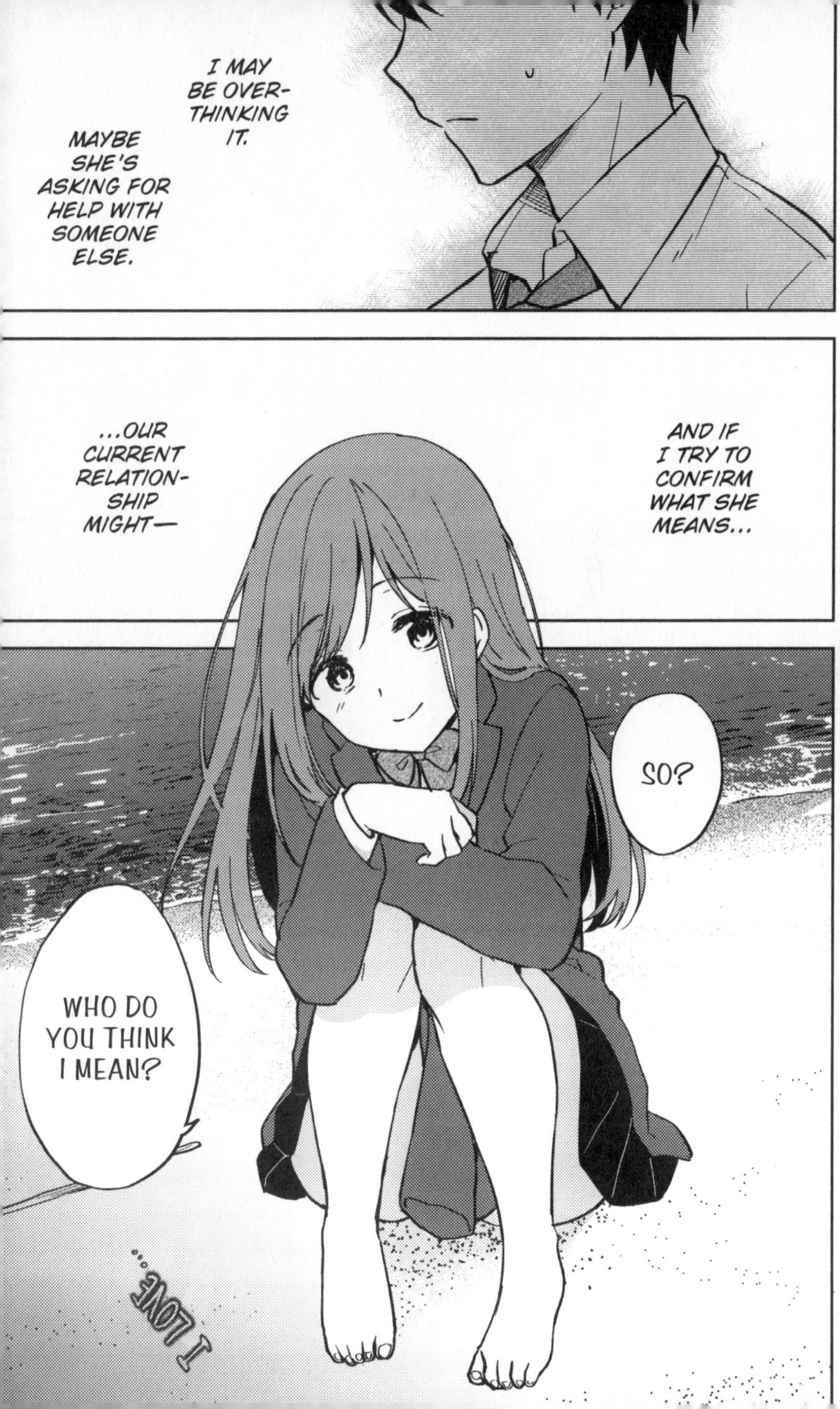
I MAY BE OVER-THINKING IT.
MAYBE SHE'S ASKING FOR HELP WITH SOMEONE ELSE.
AND IF I TRY TO CONFIRM WHAT SHE MEANS...
...OUR CURRENT RELATION-SHIP MIGHT—
SO?
WHO DO YOU THINK I MEAN?
I LOVE...

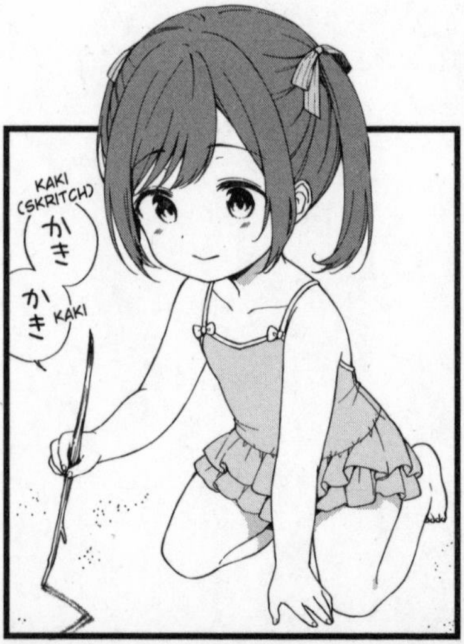

KAKI (SKRITCH)
かき
かき
KAKI

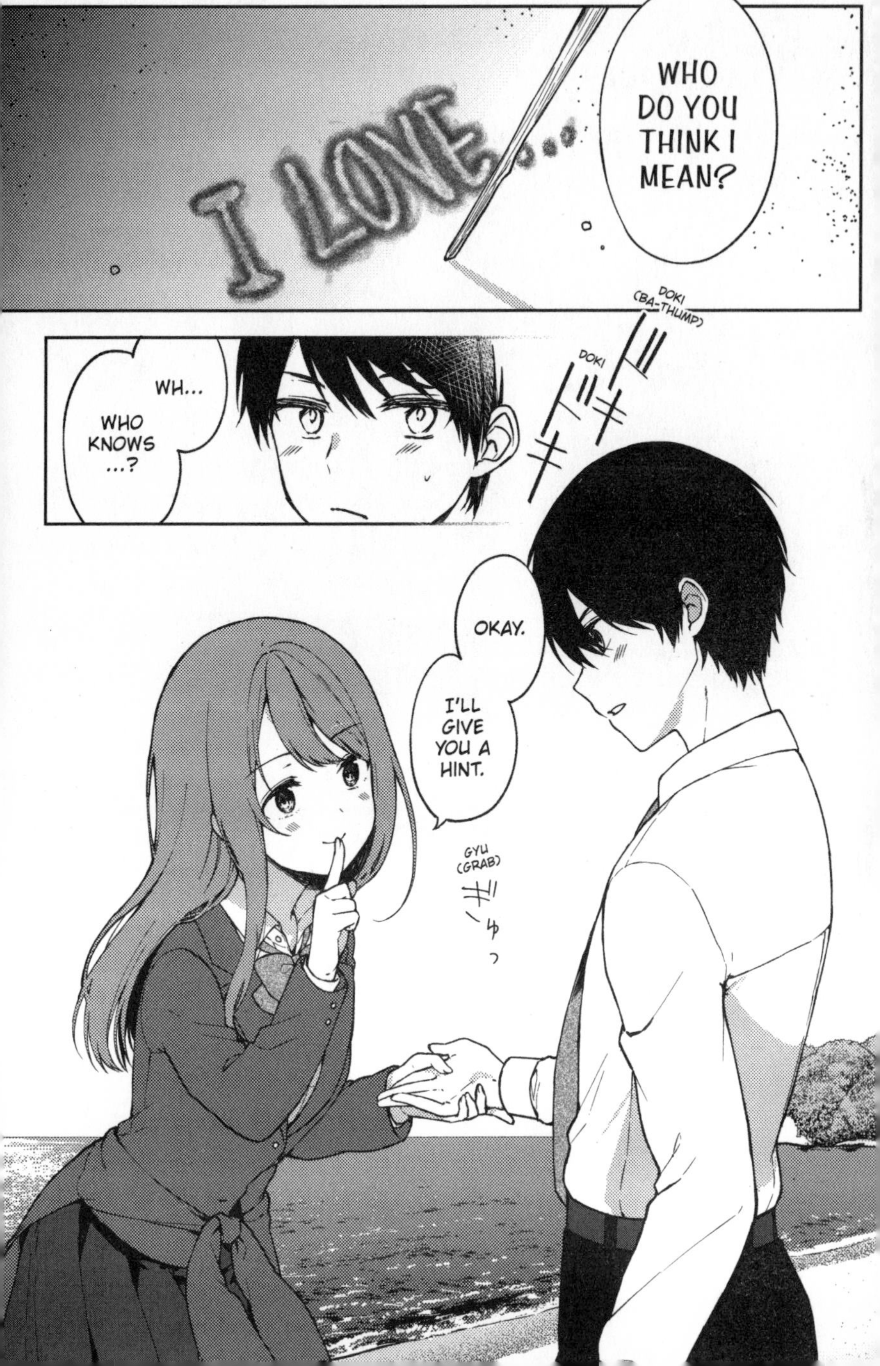
WHO DO YOU THINK I MEAN?
I LOVE...
DOKI (BA-THUMP)
DOKI
WH... WHO KNOWS ...?
OKAY.
I'LL GIVE YOU A HINT.
GYU (GRAB)

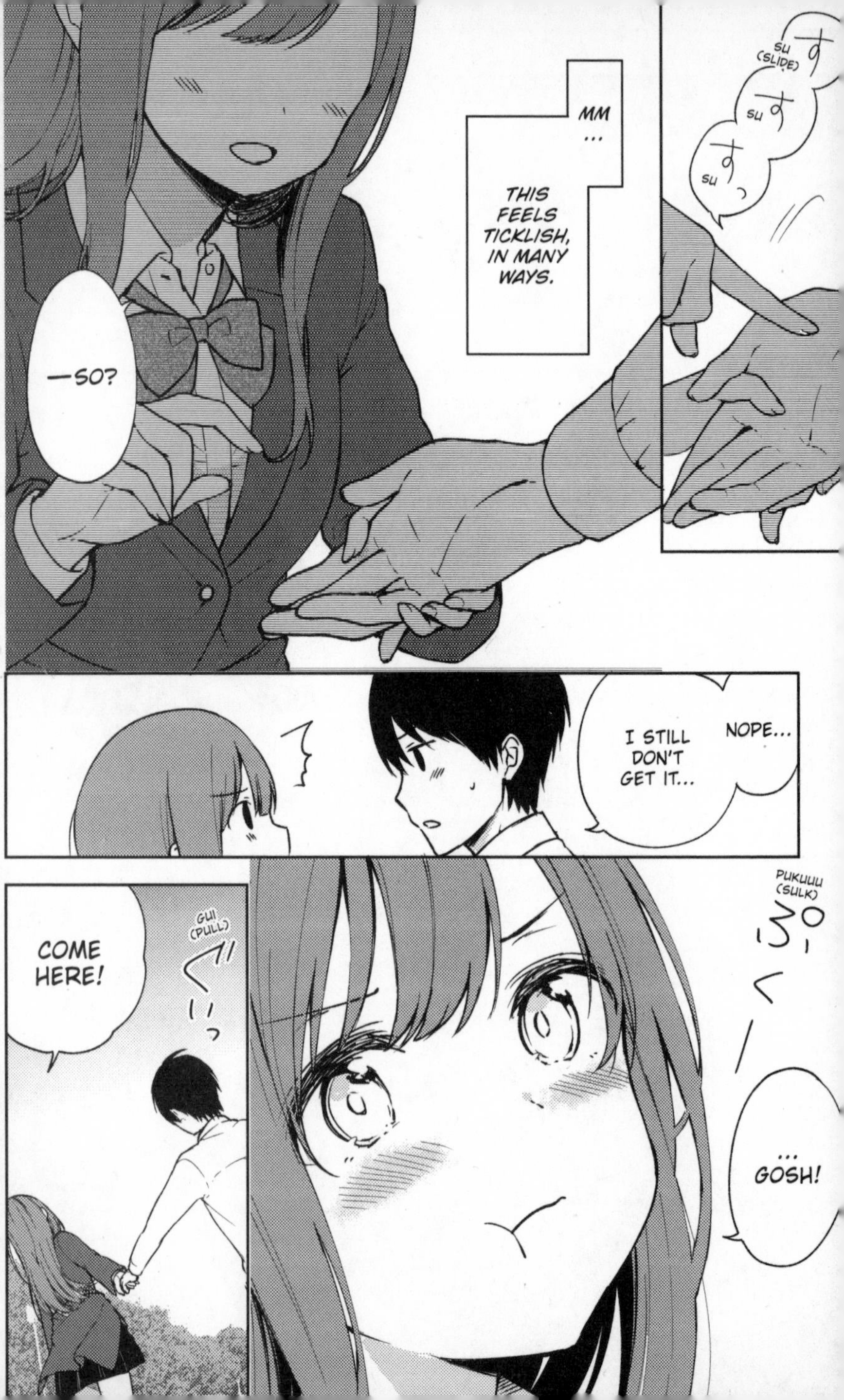

す SU (SLIDE)
す SU
すっ SU
MM... THIS FEELS TICKLISH, IN MANY WAYS.
—SO?
NOPE...
I STILL DON'T GET IT...
ぷくー PUKUUU (SULK)
...GOSH!
COME HERE!
ぐいっ GUI (PULL)

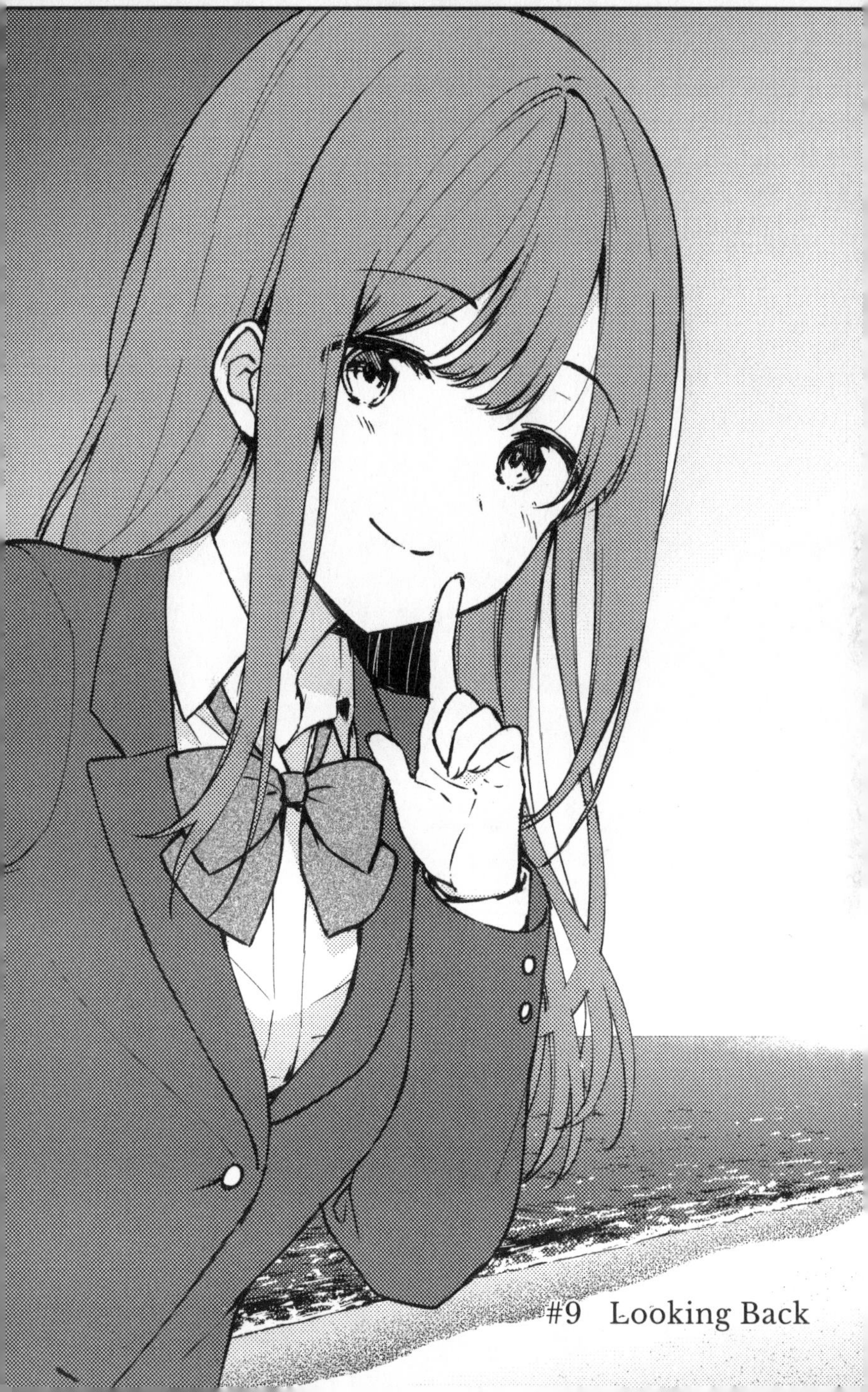

#9 Looking Back

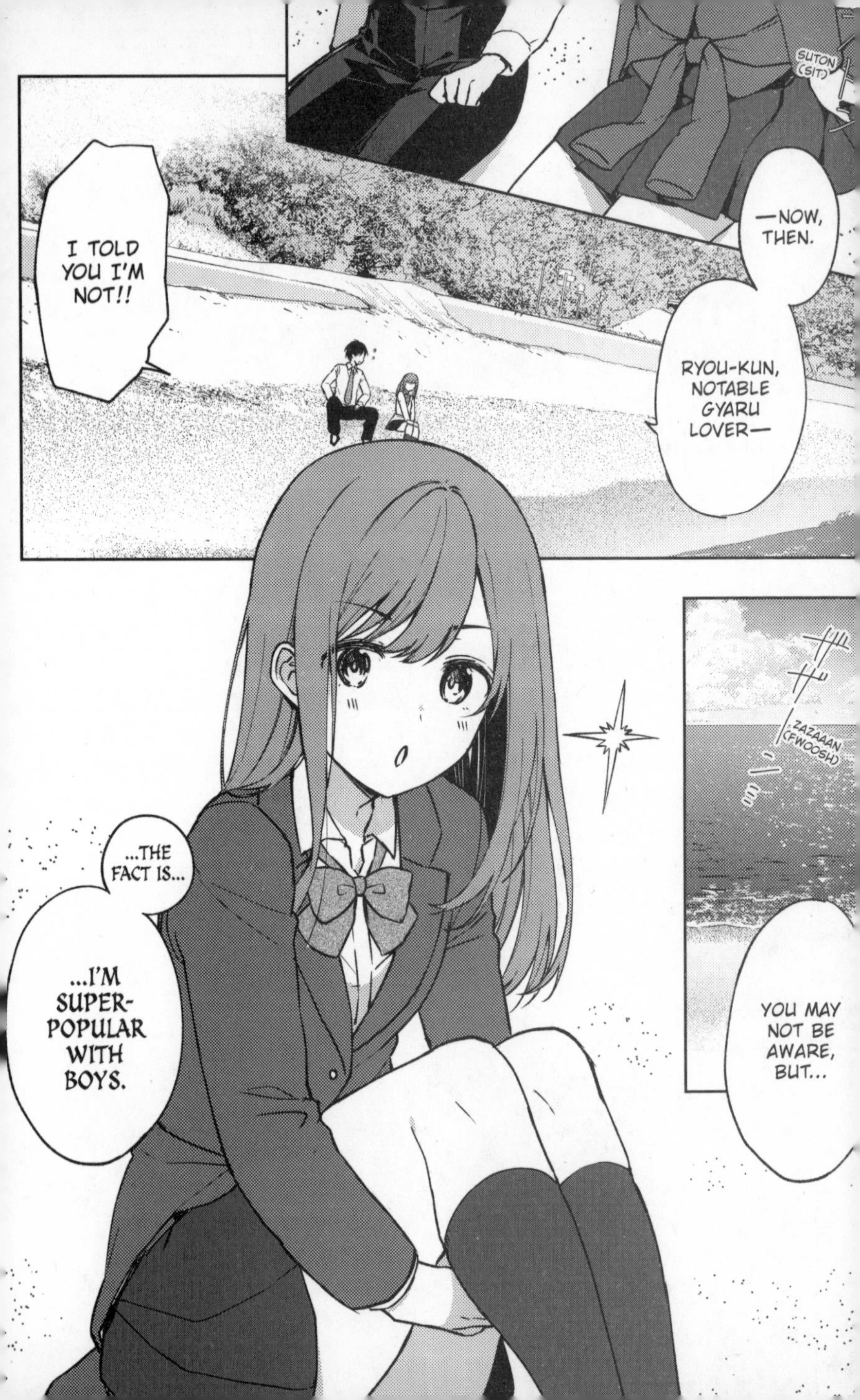
SUTON (SIT)
—NOW, THEN.
RYOU-KUN, NOTABLE GYARU LOVER—
I TOLD YOU I'M NOT!!
ZAZAAAN (FWOOSH)
YOU MAY NOT BE AWARE, BUT...
...THE FACT IS...
...I'M SUPER-POPULAR WITH BOYS.

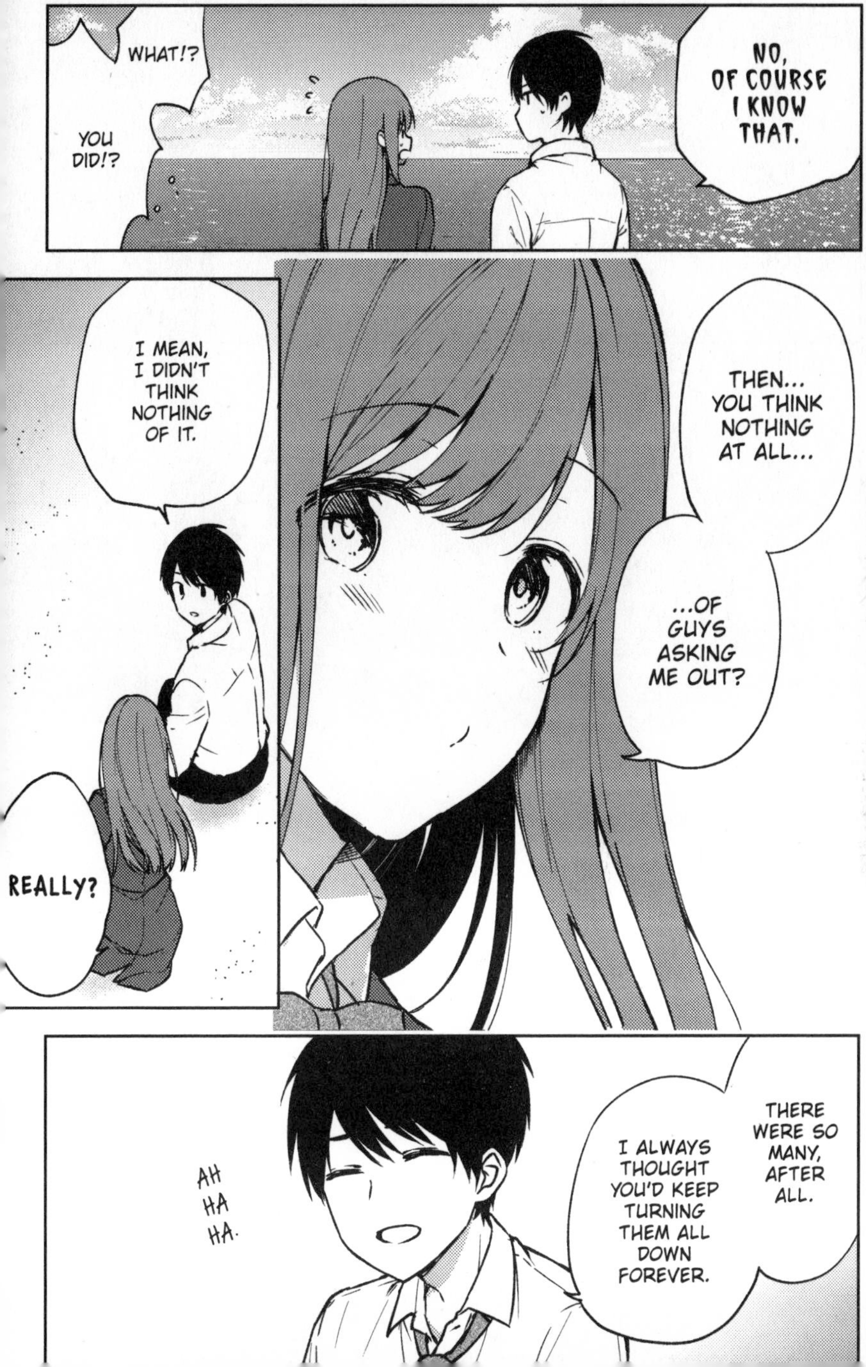
NO, OF COURSE I KNOW THAT.
WHAT!?
YOU DID!?
THEN... YOU THINK NOTHING AT ALL...
...OF GUYS ASKING ME OUT?
I MEAN, I DIDN'T THINK NOTHING OF IT.
REALLY?
THERE WERE SO MANY, AFTER ALL.
I ALWAYS THOUGHT YOU'D KEEP TURNING THEM ALL DOWN FOREVER.
AH HA HA.

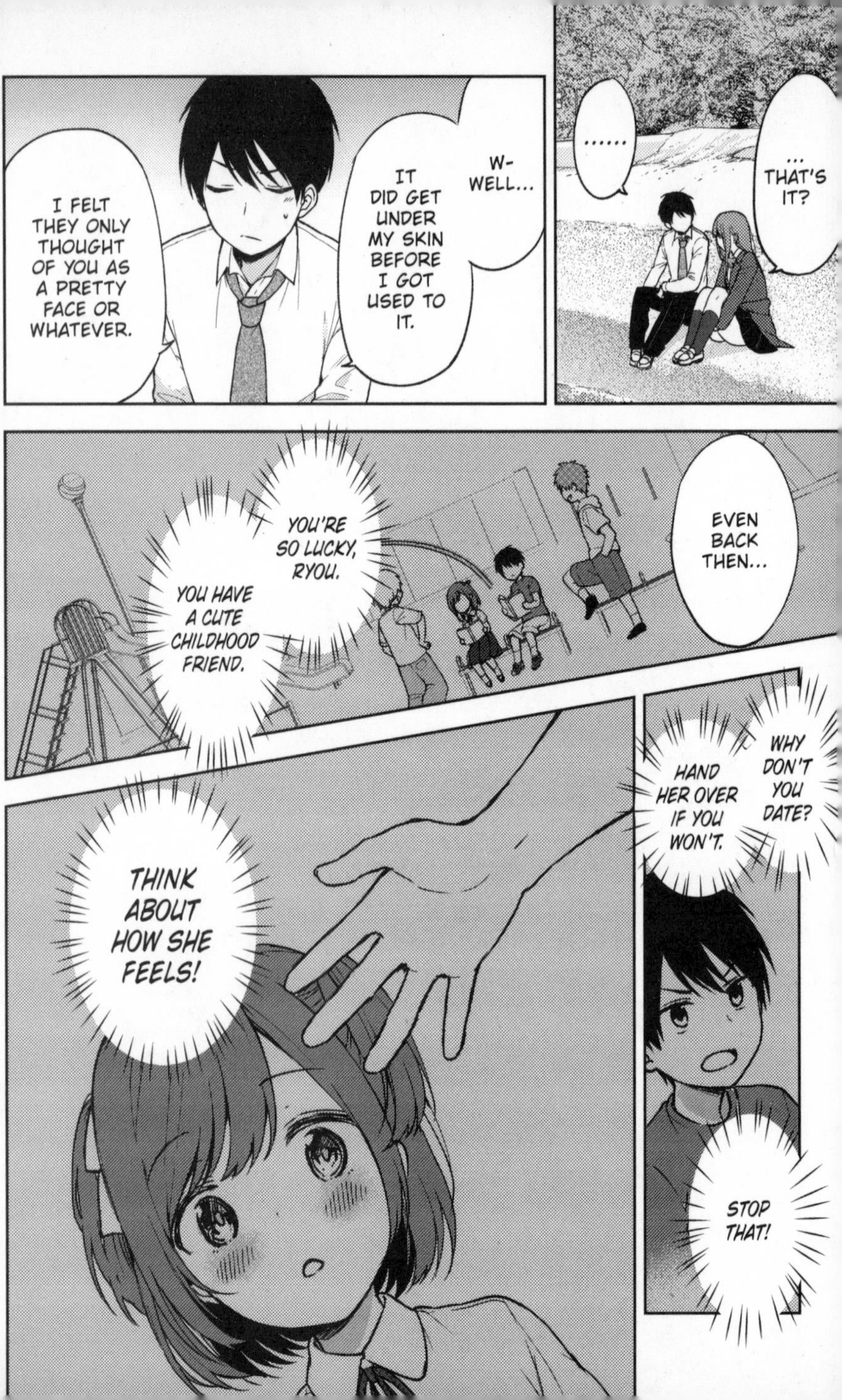
... THAT'S IT?
......
W- WELL...
IT DID GET UNDER MY SKIN BEFORE I GOT USED TO IT.
I FELT THEY ONLY THOUGHT OF YOU AS A PRETTY FACE OR WHATEVER.
EVEN BACK THEN...
YOU'RE SO LUCKY, RYOU.
YOU HAVE A CUTE CHILDHOOD FRIEND.
WHY DON'T YOU DATE?
HAND HER OVER IF YOU WON'T.
STOP THAT!
THINK ABOUT HOW SHE FEELS!

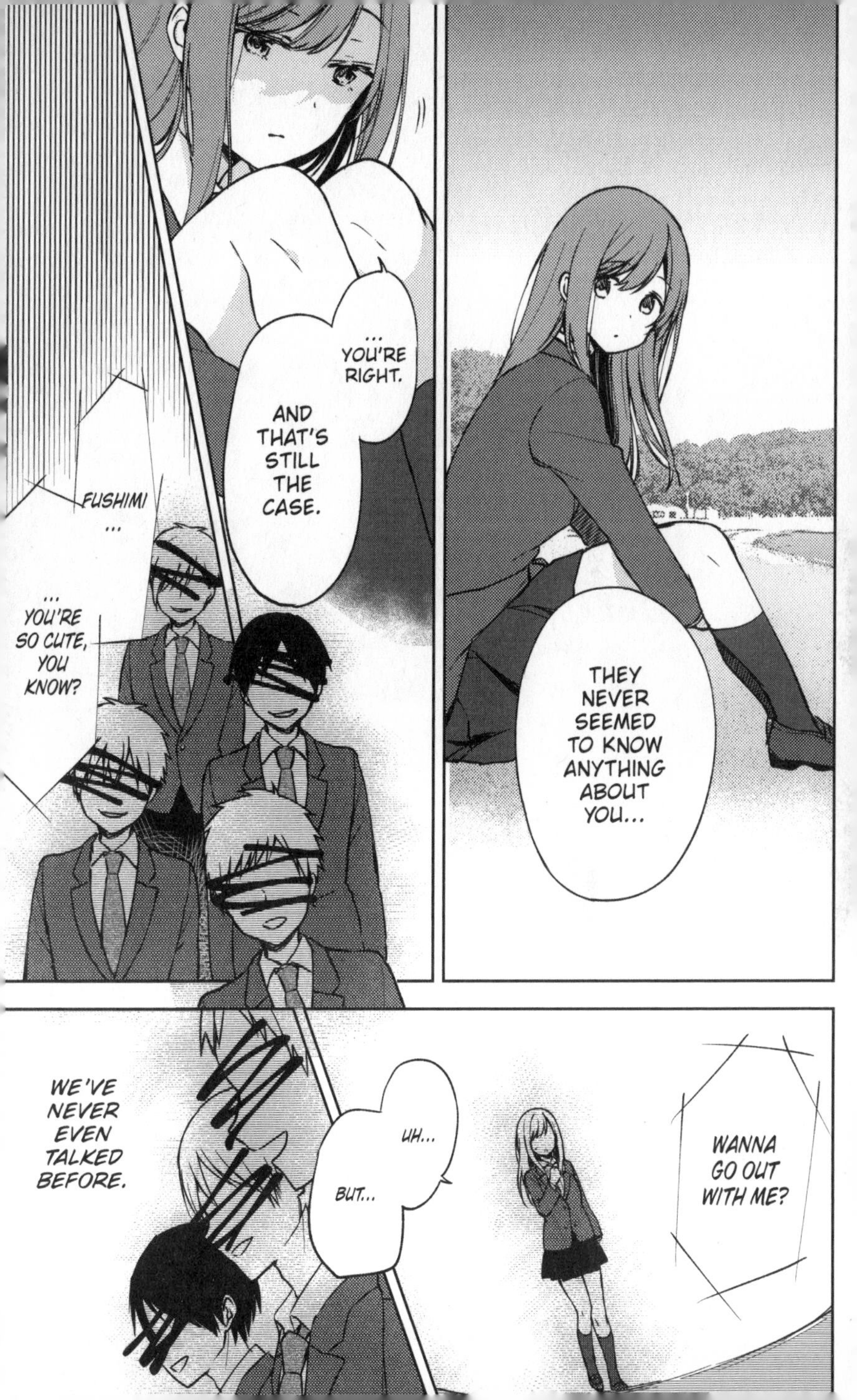
THEY NEVER SEEMED TO KNOW ANYTHING ABOUT YOU...
...YOU'RE RIGHT.
AND THAT'S STILL THE CASE.
FUSHIMI...
...YOU'RE SO CUTE, YOU KNOW?
WANNA GO OUT WITH ME?
UH...
BUT...
WE'VE NEVER EVEN TALKED BEFORE.

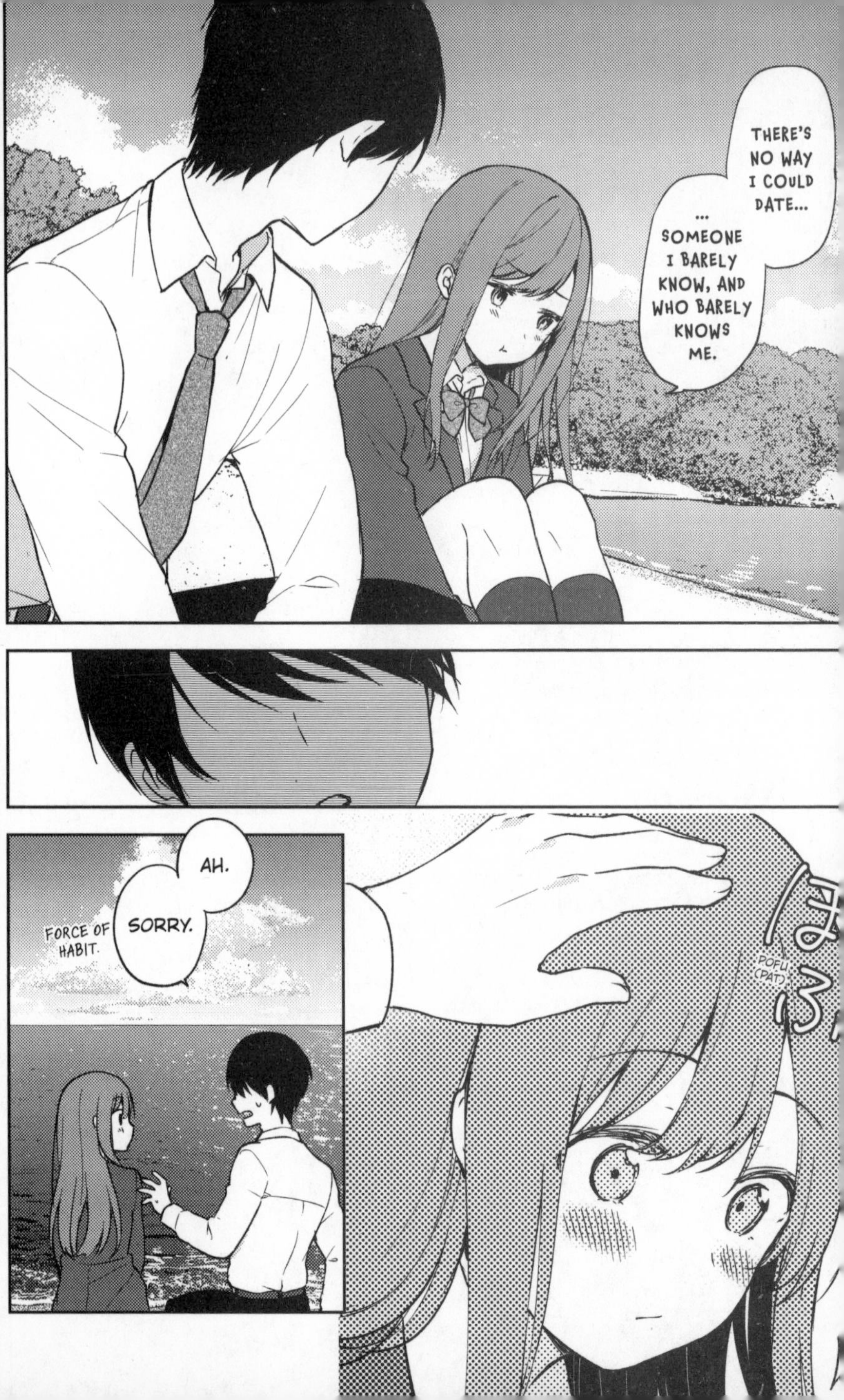
THERE'S NO WAY I COULD DATE...
...SOMEONE I BARELY KNOW, AND WHO BARELY KNOWS ME.
ぽふ
POFU (PAT)
AH.
SORRY.
FORCE OF HABIT.

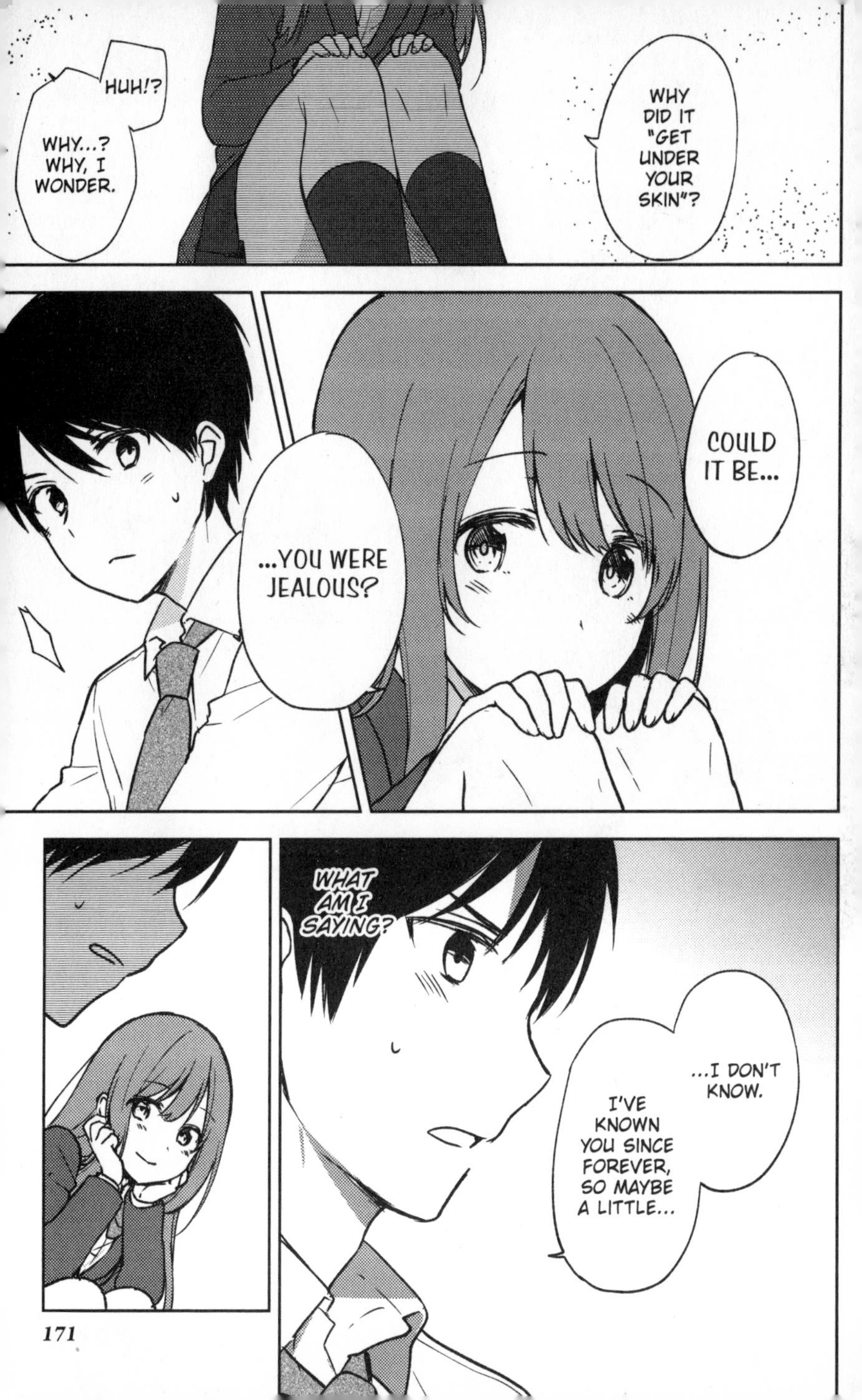
WHY DID IT "GET UNDER YOUR SKIN"?
HUH!?
WHY...? WHY, I WONDER.
COULD IT BE...
...YOU WERE JEALOUS?
WHAT AM I SAYING?
...I DON'T KNOW.
I'VE KNOWN YOU SINCE FOREVER, SO MAYBE A LITTLE...

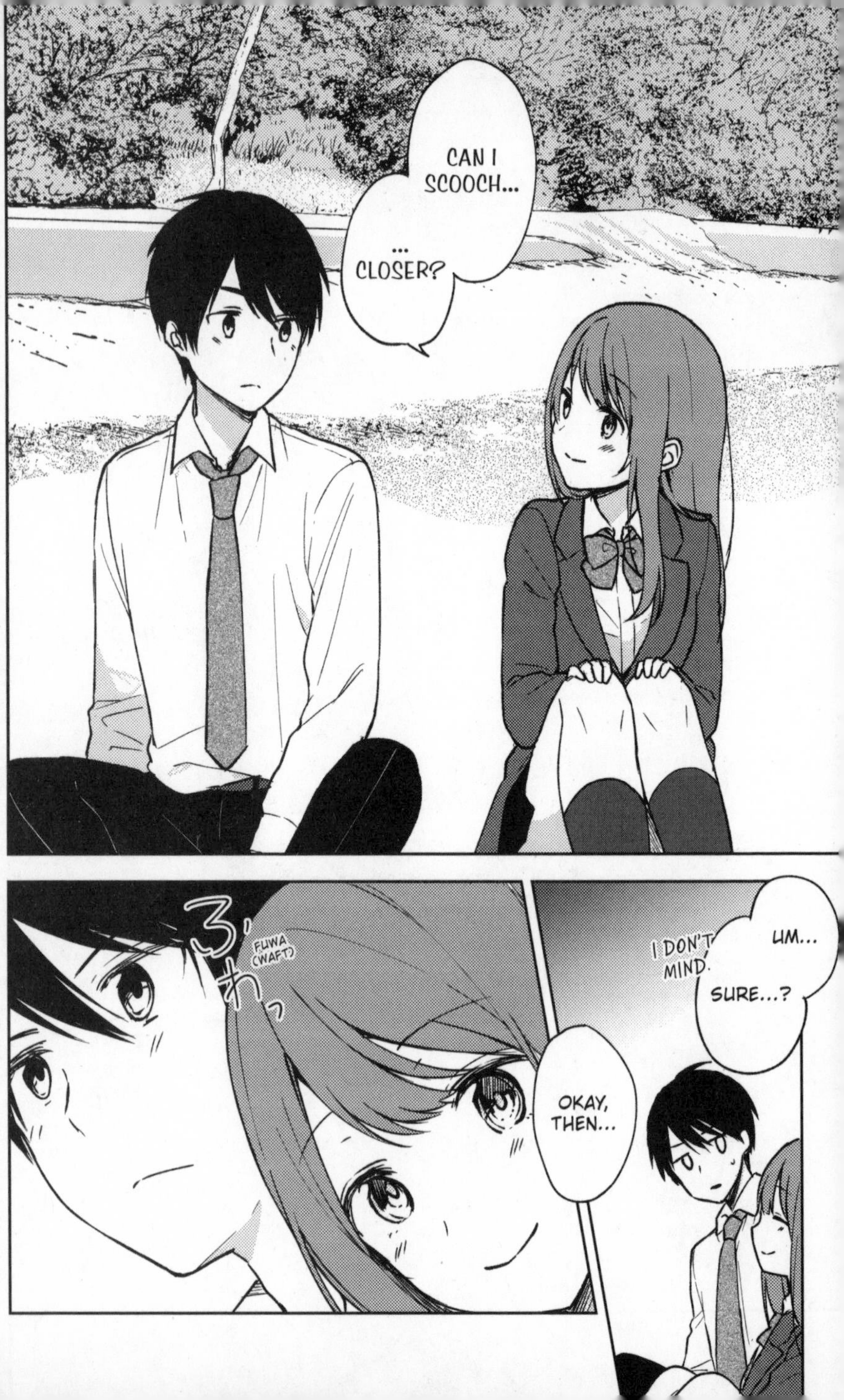
CAN I SCOOCH...
...CLOSER?
UM... SURE...?
I DON'T MIND.
OKAY, THEN...
ふわっ
FUWA (WAFT)

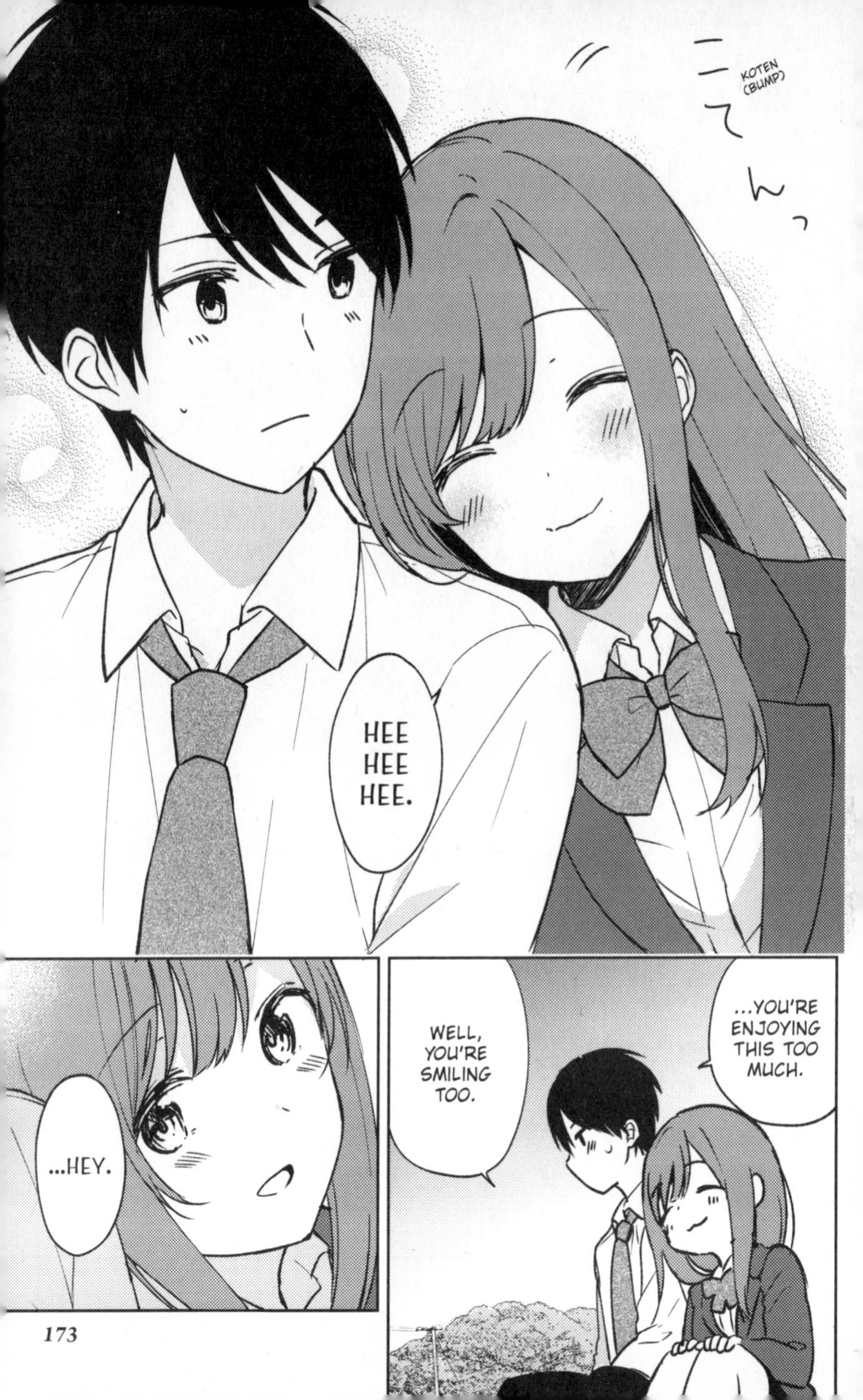
こてんっ
KOTEN (BUMP)
HEE HEE HEE.
...YOU'RE ENJOYING THIS TOO MUCH.
WELL, YOU'RE SMILING TOO.
...HEY.

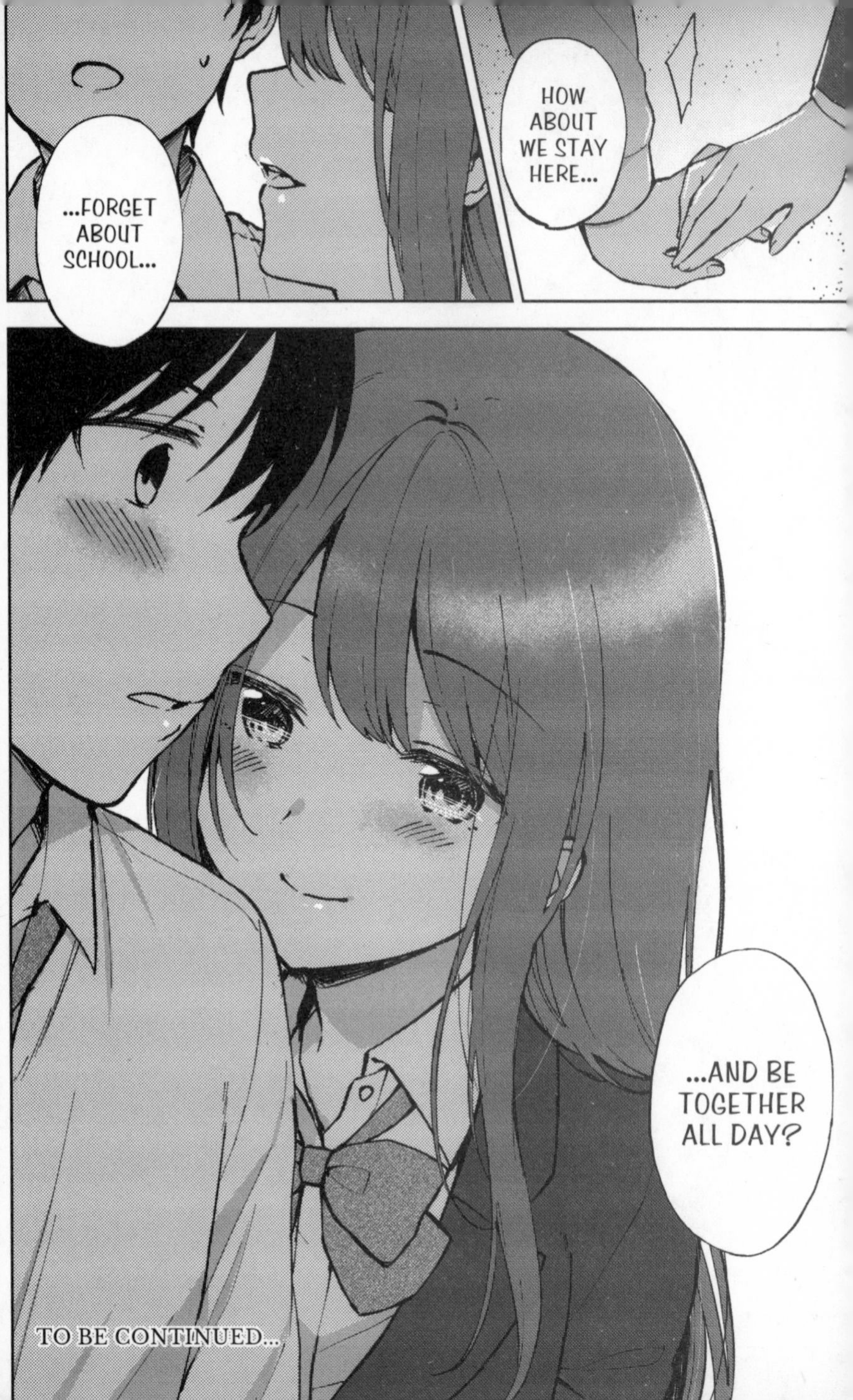
HOW ABOUT WE STAY HERE...
...FORGET ABOUT SCHOOL...
...AND BE TOGETHER ALL DAY?
TO BE CONTINUED...

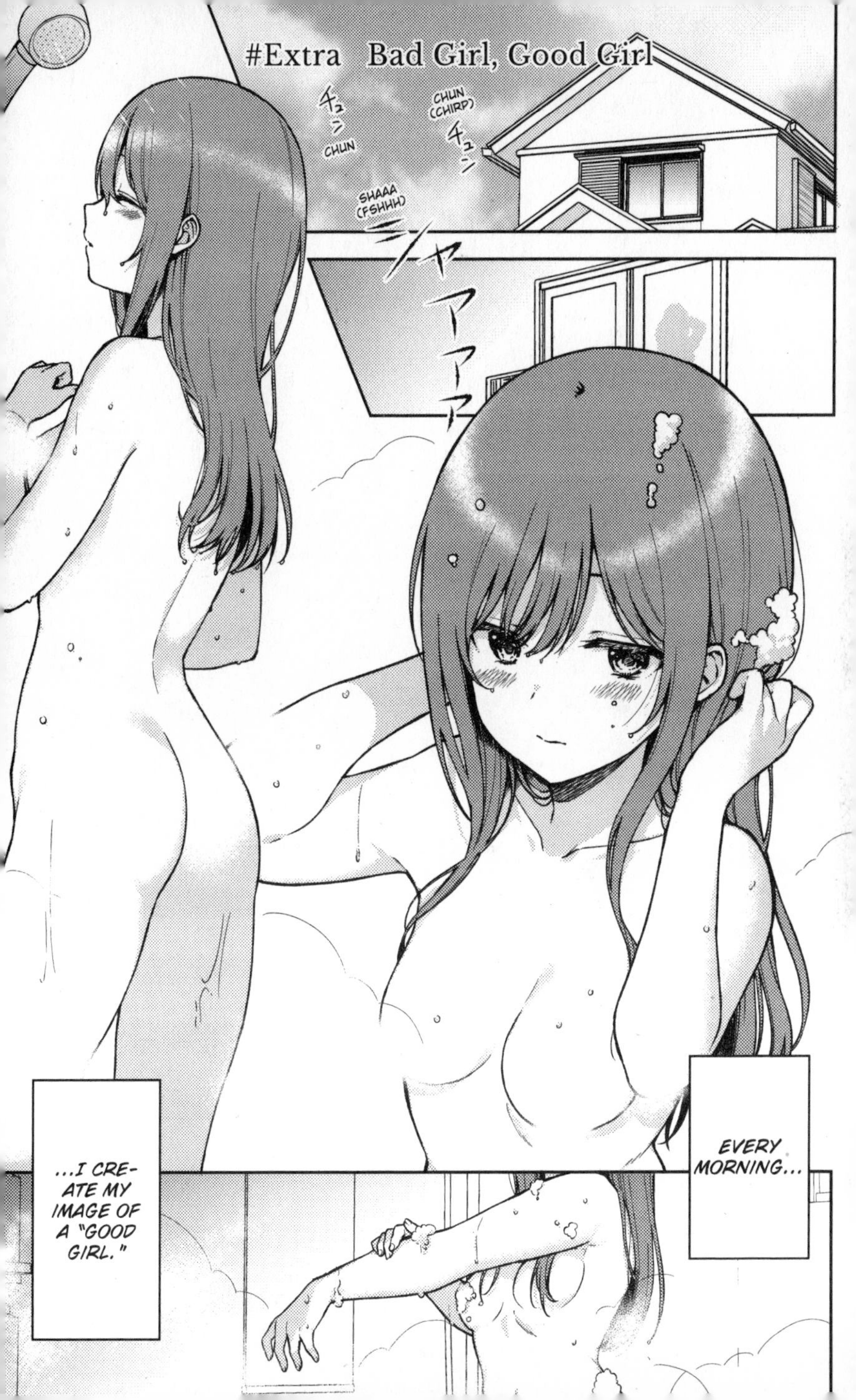
#Extra Bad Girl, Good Girl
CHUN (CHIRP)
CHUN
SHAAA (FSHHH)
EVERY MORNING...
...I CRE-ATE MY IMAGE OF A "GOOD GIRL."

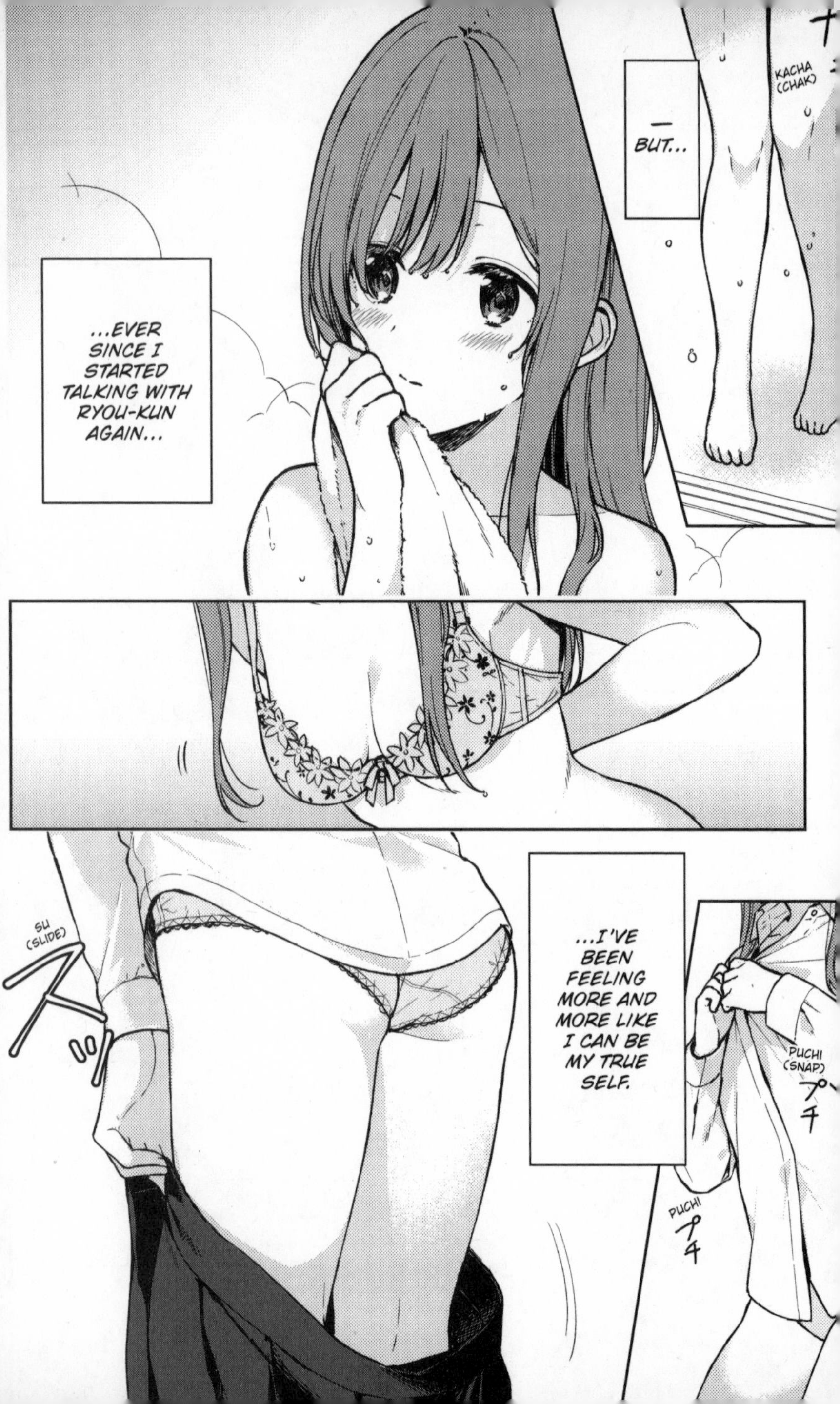
KACHA (CHAK)
—BUT...
...EVER SINCE I STARTED TALKING WITH RYOU-KUN AGAIN...
PUCHI (SNAP)
PUCHI
...I'VE BEEN FEELING MORE AND MORE LIKE I CAN BE MY TRUE SELF.
SU (SLIDE)

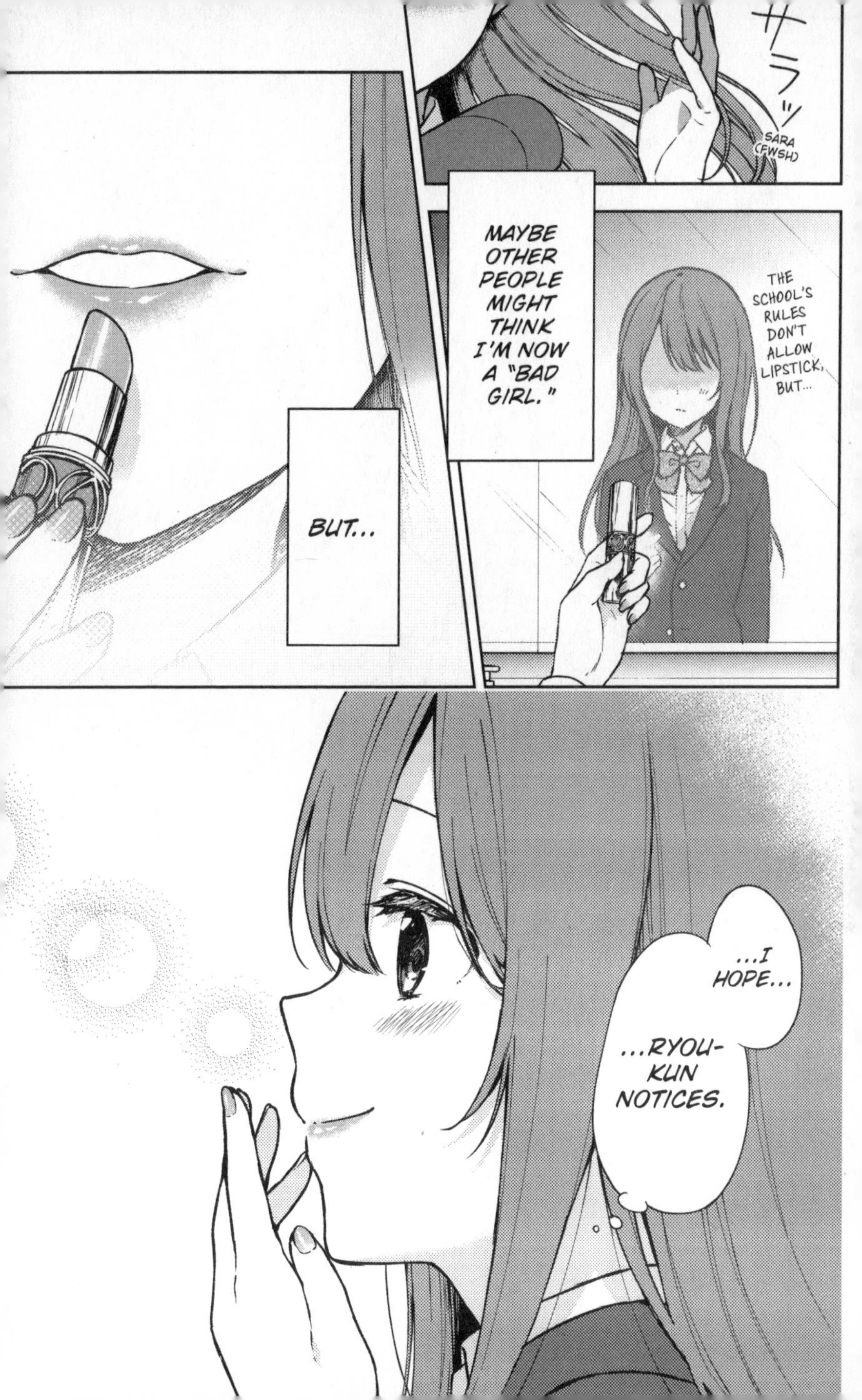
サラッ
SARA (FWSH)
THE SCHOOL'S RULES DON'T ALLOW LIPSTICK, BUT...
MAYBE OTHER PEOPLE MIGHT THINK I'M NOW A "BAD GIRL."
BUT...
...I HOPE...
...RYOU-KUN NOTICES.

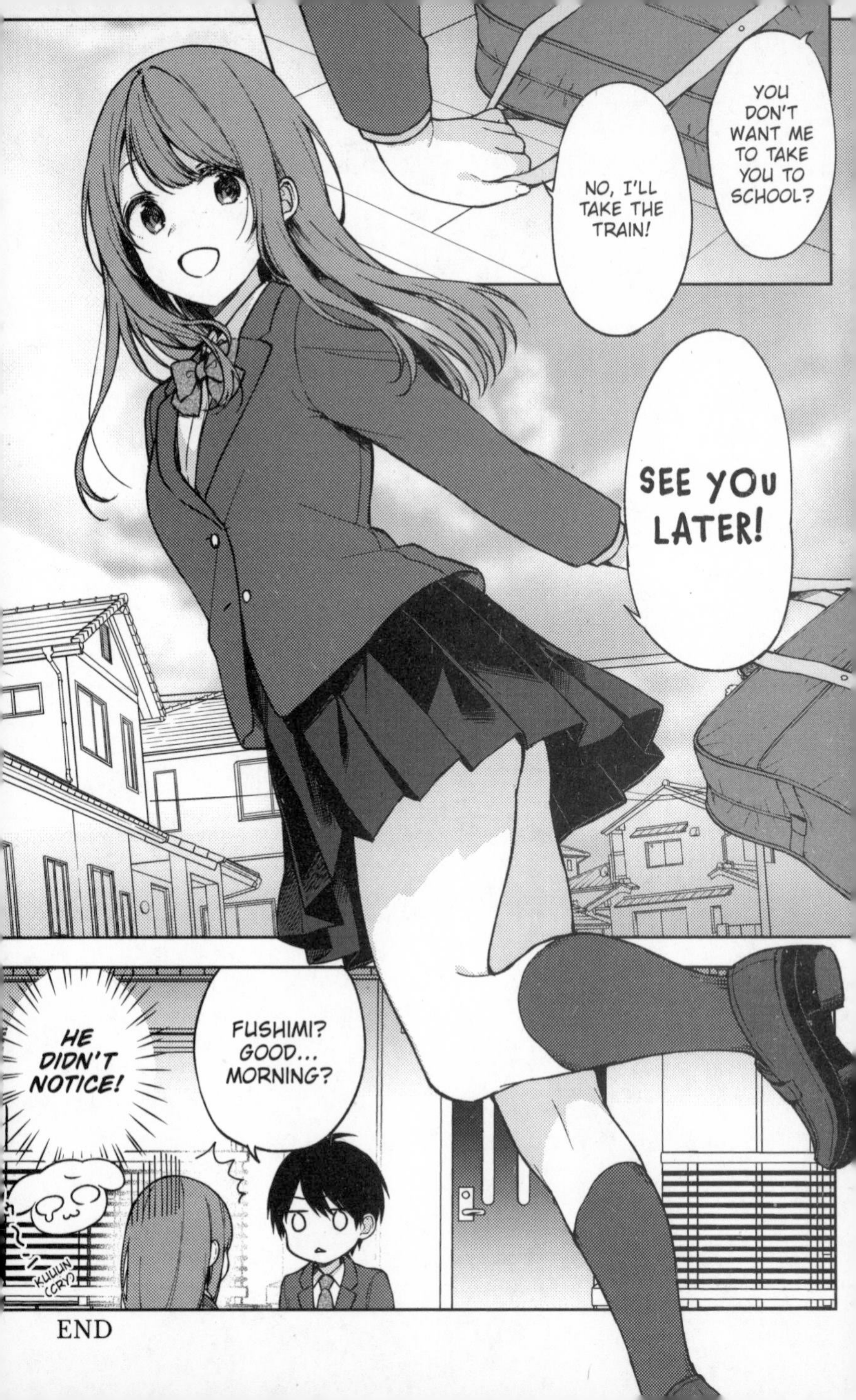
YOU DON'T WANT ME TO TAKE YOU TO SCHOOL?
NO, I'LL TAKE THE TRAIN!
SEE YOU LATER!
FUSHIMI? GOOD... MORNING?
HE DIDN'T NOTICE!
KUUUN (CRY)

END

The Girl I Saved on the
Train Turned Out to Be
My Childhood Friend

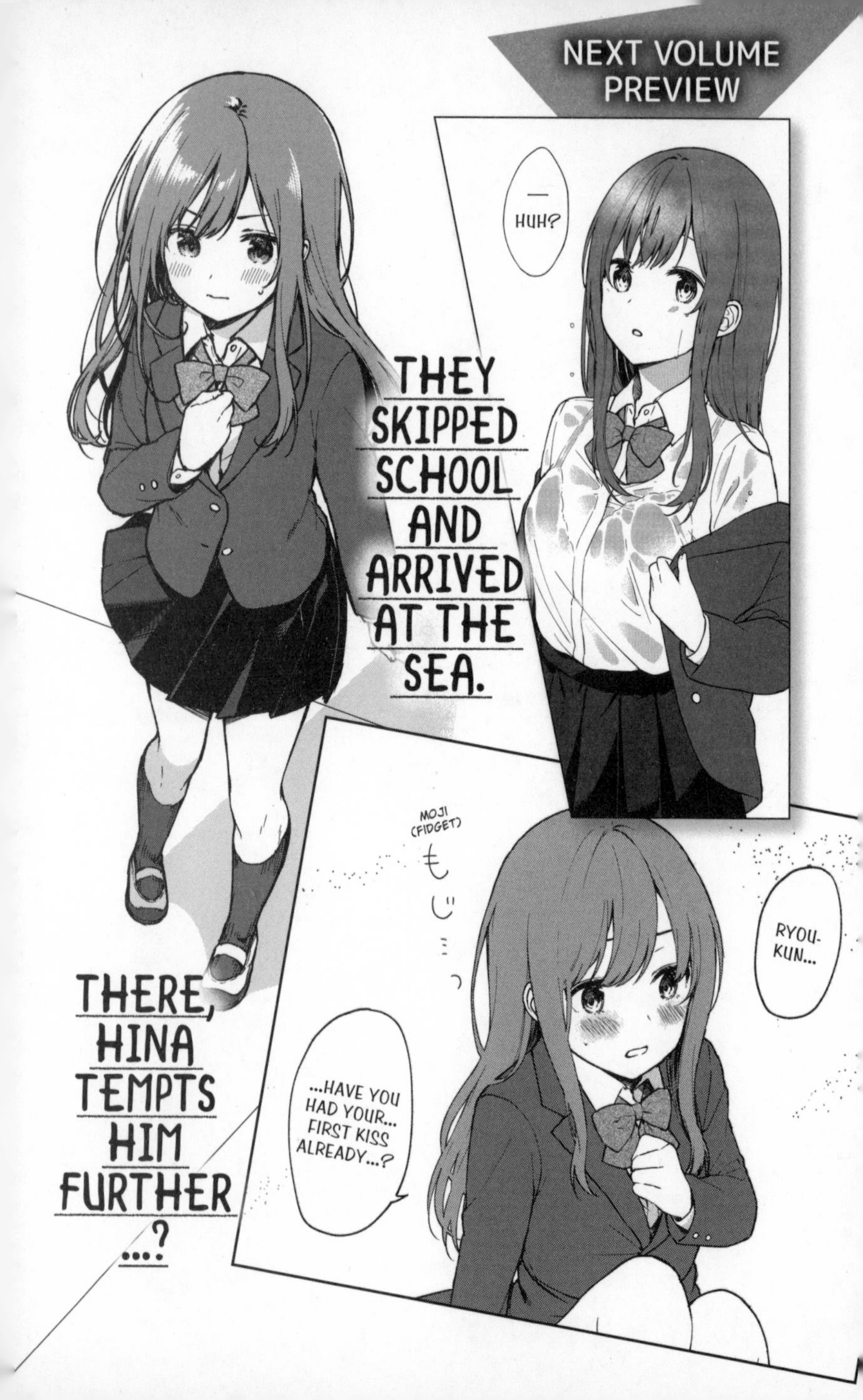
NEXT VOLUME PREVIEW
—HUH?
THEY SKIPPED SCHOOL AND ARRIVED AT THE SEA.
MOJI (FIDGET) もじっ
RYOU-KUN...
...HAVE YOU HAD YOUR... FIRST KISS ALREADY...?
THERE, HINA TEMPTS HIM FURTHER...?

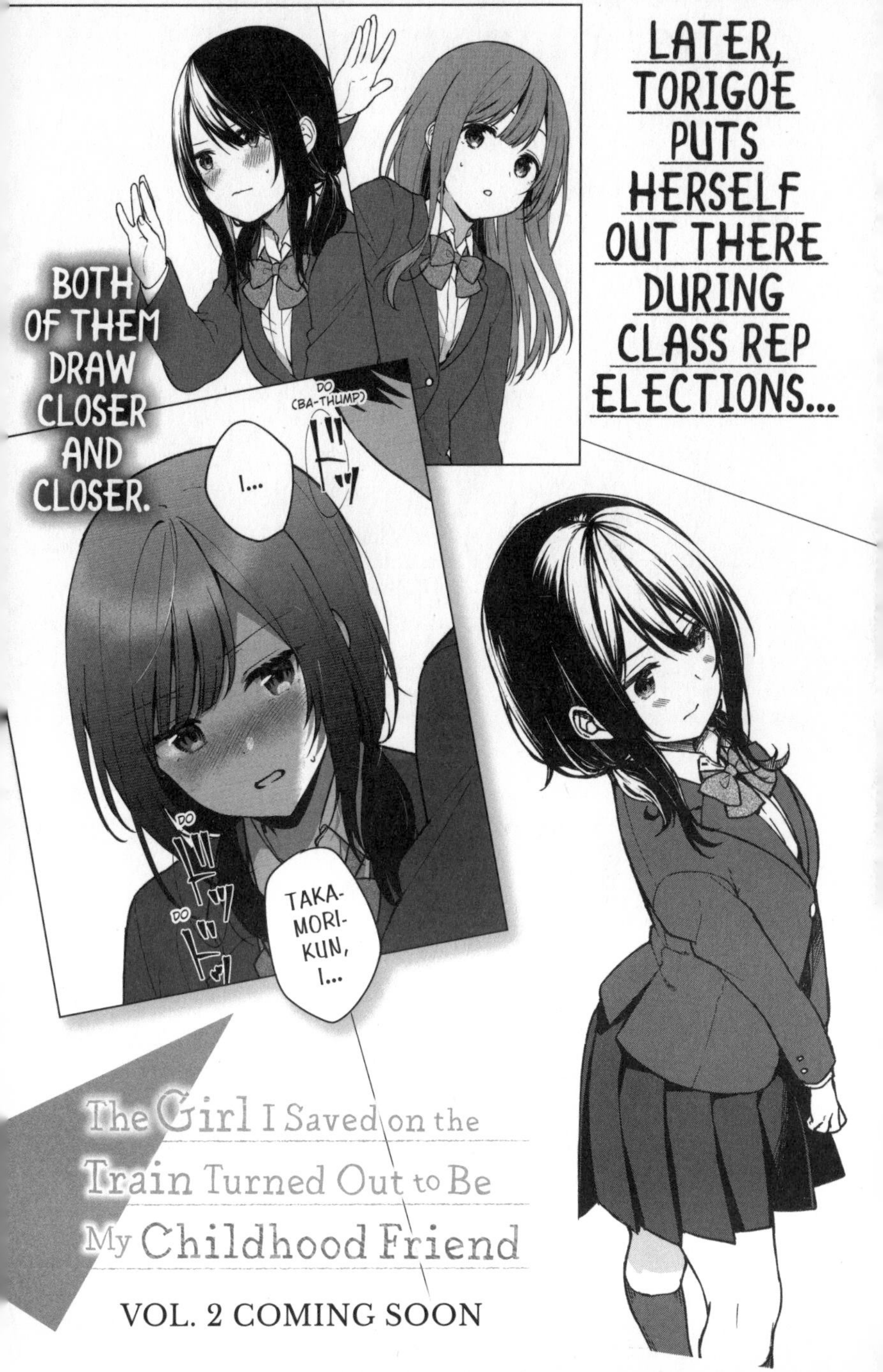
LATER, TORIGOE PUTS HERSELF OUT THERE DURING CLASS REP ELECTIONS...
BOTH OF THEM DRAW CLOSER AND CLOSER.
DO (BA-THUMP)
I...
DO
DO
TAKA-MORI-KUN, I...
The Girl I Saved on the Train Turned Out to Be My Childhood Friend
VOL. 2 COMING SOON

TRANSLATION NOTES

COMMON HONORIFICS

-san: The Japanese equivalent of Mr./Mrs./Miss.
If a situation calls for politeness, this is the fail-safe honorific.
-kun: Used most often when referring to boys, this indicates affection or
familiarity. Occasionally used by older men among their peers, but it may
also be used by anyone referring to a person of lower standing.
-chan: An affectionate honorific indicating familiarity used mostly in reference
to girls; also used in reference to cute persons or animals of either gender.
no honorific: Indicates familiarity or closeness; if used without permission or
reason, addressing someone in this manner would constitute an insult.
-niisan, nii-san, etc.: A term of endearment meaning "big brother" that may be more
widely used to address any young man who is like a brother, regardless of whether
he is related.

Page 19
Given name: Calling someone by their first name or without any honorific is done only
by those with a close relationship, such as friends. When Hina and Ryou grew apart, they
reverted to calling each other by their family names. And because their classmates are
unaware of their shared history, Hina is careful to call him Takamori-kun in front of
others.

Page 52
LINE: Hina and Ryou, and the rest of their classmates, are using the LINE app, which is
a popular messaging service in Japan that boasts a wide variety of cute stickers.

Page 60
Death from embarrassment: The Japanese word used here is *hazukashi* or 恥ずかし, which
in and of itself means "embarrassment." However, the character for *shi* has been swapped
for the Chinese character 死, which means "to die" and is also pronounced as "shi."

Page 79
Gyaru: A transliteration of the English word "gal," *gyaru* refers to someone who adheres to
the *gyaru* fashion subculture. It encompasses countless different substyles, but it loosely
refers to fashion that sticks out from the current norm. The stereotypical image of a *gyaru*
is that of a girl who dresses more risqué, sports heavy makeup and dyed hair, and heavily
uses slang.

Page 99
Niini: An affectionate nickname that is a play on *onii-san*, the Japanese word for "big
brother."

Page 144
Hina's drawing: *Aiaigasa*, or two people sharing one umbrella, can be seen as a romantic
gesture, as *ai* also sounds like the Japanese word for love. The little doodle of the umbrella
with a heart on top is a way to denote *aiaigasa*. Similar to writing a crush's name inside of
a heart in the West, one would usually write their name and the name of their crush under
the umbrella.

The Girl I Saved on the
Train Turned Out to Be
My Childhood Friend

There's something really strange about the maid I just hired!

No normal person could be so beautiful, or cook such amazingly delicious food, or know exactly what I want before I even ask. She must be using magic—right, a spell is the only thing that can explain why my chest feels so tight whenever I look at her. I swear, I'm going to get to the bottom of what makes this maid so...mysterious!

Volume 1-3 Now Available!

The Maid I Hired Recently Is Mysterious

I've Been Killing SLIMES for 300 Years and Maxed Out My Level

It's hard work taking it slow...

After living a painful life as an office worker, Azusa ended her short life by dying from overwork. So when she finds herself reincarnated as an undying, unaging witch in a new world, she vows to spend her days stress-free and as pleasantly as possible. She ekes out a living by hunting down the easiest targets—the slimes! But after centuries of doing this simple job, she's ended up with insane powers... how will she maintain her low-key life now?!

IN STORES NOW!

Light Novel Volumes 1–12

Manga Volumes 1–9

SLIME TAOSHITE SANBYAKUNEN, SHIRANAIUCHINI LEVEL MAX NI NATTEMASHITA © 2017 Kisetsu Morita © 2017 Benio / SB Creative Corp.

SLIME TAOSHITE SANBYAKUNEN, SHIRANAIUCHINI LEVEL MAX NI NATTEMASHITA ©Kisetsu Morita/SB Creative Corp. Original Character Designs: ©Benio/SB Creative Corp. ©2018 Yusuke Shiba /SQUARE ENIX CO., LTD.

For more information, visit www.yenpress.com

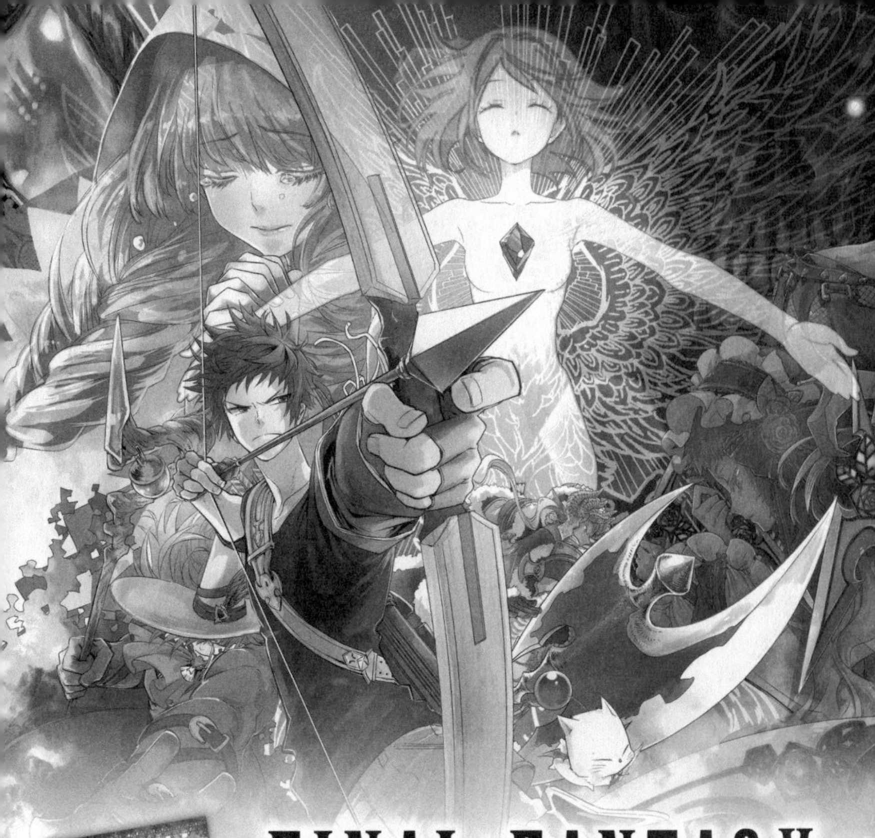

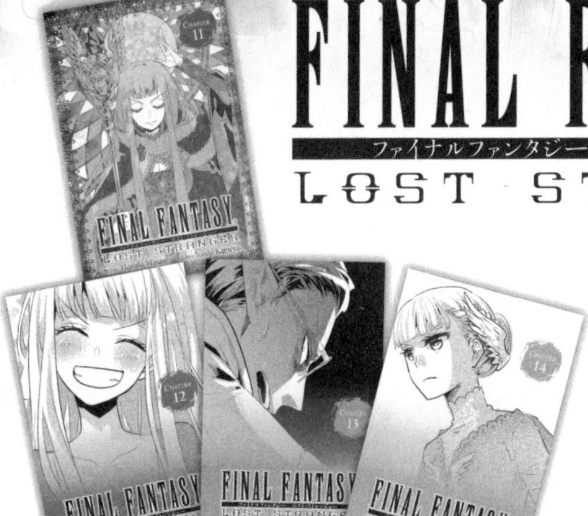

11
FINAL FANTASY
LOST STRANGER
12
13
14
FINAL FANTASY
LOST STRANGER

Toilet-bound Hanako-Kun

At Kamome Academy, rumors abound about the school's Seven Mysteries, one of which is Hanako-san. Said to occupy the third stall of the third floor girls' bathroom in the old school building, Hanako-san grants any wish when summoned. Nene Yashiro, an occult-loving high school girl who dreams of romance, ventures into this haunted bathroom...but the Hanako-san she meets there is nothing like she imagined! Kamome Academy's Hanako-san...is a boy!

PRESENTING THE LATEST SERIES FROM
JUN MOCHIZUKI

THE CASE STUDY OF VANITAS

**READ THE CHAPTERS AT
THE SAME TIME AS JAPAN!**

**AVAILABLE NOW WORLDWIDE
WHEREVER E-BOOKS ARE SOLD!**

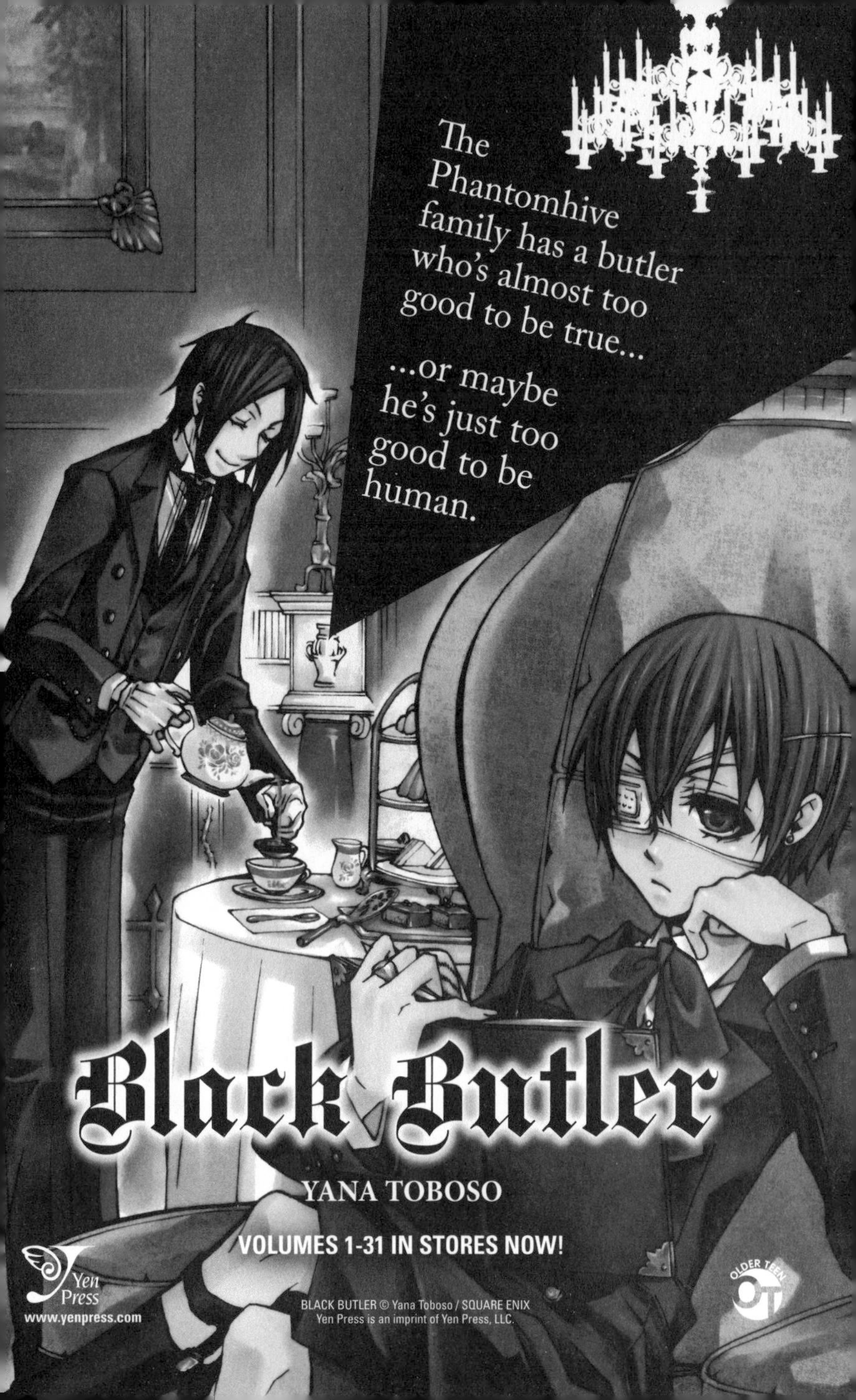
The Phantomhive family has a butler who's almost too good to be true...
...or maybe he's just too good to be human.
Black Butler
YANA TOBOSO
VOLUMES 1-31 IN STORES NOW!
Yen Press
www.yenpress.com
BLACK BUTLER © Yana Toboso / SQUARE ENIX
Yen Press is an imprint of Yen Press, LLC.
OLDER TEEN
OT

The Girl I Saved on the Train Turned Out to Be My Childhood Friend ①

Original Story by
Kennoji

Composition by
Haco Matsuura

Art by
Yoh Midorikawa

Character design by
Fly

Translation: SERGIO AVILA ★ Lettering: ELENA PIZARRO

CHIKAN SARESONINATTEIRU S-KYU BISHOJO WO TASUKETARA
TONARI NO SEKI NO OSANANAJIMI DATTA vol. 1
©Kennoji/SB Creative Corp.
Original Character Designs:©Fly/SB Creative Corp.
©2021 Haco Matsuura,Yoh Midorikawa/SQUARE ENIX CO., LTD.
First published in Japan in 2021 by SQUARE ENIX CO., LTD.
English translation rights arranged with SQUARE ENIX CO., LTD.
and Yen Press, LLC through Tuttle-Mori Agency, Inc.

English translation © 2022 by SQUARE ENIX CO., LTD.

Yen Press
150 West 30th Street, 19th Floor, New York, NY 10001

Visit us at yenpress.com ★ facebook.com/yenpress ★ twitter.com/yenpress ★ yenpress.tumblr.com ★ instagram.com/yenpress

First Yen Press Edition: June 2022
Edited by Yen Press Editorial: Won Young Seo, JuYoun Lee
Designed by Yen Press Design: Wendy Chan

Yen Press is an imprint of Yen Press, LLC.
The Yen Press name and logo are trademarks of Yen Press, LLC.

The publisher is not responsible for websites (or their content) that are not owned by the publisher.

Library of Congress Control Number: 2022934315

ISBNs: 978-1-9753-4727-7 (paperback)
        978-1-9753-4728-4 (ebook)

10 9 8 7 6 5 4 3 2 1

WOR

Printed in the United States of America